T0281500

Lecture Notes in Computer Science 14165

Founding Editors

Gerhard Goos
Juris Hartmanis

The series Lecture Notes in Computer Science (LNCS), including its subseries Lecture Notes in Artificial Intelligence (LNAI) and Lecture Notes in Bioinformatics (LNBI), has established itself as a medium for the publication of new developments in computer science and information technology research, teaching, and education.

LNCS enjoys close cooperation with the computer science R & D community, the series counts many renowned academics among its volume editors and paper authors, and collaborates with prestigious societies. Its mission is to serve this international community by providing an invaluable service, mainly focused on the publication of conference and workshop proceedings and postproceedings. LNCS commenced publication in 1973.

Anne E. Haxthausen · Wen-ling Huang ·
Markus Roggenbach
Editors

Applicable Formal Methods for Safe Industrial Products

Essays Dedicated to Jan Peleska
on the Occasion of His 65th Birthday

 Springer

Editors
Anne E. Haxthausen 🆔
Technical University of Denmark
Lyngby, Denmark

Wen-ling Huang
University of Bremen
Bremen, Germany

Markus Roggenbach 🆔
Swansea University
Swansea, UK

ISSN 0302-9743   ISSN 1611-3349 (electronic)
Lecture Notes in Computer Science
ISBN 978-3-031-40131-2   ISBN 978-3-031-40132-9 (eBook)
https://doi.org/10.1007/978-3-031-40132-9

Cover illustration: The illustration appearing on the cover of this book is the work of Jan Peleska, produced in the context of his work in the field of formal railway control systems verification. Used with permission.

This Springer imprint is published by the registered company Springer Nature Switzerland AG
The registered company address is: Gewerbestrasse 11, 6330 Cham, Switzerland

Jan Peleska – February 2023

Preface

This Festschrift is dedicated to Jan Peleska on the occasion of his 65th birthday. Its title "Applicable Formal Methods for Safe Industrial Products" mirrors Jan's research interest in the combination and application of existing methods and corresponding tools to 'real-world' problems. Most of his research activities are motivated by and applied to industrial projects in the field of safety-critical embedded systems and distributed systems, such as, for example, avionic systems and railway control systems. This Festschrift begins with a laudatio, which celebrates Jan's scientific contributions and acknowledges him as a wonderful colleague and friend.

When asked to contribute to Jan's Festschrift, no less than twenty-four friends, collaborators, and colleagues were more than happy to submit papers. Thematically, their contributions address a wide range of topics, which we grouped into the four sections of this Festschrift:

- Testing,
- Railway Verification and Safety & Security,
- Intelligent Systems and Cyber-Physical Systems, and
- Tools and Techniques for Specification, Verification and Code Generation.

Jan published research results in each of these topical areas.

Each paper was carefully read by two reviewers. We would like to thank the reviewers for their time and efforts. We would like to thank all the contributors for their efforts in making this Festschrift a reality. A special thanks goes to Jim Woodcock for his support and advice during the preparation of this Festschrift. Finally, we also would like to extend our gratitude to Springer, for their willingness to publish this Festschrift.

This Festschrift was presented to Jan on 3rd of March 2023 at the Colloquium held at the University of Bremen, Germany. The event was attended by numerous colleagues, friends and former students of Jan Peleska. We would like to express our appreciation for the financial support provided for this event by the Department of Computer Science of the University of Bremen and Verified Systems International GmbH.

March 2023

Anne E. Haxthausen
Wen-ling Huang
Markus Roggenbach

Organization

Program Committee

Jens Braband	Siemens Mobility GmbH, Germany
Jörg Brauer	Verified Systems International GmbH, Germany
Ana Cavalcanti	University of York, UK
Werner Damm	University of Oldenburg, Germany
Rolf Drechsler	University of Bremen, Germany
Alessandro Fantechi	University of Florence, Italy
John Fitzgerald	University of Newcastle, UK
Martin Fränzle	University of Oldenburg, Germany
Mario Gleirscher	University of Bremen, Germany
Gloria Gori	University of Florence, Italy
Klaus Havelund	NASA Jet Propulsion Laboratory, USA
Anne E. Haxthausen	Technical University of Denmark, Denmark
Maritta Heisel	University of Duisburg-Essen, Germany
Robert M. Hierons	University of Sheffield, UK
Wen-ling Huang	University of Bremen, Germany
Alexander Knapp	University of Augsburg, Germany
Peter Gorm Larsen	Aarhus University, Denmark
Pascale Le Gall	Paris-Saclay University, France
Thierry Lecomte	CLEARSY Safety Solutions Designer, France
Mohammad Reza Mousavi	King's College London, UK
Hoang Nga Nguyen	Coventry University, UK
Ernst-Rüdiger Olderog	University of Oldenburg, Germany
Alexander Pretschner	Technical University of Munich, Germany
Markus Roggenbach	Swansea University, UK
Robert Sachtleben	University of Bremen, Germany
Thomas Santen	Formal Assurance, Germany
Bernd-Holger Schlingloff	Fraunhofer Fokus, Germany
Jim Woodcock	University of York, UK

Jan Peleska – The Admirable Expert in Applicable Formal Methods for Safe Industrial Products (Laudatio)

Anne E. Haxthausen [iD]

DTU Compute, Technical University of Denmark, Lyngby, Denmark
aeha@dtu.dk

This is a laudatio in honour of Jan Peleska on the occasion of his 65th birthday. Rather than praising Jan's whole scientific career and achievements, which would go beyond my space and time limits, this laudatio expresses my admiration for an outstanding person, an admiration I know is shared by colleagues around the world.

The admirable expert in applicable formal methods for safe industrial products. Jan Peleska has established an outstanding international reputation for his research and leadership in the field of *Applicable Formal Methods for Safe Industrial Products*.

He has, in the most remarkable and successful way, combined a career in academia with a career in industry.

After having been employed for 10 years in industry, in 1995 he became a full professor in computer science at Bremen University. Since then, he has been conducting research in applicable formal methods for validation, verification, and test of safety-critical embedded systems, typically for the railway, avionics, automotive, and aerospace domains.

In 1998 Jan and his wife, Cornelia Zahlten, founded the company *Verified Systems International GmbH*, and since then, he has been scientific leader of the company as head of Research & Development. Today, the company has 25 employees and provides tools and services in the field of safety-critical system development, verification, validation, and test.

In the company Jan's research results from the university are adopted and used for the development of safe industrial products for customers like Siemens, Airbus, Daimler AG, and Astrium. Jan has been the brain behind Verified's flagship product, *RT-Tester*, a very comprehensive test automation tool suite for automatic test generation, test execution and real-time test evaluation. Jan is especially famous for his methods for complete testing, and in 2015, the company was awarded the runner-up trophy of the EU Innovation Radar Prize for making a novel testing strategy, developed by him and his colleague Wen-ling Huang at the university, available for industrial use. Indeed, *Verified* has verified that Jan's research results are industrial applicable!

The most wonderful colleague and friend. Besides being a brilliant researcher, Jan is the most wonderful colleague and friend.

I have collaborated with Jan since 1996. It has been wonderful to have Jan as collaborator and friend all these years. I am so grateful for that.

Jan has influenced my career in such a great way: He put me on the right track, the railway research track, when he in 1996 invited me to collaborate on the formal modelling and verification of a real-world, distributed railway control system. Since then, we have collaborated on many railway projects and we have co-authored 28 papers. Jan has inspired me a lot, always full of exciting and innovative research ideas that have led to success. He has a fantastic sense of what is needed and also knows how to achieve that.

Beyond this, Jan is also a really good friend: so caring, helpful, charming, and generous.

Jan, thank you for the most wonderful collaboration and friendship over so many years! My warmest congratulations on your birthday and my best wishes for a happy and long life.

Contents

Intelligent Systems and Cyber-Physical Systems

Tools and Techniques for Specification, Verification and Code Generation

Testing

On Testing Ethical Autonomous Decision-Making

Michael E. Akintunde$^{(\boxtimes)}$, Martim Brandão, Gunel Jahangirova,
Hector Menendez, Mohammad Reza Mousavi, and Jie Zhang

King's College London, London, UK
{michael.akintunde,martim.brandao,gunel.jahangirova,hector.menendez,
mohammad.mousavi,jie.zhang}@kcl.ac.uk

Abstract. We present an initial proposal for a testing framework for ethical decisions in autonomous agents, based on the well-known perception-action model. We identify three main components in our proposed framework for test-case generation, conformance analysis, and learning and adaptation of ethical models based on examples from stakeholders. We define a number of templates formalising the main ethical theories in the literature that can be further instantiated for testing concrete systems according to such theories.

Keywords: Testing · Ethics · Autonomous Systems

1   Introduction

Ethics, in our context, is a systematic description of principles for what is right and honourable [7,23]; examples of such behaviour include respecting the privacy of patients (of/by an agent), dealing fairly with patients, and not deceiving them in interactions. Autonomous systems are already taking decisions that are ethically charged: software that takes credit ratings for mortgages can be unfair or biased; a chatbot can be offensive and discriminatory; an assistive care robot can violate patients' privacy or make unethical decisions that damage patients' integrity.

Different stakeholders may have different ethical concerns and even subscribe to different meta-ethical frameworks. Even the opening, seemingly obvious, examples we gave above may be debated in different contexts and benefit from more scrutiny, specification, and discussion in their specific context. The diversity and ambiguity of these ethical concerns and meta-ethical frameworks have been a challenge in their system-level testing. There have been a number of recent approaches aiming to formalise specific meta-ethical frameworks for autonomous systems [24,27,41]. There are also works that focus on testing specific ethical concerns, such as fairness or bias [5,16–18]. However, we are not aware of any general framework that can be used to encode different stakeholders' ethical rules and concerns in order to test them.

Whether autonomous systems can be counted as fully-ethical agents is a philosophical concern which is outside the scope of our paper; regardless of one's

A. E. Haxthausen et al. (Eds.): Peleska Festschrift 2023, LNCS 14165, pp. 3–15, 2023.
https://doi.org/10.1007/978-3-031-40132-9_1

stance in this regard, it is helpful to have tools to evaluate autonomous decision-making.

Our aim is to automate system-level testing for ethical decision-making that is customisable to different meta-ethical frameworks. For this purpose, we propose a framework to: 1) generate challenging test scenarios/inputs, 2) analyse the test results via oracles, and 3) adjust the oracles through stakeholder engagement.

We do not aim to resolve disagreements among stakeholders; instead, we would like to give different stakeholders a tool to understand their ethical concerns better, use it to engage in a discussion with other stakeholders, and also test black-box or third-party autonomous systems against their concerns. For underrepresented stakeholders and those with less power to scrutinise the design of such systems, we would like to provide a tool to rigorously capture their concerns and reveal any deviations from what they consider ethically significant. Our goal can hence be summarised as providing a tool for providing more transparency regarding ethical concerns in complex autonomous systems.

To illustrate the concepts presented in the remainder of this paper, we use the following scenario as our motivating example.

Motivating Example. Consider an autonomous vehicle designed to drive autonomously in urban traffic. A function of this autonomous vehicle focuses on dealing with emergency vehicles such as ambulances and fire engines. Through a vehicle-to-vehicle communication method, it can learn about vehicles that are on a critical mission and their kinematics, and must react to this information. Such a function can make ethically-charged decisions, e.g., decisions that may help or harm the condition of a patient in an approaching ambulance at various costs, such as violating traffic regulations.

Considering the significant amount of studies in human ethics and the complexity of developing substantial frameworks that embed their knowledge, our work identifies the following challenges for the testing framework:

1. **Generating effective test scenarios**: there is a significant amount of scenarios, creating a wide input space for autonomous decision-making. Focusing on effective ones that are likely to reveal issues (or establish trust) is a major challenge. Another significant challenge to cope with this limitation is to define measures of effectiveness, both to steer the testing process and to evaluate and compare different techniques.
2. **Different meta-ethical frameworks**: Ethics have evolved differently in different contexts, creating a plethora of ethical frameworks. A major challenge in developing a discipline of testing is to choose one of them. However, since there is no single agreed-upon framework, this choice is significantly complex.

3. **Ethical oracles**: Even within a fixed ethical framework, defining a rigorous test oracle to judge ethical behaviours and pass verdicts about conflicting ethical concerns is a highly non-trivial challenge.
4. **Diversity and stakeholder engagement**: Developing a responsible regime of testing for ethical concerns requires interaction with a diverse population of users. Overcoming this challenge involves gathering a truly diverse population of stakeholders (both representing the diversity in their demographics and backgrounds, but also in their roles and relationships with respect to each other and the system under test). Additionally, it requires a testing regime with artefacts (e.g., test models and test cases) that are meaningful and understandable to the diverse population.

In the remainder of the paper, we propose an architecture for testing ethical decision-making in Sect. 2. Then in Sect. 3, we focus on the formalisation of ethical theories that can be used for test-case generation, test oracles, and learning from stakeholder engagement. In Sect. 4, we review some of the related work and in Sect. 5, we conclude the paper and present the directions of our ongoing research.

2 Architecture for Testing Ethics

Figure 1 demonstrates our proposed architecture to test ethics in autonomous systems. The overall workflow starts from the selected *ethical model* which along with the System Under Test (SUT) is used to generate the test cases. The generated test cases are executed on the SUT, and the resulting system traces are passed to the *conformance analyser* which checks whether the test cases pass or fail the ethical tests according to the selected oracle. A subset of both passing and failing test cases is then passed to the stakeholders for their consideration and validation. It is important at this step to perform a meaningful *test selection* so that these test executions are representative of the system's overall behaviour from the ethical perspective. The stakeholders/ethical experts can indicate the test cases for which they do not agree with the outcome provided by the conformance analyser. Such test cases become counter-examples to the adopted ethical model. The *learning module* component can use generated counter-examples to adjust the ethical model. This adjustment can be performed by applying the ideas behind existing works on online and offline learning [14,19,31,37,49], as well as search-based approaches to oracle improvement [29,30,46]. The presented iterative process can continue until no more counter-example test cases can be identified. This does not mean that the SUT eventually passes all tests but that the stakeholder(s) eventually agree with the pass/fail decision of tests generated by the system. Each stakeholder may be using the testing system separately from other stakeholders and thus learning a different ethical model that reflects their concerns. The test cases they generate can then be used for discussion and negotiation with other stakeholders.

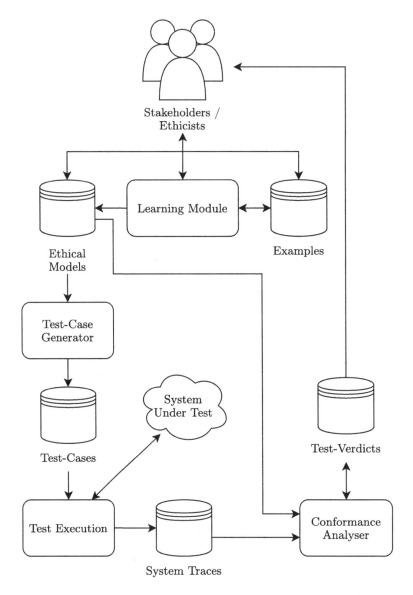

Fig. 1. Proposed Architecture for Testing Ethics.

2.1 Test Input Generation

The test cases need to capture the scenarios where the decision taken by the system puts various ethical principles of the ethical model into conflict. The aim of test case generation in this architecture is to generate such test cases out of the large space of all possible scenarios. One way to achieve this task is to cast it as a *search-based* testing problem [28,34]. The search process can be guided by two different goals: (1) detecting ethical faults more effectively (2) checking the soundness of the ethical model.

The first goal concerns generating scenarios in which the violation of an ethical model can be effectively established; in other words, we are looking for scenarios in which the choices of the agent can clearly and quickly reveal the violation of an ethical model. When generating such scenarios, we would like to maximise the diversity between them as well as the coverage of the ethical model and the space of possible scenarios. The target measure for diversity can be uniformity which can be measured by using a statistical test related to the uniform distribution, such as the L2-test [26]. As a target measure for coverage a straightforward measure is the t-wise coverage of possible choices among actions.

The second goal aims to put the agent into ethical dilemmas, e.g., to force it to make a choice between different actions that have similar ethical status. For this, we can first identify test objectives that determine how far candidate tests are from taking different ethically-charged actions. We then can guide the test generation process towards test scenarios that lead to undesired interactions between these test objectives [3] by using *many-objective optimisation* algorithms such as NSGA-II [20], HypE [12], and MOSA [36]. Game-theoretic formulations [25] and synthesising scenarios towards an expected equilibrium can provide another alternative approach.

For our motivating example, we need to first guide the scenario-generation towards situations 1) where a particular rule of the road is applicable (e.g., as specified in the Highway Code), and 2) where there is a potential conflict in the rights of way and/or the rules of the road. Regarding case 1, a generated test scenario should for example demonstrate whether a vehicle gives way to an ambulance. If it does not, this can reveal faults in ethical decision-making. A scenario pertaining to case 2 is when giving way to an ambulance involves damaging another vehicle or hitting a curb or a road user. Moreover, we would like to diversify the set of generated scenarios by considering substantially different situations and also cover various possible conflicts, e.g., all possible pairwise choices among conflicting actions.

2.2 Test Oracle Identification

Test oracle [13] identification is one of the key problems in testing ethics. Autonomous systems are typically stochastic and the ground truth is not specified a priori. Moreover, for ethics itself, even human ethics are often faced with difficult dilemmas without easy answers, in which each side might have valid arguments. In our architecture, the *conformance analyser* needs to automatically decide which decisions are acceptable and which are not. The ethical models needed for conformance analysis can be extracted from various sources, discussed below.

Ethical Models from Laws and Policies. Researchers and companies have recommended various laws and regulations from government or non-profit institutions as a means of ensuring machine ethics. There are some widely acknowledged regulations such as the "Ethics Guidelines for Trustworthy AI" from the

European Commission [44] and "Recommendation on the Ethics of AI" from the UNESCO Ad Hoc Expert Group [48]. IEEE developed an extensive process model standard for incorporating ethical concerns during system design [1]. Some of these standards have been translated into domain-specific guidelines, e.g., in the domain of autonomous vehicles [24]. The information from these sources can be extracted, in terms of rules or utility functions, to build the basis for an ethical model to be used in our automated conformance analyser. In Sect. 3, we provide the templates that can be used to encode these informal descriptions into a formal specification.

Test Oracles from Stakeholders and Human Experts. The information about the expected behaviour of the ethical model can be provided in the form of a number of examples by the stakeholders or human experts. These examples can then be generalised into ethical models using learning algorithms (such as automata learning or neural networks) in our templates for ethical theories specified below. Our ethical theories specify a relative value for different types of behaviour; when coming up with a complete model is challenging (due to lack of sufficient examples or conflict among stakeholders), abstractions of such models such as metamorphic properties can be used.

For example, for our motivating example, a specific ethical theory can 1) specify the relative value of different actions, such as giving way to an ambulance, damaging another vehicle, and hitting a road user, or 2) specify the total utility of each course of actions for the other road users (including any quantification of the resulting damage) by taking a weighted sum of the utility of actions for the individual road users involved in a scenario.

The next section describes the ethical theories that can be used as templates for ethical models.

3 Ethical Theories for Conformance Analysis

Passing a verdict on the decision-making scenarios (bottom-right corner of Fig. 1) requires defining or learning an ethical model (top-left corner of Fig. 1), e.g., through a set of rules. Modelling the ethics of autonomous agents has been the subject of machine ethics for the past few decades. It aims to understand the consequences of machine behaviour on either other machines or people [7]. The main goal of this field is to study and help construct systems that act under a specific ethical theory. Instead of committing to a particular ethical theory, in this paper, we develop a general semantic framework that can be used to define different ethical models. These models can be learned using the examples provided by the stakeholders by fitting the parameters of our semantic model.

In this section, we review the three major ethical theories, namely, deontological, consequentialist (or utilitarian), and virtue ethics [47], and present the semantic templates for them. Our templates use the simple perception-action agent model by Russel and Norvig [40], depicted in Fig. 2. This model postulates two sets of *Prc* and *Act*, for percepts and actions, respectively. Our framework is designed for black-box testing and can be further extended to take the details of the agent implementation into account. Furthermore, depending on the ethical theory we may need to model the environment or not.

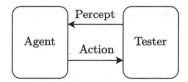

Fig. 2. A Model of Agent and Tester Interaction.

3.1   Deontological Ethics

In deontological ethics, an action is morally good if it follows a predefined set of moral values or rules [45]. There are two perspectives for defining the values of actions: agent-centred and patient-centred. The former focuses the ethics on the agent's actions, while the latter focuses the ethics on the agent who receives the action and the consequences [32]. Following the moral theory of deontological ethics, our semantic template for a deontological oracle involves defining a value for each action; the values are taken from any (pseudo-) metric space on a discrete or continuous set, i.e., a set of values with a defined distance between them. A basic domain is the discrete domain {Forbidden, Neutral, Obligatory}, with a unit distance from Forbidden to Neutral and from Neutral to Obligatory. However, more sophisticated domains define a spectrum of actions and their relative values to each other. The objective will be used to define the oracle as well as to steer the test-case generation in a direction that is more likely to reveal ethical issues. The test case input is a non-empty sequence of percepts. The considered output is the last action in the sequence of actions produced as the result of inputs. The oracle checks that the output action is not more than ϵ apart from the ideal action after the input (first row in Table 1).

Consider our running example; assume that the agent has three moral duties:

1. an agent shall respect human lives,
2. an agent shall give way to ambulances, and
3. an agent shall not damage other cars.

Obviously these three moral duties can be in conflict and we model the conflict, and the relative priority of these rules as follows. We define a model in which the value of not giving way to the ambulance is -1, damaging a car is -0.5 and hitting a human road user is -2. Note that this choice of values are a rough indication of the relative importance of the three rules; however, often the domain of values needs to be more complex, e.g., be multi-dimensional. This allows for comparing the outcomes of different scenarios based on deontological ethics. For example, based on this oracle, a scenario in which a vehicle blocks the ambulance because it may damage another vehicle while giving way to the ambulance is considered a failure, while blocking the ambulance when giving way will lead to killing or seriously injuring a pedestrian will be considered a pass.

Table 1. Model Templates for Different Theories of Ethics.

Framework	Objective	Test input	Test output	Test oracle
Deontological	$Obj: Act \rightarrow Val$	$\alpha : Prc^+$	$a : Act$, last observed action	Obj(ideal after α) - Obj(a after α) $\leq \epsilon$
Consequentialism	$Obj: Act \times Env \rightarrow Val$	$\alpha : Prc^+$	$\beta : Act^+$, sequence of observed actions	Obj(ideal after α, env) - Obj(β after α, env) $\leq \epsilon$
Virtue	$S \subseteq Prc^+ \times Act^+$, Robotic saint	$A \subseteq Prc^+$	$B \subseteq Prc^+ \times Act^+$	(1) $\forall \alpha \in B \; \exists \beta \in S \cdot dist(\alpha, \beta) \leq \epsilon \wedge \forall \beta \in B \; \exists \alpha \in S \cdot dist(\alpha, \beta) \leq \epsilon$, (2) Convergence to S

3.2   Consequentialism

Consequentialism focuses on consequences, e.g., aiming at maximising global well-being [42]. According to this moral theory, the value of an action is determined by its global utility. Two of the sub-fields of consequentialism are act utilitarianism and rule utilitarianism [42]. The former establishes that every single act must focus on maximising utility. The latter focuses on social rules. It establishes that the only rules that need to be applied are those that maximise well-being.

The semantic framework for a consequentialist oracle (second row in Table 1) involves an objective function that defines the value of actions through their effects on the environment *Env*. The form of such an objective is a weighted sum of the effect of actions (e.g., happiness) of agents in the environment. The input and output, similar to the deontological case, are non-empty traces of percepts and actions. The oracle asserts that the distance of the accumulative value of all actions is not farther than ϵ from that of the ideal sequence.

In our running example, an ethical model assigns a value to the relative damage to the different patients caused by an action (i.e., ego vehicle, other vehicles, road users, and the emergency vehicle patient) and a weighting to calculate the total utility of the scenario.

3.3   Virtue Ethics

In virtue ethics, an action is good if the agents manifest virtuosity when they act [43]. A distinct form of virtue ethics is the exemplarist virtue theory [52] where the morality of an agent is measured in terms of its similarity to an exemplary agent (a moral saint).

Virtue ethics is a challenging ethical theory to test; we model the semantic model of virtue ethics (third row of Table 1) as a robotic saint which is modelled as a set of pairs of percept and action sequences. The test input is a set of percept sequences and the test output is a set of pairs of percept- and action sequences. We propose two types of oracles for testing virtue ethics; the first type of oracle is a conformance oracle that checks for each behaviour of the saint, there is a similar behaviour of the agent that is at most ϵ apart and vice versa. The notion of distance is calculated based on a notion of action similarity akin to the objective function of deontological ethics. The second type of oracle measures the convergence of the agent's behaviour towards the behaviour of the saint, i.e., measures how much more conforming the longer traces of behaviour become compared to the shorter traces. In our running example, an ethical model is defined by learning the behaviour of an idealised driver, e.g., exploiting driving logs, taking accidents as negative examples; subsequently, measures of conformance [2] and convergence [4] can be used to measure the conformance of an agent to the model.

4 Related Work

4.1 Ethical Oracle Identification

Test Oracles that Rely on Human Judgment. One way to identify test oracles is to rely on the judgement of human (stakeholders and ethicists). Pontier and Widdershoven [39] use human judges to provide oracles to find unethical issues. Allen et al. [6] conducted a "Moral Turing Test" in which a "blind" observer is asked to compare the behaviour of a machine to humans. Similarly, Anderson et al. [8] provided a self-made Ethical Turing Test to evaluate their ethical principles: If the system performs as an ethical expert would, then it passes the test. They also argued that ethically significant behaviour of autonomous systems should be guided by ethical principles determined by ethics experts. Wu et al. [51] employed ordinary human data to derive human policies and help to learn ethical behaviours as test oracles.

Test Oracles that Rely on Laws and Policies. Asaro [11] suggests the existing legal system can be used as a starting point for deriving AI ethics. Vanderelst and Winfield [50] test robot behaviours based on Asimov's laws of robotics. The use of Asimov's laws has been extensively criticised, e.g., in [9].

Test Oracles with Simulations. The survey by Nallur [35] does not specifically mention testing ethics. However, it discusses the evaluation of ethics by simulation of ethical dilemmas. In this formulation, ethical dilemmas serve as test cases, and if the autonomous system can resolve a dilemma in a particular manner, then ethics were successfully implemented in this system.

4.2   Ethical Representation

Arkoudas et al. [10,15] propose to use Horty logic to compose ethical semantics. Dennis et al. [21] developed a framework for representing the context of ethical reasoning, which involves encoding user values as a set of rules. An ethical reasoner can then be embedded in a reasoning cycle to gather contextual information and update its ethical encoding. Dennis et al. [22] apply the AJPF model-checker to verify the behaviour of the consequence engine in a robot system.

There are also several works that mentioned the importance of ethics testing. Pontier and Hoorn talked about the importance of making ethics measurable [38]: "Ethics must be made computable in order to make it clear exactly how agents ought to behave in ethical dilemmas". Madl and Franklin [33] discuss the necessity of a set of moral tests to guarantee AI ethics and propose the idea of moral test-driven development.

AI ethics considerations can be various, including privacy, fairness, accountability, explainability and others. The testing efforts on these aspects mainly focus on fairness testing. We refer to Chen et al. [18] for a comprehensive survey of the literature on testing AI fairness. As far as we know, there is no general framework that is specially designed for testing ethical decision-making.

5   Conclusion and Future Research Roadmap

In this paper, we propose a framework for testing ethical aspects of decision-making in autonomous systems. Our framework comprises three major parts: 1) a test-case generation algorithm, 2) a conformance analyser, and 3) a learning algorithm to learn an ethical model for the former two parts and adjust it based on stakeholders' feedback. We presented three formalisations of the major ethical theories that can be used as templates for the ethical models in test-case generation, conformance analysis, and learning from examples. The purpose of our proposed framework is to provide a tool for various stakeholders, and particularly under-represented and less powerful ones, to specify their concerns and test complex autonomous systems against them.

We plan to instantiate our framework with concrete algorithms in the domain of autonomous vehicles. We are currently developing a simulation environment in order to execute the generated scenarios, present the stakeholders with tangible examples, and receive their feedback. Our framework focuses on a black-box perspective on the system under test; extensions of our framework can be developed by using more information from the agents' state, including aspects such as belief, desire, and intention as well as specifications of neuro-symbolic agents.

Acknowledgments. The support of the UKRI Trustworthy Autonomous Systems Hub (reference EP/V00784X/1) and Trustworthy Autonomous Systems Node in Verifiability (reference EP/V026801/2) is gratefully acknowledged. The authors are grateful to Peta Masters and to the anonymous reviewers for their constructive comments.

References

1. IEEE standard model process for addressing ethical concerns during system design. IEEE Std 7000–2021, pp. 1–82 (2021). https://doi.org/10.1109/IEEESTD.2021.9536679
2. Abbas, H.: Test-Based Falsification and Conformance Testing for Cyber-Physical Systems. Ph.D. thesis, Arizona State University, Tempe, USA (2015). https://hdl.handle.net/2286/R.I.29861
3. Abdessalem, R.B., Panichella, A., Nejati, S., Briand, L.C., Stifter, T.: Testing autonomous cars for feature interaction failures using many-objective search. In: 2018 33rd IEEE/ACM International Conference on Automated Software Engineering (ASE), pp. 143–154. IEEE (2018)
4. Abdessalem, R.B., Panichella, A., Nejati, S., Briand, L.C., Stifter, T.: Testing autonomous cars for feature interaction failures using many-objective search. In: Huchard, M., Kästner, C., Fraser, G. (eds.) Proceedings of the 33rd ACM/IEEE International Conference on Automated Software Engineering, ASE 2018, Montpellier, France, September 3–7, 2018, pp. 143–154. ACM (2018). https://doi.org/10.1145/3238147.3238192
5. Aggarwal, A., Lohia, P., Nagar, S., Dey, K., Saha, D.: Black box fairness testing of machine learning models. In: Proceedings of the 2019 27th ACM Joint Meeting on European Software Engineering Conference and Symposium on the Foundations of Software Engineering, pp. 625–635 (2019)
6. Allen, C., Varner, G., Zinser, J.: Prolegomena to any future artificial moral agent. J. Exper. Theor. Artif. Intell. **12**(3), 251–261 (2000)
7. Anderson, M., Anderson, S.L.: Machine ethics. Cambridge University Press (2011)
8. Anderson, M., Anderson, S.L.: Geneth: a general ethical dilemma analyzer. Paladyn, J. Behav. Robot. **9**(1), 337–357 (2018)
9. Anderson, S.L.: The Unacceptability of Asimov's Three Laws of Robotics as a Basis for Machine Ethics, pp. 285–296. Cambridge University Press (2011). https://doi.org/10.1017/CBO9780511978036.021
10. Arkoudas, K., Bringsjord, S., Bello, P.: Toward ethical robots via mechanized deontic logic. In: AAAI fall symposium on machine ethics, pp. 17–23. The AAAI Press Menlo Park, CA, USA (2005)
11. Asaro, P.M.: What should we want from a robot ethic? In: Machine Ethics and Robot Ethics, pp. 87–94. Routledge (2020)
12. Bader, J., Zitzler, E.: Hype: an algorithm for fast hypervolume-based many-objective optimization. Evol. Comput. **19**(1), 45–76 (2011)
13. Barr, E.T., Harman, M., McMinn, P., Shahbaz, M., Yoo, S.: The oracle problem in software testing: a survey. IEEE Trans. Software Eng. **41**(5), 507–525 (2015)
14. Bottou, L.: Online algorithms and stochastic approxima-p tions. Online learning and neural networks (1998)
15. Bringsjord, S., Arkoudas, K., Bello, P.: Toward a general logicist methodology for engineering ethically correct robots. IEEE Intell. Syst. **21**(4), 38–44 (2006)
16. Chakraborty, J., Majumder, S., Menzies, T.: Bias in machine learning software: why? how? what to do? In: Proceedings of the 29th ACM Joint Meeting on European Software Engineering Conference and Symposium on the Foundations of Software Engineering, pp. 429–440 (2021)
17. Chen, Z., Zhang, J., Sarro, F., Harman, M.: Maat: A novel ensemble approach to addressing fairness and performance bugs for machine learning software. In: The ACM Joint European Software Engineering Conference and Symposium on the Foundations of Software Engineering (ESEC/FSE) (2022)

18. Chen, Z., Zhang, J.M., Hort, M., Sarro, F., Harman, M.: Fairness testing: A comprehensive survey and analysis of trends. arXiv preprint arXiv:2207.10223 (2022)
19. Damasceno, C.D.N., Mousavi, M.R., da Silva Simão, A.: Learning to reuse: Adaptive model learning for evolving systems. In: Ahrendt, W., Tarifa, S.L.T. (eds.) Integrated Formal Methods - 15th International Conference, IFM 2019, Bergen, Norway, December 2–6, 2019, Proceedings. Lecture Notes in Computer Science, vol. 11918, pp. 138–156. Springer (2019). https://doi.org/10.1007/978-3-030-34968-4_8
20. Deb, K., Jain, H.: An evolutionary many-objective optimization algorithm using reference-point-based nondominated sorting approach, part i: solving problems with box constraints. IEEE Trans. Evol. Comput. **18**(4), 577–601 (2013)
21. Dennis, L.A., Bentzen, M.M., Lindner, F., Fisher, M.: Verifiable machine ethics in changing contexts. In: Proceedings of the AAAI Conference on Artificial Intelligence. vol. 35, pp. 11470–11478 (2021)
22. Dennis, L.A., Fisher, M., Winfield, A.: Towards verifiably ethical robot behaviour. In: Workshops at the Twenty-Ninth AAAI Conference on Artificial Intelligence (2015)
23. Dubber, M.D., Pasquale, F., Das, S.: The Oxford Handbook of Ethics of AI. Oxford Univ. Press (2020). https://doi.org/10.1093/oxfordhb/9780190067397.001.0001
24. Evans, K., de Moura, N., Chauvier, S., Chatila, R., Dogan, E.: Ethical decision making in autonomous vehicles: the AV ethics project. Sci. Eng. Ethics **26**(6), 3285–3312 (2020). https://doi.org/10.1007/s11948-020-00272-8
25. Gogoll, J., Zuber, N., Kacianka, S., Greger, T., Pretschner, A., Nida-Rümelin, J.: Ethics in the software development process: from codes of conduct to ethical deliberation. Philos. Technol. **34**(4), 1085–1108 (2021). https://doi.org/10.1007/s13347-021-00451-w
26. Goldreich, O., Ron, D.: On testing expansion in bounded-degree graphs. In: Goldreich, O. (ed.) Studies in Complexity and Cryptography. Miscellanea on the Interplay between Randomness and Computation. LNCS, vol. 6650, pp. 68–75. Springer, Heidelberg (2011). https://doi.org/10.1007/978-3-642-22670-0_9
27. Govindarajulu, N.S., Bringsjord, S., Ghosh, R., Sarathy, V.: Toward the engineering of virtuous machines. In: Proceedings of the 2019 AAAI/ACM Conference on AI, Ethics, and Society, pp. 29–35. AIES '19, Association for Computing Machinery, New York, NY, USA (2019)
28. Harman, M., Jia, Y., Zhang, Y.: Achievements, open problems and challenges for search based software testing. In: 2015 IEEE 8th International Conference on Software Testing, Verification and Validation (ICST), pp. 1–12. IEEE (2015)
29. Jahangirova, G., Clark, D., Harman, M., Tonella, P.: Test oracle assessment and improvement. In: Proceedings of the 25th International Symposium on Software Testing and Analysis, pp. 247–258 (2016)
30. Jahangirova, G., Clark, D., Harman, M., Tonella, P.: An empirical validation of oracle improvement. IEEE Trans. Softw. Eng. **47**(8), 1708–1728 (2019)
31. Jain, L.C., Seera, M., Lim, C.P., Balasubramaniam, P.: A review of online learning in supervised neural networks. Neural Comput. Appl. **25**(3), 491–509 (2014)
32. Kant, I.: Groundwork for the Metaphysics of Morals. Yale University Press. Commented by Jerome B Schneewind (1785)
33. Madl, T., Franklin, S.: Constrained incrementalist moral decision making for a biologically inspired cognitive architecture. In: Trappl, R. (ed.) A Construction Manual for Robots' Ethical Systems. CT, pp. 137–153. Springer, Cham (2015). https://doi.org/10.1007/978-3-319-21548-8_8

34. McMinn, P.: Search-based software test data generation: a survey. Software testing, Verification and reliability **14**(2), 105–156 (2004)
35. Nallur, V.: Landscape of machine implemented ethics. Sci. Eng. Ethics **26**(5), 2381–2399 (2020)
36. Panichella, A., Kifetew, F.M., Tonella, P.: Reformulating branch coverage as a many-objective optimization problem. In: 2015 IEEE 8th International Conference on Software Testing, Verification and Validation (ICST), pp. 1–10. IEEE (2015)
37. Parisi, G.I., Kemker, R., Part, J.L., Kanan, C., Wermter, S.: Continual lifelong learning with neural networks: a review. Neural Netw. **113**, 54–71 (2019)
38. Pontier, M., Hoorn, J.: Toward machines that behave ethically better than humans do. In: Proceedings of the Annual Meeting of the Cognitive Science Society, vol. 34 (2012)
39. Pontier, M.A., Widdershoven, G.A.M.: Robots that stimulate autonomy. In: Papadopoulos, H., Andreou, A.S., Iliadis, L., Maglogiannis, I. (eds.) AIAI 2013. IAICT, vol. 412, pp. 195–204. Springer, Heidelberg (2013). https://doi.org/10.1007/978-3-642-41142-7_20
40. Russell, S., Norvig, P.: Artificial Intelligence: A Modern Approach. Pearson, 4th edition edn. (2020)
41. Shea-Blymyer, C., Abbas, H.: Algorithmic ethics: Formalization and verification of autonomous vehicle obligations. ACM Trans. Cyber-Phys. Syst. **5**(4) (sep 2021). https://doi.org/10.1145/3460975
42. Sinnott-Armstrong, W.: Consequentialism. In: Zalta, E.N. (ed.) The Stanford Encyclopedia of Philosophy. Metaphysics Research Lab, Stanford University, Fall 2021 edn. (2021)
43. Slote, M.: Agent-based virtue ethics. Handbuch Tugend und Tugendethik, pp. 1–10 (2020)
44. Smuha, N.: Ethics guidelines for trustworthy ai. In: AI & Ethics, Date: 2019/05/28-2019/05/28, Location: Brussels (Digityser), Belgium (2019)
45. Tännsjö, T.: Understanding ethics. Edinburgh University Press (2013)
46. Terragni, V., Jahangirova, G., Tonella, P., Pezzè, M.: Evolutionary improvement of assertion oracles. In: Proceedings of the 28th ACM Joint Meeting on European Software Engineering Conference and Symposium on the Foundations of Software Engineering, pp. 1178–1189 (2020)
47. Tolmeijer, S., Kneer, M., Sarasua, C., Christen, M., Bernstein, A.: Implementations in machine ethics: a survey. ACM Comput. Surv. (CSUR) **53**(6), 1–38 (2020)
48. UNESCO: Recommendation on the Ethics of Artificial Intelligence. United Nations Educational, Scientific and Cultural Organization (2022)
49. Vaandrager, F.W.: Model learning. Commun. ACM **60**(2), 86–95 (2017). https://doi.org/10.1145/2967606
50. Vanderelst, D., Winfield, A.: An architecture for ethical robots inspired by the simulation theory of cognition. Cogn. Syst. Res. **48**, 56–66 (2018)
51. Wu, Y.H., Lin, S.D.: A low-cost ethics shaping approach for designing reinforcement learning agents. In: Proceedings of the AAAI Conference on Artificial Intelligence, vol. 32 (2018)
52. Zagzebski, L.: Exemplarist virtue theory. Metaphilosophy (2010)

Bringing RoboStar and RT-Tester Together

Ana Cavalcanti[1]($^{(\boxtimes)}$) (iD), Alvaro Miyazawa[1] (iD), Uwe Schulze[2], and Jon Timmis[3] (iD)

[1] University of York, York, UK
`Ana.Cavalcanti@york.ac.uk`
[2] Verified Systems International GmbH, Bremen, Germany
[3] University of Sunderland, Sunderland, UK

Abstract. In recent work, Cavalcanti and her group, including Miyazawa and Timmis, have developed a CSP-based framework for model-based engineering of robotic systems, called RoboStar. In this paper, we describe our current effort to ally RoboStar and RT-Tester, an award-winning tool that embodies many of Jan Peleska's beautiful results on formal testing. With our work, RoboStar users can benefit from the testing infrastructure of RT-Tester to run simulations and tests generated using the RoboStar automated techniques. The testing primitives of RT-Tester simplify the implementation of test cases, and the RT-Tester execution engine provides state-of-the-art high-performance real-time facilities to carry out and report the traceable results of test experiments.

Keywords: Testing · Formal models · CSP · Automation

1 Introduction

For many years now, we have known that "Testing can be formal, too" [21]. In this line of work, tests arise from models described using some formal notation. Back in 2006, Cavalcanti and Gaudel have presented a testing theory for models written in CSP [8], but Jan Peleska had studied that a decade earlier [30].

In a seminal paper [31], Peleska and Siegel formalise a test-automation method based on CSP. They define a conformance relation $\sqsubseteq_C$ and establish its relationship to failures and trace refinement in CSP. They also define and study two extra conformance relations: divergence refinement and robustness. They take the view that synchronisation is point-to-point and use an extra CSP event to characterise tests that do not fail (are either inconclusive or successful).

Peleska and Siegel define "may" and "must" tests and characterise the capability detections of tests. The test sets in [31] required to establish refinement are based on "may" and "must" tests for both the specification and implementation. Their approach inspired the definition in [8] of exhaustive test sets based on the traces $s \frown \langle a \rangle$ and failures (a, A) that are not admissible by the specification.

Over the years, Cavalcanti and Gaudel worked with others to enrich their theory to consider a data-rich version of CSP, namely *Circus* [10], distributed

A. E. Haxthausen et al. (Eds.): Peleska Festschrift 2023, LNCS 14165, pp. 16–33, 2023.
https://doi.org/10.1007/978-3-031-40132-9_2

testing [13], specific selection strategies [1,9,11,12,17], and inputs and outputs [2,14]. The practical impact of this theoretical work has to be via tools that mechanise test-generation and selection strategies to provide finite test suites. In [18], the results of pursuing an approach based on theorem proving are presented.

Jan Peleska, in his continuous pursuit to work both on beautiful theories and practical techniques, has encouraged us to consider a model-checking approach. Cavalcanti and Miyazawa have had the honour to collaborate with him and his team, including Schulze, in European projects (COMPASS [36] and INTO-CPS [26]). In [15], our teams have pursued together a formal link between the mathematical underpinning of Jan Peleska's practical test-generation techniques and Cavalcanti and Gaudel's testing theory for CSP using Hoare and He's Unifying Theories of Programming [23]. More recently, Peleska has taken a lead in identifying finite and complete test suites [29].

In all these lines of research, our teams have worked extensively in the area of cyber-physical systems. Currently, Cavalcanti, Miyazawa, and Timmis's team has been concerned with Software Engineering for Robotics. They are developing the RoboStar [4] framework, including domain-specific notations [16,27] for modelling, verification, and simulation, all underpinned by CSP-based semantics. In terms of testing, the RoboStar approach is based on that originally put forward in [8]. In [6], we have presented a practical approach to test generation based on RoboStar design models, but have not studied test execution.

Jan Peleska' group at the University of Bremen, together with Verified Systems[1], have developed RT-Tester [28,32]. This is a tool for automated generation of test cases, test data, and test procedures from UML and SysML models, as well as simulation and model checking. RT-Tester is distinctive in its comprehensive support for test execution, performance, and real-time capabilities.

Here, we describe our approach, depicted in Fig. 1, to use RT-Tester taking advantage of the RoboStar notations. As indicated, for a RoboStar design model, written in a notation called RoboChart [27], there is support for automatic generation of (fault-based) tests using mutation [6]. The result is a suite of test-case specifications to uncover the faults introduced by mutation.

RoboStar includes a technique to translate a RoboChart model to a simulation model, written in a notation called RoboSim [16]. An automatically generated RoboSim model is correct by construction. It is perfectly valid, however, for a development to start from a RoboSim, rather than RoboChart, model. Moreover, there is value in exercising the simulation to validate the RoboChart and RoboSim models. In our approach, however the RoboSim model is obtained, it is used to generate code that can be executed in RT-Tester. We describe in this paper our technique for generation of code. It contains a simulator independent component, capturing the behaviour of the RoboSim model, and an RT-tester specific component to connect the code to the RT-Tester infrastructure.

In this paper, we also describe how we can generate test procedures for RT-Tester from RoboStar test-case specifications. With the work presented here,

---

[1] www.verified.de/.

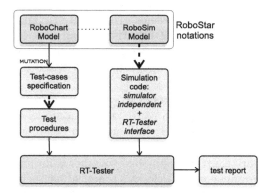

Fig. 1. RoboStar approach to testing using RT-Tester. Key: the dashed line indicates an intended or established connection that ensures preservation of properties; the solid arrow labelled "MUTATION" refers to an existing technique; dashed arrows represent the work in this paper; the solid arrows without a label indicate data flow.

we can use RT-Tests to exercise the simulation using the tests generated from RoboChart, and produce a report tracing verdicts to test procedures.

If execution of a test procedure gives a fail verdict, with our work, we can trace it back to the test case used to generate the test procedure, and from that to the mutation of the RoboChart model that has been used to generate the test case. This gives rich information about the fault revealed and its possible cause.

Next, we give a brief overview of RoboSim. Section 3 describes RT-Tester. In Sect. 4, we present our integration of RoboSim with RT-Tester, and in Sect. 5 we describe an example of its use. We conclude in Sect. 6.

2   RoboStar Technology

The RoboStar framework addresses the need to support roboticists in benefitting from a model-centric, rather than the current code-centric, approach to software development. Many have worked on modern software engineering techniques for robotics [7]. RoboStar is distinctive in its mathematical foundations to support verification by proof (model checking and theorem proving) and to justify the techniques for automatic generation of models, simulations, code, and tests.

A key line of work in RoboStar pursues mathematical foundations using process algebras for refinement that extend CSP. They have themselves a predicative relational semantics defined using the Unifying Theories of Programming [23], and cater for rich data models, and hybrid or probabilistic behaviour. So, for generation of tests, the body of work pioneered by Jan Peleska is extremely relevant. With the work presented here, we seek to take advantage of that.

RoboStar includes a number of domain-specific notations. They cater for the definition of design models for control software, of operational requirements (for the robotic platform and the environment in which the robot is to be used) [5], of simulation models, and of properties [35]. As said, the notation for designs is

RoboChart. It uses the concept of a module to describe platform-independent models of the control software. The notation to model simulations is RoboSim.

A RoboSim model has three components: a d-model, a p-model, and a platform mapping. Loosely speaking, a d-model corresponds to a RoboChart module, in that it describes the software controller of a robot using state machines and abstractions of the services provided by the platform (represented by events, variables and operations). Unlike RoboChart, however, a d-model embeds the simulation paradigm: it describes a cyclic mechanism whose control flow is determined by a time period defining the length of the cycle. As usual, computation happens infinitely fast at the sample times determined by the length of the cycle.

A p-model describes the physical structure of a robot in terms of its links, joints, sensors, and actuators, as well as a robot's behaviours in terms of a set of differential equations. A platform mapping describes how the abstract services used by the software (as defined in a d-model) can be realised in terms of the outputs of sensors and inputs of actuators (of a p-model).

For illustration, we present in Fig. 2 the d-model for a wheeled robot that moves in a straight line, turning when needed to avoid obstacles[2]. A d-model is characterised by a module: in this example, it is defined by the block named SimCMovement (bottom right). A module includes a block, in the example called Vehicle, that gives the abstract characterisation of the robotic platform. In our example, Vehicle provides (P) two operations, move(lv,av) and stop(), representing abstractions for motors defined in the interface MovementI (top left). Vehicle also includes (i) an event obstacle defined in an interface ObstacleI to represent inputs from a sensor that can detect obstacles in front of the robot.

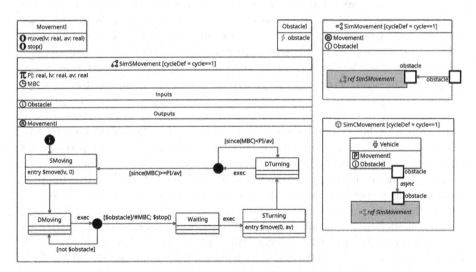

Fig. 2. RoboSim d-model for a simple ranger robot.

---

[2] Numerous more interesting examples are available at robostar.cs.york.ac.uk.

The behaviour of a module is defined by one or more parallel controllers. In Fig. 2, SimCMovement has a single controller called SimMovement, referenced in the module block, and defined in its own block (top right). The behaviour of a controller is defined by one or more parallel state machines. Again, our simple example uses one machine SimSMovement, defined on the left in Fig. 2.

The RoboSim (and RoboChart) state-machine notations are in many ways similar to that of UML and SysML, but they have a precise action language, and support for definition of time properties. First of all, in RoboSim, each module, controller, and machine defines or constrains, via a cycleDef clause, a value for cycle, a variable denoting the number of time units that specifies the length of the simulation cycle. In Fig. 2, cycle is defined to be 1 everywhere. The value of a time unit can be adjusted for different simulations or deployments.

Also, a RoboSim state machine can declare and use clocks. In SimSMovement, we declare a clock MBC to time the turn of the robot when it finds an obstacle. SimSMovement starts in the state SMoving, as indicated by the transition from the initial junction, represented by a black circle with an i in the middle. The entry action for that state calls the operation move; the argument lv (a constant declared locally) defines a linear speed and the argument 0 indicates that the movement is in a straight line (the angular speed is 0).

From SMoving, a transition without a guard or a trigger becomes immediately enabled. So, SimSMovement immediately moves to the state DMoving. Enabled transitions are urgent, so that time is predictable.

From DMoving, the only transition is guarded by the trigger exec. This indicates that no more progress can be made in the current simulation cycle. In the next cycle, however, that transition is taken to a junction, represented by a black circle. Here, SimSMovement takes a transition back to DMoving, if the input event $obstacle has not happened in the current cycle. If it has, SimSMovement resets the clock (# MBC), calls stop, and moves to Waiting.

In Waiting, SimSMovement again pauses until the next cycle. At that point, it moves to the state STurning, calls move(0,av) to turn with speed av, goes to DTurning and again waits for the next cycle. The transitions from the junction reached in the next cycle are guarded by a condition on the value of the clock. If not enough time has passed (since(MBC) ¡ PI/av), then SimSMovement returns to DTurning and waits again for the next cycle. (It is the evolution of the cycles that advances the time.) Otherwise, SimSMovement returns to SMoving.

RoboTool is an implementation of the RoboStar notations and techniques. These include RoboChart and RoboSim, as well as model transformations to convert RoboChart models into RoboSim models, and both RoboChart and RoboSim models into various formal notations (CSP, tock-CSP [3], a discrete-time version of CSP, and *CyPhyCircus* [20], a state-rich hybrid version of CSP). We also target a few tools (PRISM [25], Isabelle/UTP [19], and UPPAAL [37]), and programming languages (for example, C, used here, and Rust).

Our goal is to support testing of RoboChart models through RT-Tester. This can be achieved by (a) generating a simulation model in RoboSim; (b) generating simulation code; and (c) integrating the generated code with the RT-Tester test harness. RoboTool can be used for (a); in Sect. 4, we describe our approach and implementation to support (b) and (c).

3   RT-Tester

RT-Tester is an industrial-strength test-automation tool for automatic test execution and real-time test evaluation. Its key features include a strong C/C++-based test script language, high-performance multi-threading, and hard real-time capability. RT-Tester is associated with RT-Tester Model-Based Testing (RTT-MBT), a test-generation tool. The core RT-Tester and RTT-MBT together support all test integration levels: from unit-tests to software-in-the-loop tests (module tests) to hardware-in-the-loop tests and model-in-the-loop tests.

RTT-MBT is a commercial product arising from the adaptation by Verified Systems of the results of the project TCGen[3]. It supports the generation of test cases for different levels of model coverage allowing generation of test suites with different test strengths. Traceability data relating requirements, test cases, test procedures, and test results are generated and captured during test generation, test execution, and test-result analysis. In addition to test generation, RTT-MBT can also be used for bounded model checking of LTL formulas. We refer to [33] and [28] for more details about RT-Tester and RTT-MBT.

RTT-MBT generates test procedures, that is, scripts implementing one or more test cases, using the RT-Tester test language, called RTTL. In this way the procedures can be directly used with RT-Tester. The test generator however has been explicitly designed to support fast and easy implementation of test-procedure generation for other languages.

Because RTT-MBT uses a model of the system under test (SUT), a simulation of the SUT can be generated from that model. Generating test procedures from a model and executing these tests against a simulation generated from the same model is obviously not useful in helping to discover any flaws of the real SUT. It can however be useful in (a) discovering design weaknesses of the SUT by exercising the simulation, (b) verifying the test strength of a generated test suite (if errors are injected into the simulation), and (c) testing a partly implemented SUT or single parts of an SUT, by simulating the missing parts.

With our work, we support generation from RoboSim models of simulations that can be executed by RT-Tester based on tests generated using other models. In the future, we will also support test generation from RoboSim models.

If the SUT itself is a model, RT-Tester can be used to execute test procedures against this model, as long as the model can be executed (through code generation or a model interpreter or something similar) and the interface of the model is accessible from the outside. The implementation of the communication between the RT-Tester test procedure and the model under test depends on the concrete model and model-execution environment. This implementation

---

[3] Funded   by   BIG   Bremen   Investitions-Gesellschaft   mbH   (research   grant 2INNO1015B).

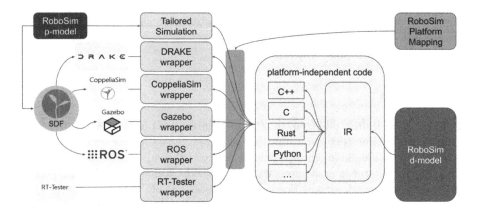

Fig. 3. RoboTool approach to code generation of simulations from RoboSim models.

is normally encapsulated in a so-called interface module that is part of the test environment used by the RT-Tester test procedure.

Our work provides, via generation of code and associated interface module, a means to execute using RT-Tester a RoboSim model, that is, use it as a model under test as part of an RT-Tester test procedure. The details of our encoding of RoboSim in RT-Tester are given in the next section.

4   RoboSim and RT-Tester

The RoboTool approach to code generation from RoboSim models is outlined in Fig. 3. The d-models (bottom right) can be used to generate platform-independent code. As further detailed in the sequel, it is this facility that we have built upon to cater for code that can be executed in RT-Tester.

The p-models (top left) can be used to generate XML-based documents, written in the SDF format[4], accepted by various off-the-shelf simulators as indicated in Fig. 3 (DRAKE[5], CoppeliaSim [34], Gazebo [24], and so on). SDF documents capture the links, joints, sensors, and actuators of a p-model, but not the user-specified equations. Instead, the simulators use physics engines to describe behaviour. An alternative indicated in Fig. 3 is the generation of a tailored simulation of the equations, rather than using an off-the-shelf simulator.

The platform mapping supports the generation of tool-specific wrappers. The platform-independent code raises service requests as defined in the RoboSim model (via the platform block of the module). These are implemented as defined in the platform mapping, using the API of specific simulation tools.

In Sect. 4.1, we give an overview of our approach to generation of platform-independent code. Section 4.2 describes the wrapper for RT-Tester.

---

[4] sdformat.org.
[5] drake.mit.edu/.

4.1 Platform-Independent Code Generation

The RoboTool code generation is based on model transformations: (1) a model-to-model (m2m) transformation between a RoboSim d-model and an intermediate representation (IR) and (2) a family of model-to-text (m2t) transformations. In Fig. 3, the first is represented by the arrow from the RoboSim d-model block (bottom right) to the block labelled IR, and the transformations in the second set are depicted by the arrows from the IR block to blocks representing code written in various programming languages, such as Rust and C.

This two-step approach separates the encoding of the semantics of RoboSim d-models from the specific details of the concrete target programming language. The m2m transformation (1) captures the semantics of RoboSim d-models in terms of an abstract procedural programming language with explicit parallelism constructs (IR), while the m2t transformations (2) implement the constructs of the IR into specific target languages. So, extending our code generator to target a new programming language requires implementing only a new m2t transformation, which is much simpler than encoding the semantics of RoboSim d-models.

The m2m transformation takes a RoboSim module as input and returns a Program of our IR; Fig. 4 shows an excerpt of the IR metamodel. A Program contains a name, any number of imports, enumerations, records, and procedures, and an entry block. Imports, Enumerations, Records, and Procedures are comparable to similar concepts in procedural programming languages like C (where we find, respectively, includes, enums, structs, and functions). The EntryBlock is the program's starting point and is similar to C's main function.

Figure 5 sketches the C rendering of the IR for our example in Fig. 2. The C code is the result of an m2t transformation specific to C. Yet, it is in direct correspondence with the IR, and so we use the code to illustrate the IR structure.

In Fig. 5, there are no imports arising from the IR (although some includes are in the code, due to requirements of C). In general the imports are used to reflect the structure of the RoboSim model in the code.

The enumerations represent (a) the execution stages of states (for instance, ENTER, EXIT), (b) the possible outcomes of an execution step (WAIT or CONTINUE), (c) the state and transition identifiers, and (d) the inputs and outputs of each component of the RoboSim model (robotic platform, controllers and state machines). In Fig. 5 (lines 1–4), M_SimCMovement_output_Type is an enumeration whose values include representations of the outputs of the module SimCMovement, namely, move and stop. An extra exec constant is used as part of the realisation of the simulation event exec. The enumeration in the IR that represents all values that can be communicated by an output of SimCMovement is rendered in C as a struct, because an enum in C can include just constants (see M_SimCMovement_output_Enum in Fig. 5 (lines 6–8)).

The records specify the inputs (events), internal status (for instance, its current active state), and the memories of the state machines. In Fig. 5 (lines 10–12), a record type sm_memory represents the memory of the occurrence of SimSMovement in SimMovement (sm is the internal name of the reference to SimSMovement

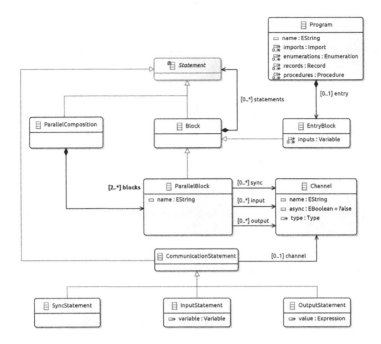

Fig. 4. Partial metamodel of the intermediate representation.

in SimMovement). In the example, the memory contains just the constant values (for Pl, lv, and av, since SimSMovement has no variables (see Fig. 2)).

The procedures implement the behaviours of a single step of the execution of states, state machines, controllers, and the module, and of the junctions and actions. In Fig. 5 (lines 14–18), stm_sm is the procedure for SimSMovement.

An EntryBlock is a special form of Block that defines the overall behaviour of a Program; a set of Variables models the inputs. A Block has a sequence of zero or more statements, and is itself a Statement. In a C program, the EntryBlock is realised as the main function. In Fig. 5, it is sketched in lines 20–40.

The IR includes statements commonly available in programming languages, such as assignment, loops, and conditionals (omitted in Fig. 4), but also an explicit construct for ParallelComposition. This is shown in Fig. 4 as a subclass of Statement. A ParallelComposition has two or more ParallelBlocks, each with a name and channels that can be used for synchronisation, input and output.

A Channel has a name, a boolean value async, which indicates whether the channel can be used for synchronous or asynchronous communication, and a type for the values that can be communicated by the channel. Besides being included in ParallelBlocks, channels are used in CommunicationStatements, which can be either SyncStatements, InputStatements or OutputStatements. InputStatements additionally include a variable in which the received value is stored. OutputStatements include the Expression (value) that is communicated. The Expressions are those commonly encountered in programming languages.

```
1  typedef enum {
2    M_SimCMovement_output_move, M_SimCMovement_output_stop,
3    M_SimCMovement_output__exec_,
4  } M_SimCMovement_output_Type;
5
6  typedef struct {
7    M_SimCMovement_output_Type type; M_SimCMovement_output_Data data;
8  } M_SimCMovement_output_Enum;
9
10 typedef struct {
11   float PI; float av; float lv;
12 } sm_memory;
13
14 void *stm_sm(void *arg) {
15   stm_sm_Channels* channels = (stm_sm_Channels*) arg;
16   sm_input_Enum_Channel* registerRead_sm = channels->registerRead_sm;
17   sm_output_Enum_Channel* registerWrite_sm = channels->registerWrite_sm; ...
18 }
19 ...
20 int main(int argc, char* argv[]) {
21   sm_input_Enum_Channel* registerRead_sm =
22     (sm_input_Enum_Channel*)malloc(sizeof(sm_input_Enum_Channel));
23   sm_output_Enum_Channel* registerWrite_sm =
24     (sm_output_Enum_Channel*)malloc(sizeof(sm_output_Enum_Channel));
25   ...
26   pthread_t stm_sm_id;
27   stm_sm_Channels* stm_sm_channels =
28     (stm_sm_Channels*)malloc(sizeof(stm_sm_Channels));
29
30   status = pthread_create(&stm_sm_id, NULL, stm_sm, stm_sm_channels);
31   if (status != 0) err_abort(status, "Create stm_sm thread");
32   ...
33   status = pthread_create(&control_id, NULL, control, control_channels);
34   status = pthread_create(&mod_SimCMovement_thread_id, NULL,
35
36   status = pthread_join(stm_sm_id, NULL);
37   if (status != 0)
38     err_abort(status, "Join stm_sm thread"); ...
39   return 0;
40 }
```

Fig. 5. Realisation of automatically generated IR in C.

In general terms, the semantics of a RoboSim module is given by the parallel composition of (CSP) processes for each controller communicating via channels representing their inputs and outputs. Similarly, the semantics of a controller is the parallel composition of processes for its machines. The notions of ParallelBlocks and Channels facilitates the encoding of this semantics in the IR; the statements of the EntryBlock define this parallel composition.

For our C encoding, we have implemented a notion of channel. In Fig. 5, stm_sm takes the representation of the channels used to describe the behaviour of SimSMovement in CSP as argument. They are called locally registerRead_sm and registerWrite_sm. The main function creates the channels needed by all ParallelBlocks and execute the functions that represent the controllers and machines in separate threads (see lines 21–24 for an example).

In line 26 of Fig. 5, a thread pthread_t is declared to represent the process that captures the semantics of SimSMovement. Lines 27–28 declare and create stm_sm_channels, whose components include the channels for SimSMovement. Line 30 shows the creation of the thread (pthread_create), using the function stm_sm and its channels stm_sm_channels for SimSMovement.

As shown in Line 31, if the creation fails, the program is aborted. Otherwise, other threads are created; in the example, we have one for the controller (line 33) and one for the module (line 34). The pthread_create function starts as well as creates a thread. After all threads start, the main function waits for their conclusion: lines 36–38 show the command for the stm_sm_id thread.

4.2   Connecting to RT-Tester

The parallel composition additionally includes a control Block to provide the means for interacting with the Program. In its simplest form, the Block requests inputs via the terminal, communicates them to the module Block, waits for outputs, and prints them to the terminal. The control Block is the component that links the platform-independent code and the actual platform, be it a terminal, a simulator, or a testing tool. The latter is our focus here.

The rendering of this control block in C is sketched in Fig. 6; it connects RT-Tester and our simulation. In general, every control block needs to use a communication mechanism to connect the platform-independent simulation code for the RoboSim model with the simulator. For RT-Tester, we use shared memory.

In detail, the control block (for RT-Tester) extracts the RoboSim events from the thread parameter (elided in line 5), initialises the shared memory (line 3), declares variables that record the input events, the output events, and a termination flag terminate__ (lines 5–7) that can be used by the simulator to interrupt the simulation, and starts the control loop (lines 9–34). (A semaphore, omitted in Fig. 6, controls the cycle, that is, passage of time.)

The control loop is active while the termination flag is false and at each step, it reads inputs in a loop (lines 10–22), produces outputs in a second loop (lines 23–32), and waits the next cycle. The input loop is controlled by the boolean variable inputdone, which becomes true once a done event is received from the simulator. This event can be sent by a test or by (a simulation of) the platform to indicate that no more inputs are available in the current cycle.

The loop to read inputs iteratively reads a value from the shared memory (line 12), and treats each event accordingly (lines 13–21). In particular, for the input event obstacle (line 15), an equivalent event of the RoboSim module is created and written to the module's registerRead channel (lines 15–17). The treatment of the remaining events (including the simulation events done and end, omitted in Fig. 6) is similar, with additional assignments to control the termination of the input and control loops.

The output loop is similarly controlled by a boolean variable outputdone. Each iteration of the loop waits for an event on the module's registerWrite channel (lines 25–26) and processes it according to its type. For instance, if the event is stop (line 27), the output variable is initialised (line 28) so that its event type is set to stop (line 29) and the variable is written to the shared memory (line 30). The event move is treated similarly, with additional steps to record the values of the parameters. The simulation event exec is treated by assigning true to the guard variable outputdone (omitted in Fig. 6).

```
1  void *control(void *arg) {
2    ...
3    attach_shmlib_shm(); init_shmlib_shm();
4
5    asts2sut_shm_event_t input;
6    sut2asts_shm_event_t output;
7    bool terminate__ = false;
8
9    while (!terminate__) {
10     bool inputdone = false;
11     while (!inputdone) {
12       input = getShmlib_asts2sut();
13       switch (input.event) {
14         case obstacle: {
15           M_SimCMovement_input_write(
16             registerRead_SimCMovement , create_M_SimCMovement_input_obstacle()
17           );
18           break;
19         }
20         ...
21       }
22     }
23     bool outputdone = false;
24     while (!outputdone) {
25       M_SimCMovement_output_Enum _output_ =
26         M_SimCMovement_output_read(registerWrite_SimCMovement);
27       if (_output_.type == M_SimCMovement_output_stop) {
28         memset(&output, 0, sizeof(output));
29         output.event = stop;
30         putShmlib_sut2asts(output);
31       } else ...
32     }
33     ...
34   }
35 }
36
```

Fig. 6. Control block connecting RT-Tester and simulation in C.

The control over the passage of simulation cycles is in the tests to allow precise control over when events can or must happen. This is discussed next.

5   Example: Testing the Simple Ranger Robot

Our approach to testing using RoboChart is based on the testing theories for its (tock-)CSP semantics that we have mentioned above. For our example, a RoboChart model, as well as several other RoboStar artefacts, are available[6].

The RoboSim model, presented in Sect. 2, is a simplification (for didactic reasons) of the model that has been automatically generated from the RoboChart model. So, tests generated from the RoboChart model have the potential to reveal mistakes of the RoboSim model (or of our code generator). Moreover, as said in Sect. 3, there is value in running the tests, even if there is a connection between the models used for generation of the tests and the simulation.

The tests generated from the RoboChart model are based on traces that define negative (forbidden) behaviours. They have the form $s \frown \langle r \rangle$, where s is a sequence of allowed events and r is a forbidden event. For

---

[6] http://www.robostar.cs.york.ac.uk/case_studies/sranger/.

example, a simple forbidden trace generated for our example is specified as $\langle move.out.lv.0, obstacle.in \rangle$. This trace indicates that after the occurrence of a call move(lv,0), the input event obstacle cannot be accepted immediately. In the testing theory for tock-CSP, the test for this trace can be described as follows.

$$inc \rightarrow_U move.out.lv.0 \rightarrow_U pass \rightarrow_U obstacle.in \rightarrow_U fail \rightarrow_U Stop_U$$

Here, we use inc, $pass$ and $fail$ to indicate the test verdicts **inconclusive, pass,** and **fail**. This description can be interpreted as follows: (1) initially, the test is **inconclusive**; (2) after the output $move.out.lv.0$ is observed, the test **passes**; and if immediately after (2) an input $obstacle.in$ is accepted, the test **fails** and finishes. We note that operation calls are regarded as outputs of the simulation.

To implement and execute such tests in RT-Tester, we create test procedures that describe particular executions of the controller. They all follow a pattern (illustrated in Fig. 7) where input and output ports implemented through the shared memory are declared (lines 2–3), the controller is executed in a separate process (forked from the @INIT block – line 4), and a sequence of interactions is defined (lines 5–39) that implement the test. In the example, we illustrate that we can send events to the controller (lines 9–10), wait for events from the controller (lines 14–15), and allow time to pass (omitted in Fig. 7).

In detail, the core of the test implementation is the @PROCESS component, which declares the variables status, to record the results of communications, robot_action, to store observed outputs of the simulation, and stimulation, to construct events sent to the simulation. Afterwards, @PROCESS defines three TestSteps (delimited by @rttBeginTestStep and @rttEndTestStep).

The first test step (lines 8–11) sends the IR event done to inform the simulation that no input events are being sent, since the first RoboSim event of the test is an output $move.out.lv.0$ (representing an operation call).

The second test step (lines 13–23) first attempts to read (@rttSelect) an event from the simulation (line 14) by waiting for a message on the input port (shm_sut2asts_p). An upper bound of 1000 ms is imposed to allow for execution delays, but this does not reflect the passing of simulation time : the trace determines that no time must pass before $move.out.lv.0$, but in simulation terms this means that the cycle cannot advance, but real execution time might.

Afterwards, in line 15, if the attempt to read is successful (status==0), we retrieve the message from shm_sut2asts_p and store it in robot_action. In lines 16–19, we check the negation of the requirement that $move.out.lv.0$ must happen (line 16): the communication is successful and the event communicated is $move.out.lv.0$. This is implemented by checking the value of status again, and inspecting the event communicated to ensure it is $move$ with arguments 1.0 and 0.0. If the negation is true, then, in lines 20–21, the test step is ended and the test procedure stops. This corresponds to the situation where the trace of the test (containing just the event $move.out.lv.0$) cannot be reached. By stopping the test without a verdict, RT-Tester implicitly records the inconclusive result.

The third test step (lines 25–37) sends, in order, the event $obstacle$ and the IR event done to the simulation, clears the port shm_sut2asts_p (line 33), waits

```
1   @abstract machine test1(){
2     @input   queuing port shm_sut2asts_p on shm_sut2asts;
3     @output queuing port shm_asts2sut_p on shm_asts2sut;
4     @INIT: { ... } ...
5     @PROCESS: { ...
6       shm_sut2asts_t robot_action; shm_asts2sut_t stimulation;
7
8       @rttBeginTestStep("cycle 1 inputs -- no inputs"); {
9         memset(&stimulation, 0, sizeof(stimulation)); stimulation.event = done;
10        @rttPut(shm_asts2sut_p, &stimulation);
11      } @rttEndTestStep;
12
13      @rttBeginTestStep("cycle 1 outputs -- move.lv.0"); { ...
14        status = @rttSelect(0, 1000 _ms, shm_sut2asts_p);
15        if (status == 0) @rttGet(shm_sut2asts_p, &robot_action);
16        if (!status == 0 || !(robot_action.event == move &&
17          abs(robot_action.values[0]- 1.0) <= EPSILON &&
18          abs(robot_action.values[1]- 0.0) <= EPSILON
19        )) {
20          @rttEndTestStep;
21          @rttStopTest;
22        }
23      } @rttEndTestStep;
24
25      @rttBeginTestStep("cycle 1 -- send obstacle and wait for reaction"); {...
26        memset(&stimulation, 0, sizeof(stimulation));
27        stimulation.event = obstacle;
28        @rttPut(shm_asts2sut_p, &stimulation);
29
30        memset(&stimulation, 0, sizeof(stimulation)); stimulation.event = done;
31        @rttPut(shm_asts2sut_p, &stimulation);
32
33        @rttClearPort(shm_sut2asts_p);
34        status = @rttSelect(0, 1000 _ms, shm_sut2asts_p);
35        if (status == 0) @rttGet(shm_sut2asts_p, &robot_action);
36        @rttAssert(!status == 0 || !(robot_action.event == obstacle_treated));
37      } @rttEndTestStep;
38      @rttStopTest;
39    }
40 }
41
```

Fig. 7. Control block connecting RT-Tester and a simulation in C. This example is for the test for the trace $\langle move.lv.0, obstacle \rangle$. Details such as forking and killing simulation processes, and documentation of tests, are omitted.

for an event on this port (lines 34–35), and asserts that either an event has not occurred or that it is not obstacle_treated (line 66). So, if the event obstacle_treated is observed, the test fails. The obstacle_treated event reflects the use of the input obstacle by the simulation. (This is recorded by a platform-independent log, that is implemented for RT-Tester as extra events: one for each input). Finally, the test is stopped (line 49).

In summary, a test implementation is obtained as follows, for a trace $s \frown \langle r \rangle$ with two parts, a trace s followed by a final forbidden event r. The events in s are implemented as test steps that may cause the test to end early with an inconclusive verdict or allow the test to proceed. The forbidden event r is implemented as a final test step that asserts that r does not occur. An output, such as $move.lv.0$, is implemented by selecting a port, reading an event, and checking whether it is r. An input event, such as $obstacle$, is implemented by sending r and done to the simulation, since no other input events need to be sent, and inspecting a log to determine whether the input has been accepted.

Our example does not explicitly include time information, although the absence of a *tock* event indicates that the interactions must happen urgently: in the current cycle. We can also handle tests that go over several cycles. For instance, the trace $\langle move.out.lv.0, tock, move.out.lv.0 \rangle$ checks an output $move.out.lv.0$ in the second cycle of the simulation. It gives rise to the following test.

$$inc \rightarrow_U move.out.lv.0 \rightarrow_U$$
$$inc \rightarrow_U (move.out?x?y \rightarrow_U Stop_U \square stop.out \rightarrow_U Stop_U)$$
$$\triangle_1 pass \rightarrow_U move.out.lv.0 \rightarrow_U fail \rightarrow_U Stop_U$$

Here, $\square$ indicates that after $move.out.lv.0$, there is a choice of outputs: either $move.out?x?y$, representing calls to move with arbitrary arguments, or $stop.out$, representing a call to stop, in the same cycle. If one of those outputs happen, we have an *inc*onclusive verdict. If, however, the cycle advances, as indicated by $\triangle_1$, then the test *pass*es, unless we observe $move.out.lv.0$, then the test *fail*s.

We implement such a test much in the same way as above. The choice ($\square$) is implemented by waiting for an event from the simulation and checking it. If an event listed in the choice happens (in the example, if it is a call to the move operation or stop event), the test ends (@rttStopTest). Otherwise, the test continues. The $\triangle$ operator is implemented by requesting the simulation to advance the cycle (by sending the IR event next_cycle).

In the future, the approach illustrated here will be generalised in the form of translation rules from tests to RT-Tester test specifications.

6   Conclusions and Vision for the Future

Our focus in this paper has been to support the simulation of RoboSim models with RT-Tester. This contribution has shown how it is possible to bring together distinct but complementary pieces of work: test generation using RoboChart, simulation of RoboSim models, and automated testing with RT-Tester. Whilst each aspect of work has their own strengths, as we have discussed, by integrating the tools in the way described, there are significant benefits that can be gained.

From a robotics perspective, being able to define clearly the model of the software and hardware, and having a mechanism to test to a much more rigorous and extensive standard then has been previously possible, opens up new possibilities. From the RT-Tester perspective, RoboSim, and its connection to the other RoboStar notations and techniques, opens a door to tackle robotics applications using a domain-specific notation.

Further work is required for the evaluation of several aspects of our approach. Further examples will support an analysis of the scalability of our approach, in terms of automatic generation of test procedures and test execution. Automation will also enable study of the detection capabilities of the various approaches to test generation from RoboChart models. They vary in the set of mutation operators used and how they are applied, and in the form of test cases considered: timed or untimed, and for traces or failures refinement.

To improve testing efficiency, the tests generated from RoboChart can be factorised, so that several forbidden traces are used to define a single adaptive test that can cope with a choice of inputs and outputs. We plan to improve our test procedures by considering factorisation and additional use of RT-Tester embedded facilities to determine the verdicts.

The most relevant aspect of the RoboTool approach to code generation for the work we present here is that concerning the d-model (right and bottom of Fig. 3). This is because we have focussed on simulating and testing the software component of a robotic system in isolation. Being able to integrate simulations of the robotic platform, with the robotic control software in that platform, will enable that wider testing of complete robotic systems before deployment. We aim to work further on this as part of our on-going and future work.

Another ambitious goal is to support model-based testing from RoboChart and RoboSim models entirely using RT-Tester. This objective requires encoding into RT-Tester of the operational semantics of RoboChart and RoboSim, but has the potential to yield very rich outcomes.

The RoboStar team looks forward to continued collaboration with Jan Peleska, at least via his group and Verified Systems International GmbH, to push forward the agenda to support further use of formal methods in industry [22]. The fruits of Jan Peleska's work will no doubt have long-term impact in all applications of embedded and cyber-physical systems.

Acknowledgements. The work of Cavalcanti, Miyazawa, and Timmis has been funded by the UK EPSRC Grants EP/R025479/1, and EP/V026801/2, and by the UK Royal Academy of Engineering Grant No CiET1718/45.

References

1. Alberto, A., Cavalcanti, A.L.C., Gaudel, M.C., Simao, A.: Formal mutation testing for *Circus*. Inf. Softw. Technol. **81**, 131–153 (2017)
2. Baxter, J., Cavalcanti, A.L.C., Gazda, M., Hierons, R.: Testing using CSP models: time, inputs, and outputs - extended version. Technical report, RoboStar Centre on Software Engineering for Robotics (2022). robostar.cs.york.ac.uk/publications/reports/BCGH22.pdf
3. Baxter, J., Ribeiro, P., Cavalcanti, A.L.C.: Sound reasoning in tock-CSP. Acta Informatica **59**, 125–162 (2022)
4. Cavalcanti, A., et al.: RoboStar technology: a roboticist's toolbox for combined proof, simulation, and testing. In: Software Engineering for Robotics, pp. 249–293. Springer, Cham (2021). https://doi.org/10.1007/978-3-030-66494-7_9
5. Cavalcanti, A., Baxter, J., Carvalho, G.: RoboWorld: where can my robot work? In: Calinescu, R., Păsăreanu, C.S. (eds.) SEFM 2021. LNCS, vol. 13085, pp. 3–22. Springer, Cham (2021). https://doi.org/10.1007/978-3-030-92124-8_1
6. Cavalcanti, A., Baxter, J., Hierons, R.M., Lefticaru, R.: Testing robots using CSP. In: Beyer, D., Keller, C. (eds.) TAP 2019. LNCS, vol. 11823, pp. 21–38. Springer, Cham (2019). https://doi.org/10.1007/978-3-030-31157-5_2

7. Cavalcanti, A.L.C., Dongol, B., Hierons, R., Timmis, J., Woodcock, J.C.P. (eds.): Software Engineering for Robotics. Springer, Cham (2021). https://doi.org/10.1007/978-3-030-66494-7

8. Cavalcanti, A., Gaudel, M.-C.: Testing for refinement in CSP. In: Butler, M., Hinchey, M.G., Larrondo-Petrie, M.M. (eds.) ICFEM 2007. LNCS, vol. 4789, pp. 151–170. Springer, Heidelberg (2007). https://doi.org/10.1007/978-3-540-76650-6_10

9. Cavalcanti, A., Gaudel, M.-C.: Specification coverage for testing in *Circus*. In: Qin, S. (ed.) UTP 2010. LNCS, vol. 6445, pp. 1–45. Springer, Heidelberg (2010). https://doi.org/10.1007/978-3-642-16690-7_1

10. Cavalcanti, A.L.C., Gaudel, M.C.: Testing for refinement in *Circus*. Acta Informatica **48**(2), 97–147 (2011)

11. Cavalcanti, A., Gaudel, M.-C.: Data flow coverage for *Circus*-based testing. In: Gnesi, S., Rensink, A. (eds.) FASE 2014. LNCS, vol. 8411, pp. 415–429. Springer, Heidelberg (2014). https://doi.org/10.1007/978-3-642-54804-8_29

12. Cavalcanti, A.L.C., Gaudel, M.C.: Test selection for traces refinement. Theoret. Comput. Sci. **563**, 1–42 (2015)

13. Cavalcanti, A., Gaudel, M.-C., Hierons, R.M.: Conformance relations for distributed testing based on CSP. In: Wolff, B., Zaïdi, F. (eds.) ICTSS 2011. LNCS, vol. 7019, pp. 48–63. Springer, Heidelberg (2011). https://doi.org/10.1007/978-3-642-24580-0_5

14. Cavalcanti, A.L.C., Hierons, R., Nogueira, S.: Inputs and outputs in CSP: a model and a testing theory. ACM Trans. Comput. Logic (2020)

15. Cavalcanti, A., Huang, W., Peleska, J., Woodcock, J.: CSP and Kripke structures. In: Leucker, M., Rueda, C., Valencia, F.D. (eds.) ICTAC 2015. LNCS, vol. 9399, pp. 505–523. Springer, Cham (2015). https://doi.org/10.1007/978-3-319-25150-9_29

16. Cavalcanti, A.L.C., et al.: Verified simulation for robotics. Sci. Comput. Program. **174**, 1–37 (2019)

17. Cavalcanti, A.L.C., Simao, A.: Fault-based refinement-testing for CSP. Softw. Q. J. (2019)

18. Feliachi, A., Gaudel, M.-C., Wenzel, M., Wolff, B.: The *Circus* testing theory revisited in Isabelle/HOL. In: Groves, L., Sun, J. (eds.) ICFEM 2013. LNCS, vol. 8144, pp. 131–147. Springer, Heidelberg (2013). https://doi.org/10.1007/978-3-642-41202-8_10

19. Foster, S., Baxter, J., Cavalcanti, A., Miyazawa, A., Woodcock, J.: Automating verification of state machines with reactive designs and Isabelle/UTP. In: Bae, K., Ölveczky, P.C. (eds.) FACS 2018. LNCS, vol. 11222, pp. 137–155. Springer, Cham (2018). https://doi.org/10.1007/978-3-030-02146-7_7

20. Foster, S., Cavalcanti, A.L.C., Canham, S., Woodcock, J.C.P., Zeyda, F.: Unifying theories of reactive design contracts. Theoret. Comput. Sci. **802**, 105–140 (2020)

21. Gaudel, M.-C.: Testing can be formal, too. In: Mosses, P.D., Nielsen, M., Schwartzbach, M.I. (eds.) CAAP 1995. LNCS, vol. 915, pp. 82–96. Springer, Heidelberg (1995). https://doi.org/10.1007/3-540-59293-8_188

22. Gleirscher, M., Marmsoler, D.: Formal methods in dependable systems engineering: a survey of professionals from Europe and north America. Empir. Softw. Eng. **25**(6), 4473–4546 (2020)

23. Hoare, C.A.R., Jifeng, H.: Unifying Theories of Programming. Prentice-Hall (1998)

24. Koenig, N., Andrew, H.: Design and use paradigms for gazebo, an open-source multi-robot simulator. In: 2004 IEEE/RSJ International Conference on Intelligent Robots and Systems, vol. 3, pp. 2149–2154. IEEE (2004)

25. Kwiatkowska, M., Norman, G., Parker, D.: Probabilistic symbolic model checking with PRISM: a hybrid approach. Int. J. Softw. Tools Technol. Transfer **6**(2), 128–142 (2004)
26. Larsen, P.G., et al.: Integrated tool chain for model-based design of cyber-physical systems: the INTO-CPS project. In: 2nd International Workshop on Modelling, Analysis, and Control of Complex CPS, pp. 1–6 (2016)
27. Miyazawa, A., Ribeiro, P., Li, W., Cavalcanti, A.L.C., Timmis, J., Woodcock, J.C.P.: RoboChart: modelling and verification of the functional behaviour of robotic applications. Softw. Syst. Model. **18**(5), 3097–3149 (2019)
28. Peleska, J., Huang, W.: Industrial-strength model-based testing of safety-critical systems. In: Fitzgerald, J., Heitmeyer, C., Gnesi, S., Philippou, A. (eds.) FM 2016. LNCS, vol. 9995, pp. 3–22. Springer, Cham (2016). https://doi.org/10.1007/978-3-319-48989-6_1
29. Peleska, J.l., Huang, W., Cavalcanti, A.L.C.: Finite complete suites for CSP refinement testing: Sci. Comput. Program. **179**, 1–23 (2019)
30. Peleska, J.: Test automation for safety-critical systems: industrial application and future developments. In: Gaudel, M.-C., Woodcock, J. (eds.) FME 1996. LNCS, vol. 1051, pp. 39–59. Springer, Heidelberg (1996). https://doi.org/10.1007/3-540-60973-3_79
31. Peleska, J., Siegel, M.: Test automation of safety-critical reactive systems. South Afr. Comput. J. **19**, 53–77 (1997)
32. Peleska, J., Vorobev, E., Lapschies, F.: Automated test case generation with SMT-solving and abstract interpretation. In: Bobaru, M., Havelund, K., Holzmann, G.J., Joshi, R. (eds.) NFM 2011. LNCS, vol. 6617, pp. 298–312. Springer, Heidelberg (2011). https://doi.org/10.1007/978-3-642-20398-5_22
33. Peleska, J., Vorobev, E., Lapschies, F., Zahlten, C.: Automated model-based testing with RT-tester. Technical report (2011). http://www.informatik.uni-bremen.de/agbs/testingbenchmarks/turn_indicator/tool/rtt-mbt.pdf
34. Rohmer, E., Singh, S.P.N., Freese, M.: V-REP: a versatile and scalable robot simulation framework. In: IEEE/RSJ International Conference on Intelligent Robots and Systems, vol. 1, pp. 1321–1326. IEEE (2013)
35. Windsor, M., Cavalcanti, A.L.C.: RoboCert: property specification in robotics. In: Riesco, A., Zhang, M. (eds.) International Conference on Formal Engineering Methods. Lecture Notes in Computer Science, vol. 13478, pp. 386–403. Springer, Cham (2022). https://doi.org/10.1007/978-3-031-17244-1_23
36. Woodcock, J., Cavalcanti, A., Fitzgerald, J., Foster, S., Larsen, P.G.: Contracts in CML. In: Margaria, T., Steffen, B. (eds.) ISoLA 2014. LNCS, vol. 8803, pp. 54–73. Springer, Heidelberg (2014). https://doi.org/10.1007/978-3-662-45231-8_5
37. Zhang, M., Du, D., Sampaio, A.C.A., Cavalcanti, A.L.C., Filho, M.C., Zhang, M.: Transforming RoboSim models into UPPAAL. In: 15th International Symposium on Theoretical Aspects of Software Engineering, pp. 71–78. IEEE (2021)

Implementation Relations for Distributed Testing

Robert M. Hierons[1]([✉]), Mercedes G. Merayo[2], and Manuel Núñez[2]

[1] Department of Computer Science, The University of Sheffield,
Sheffield S1 4GG, UK
`r.hierons@sheffield.ac.uk`
[2] Design and Testing of Reliable Systems Research Group, Universidad Complutense
de Madrid, Madrid, Spain

Abstract. When testing a system that interacts with its environment at several physically distributed interfaces (ports) it is normal to place a local tester at each port. If the local testers do not synchronise their actions then the local tester at port p can only observe the sequence of inputs and outputs that occur at p. If, in addition, there is no global clock then it may be impossible to reconstruct the global trace that occurred in testing and testing is then using the distributed test architecture. As a result, the System Under Test (SUT) might be able to produce a global trace that is not allowed by the specification, and so would normally represent a failure, but where the local testers cannot observe this difference. The use of the distributed test architecture thus affects the ability of testing to distinguish between a specification and an SUT and so leads to the need for a different notion of correctness (implementation relation). This paper explores alternative implementation relations for distributed testing and how they relate.

1 Introduction

Jan Peleska has made a significant long-term contribution to the development of systematic test generation techniques based on formal models (see, for example, [19]) and has shown how such techniques can be used in an industrial setting [24–26]. This is an important contribution since testing is a core part of software development. As Peleska has shown, if there is a model of the required behaviour of the *system under test (SUT)* then there is potential to automate test generation based on this model, with this approach often being called *model-based testing (MBT)*. Further, if the model has a formal semantics then automated test generation can be systematic, in the sense that one can formally reason about the types of faults that test cases can find (see, for example, [1, 7, 19, 20, 24, 27, 28, 30]).

Most work on MBT uses models in the form of a finite state machine (FSM) or labelled transition system (LTS). However, the user is not expected to produce FSM or LTS models: the user can produce models written using a state-based language such as Statecharts, with these models being mapped to FSMs

A. E. Haxthausen et al. (Eds.): Peleska Festschrift 2023, LNCS 14165, pp. 34–48, 2023.
https://doi.org/10.1007/978-3-031-40132-9_3

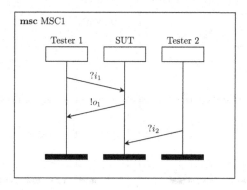

Fig. 1. A controllability problem [15]

or LTSs [6,7,20]. Testing is typically then a process in which a tester interacts with the SUT, through providing inputs and observing outputs, and the
resultant sequence of inputs and outputs (*trace*) is checked against the original model/specification. Although this captures how testing is often carried out,
testing can be rather different. For example, the communication between the
tester and the SUT might be through a medium that introduces a delay. Testing
is then asynchronous, with the trace that is observed by the tester potentially
not being the trace produced by the SUT since the tester observes inputs before
the SUT does and the SUT produces outputs before they are observed by the
tester [9,12,32]. The SUT might also interact with its environment at multiple
physically distributed interfaces, called *ports*, with there being a *local tester* at
each port. If the local testers do not synchronise their actions and there is no
global clock then testing is taking place in the distributed test architecture [21].
We use the term *distributed testing* when we refer to testing in the distributed
test architecture.

    In the distributed test architecture, an observation consists of a number of
local traces, one for each port, as opposed to a single (global) trace. Early work on
distributed testing noted that it can lead to *controllability problems*, which occur
because a tester cannot observe the interactions at other ports and, therefore,
sometimes does not know when to supply an input [4,29]. To see how controllability problems can occur, consider the scenario shown in Fig. 1 in which three
processes interact (two testers and the SUT), arrows represent the exchange of
messages, and time progresses as we move down the line associated with a process. Here, Tester 1 starts by sending input $?i_1$ to the SUT and should then
receive output $!o_1$. After this, Tester 2 should send input $?i_2$. However Tester 2
cannot observe the interactions between Tester 1 and the SUT and so does not
know when to send its input.

    There can also be *observability problems*, where a global trace not allowed
by the specification occurs but the observation made (the set of local traces)
is consistent with a behaviour of the specification [5]. To see how observability
problems can occur, consider the two scenarios shown in Fig. 2. Here, there are

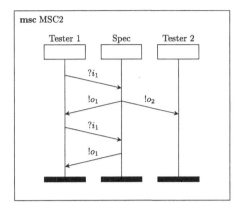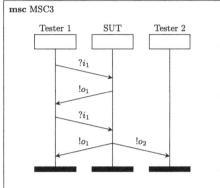

Fig. 2. Observationally equivalent scenarios [15]

two different global traces but in each case Tester 1 observes $?i_1!o_1?i_1!o_1$ and Tester 2 observes $!o_2$. As a result, these global traces are indistinguishable when testing in the distributed test architecture.

Much of the early work on distributed testing aimed to produce test generation techniques that returned test sequences that do not suffer from controllability or observability problems. This previous work thus used traditional implementation relations such as **ioco** [30]: the implementation relation did not reflect the reduced ability of testing to distinguish between different global traces and so also different processes. As a result, for example, such work might consider a test case to be sufficient to find a given fault even when no tester can observe a difference in behaviour (again, see Fig. 2). This paper focuses on later work that developed new implementation relations that reflected the nature of the distributed test architecture and the ability of testing to distinguish processes in this test architecture.

This paper is structured as follows. Section 2 defines the types of models considered and introduces notation used throughout the paper. Section 3 then formalises what we mean by distributed testing and Sect. 4 defines and compares the implementation relations. Section 5 then outlines some related and future work and Sect. 6 draws conclusions.

2   Preliminaries

In software testing, typically a tester applies inputs and observes outputs produced by the SUT. Throughout this paper we use I to denote the set of possible inputs and O to denote the set of possible outputs. The sets I and O are therefore disjoint. We will normally precede the name of an input by '?' and the name of an output by '!'. We will use a running example to illustrate the key principles.

Example 1. The system depicted in Fig. 3 represents a simplified version of the diagnosis protocol of a gynaecological cancer screening centre management system. It focuses on the functionality associated with the process that begins at the moment a patient makes a date with the doctor. When a patient visits the doctor, they can either prescribe some tests or diagnose an illness. In the first case, the patient must go to the laboratory and image diagnosis section and make the corresponding appointments. Once the results of the tests are available, the patient will visit the doctor. If the results of the tests provide enough information, then the doctor will diagnose the patient and prescribe the appropriate medication. However, the doctor may need more tests to give a final diagnosis and then the patient will begin the cycle again. The protocol is very close to a *real* system. In order to simplify the presentation we only consider one battery of tests: an ultrasound, a mammography and a smear test. After the test results are received in the doctor's office and the patient makes an appointment, the patient will visit the doctor for a diagnosis.

The main type of model we use is an input output transition system, which is a labelled transition system in which the set of actions is partitioned into inputs and outputs.

Definition 1 (Input Output Transition System). *An input output transition system (IOTS) r is defined by a tuple (Q, I, O, T, q_{in}) in which Q is a countable set of states, $q_{in} \in Q$ is the initial state, I is a countable set of inputs, O is a countable set of outputs, and $T \subseteq Q \times (I \cup O \cup \{\tau\}) \times Q$ is the transition relation. Here, τ represents an internal action, which cannot be observed.*

We say that state $q \in Q$ is stable if there is no $q' \in Q$ and $y \in O \cup \{\tau\}$ such that $(q, y, q') \in T$. This represents the situation in which r cannot change state without first receiving input. The process r is input-enabled *if for all $q \in Q$ and $?i \in I$ there is some $q' \in Q$ such that $(q, ?i, q') \in T$.*

We make the normal assumption that the SUT is input-enabled. In defining implementation relations for distributed testing, we will also require that specifications are input-enabled[1]. Some of the implementation relations described in this paper have been generalised to the case where the specification need not be input-enabled [17].

Example 2. The specification depicted in Fig. 3 is an *IOTS* in which input actions represent different actions, such as the request of the different appointments (*?app_smear_test, ?app_ultrasound, ...*), the inclusion in the system of the images or samples obtained by means of tests (*?smear_test, ?mammography, ...*), the registration of the diagnosis (*?diagnosis*) or the prescription of tests (*?tests_presc*). The output actions correspond to the information provided by the system to the users. For example, the dates of the requested appointments (*!date_smear_test, !date_ultrasound, ...*) or the results obtained from the tests

---

[1] The alternative term Input Output Labelled Transition System is often used if a process does not have to be input-enabled.

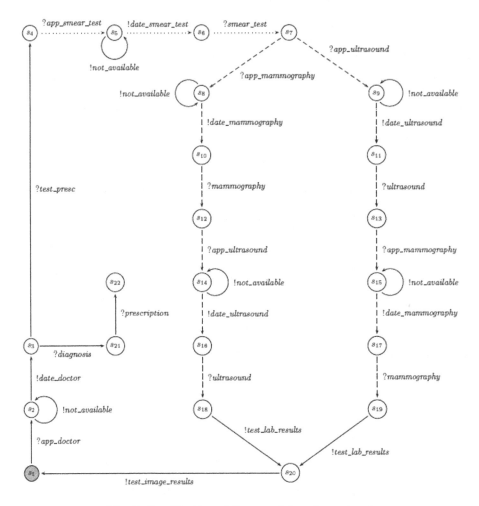

Fig. 3. Specification of the appointments protocol

carried out (!*test_lab_results*, !*test_image_results*). The initial state, s_1, is shaded. For the sake of clarity, not all transitions are included in the figure since this would overload the graph. Specifically, we have omitted those required to ensure that the system is input-enabled (the missing transitions lead to no change in state).

We also introduce notation that can be used to define processes. Given action a and process r, we use $a.r$ to denote the process that becomes r after engaging in action a. Further, if S is a countable set of processes then we use $\sum S$ to denote the process that non-deterministically chooses to be any process in S.

As is usually done when testing from an IOTS, we assume that the tester can observe the SUT being in a stable state (being *quiescent*). In practice, the tester will do this via a timeout, with the time Δ_T used being problem-specific.

There is thus the associated test hypothesis (assumption) that if the SUT does not receive input or produce output for time Δ_T then the SUT is in a stable state. We use δ to denote quiescence.

Definition 2. *Given IOTS $r = (Q, I, O, T, q_{in})$, we can extend the transition relation T to T_δ by adding the transition (q, δ, q) for each stable state q of r. We use $\mathcal{A}ct$ to denote the set of observable actions and so $\mathcal{A}ct = I \cup O \cup \{\delta\}$.*

Note that traces that (can) include quiescence are often called *suspension traces*; we simply call them traces since we do not consider other types of traces. The following standard notation is often used in the context of the standard implementation relation **ioco** (see, for example, [30]).

Definition 3. *Let $r = (Q, I, O, T, q_{in})$ be an IOTS. We use the following notation.*

1. *If $(q, a, q') \in T_\delta$, for $a \in \mathcal{A}ct \cup \{\tau\}$, then we write $q \xrightarrow{a} q'$.*
2. *We write $q \xRightarrow{a} q'$, for $a \in \mathcal{A}ct$, if there exist $q_0, \ldots, q_m$ and $k \geq 0$ such that $q = q_0$, $q' = q_m$, $q_0 \xrightarrow{\tau} q_1, \ldots q_{k-1} \xrightarrow{\tau} q_k$, $q_k \xrightarrow{a} q_{k+1}$, $q_{k+1} \xrightarrow{\tau} q_{k+2}, \ldots, q_{m-1} \xrightarrow{\tau} q_m$.*
3. *We write $q \xRightarrow{\epsilon} q'$ if there exist $q_1, \ldots, q_k$, for $k \geq 1$, such that $q = q_1$, $q' = q_k$, $q_1 \xrightarrow{\tau} q_2, \ldots q_{k-1} \xrightarrow{\tau} q_k$.*
4. *We write $q \xRightarrow{\sigma} q'$ for $\sigma = a_1 \ldots a_m \in \mathcal{A}ct^*$ if there exist $q_0, \ldots, q_m$, $q = q_0$, $q' = q_m$ such that for all $1 \leq i < m$ we have that $q_i \xRightarrow{a_{i+1}} q_{i+1}$.*
5. *We write $r \xRightarrow{\sigma}$ if there exists q' such that $q_{in} \xRightarrow{\sigma} q'$ and we say that σ is a trace of r.*
6. *We let $\mathcal{T}r^*(r)$ denote the set of finite traces of r.*

Let $q \in Q$ and $\sigma \in \mathcal{A}ct^*$ be a trace. We consider

1. *q **after** $\sigma = \{q' \in Q | q \xRightarrow{\sigma} q'\}$.*
2. *r **after** $\sigma = q_{in}$ **after** σ.*
3. *$out(q) = \{!o \in O \cup \{\delta\} | q \xRightarrow{!o}\}$.*

The last function can be extended to deal with sets in the expected way: Given $Q' \subseteq Q$ we define $out(Q') = \cup_{q \in Q'} out(q)$.

We say that the process r is deterministic *if for every state q and $a \in \mathcal{A}ct$ there is at most one state q' such that $(q, a, q') \in T_\delta$. We say that r is output-divergent if it can reach a state from which there is an infinite trace that contains outputs and internal actions only.*

We will consider processes that are output-divergent but a number of the definitions will require us to restrict attention to processes that are not output-divergent. Note that output divergence can be undesirable in testing since a process can choose to keep on providing outputs and not allow the tester to supply inputs. We can now define the standard implementation relation **ioco**.

Definition 4 (Implementation relation ioco). *Given IOTSs i and s we have that i **ioco** s if for every trace σ of s we have that $out(i$ **after** $\sigma) \subseteq out(s$ **after** $\sigma)$.*

3   Distributed Testing

Implementation relations such as **ioco** implicitly assume that there is a single *global tester* and this global tester is able to observe all of the actions in which the SUT engages, as well as quiescence, and determine the order in which these actions occurred. For example, if the SUT corresponding to the specification presented in Fig. 3 produced output !*test_lab_results* and then !*test_image_results* then the tester can observe both outputs and know that they were produced in this order. For many systems, this is a reasonable assumption and so one can use this type of implementation relation.

Research in the 1980 s, on testing implementations of communication protocols [4,5] against an FSM specification, observed that sometimes one requires multiple testers. In this work, there was an upper tester, which acted as the software that was using the protocol, and a lower tester, which interacted with the SUT through a communications network. For such systems, the SUT has multiple (two) physically distributed interfaces (called *ports*), there is a separate *local tester* at each port, and these local testers are not synchronised. This results in the local tester at port p observing a local trace (the sequence of events at port p) and so the overall observation made being a set of local traces: one local trace for each port of the SUT.

Figure 4 shows two architectures that can be used when testing a system that has multiple ports [17]. Figure 4(a) shows the case where there is a single global tester that provides inputs at all of the ports and observes the outputs; this is consistent with implementation relations such as **ioco**. Such a global tester can reconstruct the global trace that occurred during testing, although sometimes it may be difficult for the global tester to achieve this if the observation of an event is given a local timestamp and the clocks used are not perfectly synchronised. Figure 4(b) shows the *distributed test architecture* in which there is a separate local tester at each port and each local tester observes a local trace. It is possible to combine the two test architectures, leading to there being both a centralised tester and local testers [13] but we will not discuss such a combined architecture.

As previously mentioned, early work on distributed testing observed that it can lead to additional controllability and observability problems. The initial response was to try to find test sequences that avoid controllability and observability problems. These are test sequences (traces) where, for example, one can establish a global order of actions (see, for example, [2,11,22,23,31]). Later, it was recognised that the distributed test architecture introduces inherent limitations into testing and these limitations cannot be avoided unless some mechanism can be established to synchronise the local testers [18]. As a result, if it is not possible to synchronise the local testers then any test generation technique that returns test sequences that overcome the limitations imposed by the distributed test architecture must either be incomplete (misses some 'faults') or restricted to a special class of FSMs. Naturally, similar observations apply to IOTSs. This led to the definition of a new implementation relation for FSMs [18]; in this section we focus on the corresponding implementation relations defined for IOTSs. We need to include information about ports into models.

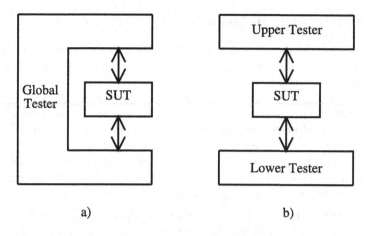

Fig. 4. Testing architectures in systems with multiple ports

Definition 5. *A distributed $\mathcal{IOTS}$ (d$\mathcal{IOTS}$) is a pair $(M, \mathcal{P})$, where $M = (Q, I, O, T, q_{in})$ is an $\mathcal{IOTS}$ and $\mathcal{P}$ is the set of ports. We partition I into pairwise disjoint sets I_p, for all $p \in \mathcal{P}$, containing those inputs that can be received at port p. Similarly, O is partitioned into pair-wise disjoint sets O_p, for all $p \in \mathcal{P}$, containing those outputs that can be produced at port p.*

Act_p denotes the set of observations that can be made at p, that is, $Act_p = I_p \cup O_p \cup \{\delta\}$.

Example 3. Let us consider the $\mathcal{IOTS}$ depicted in Fig. 3, which is actually a d$\mathcal{IOTS}$. The system has three different ports that correspond to the laboratory, the image diagnosis section and the consultations. These ports are connected to the central server where information related to patients is stored. The different types of lines used to draw the transitions are related to the different ports: solid for the doctor's office, dashed for the image diagnosis office and dotted for the laboratory office.

Given port p and a (global) trace $\sigma \in Act^*$, we let $\pi_p(\sigma)$ denote the projection of σ onto port p and this is called a *local trace*.

Definition 6 (Projection onto port p). *Let $p \in \mathcal{P}$ and $\sigma \in Act^*$ be a sequence of actions. We let $\pi_p(\sigma)$ denote the projection of σ onto port p and $\pi_p(\sigma)$ is called a* local trace. *Formally,*

$$\pi_p(\sigma) = \begin{cases} \epsilon & \text{if } \sigma = \epsilon \\ a\pi_p(\sigma') & \text{if } \sigma = a\sigma' \wedge a \in Act_p \\ \pi_p(\sigma') & \text{if } \sigma = a\sigma' \wedge a \in Act \setminus Act_p \end{cases}$$

Given $\sigma, \sigma' \in Act^*$ we write $\sigma \sim \sigma'$ if σ and σ' cannot be distinguished when making local observations, that is, for all $p \in \mathcal{P}$ we have that $\pi_p(\sigma) = \pi_p(\sigma')$.

Note that quiescence is observed at all ports.

4   Implementation Relations

Recall that in the distributed test architecture, there is a separate local tester at each port. These testers make local observations and the local observations are used in order to produce a test verdict such as pass (if the observed behaviour is consistent with the specification) or fail (if the observed behaviour is not consistent with the specification). The initial focus was on two main alternatives. In the first of these alternatives, the local tester at port p produces a local verdict v_p: the tester determines whether the local observation at p is one allowed by the specification. The local verdicts are then combined, with the overall verdict being fail if and only if one or more of the local verdicts are fail. This leads to the following implementation relation [17].

Definition 7 (The pdioco implementation relation). *Let* i, s *be dIOTSs with port set* $\mathcal{P}$. *We write* i **pdioco** s *if for every trace* $\sigma \in \mathcal{T}r^*(i)$ *and for every port* $p \in \mathcal{P}$ *there exists some trace* $\sigma' \in \mathcal{T}r^*(s)$ *such that* $\pi_p(\sigma) = \pi_p(\sigma')$.

Let us suppose that σ is a global trace. Clearly, σ uniquely defines the corresponding local traces but, in addition, the converse is not the case: there may be some different global trace σ' that has the same set of local traces. It is therefore unsurprising that **pdioco** is strictly weaker than **ioco**.

Proposition 1. *Let* i, s *be dIOTSs. We have that* i **ioco** s *implies* i **pdioco** s. *However, there exist processes* s *and* i *such that* i **pdioco** s *but where we do not have that* i **ioco** s.

A practical benefit of **pdioco** is that the test infrastructure for such an implementation relation may be relatively simple: each local tester records its local verdict and these local verdicts are either sent to a central tester that combines them or are locally stored and combined later. Thus, the complexity of the *oracle problem*[2] is essentially the same as that of **ioco** (there is a multiplier of $|\mathcal{P}|$). Note also that it has been shown that i **pdioco** s holds if and only if, for every $p \in \mathcal{P}$, the projection of i onto p conforms, under **ioco**, to the projection of s onto p [17].

Although **pdioco** is appealing, the local testers might have observed projections of different global traces of the specification. As a result, the verdict might be pass despite the global trace that occurred being very different from any global trace of the specification. For example, consider the global trace $?app\_doctor!date\_doctor?test\_presc?app\_smear\_test$ $?app\_mammography\,!date\_mammography!date\_smear\_test$. This global trace is not allowed by our specification. However, the projection of this trace onto each port ($?app\_doctor!date\_doctor?test\_presc$, $?app\_smear\_test!date\_smear\_test$ and $?app\_mammography!date\_mammography$) will lead to a pass verdict. Testing can be strengthened by allowing the local testers to log their observations (local traces), with these logs being brought together after testing is complete. This leads to a different implementation relation [16, 17].

---

[2] The oracle problem is the problem of deciding whether an observation made in testing is one allowed by the specification.

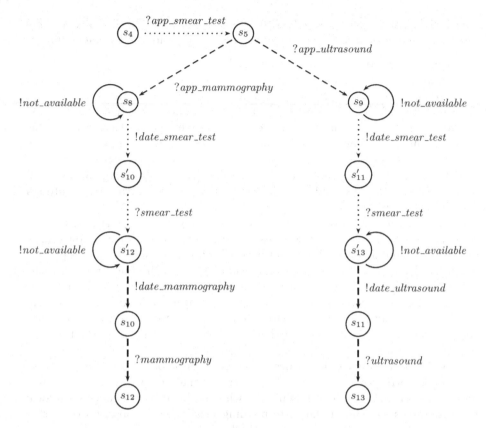

Fig. 5. A variant of the protocol

Definition 8 (The dioco implementation relation). *Let i, s be $dIOTSs$. We write i **dioco** s if for every trace σ such that $i \stackrel{\sigma}{\Longrightarrow} i'$ for some i' that is in a stable state, there exists a trace σ' such that $s \stackrel{\sigma'}{\Longrightarrow} s'$ and $\sigma' \sim \sigma$.*

Example 4. Let us consider the specification presented in Fig. 3. If we replace its subgraph starting at s_4 and ending at s_{12} and s_{13} by the subgraph depicted in Fig. 5 we obtain an alternative protocol. This new protocol does not conform to the original one with respect to **dioco**. For example, if we consider the trace reaching the stable state s'_{10} in this new protocol, $\sigma = ?app\_doctor!date\_doctor$ $?test\_presc?app\_smear\_test?app\_mammography!date\_smear\_test$, there does not exist any trace σ' in the original model such that $\sigma' \sim \sigma$. This is due to the fact that, in the original model, the projection of the traces corresponding to the laboratory office and reaching the transitions labelled with $?app\_mammography$ present the input $?smear\_test$. This action does not appear in σ. However, the changes included in the new protocol do not modify the original order of the actions at the different ports and, therefore, it does conform to the original one if we use **pdioco**.

Proposition 2. *There exist dIOTSs s and i such that i* **dioco** *s but not i* **ioco** *s. There also exist dIOTSs s and i such that i* **pdioco** *s but not i* **dioco** *s.*

Although **dioco** has the advantage of being stronger than **pdioco**, it has the disadvantage that one can no longer express the oracle problem in terms of separate instances of the oracle problem for the local testers. In fact, even for a deterministic FSM specification, the oracle problem becomes NP-Complete [10].

Notice that the definition of **dioco** only considers traces that reach stable states of the SUT. The reason for this is that the local testers can effectively 'stop testing' at such stable states: the local testers all observe quiescence at the end of the trace. In practice, the local testers can keep on observing outputs until a stable state is reached and then determine that the state was stable through a sufficiently long timeout.

This approach, of only considering traces that reach stable states, has the benefit of relatively simplicity and leads to an implementation relation that is defined in a similar way to **ioco**. However, **dioco** can be unsuitable if a process is output divergent. To see why this is the case, consider some trace σ of the SUT that reaches a quiescent state and an infinite extension $\sigma.\sigma'$ such that none of the states after σ are stable: for every non-empty prefix σ'' of σ' we have that $\sigma.\sigma''$ does not reach a stable state. The above definition of **dioco** does not consider any of these $\sigma.\sigma''$, even if they are clearly 'different' from the traces of the specification.

An alternative approach has been defined in terms of *observations* of a process; these correspond to tuples of local traces that might be observed when interacting with the process. Essentially, when a global trace occurs, each local tester observes a prefix of the corresponding local trace (it observes the entire local trace if it waits long enough). In the following, given a (local) trace σ_p we let $pref(\sigma_p)$ denote the set of prefixes of σ_p.

Definition 9 (Observation). *Given dIOTS r with m ports, we say that obs = $(\sigma_1, \ldots, \sigma_m)$ is an observation of r if there exists a global trace $\sigma \in \mathcal{T}r^*(r)$ such that for all $p \in \mathcal{P}$, we have that $\sigma_p \in pref(\pi_p(\sigma))$. We let Obs(r) denote the set of possible observations of r.*

Given IOTS r' we say that obs is allowed by *r' if and only if obs $\in$ Obs(r').*

If one considers the above definition and a specification s, then we can give an observation *obs* verdict *pass* if and only if *obs* is allowed by s. The idea simply is that although the testers do not know that the local traces they have observed are all projections of the same global trace of the SUT, they do know that they are all prefixes of projections of a global trace of the SUT.

We can now define an alternative implementation relation on the basis of the above: it essentially says that an SUT conforms to a specification if and only if all observations regarding the SUT are also observations regarding the specification [15].

Definition 10 (The dioco$_o$ implementation relation). *Given dIOTSs i and s with the same input and output alphabets and the same set of ports, we write i* **dioco$_o$** *s if and only if Obs(i) $\subseteq$ Obs(s).*

Note that the oracle problem for **dioco**$_o$ is also NP-Complete [15]. The above implementation relation is suitable for processes that are output-divergent and is equivalent to **dioco** if the processes are not output-divergent [15].

Proposition 3. *Given dIOTSs i and s that are not output-divergent, i* **dioco** *s if and only if i* **dioco**$_o$ *s.*

The implementation relation **dioco**$_o$ is thus a conservative generalisation of **dioco**. A different conservative generalisation of **dioco** has been defined in terms of infinite traces of processes [17]. However, this alternative generalisation has been shown to be too strong in the sense that an implementation i might fail to be a correct implementation of a specification s even though no finite observation can distinguish the SUT and specification [15].

5   Related and Future Work

The focus of this paper has been on defining suitable implementation relations, which formalise what it means for an SUT to be a correct implementation of a *dIOTS*. Such implementation relations can support systematic testing but they do not, on their own, address the problem of generating test cases for use in testing. There have been two main approaches to test generation for testing in the Distributed Test Architecture. One class of approaches, developed for testing from an FSM, involves producing test sequences that have no controllability and/or observability problems (see, for example, [3,23]). Naturally, these techniques lack generality (there are FSMs for which there is no such test sequence) but are potentially powerful where they can be applied. A second class of approaches allows the local testers to exchange synchronisation messages and typically aims to minimise the number of messages or communications channels required in order to overcome controllability and/or observability problems in a given test sequence (see, for example, [22,33]).

Some work has taken into account the nature of distributed testing during test generation. One proposal is to generate test cases in the form of tuples of (local) test cases: one local test case per port [17]. It is then possible to check whether such a test case introduces controllability and/or observability problems. It is unclear, however, how one might generate suitable test cases that are guaranteed to be free from such problems; it may be best to simply generate test cases and accept that controllability problems may lead to nondeterminism in the interaction between a test case and an SUT even if the SUT is deterministic. A second disadvantage of this approach, in which one generates a separate local test case for each port, is that it is more difficult to relate these test cases to test objectives, such as covering part of a model. If one is interested in generating test cases to cover part of a model then one might instead represent test generation as a multi-player game problem, although it transpires that the existence of test cases guaranteed to lead to, for example, a given state being reached is undecidable [8]. A third approach limits the aim of testing to finding faults that can be found using controllable test cases [14] and returns test suites that find all such faults (subject to the standard FSM testing assumption that we have a known upper bound on the number of states of the SUT).

Recent work by Huang and Peleska [20] has devised a model-independent approach to testing. They observe that the semantics of a state-based model is a set L of traces and if the original model is finite-state then L is regular. The semantics L thus induces an LTS $LTS(L)$, which can be defined largely through the use of Nerode-equivalence (two traces σ and σ' reach the same state of the induced LTS if they have the same set of continuations in L). Testing can then be based on the induced model $LTS(L)$. This approach addresses a weakness of test generation based on coverage, which is that two models may be equivalent (have the same semantics) and yet lead to different test suites. It also moves coverage away from the coverage of syntax and towards the coverage of semantics. It would be interesting to adapt this approach to distributed testing and there appear to be at least two possible routes. First, one could define a language whose elements are tuples of (local traces) and define a notion similar to Nerode-equivalence for such a language. Alternatively, one could extend the language L defined by an LTS by including all traces that are observationally equivalent to traces of L and use this extended language as the basis for inducing an LTS.

6 Conclusions

Although testing is an important part of software development, it is often manual and so expensive and error-prone. If there is a model (specification) of the required behaviour of the SUT and this model has a formal semantics then there is potential to base systematic test generation on this model. However, it is important to use a suitable implementation relation since otherwise, for example, testing might incorrectly suggest that a correct SUT is faulty or a faulty SUT is correct.

Most approaches to model-based testing (MBT) assume that there is a single tester that interacts with the SUT and can observe the global trace produced by the SUT. Sometimes, however, the SUT has multiple physically distributed ports and there is a local tester at each port. If the distributed test architecture is used then no tester can observe the global trace produced by the SUT and verdicts must instead be based on local traces (projections of the global trace).

We have described several different implementation relations defined for the distributed test architecture. The simplest approach is for each local tester to compare its observation (local trace) against the local traces allowed by the specification, with the overall verdict being fail if and only if one of these local verdicts is fail. The corresponding implementation relation **pdioco** is equivalent to the one produced if one compares the projections of the SUT and specification using the standard implementation relation **ioco**. However, we have seen that **pdioco** can hold between an SUT and a specification even if the SUT has behaviours (global traces) that are very different from those of the specification. This motivated the definition of a stronger implementation relation, **dioco**, that corresponds to a scenario in which the local tester observe local traces and the local traces are brought together. We have also seen that this can be generalised to remove the constraint that processes are not output-divergent.

The implementation relations provide a formal basis for testing within the distributed test architecture. However, much remains to be done. For example, we have also seen that there has been relatively little work on test generation algorithms that target these implementation relations. In this context, it may be possible to extend the approach of Huang and Peleska [20], which bases test generation on a model induced by the language defined by the specification.

References

1. Braunstein, C., et al.: Complete model-based equivalence class testing for the ETCS ceiling speed monitor. In: Merz, S., Pang, J. (eds.) ICFEM 2014. LNCS, vol. 8829, pp. 380–395. Springer, Cham (2014). https://doi.org/10.1007/978-3-319-11737-9_25
2. Cacciari, L., Rafiq, O.: Controllability and observability in distributed testing. Inf. Softw. Technol. **41**(11–12), 767–780 (1999)
3. Chen, W., Ural, H.: Synchronizable checking sequences based on multiple UIO sequences. IEEE/ACM Trans. Netw. **3**, 152–157 (1995)
4. Dssouli, R., von Bochmann, G.: Error detection with multiple observers. In: 5th WG6.1 International Conference on Protocol Specification, Testing and Verification, PSTV 1985, pp. 483–494. North-Holland (1985)
5. Dssouli, R..., von Bochmann, G.: Conformance testing with multiple observers. In: 6th WG6.1 International Conference on Protocol Specification, Testing and Verification, PSTV 1986, pp. 217–229. North-Holland (1986)
6. Grieskamp, W., Gurevich, Y., Schulte, W., Veanes, M.: Generating finite state machines from abstract state machines. In: ACM SIGSOFT Symposium on Software Testing and Analysis, ISSTA 2002, pp. 112–122. ACM Press (2002)
7. Grieskamp, W., Kicillof, N., Stobie, K., Braberman, V.: Model-based quality assurance of protocol documentation: tools and methodology. Softw. Testing Verification Reliab. **21**(1), 55–71 (2011)
8. Hierons, R.M.: Reaching and distinguishing states of distributed systems. SIAM J. Comput. **39**(8), 3480–3500 (2010)
9. Hierons, R.M.: The complexity of asynchronous model based testing. Theor. Comput. Sci. **451**, 70–82 (2012)
10. Hierons, R.M.: Oracles for distributed testing. IEEE Trans. Softw. Eng. **38**(3), 629–641 (2012)
11. Hierons, R.M.: Overcoming controllability problems in distributed testing from an input output transition system. Distrib. Comput. **25**(1), 63–81 (2012)
12. Hierons, R.M.: Implementation relations for testing through asynchronous channels. Comput. J. **56**(11), 1305–1319 (2013)
13. Hierons, R.M.: Combining centralised and distributed testing. ACM Trans. Softw. Eng. Methodol. **24**(1), article 5 (2014)
14. Hierons, R.M.: Generating complete controllable test suites for distributed testing. IEEE Trans. Softw. Eng. **41**(3), 279–293 (2015)
15. Hierons, R.M.: A more precise implementation relation for distributed testing. Comput. J. **59**(1), 33–46 (2016)

16. Hierons, R.M., Merayo, M.G., Núñez, M.: Implementation relations for the distributed test architecture. In: Suzuki, K., Higashino, T., Ulrich, A., Hasegawa, T. (eds.) FATES/TestCom -2008. LNCS, vol. 5047, pp. 200–215. Springer, Heidelberg (2008). https://doi.org/10.1007/978-3-540-68524-1_15

17. Hierons, R.M., Merayo, M.G., Núñez, M.: Implementation relations and test generation for systems with distributed interfaces. Distrib. Comput. **25**(1), 35–62 (2012)

18. Hierons, R.M., Ural, H.: The effect of the distributed test architecture on the power of testing. Comput. J. **51**(4), 497–510 (2008)

19. Hörcher, H.-M., Peleska, J.: Using formal specifications to support software testing. Softw. Qual. J. **4**(4), 309–327 (1995)

20. Huang, W., Peleska, J.: Model-based testing strategies and their (in)dependence on syntactic model representations. Int. J. Softw. Tools Technol. Transfer **20**(4), 441–465 (2018)

21. Joint Technical Committee ISO/IEC JTC 1. International Standard ISO/IEC 9646-1. Information Technology - Open Systems Interconnection - Conformance testing methodology and framework - Part 1: general concepts. ISO/IEC (1994)

22. Jourdan, G.-V., Ural, H., Yenigün, H.: Minimizing coordination channels in distributed testing. In: Najm, E., Pradat-Peyre, J.-F., Donzeau-Gouge, V.V. (eds.) FORTE 2006. LNCS, vol. 4229, pp. 451–466. Springer, Heidelberg (2006). https://doi.org/10.1007/11888116_32

23. Luo, G., Dssouli, R., von Bochmann, G.: Generating synchronizable test sequences based on finite state machine with distributed ports. In: 6th IFIP Workshop on Protocol Test Systems, IWPTS 1993, pp. 139–153. North-Holland (1993)

24. Peleska, J.: Industrial-strength model-based testing - state of the art and current challenges. In: 8th Workshop on Model-Based Testing, MBT 2013, EPTCS 111, pp. 3–28 (2013)

25. Peleska, J.: Model-based avionic systems testing for the airbus family. In: 23rd IEEE European Test Symposium, ETS 2018, pp. 1–10. IEEE Computer Society (2018)

26. Peleska, J., et al.: A real-world benchmark model for testing concurrent real-time systems in the automotive domain. In: Wolff, B., Zaïdi, F. (eds.) ICTSS 2011. LNCS, vol. 7019, pp. 146–161. Springer, Heidelberg (2011). https://doi.org/10.1007/978-3-642-24580-0_11

27. Peleska, J., Siegel, M.: Test automation of safety-critical reactive systems. S. Afr. Comput. J. **19**, 53–77 (1997)

28. Sachtleben, R., Peleska, J.: Effective grey-box testing with partial FSM models. Softw. Testing, Verification Reliab. **32**(2) (2022)

29. Sarikaya, B., von Bochmann, G.: Synchronization and specification issues in protocol testing. IEEE Trans. Commun. **32**, 389–395 (1984)

30. Tretmans, J.: Model based testing with labelled transition systems. In: Hierons, R.M., Bowen, J.P., Harman, M. (eds.) Formal Methods and Testing. LNCS, vol. 4949, pp. 1–38. Springer, Heidelberg (2008). https://doi.org/10.1007/978-3-540-78917-8_1

31. Ural, H., Whittier, D.: Distributed testing without encountering controllability and observability problems. Inf. Process. Lett. **88**(3), 133–141 (2003)

32. Weiglhofer, M., Wotawa, F.: Asynchronous input-output conformance testing. In: 33rd Annual IEEE Computer Software and Applications Conference, COMPSAC 2009, pp. 154–159. IEEE Computer Society (2009)

33. Wu, W.-J., Chen, W.-H., Tang, C.Y.: Synchronizable test sequence for multi-party protocol conformance testing. Comput. Commun. **21**(13), 1177–1183 (1998)

Conformance Relations Between Input/Output Languages

Wen-ling Huang[iD] and Robert Sachtleben[(✉)][iD]

Department of Mathematics and Computer Science, University of Bremen,
Bremen, Germany
{huang,rob_sac}@uni-bremen.de

Abstract. In this paper, we propose a novel unifying approach to characterising well-known conformance relations between finite state machines, including equivalence, reduction, and variations thereof. This approach is based on languages over input/output alphabets. It allows for easier comparison between conformance relations, and gives rise to a fundamental necessary and sufficient criterion for conformance testing.

Keywords: Languages · Model-based testing · Conformance testing · Complete testing theories

1 Introduction

Motivation. In the field of model-based testing (MBT), a large variety of conformance relations have been developed that describe the conditions under which a system-under-test (SUT) conforms to the reference model. Examples of such relations include *equivalence*, requiring both systems to exhibit the exact same behaviour (see [18]), and *quasi-reduction* (see [11]), which allows the SUT to differ from the reference model. Unfortunately, little effort has been made to develop a unifying framework of these conformance relations,[1] hindering direct comparisons between them and the development of generalised testing strategies. Also, the test strength of such strategies often depends on the syntactic representation of reference models, despite the relations being defined only over their behavioural semantics. Examples of this are discussed in [8].

Main Contributions. In this paper, we propose a unifying treatment of conformance relations, allowing for easier comparisons between them. The approach is independent of the syntactic representation of the reference model and not based on a particular modelling formalism such as finite state machines (FSM). Instead, we define the relations purely over languages which represent the behavioural semantics of the model. We derive a fundamental necessary and sufficient criterion for conformance that applies to any conformance relations definable via

---

[1] Compare, for example, the various definitions of quasi-equivalence in [4,5,11–13].

© The Author(s), under exclusive license to Springer Nature Switzerland AG 2023
A. E. Haxthausen et al. (Eds.): Peleska Festschrift 2023, LNCS 14165, pp. 49–67, 2023.
https://doi.org/10.1007/978-3-031-40132-9_4

our characterisation. For this criterion, we sketch how it may serve as a foundation for the generation of test algorithms. Finally, we show that testing for quasi-equivalence, quasi-reduction and strong-reduction can be transformed into testing for reduction.

Related Work. Model-based testing strategies which are independent of the syntactic representation of the model have been considered in [8]. Based on an existing strategy from FSMs [1,18], the authors develop a strategy for testing for language equivalence. Some other conformance relations we consider have also been introduced together with complete testing methods, as in the case of *reduction* for completely specified FSMs (see [3,14]), *quasi-equivalence* and *quasi-reduction* (see [4,5,11–13]) or *strong-reduction* for partial FSMs (see [15]). It has been shown in [7] that such strategies may be lifted to more expressive formalisms such as reactive IO-state-transition systems (RIOSTS) via partitioning of states and inputs into equivalence classes.

Overview. Sect. 2 introduces basic definitions and notation used throughout this paper. Next, Sect. 3 introduces our approach, defines several conformance relations and derives relations between them. Examples of conformance relations studied in this paper are presented via FSMs. A fundamental criterion for conformance is developed and discussed in Sect. 4, which also showcases how conformance relations may be expressed in terms of reductions, with detailed proofs presented in Appendix A. Finally, Sect. 5 presents the conclusion.

2   Preliminaries

In this section, we give some basic definitions and notation used in this paper.

An input (output) alphabet Σ_I (Σ_O) is a non-empty set. Elements of Σ_I are called inputs and elements of Σ_O are called outputs. Σ^* is the set of all finite sequences over $\Sigma = \Sigma_I \times \Sigma_O$ and, as usual, $\varepsilon \notin \Sigma \cup \Sigma_I \cup \Sigma_O$ denotes the empty sequence. Σ_O^* and Σ_I^* are defined analogously. For $\sigma = (x, y) \in \Sigma$ we also use the notation $\sigma = x/y$, and for input and output sequences $\overline{x} = x_1 x_2 \ldots x_k$, $\overline{y} = y_1 y_2 \ldots y_k$ of the same length we use $\overline{x}/\overline{y}$ to denote $(x_1/y_1)(x_2/y_2)\ldots(x_k/y_k)$. Elements of Σ^* are called words and will be denoted by lower case Greek letters α, β, etc. Given two words α and β we denote by $\alpha.\beta$ the concatenation of α and β. We say that α is a prefix of β if there exists a word γ such that $\alpha.\gamma = \beta$. A subset $\mathcal{L} \subseteq \Sigma^*$ is called a language over Σ. We say that $\mathcal{L}$ is prefix closed if for any word $\beta \in \mathcal{L}$ and each prefix α of β we have $\alpha \in \mathcal{L}$. The subset $L_{\mathcal{L}}(\pi)$ for any word $\pi \in \Sigma^*$ is defined as $L_{\mathcal{L}}(\pi) = \{\tau \in \Sigma^* \mid \pi.\tau \in \mathcal{L}\}$. Two words α, β are $\sim_L$ [2] equivalent, if $L_{\mathcal{L}}(\alpha) = L_{\mathcal{L}}(\beta)$. In this paper we restrict our study to non-empty prefix closed languages.

Let $\mathcal{L}$ be a non-empty prefix closed language over $\Sigma = \Sigma_I \times \Sigma_O$. An input sequence $\overline{x}$ is said to be *defined* or *executable* in a word π of $\mathcal{L}$ if there is an

---

[2] There is no difference between $\sim_L$ and Nerode congruence [9].

output sequence $\overline{y}$ such that $\pi.\overline{x}/\overline{y} \in \mathcal{L}$. We use $\mathrm{exec}_{\mathcal{L}}(\pi)$ to denote the set of all defined input in π of $\mathcal{L}$, i.e.,

$$\mathrm{exec}_{\mathcal{L}}(\pi) = \{x \in \Sigma_I \mid \exists y \in \Sigma_O, \pi.x/y \in \mathcal{L}\}.$$

Definition 1. *For any $\pi \in \Sigma^*$ and any $\overline{x} \in \Sigma_I^*$ define the set of all outputs or responses to $\overline{x}$ after π as*

$$\mathrm{out}_{\mathcal{L}}(\pi, \overline{x}) = \{\overline{y} \in \Sigma_O^* \mid \pi.(\overline{x}/\overline{y}) \in \mathcal{L}\}. \tag{1}$$

Hence, $\mathrm{out}_{\mathcal{L}}(\pi, \overline{x}) = \emptyset$ if and only if $\pi \notin \mathcal{L}$ or $\overline{x}$ is not defined in π.

Language $\mathcal{L}$ is called completely specified, if for any word $\pi \in \mathcal{L}$ and any input $x \in \Sigma_I$, $\mathrm{out}_{\mathcal{L}}(\pi, x) \neq \emptyset$ holds. This is equivalent to $\mathrm{exec}_{\mathcal{L}}(\pi) = \Sigma_I$, for any word $\pi \in \mathcal{L}$.

In subsequent sections, when using indexed identifiers $\mathcal{L}_i$ for languages, we omit symbol $\mathcal{L}$ in terms over $\mathcal{L}_i$ such as $L_{\mathcal{L}_i}$, $\mathrm{exec}_{\mathcal{L}_i}$, and $\mathrm{out}_{\mathcal{L}_i^\dagger}$, and simply write L_i, exec_i, and $\mathrm{out}_{i^\dagger}$, respectively.

3 Conformance Relations

In this section, we study two classes of conformance relations on non-empty prefix closed languages over $\Sigma = \Sigma_I \times \Sigma_O$. The first class is introduced in Subsect. 3.1. It arises from a unifying characterisation of several conformance relations previously proposed for finite state machines. As examples of this class, we provide characterisations of *equivalence* (see [1,18]), *reduction* (see [3]), *quasi-equivalence* (see [11]), *quasi-reduction* (see [4]) and *strong-reduction* (see [15]).

Subsection 3.2 thereafter introduces a modification of this characterisation which gives rise to a novel class of conformance relations. As examples of this class we describe four novel conformance relations: *semi-equivalence*, *strong-semi-equivalence*, *semi-reduction*, and *strong-semi-reduction*. To the best of our knowledge, these have not been considered in the literature before.

For the conformance relations employed as examples, we examine in Subsect. 3.3 whether conformance with respect to one relation implies conformance w.r.t. another. An overview of the obtained results is given in Fig. 2 on page 10.

Running Example. Throughout this section, we present concrete examples for the considered conformance relations using finite state machines. For these examples it is sufficient to view FSMs as directed graphs whose nodes are called *states* and whose edges are called *transitions* and labelled with input-output (IO) pairs in $\Sigma_I \times \Sigma_O$. Each FSM M exhibits an initial state, represented in the following by an incoming edge with no source. Finally, the language $\mathcal{L}(M)$ of M is the set of all IO-traces obtained by projecting finite paths from the initial state of M to the labels of their transitions. Thus $\mathcal{L}(M)$ always includes ε and is prefix closed. A more formal definition can be found in [5].

FSM M_1 shown in Fig. 1a models a simple vending machine. It exhibits a simple graphical user interface which in initially displays two buttons (C) and (T) for coffee and tea, respectively. Upon pressing one of these buttons, the machine requests payment (RP) and enters state C or T. These can be exited only by offering payment (P), which releases the selected beverage, represented as outputs (RC) and (RT). In the initial state S, a request for tea may alternatively and nondeterministically be fulfilled without payment. Offering payment in the initial state is rejected and a rejection message is displayed, which is represented by output $(-)$. In states C and T, the machine does not display buttons (C) and (T), which is represented by these inputs not being defined in these states.

In the following, we consider the FSMs shown in Fig. 1 and check their conformance to M_1 under the discussed relations. Table 1 provides a summary.

3.1 Equivalence, Quasi-equivalence, Reduction, Quasi-reduction, and Strong-Reduction

Two of the most widely employed conformance relations in model-based testing are (language) *equivalence* and *reduction* (see [1,3,18]). A system-under-test (SUT) with language $\mathcal{L}_1$ conforms to a reference model with language $\mathcal{L}_2$ with respect to equivalence if $\mathcal{L}_1 = \mathcal{L}_2$ holds, that is, if and only if it exhibits exactly the same set as behaviours as the reference model. Conformance with respect to reduction only requires $\mathcal{L}_1 \subseteq \mathcal{L}_2$ to hold, where $\mathcal{L}_2$ often represents the set of all safe behaviours. Thus, a conforming SUT may omit behaviours of the reference model, but may not add any.

Of the FSMs in Fig. 1, no FSM other than M_1 is equivalent to M_1, as they add or omit behaviour. For example, M_3 implements $(T/RP).(C/RP) \notin \mathcal{L}(M_1)$. Any FSM equivalent to M_1 must in particular allow arbitrary many repetitions of the T/RT self-loop, excluding FSMs with finite languages such as M_2. M_2 here represents a system that allows selecting tea in the GUI once but does not allow any further action. Thus, it drastically reduces the capabilities of M_1, but does not introduce any additional behaviour, and hence is a reduction. In contrast, M_3 is not a reduction of M_1, as it adds a button for coffee in state T.

Instead of directly comparing $\mathcal{L}_1$ and $\mathcal{L}_2$ in their entirety, we propose a characterisation of conformance relations that is based on comparing the outputs produced for each input after each trace in both languages. To this end, we introduce conformance relation $\preceq_H$ parameterised over relation $H \subseteq 2^{\Sigma_O} \times 2^{\Sigma_O}$.

Definition 2. *Let $H \subseteq 2^{\Sigma_O} \times 2^{\Sigma_O}$ be a relation on the power set of Σ_O. A language $\mathcal{L}_1$ is called $\preceq_H$-conform to a language $\mathcal{L}_2$, in notation $\mathcal{L}_1 \preceq_H \mathcal{L}_2$, if $\forall \pi \in \mathcal{L}_1 \cap \mathcal{L}_2, \forall x \in \Sigma_I,$*

$$(\text{out}_{\mathcal{L}_1}(\pi, x), \text{out}_{\mathcal{L}_2}(\pi, x)) \in H. \tag{2}$$

By selecting suitable relations H, it is then possible to represent a large class of practically relevant conformance relations. For example, equivalence and

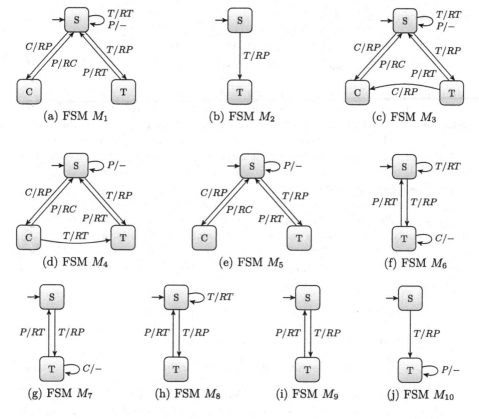

Fig. 1. Example FSMs

Table 1. Overview of the satisfaction of the discussed conformance relations by the example FSMs provided in Fig. 1 with respect to reference model M_1 described in Fig. 1a. A check mark in column M_i indicates that M_i conforms to M_1 w.r.t. the conformance relation given in the corresponding row.

	M_1	M_2	M_3	M_4	M_5	M_6	M_7	M_8	M_9	M_{10}
$\preceq_{equiv} M_1$	✓									
$\preceq_{red} M_1$	✓	✓			✓			✓	✓	
$\preceq_{quasieq} M_1$	✓		✓							
$\preceq_{quasired} M_1$	✓		✓	✓	✓					
$\preceq_{strongred} M_1$	✓				✓					
$\leq_{semieq} M_1$	✓		✓			✓		✓		
$\leq_{semired} M_1$	✓		✓	✓	✓	✓	✓	✓	✓	✓
$\leq_{strongsemieq} M_1$	✓							✓		
$\leq_{strongsemired} M_1$	✓				✓			✓	✓	

reduction can be defined as

$$\mathcal{L}_1 = \mathcal{L}_2 \iff \mathcal{L}_1 \preceq_{equiv} \mathcal{L}_2 \qquad \text{where } \boldsymbol{equiv} = \{(A, A) \mid A \subseteq \Sigma_O\} \qquad (3)$$

$$\mathcal{L}_1 \subseteq \mathcal{L}_2 \iff \mathcal{L}_1 \preceq_{red} \mathcal{L}_2 \qquad \text{where } \boldsymbol{red} = \{(A, B) \mid A \subseteq B \subseteq \Sigma_O\} \qquad (4)$$

A detailed proof of (3) and (4) is given in Appendix A.

Based on equivalence and reduction, the conformance relations *quasi-equivalence*, *quasi-reduction* and *strong-reduction* have been proposed in the literature (see [5,11,15]), which pose more elaborate constraints on how a conforming SUT should behave with respect to defined and undefined inputs of the reference model. In the following, we show how these conformance relations can be characterised via $\preceq_H$-conformance.

Quasi-equivalence and quasi-reduction respectively modify equivalence and reduction by allowing the SUT to have arbitrary responses to undefined inputs. More precisely, language $\mathcal{L}_1$ is called *quasi-equivalent* to $\mathcal{L}_2$ if for any $\pi \in \mathcal{L}_1 \cap \mathcal{L}_2$ and any input $x \in \Sigma_I$ defined in π of $\mathcal{L}_2$, i.e., $x \in \text{exec}_2(\pi)$, it holds that $\text{out}_1(\pi, x) = \text{out}_2(\pi, x)$. For any input $x \in \Sigma_I$ which is not defined in π of $\mathcal{L}_2$, $\text{out}_1(\pi, x)$ can be arbitrary. Hence

$$\boldsymbol{quasieq} = \{(A, A) \mid A \subseteq \Sigma_O\} \cup \{(A, \emptyset) \mid A \subseteq \Sigma_O\}. \qquad (5)$$

is a suitable relation to characterise quasi-equivalence:

$$\mathcal{L}_1 \text{ is quasi-equivalent to } \mathcal{L}_2 \iff \mathcal{L}_1 \preceq_{quasieq} \mathcal{L}_2. \qquad (6)$$

Similarly, language $\mathcal{L}_1$ is a *quasi-reduction* of language $\mathcal{L}_2$ if for any $\pi \in \mathcal{L}_1 \cap \mathcal{L}_2$ and any input $x \in \Sigma_I$ defined in π of $\mathcal{L}_2$, x is defined in π of $\mathcal{L}_1$ as well and $\text{out}_1(\pi, x) \subseteq \text{out}_2(\pi, x)$. Hence

$$\boldsymbol{quasired} = \{(A, B) \mid \emptyset \neq A, A \subseteq B \subseteq \Sigma_O\} \cup \{(C, \emptyset) \mid C \subseteq \Sigma_O\}. \qquad (7)$$

is a suitable relation to characterise quasi-reduction:

$$\mathcal{L}_1 \text{ is a quasi-reduction of } \mathcal{L}_2 \iff \mathcal{L}_1 \preceq_{quasired} \mathcal{L}_2. \qquad (8)$$

Quasi-equivalence and quasi-reduction are employed if the reference model is not completely specified and undefined inputs may be implemented by the SUT, in which case arbitrary responses are allowed. In example FSM M_1, input C is not defined after traces ending on T/RP (i.e. in state T). Thus, a conforming SUT may behave arbitrarily on this input, for example by switching the order to coffee as implemented in M_3. It is not allowed, however, to add a new response to a defined input, as with $(T/RP).(P/-) \in \mathcal{L}(M_{10}) \setminus \mathcal{L}(M_1)$, or to omit a defined input, as occurs in M_2, which does not offer button C in the initial state. Quasi-equivalence differs from quasi-reduction by additionally not allowing any response to a defined input to be omitted, as occurs in M_4, which does not support tea to be released in the initial state.

Strong-reduction, introduced in [15], can be derived from quasi-reduction by adding conditions to ensure that undefined inputs remain undefined. It can also be derived from reduction by requiring defined inputs to remain defined. That is, language $\mathcal{L}_1$ is a *strong-reduction* of language $\mathcal{L}_2$ if $\mathcal{L}_1$ is a quasi-reduction of $\mathcal{L}_2$ and for any $\pi \in \mathcal{L}_1 \cap \mathcal{L}_2$ and any input $x \in \Sigma_I$ it holds that if $\text{out}_2(\pi, x) = \emptyset$, then also $\text{out}_1(\pi, x) = \emptyset$. Thus, strong-reduction may be characterised by removing all $(A, \emptyset)$, $A \neq \emptyset$, from *quasired* or by removing all $(\emptyset, A)$, $A \neq \emptyset$, from *red*:

$$strongred = \{(A, B) \mid \emptyset \neq A \subseteq B \subseteq \Sigma_O\} \cup \{(\emptyset, \emptyset)\}, \tag{9}$$

which is the intersection of *quasired* and *red*:

$$\mathcal{L}_1 \text{ is a strong-reduction of } \mathcal{L}_2 \iff \mathcal{L}_1 \preceq_{strongred} \mathcal{L}_2. \tag{10}$$

In the running example, strong-reductions of example FSM M_1 do not include M_2, which omits inputs, or M_4, which adds inputs not present in M_1. An example for a strong-reduction can be found in M_5, which, compared to M_1, merely drops the release of tea in the initial state.

3.2 Semi-equivalence, Strong-semi-equivalence, Semi-reduction, Strong-semi-reduction

As previously discussed for quasi-equivalence and quasi-reduction, the condition $(A, \emptyset) \in H$, $A \subseteq \Sigma_O$ indicates that the SUT's response to inputs that are not defined in the reference model can be arbitrary. To allow the SUT to reject some inputs that are defined in the reference model, we can add pairs $(\emptyset, A)$ to H. However, it is often desirable for the SUT not to reject every defined input and to produce an expected output for at least one defined input. To achieve this, we need to specify an additional condition that reflects this requirement.

Definition 3. *Let $\mathcal{L}_1$ and $\mathcal{L}_2$ be languages over Σ and $H \subseteq 2^{\Sigma_O} \times 2^{\Sigma_O}$. We say $\mathcal{L}_1$ is $\leq_H$-conform to $\mathcal{L}_2$, denoted $\mathcal{L}_1 \leq_H \mathcal{L}_2$, if*

1. $\forall \pi \in \mathcal{L}_1 \cap \mathcal{L}_2, \forall x \in \Sigma_I : (\text{out}_1(\pi, x), \text{out}_2(\pi, x)) \in H$,
2. $\forall \pi \in \mathcal{L}_1 \cap \mathcal{L}_2 : \big(\text{exec}_2(\pi) \neq \emptyset \implies \exists x \in \Sigma_I : \text{out}_1(\pi, x) \cap \text{out}_2(\pi, x) \neq \emptyset\big).$

That is, $\mathcal{L}_1 \leq_H \mathcal{L}_2$ if and only if $\mathcal{L}_1 \preceq_H \mathcal{L}_2$ and we can not find a deadlock $\pi \in \mathcal{L}_1 \cap \mathcal{L}_2$ which is not already a deadlock in $\mathcal{L}_2$. Here, we say a word $\pi \in \mathcal{L}$ is a deadlock, if $L_{\mathcal{L}}(\pi) = \{\tau \in \Sigma^* \mid \pi.\tau \in \mathcal{L}\} = \{\varepsilon\}$. By the definition of $\text{exec}_{\mathcal{L}}(\pi)$, we can reformulate the definition for $\leq_H$-conformance as follows

$$\mathcal{L}_1 \leq_H \mathcal{L}_2 \iff \forall \pi \in \mathcal{L}_1 \cap \mathcal{L}_2, \forall x \in \Sigma_I : (\text{out}_1(\pi, x), \text{out}_2(\pi, x)) \in H$$
$$\land\, (\text{out}_2(\pi, x) \neq \emptyset \implies \exists x' \in \Sigma_I : \text{out}_1(\pi, x') \cap \text{out}_2(\pi, x') \neq \emptyset). \tag{11}$$

From this definition it follows that $M_2 \not\leq_H M_1$ for any relation H, since T/RP is a deadlock in M_2 but not in M_1.

Example 1 (Semi-equivalence). We introduce a modification of quasi-equivalence that allows a conforming SUT to omit some (but not all) defined inputs. Language $\mathcal{L}_1$ is called *semi-equivalent* to language $\mathcal{L}_2$ if for any $\pi \in \mathcal{L}_1 \cap \mathcal{L}_2$ and any input $x \in \Sigma_I$ satisfying $\text{out}_2(\pi, x) \neq \emptyset$, we have

$$\text{out}_1(\pi, x) = \emptyset \vee \text{out}_1(\pi, x) = \text{out}_2(\pi, x), \text{ and}$$
$$\exists x' \in \Sigma_I : \text{out}_1(\pi, x') \cap \text{out}_2(\pi, x') \neq \emptyset.$$

Hence, for any $\pi \in \mathcal{L}_1 \cap \mathcal{L}_2$ and any input $x \in \Sigma_I$, we have

$$\text{out}_2(\pi, x) = \emptyset \implies \text{out}_1(\pi, x) \text{ is arbitrary, and}$$
$$\text{out}_2(\pi, x) \neq \emptyset \implies \text{out}_1(\pi, x) = \emptyset \vee \text{out}_1(\pi, x) = \text{out}_2(\pi, x).$$

This can be expressed by

$$\text{out}_1(\pi, x) = \text{out}_2(\pi, x) \vee \left(\text{out}_i(\pi, x) = \emptyset \wedge \text{out}_j(\pi, x) \neq \emptyset, \{i, j\} = \{1, 2\} \right).$$

Hence, $\mathcal{L}_1$ is semi-equivalent to $\mathcal{L}_2$ if and only if $\mathcal{L}_1 \leq_{semieq} \mathcal{L}_2$, where

$$semieq = \{(A, A) \mid A \subseteq \Sigma_O\} \cup \{(\emptyset, A) \mid A \subseteq \Sigma_O\} \cup \{(A, \emptyset) \mid A \subseteq \Sigma_O\}. \quad (12)$$

In Fig. 1, $M_6 \leq_{semieq} M_1$, where M_6 omits inputs C and P after ε and exhibits both responses to T exhibited by M_1. In state T, M_6 furthermore adds response $-$ to input C (undefined in M_1), notifying the user that the order cannot be switched to coffee. In contrast, $M_7 \nleq_{semieq} M_1$, as it omits one of the responses to T in M_1.

Example 2 (Semi-reduction). A similar modification can be made to quasi-reduction by adding to **quasired** all $(\emptyset, A)$ where $A \subseteq \Sigma_O$. We say that language $\mathcal{L}_1$ is a *semi-reduction* of language $\mathcal{L}_2$ if $\mathcal{L}_1 \leq_{semired} \mathcal{L}_2$, where

$$semired = \{(A, B) \mid A \subseteq B \subseteq \Sigma_O\} \cup \{(C, \emptyset) \mid C \subseteq \Sigma_O\}. \quad (13)$$

Example 3 (Strong-semi-equivalence). Semi-equivalence allows SUT to have arbitrary responses to undefined inputs. This feature is not available for strong-semi-equivalence. Strong-semi-equivalence requires SUT to leave undefined inputs as undefined. This can be achieved by removing all $(A, \emptyset)$, $A \neq \emptyset$, from **semieq**. We define that $\mathcal{L}_1$ is called *strongly semi-equivalent* to language $\mathcal{L}_2$ if $\mathcal{L}_1 \leq_{strongsemieq} \mathcal{L}_2$, where

$$strongsemieq = \{(A, A) \mid A \subseteq \Sigma_O\} \cup \{(\emptyset, A) \mid A \subseteq \Sigma_O\} = semieq \cap red. \quad (14)$$

In Fig. 1, $M_8 \leq_{strongsemieq} M_1$, where M_8 is a very simple but practically useful implementation that allows arbitrarily many repetitions of the process of requesting, possibly paying for and finally receiving tea. Additional behaviour such as adding input C to state T in M_6 are not allowed. Furthermore, dropping behaviour on the remaining defined inputs, as for example the release of tea without payment in M_9, is forbidden.

Example 4 (Strong-semi-reduction). Analogous to strong-semi-equivalence, we define strong-semi-reduction by removing all $(A, \emptyset)$, $A \neq \emptyset$, from **semired**. That is, $\mathcal{L}_1$ is called a *strong-semi-reduction* of $\mathcal{L}_2$ if $\mathcal{L}_1 \leq_{strongsemired} \mathcal{L}_2$, where

$$strongsemired = \{(A, B) \mid A \subseteq B \subseteq \Sigma_O\} = semired \cap red = red. \tag{15}$$

These differences to strong-semi-equivalence allow $M_9 \leq_{strongsemired} M_1$ but still forbid the additions in M_6.

3.3 Comparing Conformance Relations

The parameterisation of $\preceq_H$-conformance and $\leq_H$-conformance by a relation H enables abstract comparisons between conformance relations based on comparisons between their parameters. For example, if $H_1 \subseteq H_2$ holds, then $\preceq_{H_1}$ and $\preceq_{H_2}$ are related as follows for arbitrary H_1, H_2.

Lemma 1. *Let $\mathcal{L}_1, \mathcal{L}_2$ be any languages over $\Sigma = \Sigma_I \times \Sigma_O$. Let $H_1, H_2 \subseteq 2^{\Sigma_O} \times 2^{\Sigma_O}$ be any relations on the power set of Σ_O. Suppose $H_1 \subseteq H_2$. Then $\mathcal{L}_1 \preceq_{H_1} \mathcal{L}_2 \implies \mathcal{L}_1 \preceq_{H_2} \mathcal{L}_2$.*

Proof. Suppose that $H_1 \subseteq H_2$. Then by Definition 2,

$$\mathcal{L}_1 \preceq_{H_1} \mathcal{L}_2 \iff \forall \pi \in \mathcal{L}_1 \cap \mathcal{L}_2, \forall x \in \Sigma_I : (\mathrm{out}_1(\pi, x), \mathrm{out}_2(\pi, x)) \in H_1$$
$$\implies \forall \pi \in \mathcal{L}_1 \cap \mathcal{L}_2, \forall x \in \Sigma_I : (\mathrm{out}_1(\pi, x), \mathrm{out}_2(\pi, x)) \in H_2$$
$$\iff \mathcal{L}_1 \preceq_{H_2} \mathcal{L}_2.$$

Hence $\mathcal{L}_1 \preceq_{H_1} \mathcal{L}_2 \implies \mathcal{L}_1 \preceq_{H_2} \mathcal{L}_2$. $\qquad\qquad\square$

From this lemma, the following properties over relations discussed in 3.1 follow immediately after unfolding the definitions of the employed relations (see (3), (4), (5), (7), (9)):

Theorem 1. *Let $\mathcal{L}_1, \mathcal{L}_2$ be any two languages over Σ. Then*

$$\mathcal{L}_1 \preceq_{equiv} \mathcal{L}_2 \implies \mathcal{L}_1 \preceq_{strongred} \mathcal{L}_2 \implies \mathcal{L}_1 \preceq_{red} \mathcal{L}_2,$$
$$\mathcal{L}_1 \preceq_{equiv} \mathcal{L}_2 \implies \mathcal{L}_1 \preceq_{strongred} \mathcal{L}_2 \implies \mathcal{L}_1 \preceq_{quasired} \mathcal{L}_2,$$
$$\mathcal{L}_1 \preceq_{equiv} \mathcal{L}_2 \implies \mathcal{L}_1 \preceq_{quasieq} \mathcal{L}_2 \implies \mathcal{L}_1 \preceq_{quasired} \mathcal{L}_2.$$

The following Lemma is analogous to Lemma 1 for $\leq_H$-conformance. We omit the analogous proof.

Lemma 2. *Let $\mathcal{L}_1, \mathcal{L}_2$ be any languages over Σ. Let $H_1, H_2 \subseteq 2^{\Sigma_O} \times 2^{\Sigma_O}$. Suppose $H_1 \subseteq H_2$. Then $\mathcal{L}_1 \leq_{H_1} \mathcal{L}_2 \implies \mathcal{L}_1 \leq_{H_2} \mathcal{L}_2$.*

We can also compare $\preceq_H$-conformances and $\leq_H$-conformances using the following criterion.

Lemma 3. *Let $\mathcal{L}_1, \mathcal{L}_2$ be any two languages over Σ and $H_1, H_2 \subseteq 2^{\Sigma_O} \times 2^{\Sigma_O}$. Suppose $H_1 \subseteq H_2$ and for any $(A, B) \in H_1$ it holds $B \neq \emptyset \Rightarrow A \cap B \neq \emptyset$. Then $\mathcal{L}_1 \preceq_{H_1} \mathcal{L}_2 \implies \mathcal{L}_1 \leq_{H_2} \mathcal{L}_2$.*

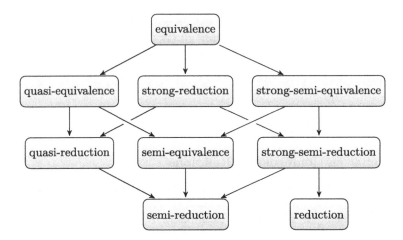

Fig. 2. Overview of the inclusion relations on the conformance relations discussed in Sect. 3 and established in Theorems 1 and 2. An arrow from A to B indicates that if $\mathcal{L}_1$ conforms to $\mathcal{L}_2$ w.r.t. relation A, then it also does so w.r.t. B.

Proof. Suppose $\mathcal{L}_1 \preceq_{H_1} \mathcal{L}_2$ and $H_1 \subseteq H_2$. Then for any $\pi \in \mathcal{L}_1 \cap \mathcal{L}_2$, and any $x \in \Sigma_I$, $(\mathrm{out}_1(\pi, x), \mathrm{out}_2(\pi, x)) \in H_1 \subseteq H_2$. Furthermore, suppose that $\mathrm{out}_2(\pi, x) \neq \emptyset$. Since for any $(A, B) \in H_1$, $B \neq \emptyset \Rightarrow A \cap B \neq \emptyset$ holds, we have that $\mathrm{out}_1(\pi, x) \cap \mathrm{out}_2(\pi, x) \neq \emptyset$. Consequently, $\mathcal{L}_1 \preceq_{H_1} \mathcal{L}_2 \implies \mathcal{L}_1 \leq_{H_2} \mathcal{L}_2$. □

From Lemma 2, Lemma 3 and unfolding definitions (18), (19), (20) and (21), the following relations between conformance relations discussed in Subsects. 3.2 and 3.1 then follow. Together with those shown in Theorem 1, these are visualised in Fig. 2.

Theorem 2. *Let $\mathcal{L}_1$, $\mathcal{L}_2$ be any languages over Σ. By definition we have*

$$\mathcal{L}_1 \leq_{strongsemieq} \mathcal{L}_2 \implies \mathcal{L}_1 \leq_{semieq} \mathcal{L}_2 \wedge \mathcal{L}_1 \preceq_{red} \mathcal{L}_2,$$
$$\mathcal{L}_1 \leq_{strongsemired} \mathcal{L}_2 \implies \mathcal{L}_1 \leq_{semired} \mathcal{L}_2 \wedge \mathcal{L}_1 \preceq_{red} \mathcal{L}_2.$$

Furthermore,

$$\mathcal{L}_1 \leq_{semieq} \mathcal{L}_2 \implies \mathcal{L}_1 \leq_{semired} \mathcal{L}_2, \tag{16}$$
$$\mathcal{L}_1 \leq_{strongsemieq} \mathcal{L}_2 \implies \mathcal{L}_1 \leq_{strongsemired} \mathcal{L}_2, \tag{17}$$

and

$$\mathcal{L}_1 \preceq_{quasieq} \mathcal{L}_2 \implies \mathcal{L}_1 \leq_{semieq} \mathcal{L}_2, \tag{18}$$
$$\mathcal{L}_1 \preceq_{quasired} \mathcal{L}_2 \implies \mathcal{L}_1 \leq_{semired} \mathcal{L}_2, \tag{19}$$
$$\mathcal{L}_1 \preceq_{equiv} \mathcal{L}_2 \implies \mathcal{L}_1 \leq_{strongsemieq} \mathcal{L}_2, \tag{20}$$
$$\mathcal{L}_1 \preceq_{strongred} \mathcal{L}_2 \implies \mathcal{L}_1 \leq_{strongsemired} \mathcal{L}_2. \tag{21}$$

Remark 1 (Completely specified languages). When considering $\preceq_H$-conformance or $\leq_H$-conformance on completely specified languages, we may remove from H all pairs containing the empty set. Let Π denote the set of such pairs. That is, let $\Pi = \{(A, \emptyset) \mid A \subseteq \Sigma_O\} \cup \{(\emptyset, A) \mid A \subseteq \Sigma_O\}$. By definition, the relations discussed above collapse into two classes under removal of Π:

$$equiv \setminus \Pi = quasieq \setminus \Pi \ = semieq \setminus \Pi = strongsemieq \setminus \Pi, \text{ and}$$
$$red \setminus \Pi = quasired \setminus \Pi = strongred \ = semired \setminus \Pi = strongsemired \setminus \Pi.$$

Also note that, by Definition 3, for any completely specified languages $\mathcal{L}_1$, $\mathcal{L}_2$ and any relation H, we have that $\mathcal{L}_1 \preceq_H \mathcal{L}_2$ and $\mathcal{L}_1 \leq_H \mathcal{L}_2$ are equivalent. Thus, for completely specified languages, there is no difference between equivalence and quasi-, semi-, or strong-semi-equivalence. Similarly, the reduction relation, quasi-reduction, strong-reduction, semi-reduction and strong-semi-reduction define the same conformance relations between completely specified languages.

4   Conformance Testing

In this section, we present a fundamental necessary and sufficient criterion for conformance testing for $\preceq_H$-conformance and $\leq_H$-conformance. Furthermore, we present different ways of completing languages such that testing for quasi-equivalence, quasi-reduction and strong-reduction can be transformed into testing for reduction, allowing for the re-use of test generation algorithms.

4.1   A Fundamental Criterion for Conformance Testing

To determine if $\mathcal{L}_1 \preceq_H \mathcal{L}_2$ or $\mathcal{L}_1 \leq_H \mathcal{L}_2$, a comparison must be made between the sets $out_1(\pi, x)$ and $out_2(\pi, x)$ for all $\pi \in \mathcal{L}_1 \cap \mathcal{L}_2$ and all $x \in \Sigma_I$. However, if $\alpha \in \Sigma^*$ satisfies

$$L_1(\pi) = L_1(\alpha) \wedge L_2(\pi) = L_2(\alpha) \tag{22}$$

we can replace the use of π with α, as they both exhibit the same information on $\mathcal{L}_1$ and $\mathcal{L}_2$. This means, it is sufficient to only examine one representative from each equivalence class, where the equivalence relation on Σ^* is defined by (22)[3].

To this end, we introduce *state cover* and *transition cover* of $\mathcal{L}_1 \parallel \mathcal{L}_2 :=$ $\{(\pi, \pi) \mid \pi \in \mathcal{L}_1 \cap \mathcal{L}_2\}$, the parallel composition of $\mathcal{L}_1$ and $\mathcal{L}_2$.

Definition 4. *We call set $V \subseteq \Sigma^*$ a state cover and set $P = V \times \Sigma_I$ a transition cover of $\mathcal{L}_1 \parallel \mathcal{L}_2$, if*

$$\forall \pi \in \mathcal{L}_1 \cap \mathcal{L}_2, \exists \alpha \in V : L_1(\pi) = L_1(\alpha) \wedge L_2(\pi) = L_2(\alpha).$$

The following two theorems show that checking for $\preceq_H$-conformance and $\leq_H$-conformance reduces to checking conformance over a transition cover.

---

[3] Recall that $L(\pi) = \{\tau \in \Sigma^* \mid \pi.\tau \in \mathcal{L}\}$ for any $\pi \in \Sigma^*$.

Theorem 3 (Fundamental Criterion for $\preceq_H$-conformance). *Let $\mathcal{L}_1, \mathcal{L}_2$ be two languages over Σ and $H \subseteq 2^{\Sigma_O} \times 2^{\Sigma_O}$. Suppose V is a state cover of $\mathcal{L}_1 \parallel \mathcal{L}_2$ and $P = V \times \Sigma_I$. Then*

$$\mathcal{L}_1 \preceq_H \mathcal{L}_2 \iff \forall (\pi, x) \in P \wedge \pi \in \mathcal{L}_1 \cap \mathcal{L}_2 : (\mathrm{out}_1(\pi, x), \mathrm{out}_2(\pi, x)) \in H.$$

Proof. Let $\pi \in \mathcal{L}_1 \cap \mathcal{L}_2$ and $x \in \Sigma_I$ be any input. Since V is a state cover of $\mathcal{L}_1 \parallel \mathcal{L}_2$, there exists some $\alpha \in V$ such that $L_i(\pi) = L_i(\alpha)$, for $i = 1, 2$. Then for any output $y \in \Sigma_O$, it holds $x/y \in L_i(\pi) \iff x/y \in L_i(\alpha)$. Hence, $\mathrm{out}_i(\pi, x) = \mathrm{out}_i(\alpha, x)$, for $i = 1, 2$, and consequently,

$$(\mathrm{out}_1(\pi, x), \mathrm{out}_2(\pi, x)) \in H \iff (\mathrm{out}_1(\alpha, x), \mathrm{out}_2(\alpha, x)) \in H.$$

Thus, we obtain the claim by unfolding the definition of $\preceq_H$:

$$\mathcal{L}_1 \preceq_H \mathcal{L}_2 \iff \forall \pi \in \mathcal{L}_1 \cap \mathcal{L}_2, x \in \Sigma_I : (\mathrm{out}_1(\pi, x), \mathrm{out}_2(\pi, x)) \in H$$
$$\iff \forall (\alpha, x) \in P \wedge \alpha \in \mathcal{L}_1 \cap \mathcal{L}_2 : (\mathrm{out}_1(\alpha, x), \mathrm{out}_2(\alpha, x)) \in H. \qquad \square$$

Theorem 4 (Fundamental Criterion for $\leq_H$-conformance). *Let $\mathcal{L}_1, \mathcal{L}_2$ be two languages over Σ and $H \subseteq 2^{\Sigma_O} \times 2^{\Sigma_O}$. Suppose V is a state cover of $\mathcal{L}_1 \parallel \mathcal{L}_2$ and $P = V \times \Sigma_I$. Then*

$$\mathcal{L}_1 \leq_H \mathcal{L}_2 \iff \forall (\pi, x) \in P \wedge \pi \in \mathcal{L}_1 \cap \mathcal{L}_2 : (\mathrm{out}_1(\pi, x), \mathrm{out}_2(\pi, x)) \in H$$
$$\wedge \, \mathrm{out}_2(\pi, x) \neq \emptyset \implies$$
$$\exists (\pi, x') \in P : \mathrm{out}_1(\pi, x') \cap \mathrm{out}_2(\pi, x') \neq \emptyset.$$

We omit the proof here, as it is analogous to that of Theorem 3.

Theorems 3 and 4 show that complete (sound and exhaustive) testing algorithms for $\preceq_H$-conformance and $\leq_H$-conformance may be generated by selecting an algorithm that computes state covers, extending its output to a transition cover P, and applying for all $(\pi, x) \in P$ first π and then x to the reference model and the system-under-test, in order to obtain $\mathrm{out}_1(\pi, x)$ and $\mathrm{out}_2(\pi, x)$. These responses are then compared as described in Theorems 3 and 4, respectively, in order to obtain a verdict.

In practice, further assumptions are placed on $\mathcal{L}_1$ and $\mathcal{L}_2$, in order to obtain finite state covers. For example, the following lemma obtains a finite state cover if both languages are regular. It can be proven using standard techniques.

Lemma 4. *We call each $L(\pi)$ with $\pi \in \mathcal{L}$ state of $\mathcal{L}$. Suppose $\mathcal{L}_1$ has at most n states and $\mathcal{L}_2$ has at most m states. Then*

$$V = \{\pi \in \Sigma^* \mid |\pi| \leq mn - 1\}$$

is a state cover of $\mathcal{L}_1 \parallel \mathcal{L}_2$.

Employing this result to compute state covers for finite state machines, whose languages are regular, and extending these to transition covers by appending all $x \in \Sigma_I$ results in the so-called 'brute-force' testing strategy[4].

---

[4] This strategy has been described, for example, in the lecture notes provided by Peleska and Huang in [10, Section 4.5].

The size of the state covers may be reduced by considering the selected conformance relation $\preceq_H$ or $\leq_H$ during the computation of the state cover. For example, the complete test suites generated for $\preceq_{equiv}$ on FSMs with upper size bounds n and m using the H-Method (see [2]) are of size at most $\mathcal{O}(n^2 \cdot |\Sigma|^{m-n+1})$. This is significantly smaller than the general result of Lemma 4. In future research, we would like to examine the possibility of deriving efficient algorithms for computing state covers for $\preceq_H$ or $\leq_H$ and arbitrary relations H by generalising from techniques proposed for specific conformance relations (see, for example, [2,3,12,16]), analogously to our development of Definitions 2 and 3.

Theorems 3 and 4 describe conditions for conformance that are both necessary and sufficient. They can be employed to verify whether a given test strategy is complete. Also note that Theorem 3 is closely related to the so-called *SPY-condition* for completeness of test suites (see [16, Theorem 1]).

4.2   Quasi-equivalence, Quasi-reduction and Strong-Reduction as Reductions

In the selection of test algorithms for $\preceq_{H_1}$-conformance for a given relation H_1, it is also interesting to examine whether this task may be reduced to checking another conformance relation by augmenting the considered languages. That is, given H_1, we search for a relation H_2 and a function f such that for all $\mathcal{L}_1, \mathcal{L}_2$, $\mathcal{L}_1 \preceq_{H_1} \mathcal{L}_2$ holds if and only if $f(\mathcal{L}_1) \preceq_{H_2} f(\mathcal{L}_2)$ holds. In the following, we show that quasi-equivalence can be expressed via quasi-reduction, which in turn can be expressed via reduction, as can strong-reduction. Thus, test strategies for these conformance relations may be generated from test strategies for reduction. Proofs for the theorems in this subsection are available in Appendix A.

To express quasi-equivalence through quasi-reduction, both languages need to be augmented. This augmentation can be achieved by adding a new symbol $y^\dagger$ to the output alphabet for each output symbol y, which indicates the *absence* of output y whenever some defined input fails to produce output y. This technique was first introduced in [5] for finite state machines.

Definition 5. *Let $\Sigma_O^\dagger = \{y^\dagger \mid y \in \Sigma_O\}$ and assume that $\Sigma_O \cap \Sigma_O^\dagger = \emptyset$. For any language $\mathcal{L}$ over $\Sigma = \Sigma_I \times \Sigma_O$, $\mathcal{L}^\dagger$ is a language over $\Sigma_I \times (\Sigma_O \cup \Sigma_O^\dagger)$ defined as follows*

$$\mathcal{L}^\dagger = \mathcal{L} \cup \{\pi.x/y^\dagger.\tau \mid (\pi, x) \in \mathcal{L} \times \Sigma_I, \mathrm{out}(\pi, x) \neq \emptyset,$$

$$y \in \Sigma_O \setminus \mathrm{out}(\pi, x), \tau \in (\Sigma_I \times \Sigma_O^\dagger)^*\}.$$

Note that $\mathcal{L}^\dagger$ is non-empty and prefix closed, since $\mathcal{L}$ is non-empty and prefix closed by assumption. Furthermore, $\mathcal{L}^\dagger$ is completely specified if and only if $\mathcal{L}$ is completely specified .

The following theorem shows that quasi-equivalence can be expressed via quasi-reduction without the restriction that $\mathcal{L}_1$ is completely specified, as required in [5].

Theorem 5. $\mathcal{L}_1 \preceq_{quasieq} \mathcal{L}_2 \iff \mathcal{L}_1^\dagger \preceq_{quasired} \mathcal{L}_2^\dagger$.

Next, to express quasi-reduction via reduction, we modify both languages by augmenting them so that all inputs are defined. More precisely, we first add an output symbol $\bot$ that is not part of Σ_O, resulting in the set $\Sigma_O^\bot = \Sigma_O \cup \{\bot\}$. Then we append after each trace π in the language all sequences over $\Sigma_I \times \Sigma_O^\bot$ whose first input symbol is undefined in π. This effectively allows arbitrary behaviour after undefined inputs.

Definition 6. *For any language $\mathcal{L}$ over $\Sigma_I \times \Sigma_O$ define language $D(\mathcal{L})$ over $\Sigma_I \times \Sigma_O^\bot$ by*

$$D(\mathcal{L}) = \mathcal{L} \cup \{\pi.x/y.\tau \mid \pi \in \mathcal{L}, out(\pi, x) = \emptyset, y \in \Sigma_O^\bot, \tau \in (\Sigma_I \times \Sigma_O^\bot)^*\}.$$

Since $\mathcal{L}$ is non-empty and prefix closed, $D(\mathcal{L})$ is non-empty and prefix closed as well. Moreover, $D(\mathcal{L})$ is completely specified.

This augmentation is sufficient to express quasi-reduction via reduction:

Theorem 6. $\mathcal{L}_1 \preceq_{quasired} \mathcal{L}_2 \iff D(\mathcal{L}_1) \preceq_{red} D(\mathcal{L}_2)$.

Finally, we show the novel result that strong-reduction can also be expressed by reduction. To this purpose, we again employ $\bot$ and $\Sigma_O^\bot$. We then augment a language by considering each contained trace π and allowing after each prefix of π the insertion of $x/\bot$ if x is not defined after the prefix. Thus, in contrast to the previous construction for quasi-reduction, we do not insert arbitrary behaviour after undefined inputs.

Definition 7. *For any language $\mathcal{L}$ over $\Sigma_I \times \Sigma_O$ define language $\mathcal{L}^\bot$ over $\Sigma_I \times \Sigma_O^\bot$ by*

$$\mathcal{L}^\bot = \{\pi_1.\tau_1.\pi_2.\tau_2 \ldots \pi_k.\tau_k \mid \pi_1 \ldots \pi_k \in \mathcal{L}, k \geq 1,$$
$$\tau_i \in \{x/\bot \mid x \in \Sigma_I, out(\pi_1 \ldots \pi_i, x) = \emptyset\}^*\}.$$

We note that $\mathcal{L} \subseteq \mathcal{L}^\bot$ and for any $\pi \in \mathcal{L}^\bot$, $\pi|_\Sigma \in \mathcal{L}$. Moreover, for any $x \in \Sigma_I$,

$$out_\bot(\pi, x) = out_\bot(\pi|_\Sigma, x) = \begin{cases} out(\pi|_\Sigma, x) \subseteq \Sigma_O & \text{if } out(\pi|_\Sigma, x) \neq \emptyset, \\ \{\bot\} & \text{if } out(\pi|_\Sigma, x) = \emptyset, \end{cases}$$

is always non-empty. Hence $\mathcal{L}^\bot$ is completely specified.

The following theorem shows that the augmentation is suitable to express strong-reduction via reduction

Theorem 7. $\mathcal{L}_1 \preceq_{strongred} \mathcal{L}_2 \iff \mathcal{L}_1^\bot \preceq_{red} \mathcal{L}_2^\bot$.

5   Conclusions

In this paper, we present a unifying treatment of well-known conformance relations that does not depend on the syntactic representation or modelling formalism of reference models. We derive a simple method to compare conformance relations and a fundamental necessary and sufficient criterion for conformance, which may be employed to generate test algorithms. We also show that quasi-equivalence, quasi-reduction and strong-reduction can be characterised in terms of reductions.

For future work, we plan to develop efficient test algorithms based on this criterion, extending the previous work [8]. Another direction could be to extend our framework to other conformance relations such as *safety*-related ones (see [6]) or conformance relations appearing in labelled transition systems (see [17] for an overview).

Acknowledgement. We would like to express our gratitude to Jan Peleska for the opportunity to collaborating with him and for his guidance in the field of testing. This paper was supported by the German Federal Ministry of Economic Affairs, Project "HiDyVe – Highly Dynamic Virtual and Hybrid Validation and Verification" under grant agreement 20X1908E.

A   Proofs

In this appendix, we present proofs for equivalences (3) and (4), as well as for Theorems 5, 6, and 7 discussed in Subsect. 4.2.

First recall equivalences (3) and (4), which state how the conformance relations equivalence and reduction can be expressed as $\preceq_H$-conformances:

$$\mathcal{L}_1 = \mathcal{L}_2 \iff \mathcal{L}_1 \preceq_{equiv} \mathcal{L}_2 \qquad \text{where } equiv = \{(A, A) \mid A \subseteq \Sigma_O\} \tag{3}$$

$$\mathcal{L}_1 \subseteq \mathcal{L}_2 \iff \mathcal{L}_1 \preceq_{red} \mathcal{L}_2 \qquad \text{where } red = \{(A, B) \mid A \subseteq B \subseteq \Sigma_O\} \tag{4}$$

Proof. To prove (3) and (4), we first show that (4) holds. To this end, let $\pi \in \mathcal{L}_1 \cap \mathcal{L}_2$ and $x \in \Sigma_I$. Suppose that $\mathcal{L}_1 \subseteq \mathcal{L}_2$. For any $y \in \Sigma_O$, $y \in \text{out}_1(\pi, x)$ holds if an only if $\pi.x/y \in \mathcal{L}_1$, which by $\mathcal{L}_1 \subseteq \mathcal{L}_2$ implies $\pi.x/y \in \mathcal{L}_2$ and hence $y \in \text{out}_2(\pi, x)$. Thus, we obtain that $\text{out}_1(\pi, x) \subseteq \text{out}_2(\pi, x)$, and therefore that the pair $(\text{out}_1(\pi, x), \text{out}_2(\pi, x))$ is contained in the relation *red*. Consequently, $\mathcal{L}_1 \preceq_{red} \mathcal{L}_2$.

To prove the other direction, suppose $\mathcal{L}_1 \preceq_{red} \mathcal{L}_2$. Let $\pi \in \mathcal{L}_1$ be any word in $\mathcal{L}_1$. We show by induction on $|\pi| \geq 0$ that $\pi \in \mathcal{L}_2$. Since $\varepsilon \in \mathcal{L}_1 \cap \mathcal{L}_2$ is the only word of length 0, $|\pi| = 0 \implies \pi \in \mathcal{L}_2$. Suppose for some $k \geq 0$ that $|\pi| \leq k$ implies $\pi \in \mathcal{L}_2$. Let $\pi.x/y \in \mathcal{L}_1$ be any word in $\mathcal{L}_1$ with $|\pi| = k$, $x \in \Sigma_I$ and $y \in \Sigma_O$. Then by definition of $\mathcal{L}_1 \preceq_{red} \mathcal{L}_2$ and the induction assumption that $\pi \in \mathcal{L}_1 \cap \mathcal{L}_2$, we have $\text{out}_1(\pi, x) \subseteq \text{out}_2(\pi, x)$. Since $\pi.x/y \in \mathcal{L}_1$, $y \in \text{out}_1(\pi, x)$, and then $y \in \text{out}_2(\pi, x)$, consequently $\pi.x/y \in \mathcal{L}_2$ and $\mathcal{L}_1 \subseteq \mathcal{L}_2$. This proves (4). To prove (3), we first note that

$$\mathcal{L}_1 = \mathcal{L}_2 \iff \mathcal{L}_1 \subseteq \mathcal{L}_2 \wedge \mathcal{L}_2 \subseteq \mathcal{L}_1, \tag{23}$$

and derive

$$\mathcal{L}_1 \preceq_{equiv} \mathcal{L}_2 \iff \mathcal{L}_1 \preceq_{red} \mathcal{L}_2 \wedge \mathcal{L}_2 \preceq_{red} \mathcal{L}_1 \tag{24}$$

by considering that for any $\pi \in \mathcal{L}_1 \cap \mathcal{L}_2, x \in \Sigma_I$,

$$(\mathrm{out}_1(\pi, x), \mathrm{out}_2(\pi, x)) \in \boldsymbol{equiv}$$
$$\iff \mathrm{out}_1(\pi, x) = \mathrm{out}_2(\pi, x)$$
$$\iff \mathrm{out}_1(\pi, x) \subseteq \mathrm{out}_2(\pi, x) \wedge \mathrm{out}_2(\pi, x) \subseteq \mathrm{out}_1(\pi, x)$$
$$\iff (\mathrm{out}_1(\pi, x), \mathrm{out}_2(\pi, x)) \in \boldsymbol{red} \wedge (\mathrm{out}_2(\pi, x), \mathrm{out}_1(\pi, x)) \in \boldsymbol{red},$$

(3) then follows directly from (24), (4) and (23).   □

Theorem 5. $\mathcal{L}_1 \preceq_{quasieq} \mathcal{L}_2 \iff \mathcal{L}_1^\dagger \preceq_{quasired} \mathcal{L}_2^\dagger.$

Proof. First note the following properties of the augmented languages, which follow from Definition 5.

For any $\pi \in \mathcal{L}^\dagger$ and $x \in \Sigma_I$, it holds

$$\mathrm{out}_\dagger(\pi, x) = \begin{cases} \mathrm{out}(\pi, x) \cup \{y^\dagger \in \Sigma_O^\dagger \mid y \notin \mathrm{out}(\pi, x)\} & \text{if } \mathrm{out}(\pi, x) \neq \emptyset, \\ \emptyset & \text{if } \pi \in \mathcal{L} \wedge \mathrm{out}(\pi, x) = \emptyset, \\ \Sigma_O^\dagger & \text{if } \pi \notin \mathcal{L}. \end{cases}$$

Furthermore, for any languages $\mathcal{L}_1, \mathcal{L}_2$ over Σ,

$$\pi \in \mathcal{L}_1^\dagger \cap \mathcal{L}_2^\dagger \implies \begin{cases} \pi \in \mathcal{L}_1 \cap \mathcal{L}_2 & \text{if } \pi \in \Sigma^*, \\ \pi \in \mathcal{L}_1^\dagger \cap \mathcal{L}_2^\dagger \setminus (\mathcal{L}_1 \cup \mathcal{L}_2) & \text{if } \pi \notin \Sigma^*. \end{cases}$$

Hence, for any $\pi \in (\mathcal{L}_1^\dagger \cap \mathcal{L}_2^\dagger) \setminus \Sigma^*$ and any $x \in \Sigma_I$, $\mathrm{out}_{1\dagger}(\pi, x) = \Sigma_O^\dagger = \mathrm{out}_{2\dagger}(\pi, x)$.

By definitions (5), (7), (2) and the above, we then have

$$\mathcal{L}_1^\dagger \preceq_{quasired} \mathcal{L}_2^\dagger$$
$$\iff \forall \pi \in \mathcal{L}_1^\dagger \cap \mathcal{L}_2^\dagger, \forall x \in \Sigma_I : \emptyset \neq \mathrm{out}_{1\dagger}(\pi, x) \subseteq \mathrm{out}_{2\dagger}(\pi, x) \vee \mathrm{out}_{2\dagger}(\pi, x) = \emptyset$$
$$\iff \forall \pi \in (\mathcal{L}_1^\dagger \cap \mathcal{L}_2^\dagger) \setminus \Sigma^*, \forall x \in \Sigma_I : \emptyset \neq \mathrm{out}_{1\dagger}(\pi, x) \subseteq \mathrm{out}_{2\dagger}(\pi, x)$$
$$\vee \mathrm{out}_{2\dagger}(\pi, x) = \emptyset$$
$$\wedge \forall \pi \in \mathcal{L}_1 \cap \mathcal{L}_2, \forall x \in \Sigma_I : \emptyset \neq \mathrm{out}_{1\dagger}(\pi, x) \subseteq \mathrm{out}_{2\dagger}(\pi, x) \vee \mathrm{out}_{2\dagger}(\pi, x) = \emptyset$$
$$\iff \forall \pi \in (\mathcal{L}_1^\dagger \cap \mathcal{L}_2^\dagger) \setminus \Sigma^*, \forall x \in \Sigma_I : \mathrm{out}_{1\dagger}(\pi, x) = \Sigma_O^\dagger = \mathrm{out}_{2\dagger}(\pi, x)$$
$$\wedge \forall \pi \in \mathcal{L}_1 \cap \mathcal{L}_2, \forall x \in \Sigma_I : \emptyset \neq \mathrm{out}_{1\dagger}(\pi, x) \subseteq \mathrm{out}_{2\dagger}(\pi, x) \vee \mathrm{out}_{2\dagger}(\pi, x) = \emptyset$$
$$\iff \forall \pi \in \mathcal{L}_1 \cap \mathcal{L}_2, \forall x \in \Sigma_I : \emptyset \neq \mathrm{out}_{1\dagger}(\pi, x) \subseteq \mathrm{out}_{2\dagger}(\pi, x) \vee \mathrm{out}_{2\dagger}(\pi, x) = \emptyset$$
$$\iff \forall \pi \in \mathcal{L}_1 \cap \mathcal{L}_2, \forall x \in \Sigma_I : \mathrm{out}_2(\pi, x) = \emptyset \vee (\emptyset \neq \mathrm{out}_1(\pi, x) \wedge$$

$$\text{out}_1(\pi, x) \cup \{y^\dagger \in \Sigma_O^\dagger \mid y \notin \text{out}_1(\pi, x)\} \subseteq$$
$$\text{out}_2(\pi, x) \cup \{y^\dagger \in \Sigma_O^\dagger \mid y \notin \text{out}_2(\pi, x)\})$$
$$\iff \forall \pi \in \mathcal{L}_1 \cap \mathcal{L}_2, \forall x \in \Sigma_I : \text{out}_2(\pi, x) = \emptyset \vee (\emptyset \neq \text{out}_1(\pi, x) \wedge$$
$$\text{out}_1(\pi, x) = \text{out}_2(\pi, x))$$
$$\iff \mathcal{L}_1 \preceq_{quasieq} \mathcal{L}_2 \qquad \qquad \square$$

Theorem 6. $\mathcal{L}_1 \preceq_{quasired} \mathcal{L}_2 \iff D(\mathcal{L}_1) \preceq_{red} D(\mathcal{L}_2)$.

Proof. First note the following properties of the augmented languages, which follow from Definition 6. Let $\mathcal{L}$ be any language over Σ. We use notation $\text{out}_D(\pi, x)$ for $\text{out}_{D(\mathcal{L})}(\pi, x)$. Then

$$\text{out}_D(\pi, x) = \begin{cases} \text{out}(\pi, x) \subseteq \Sigma_O & \text{if } \text{out}(\pi, x) \neq \emptyset, \\ \Sigma_O^\perp & \text{if } \text{out}(\pi, x) = \emptyset. \end{cases}$$

We show first that from $\mathcal{L}_1 \preceq_{quasired} \mathcal{L}_2$ follows

$$\forall \pi \in D(\mathcal{L}_1) \cap D(\mathcal{L}_2) \setminus (\mathcal{L}_1 \cap \mathcal{L}_2), \forall x \in \Sigma_I : \text{out}_2(\pi, x) = \emptyset. \qquad (25)$$

Suppose not, there exists some $\pi \in D(\mathcal{L}_1) \cap D(\mathcal{L}_2) \setminus (\mathcal{L}_1 \cap \mathcal{L}_2)$ and $x \in \Sigma_I$ such that $\text{out}_2(\pi, x) \neq \emptyset$. Since $\mathcal{L}_1 \preceq_{quasired} \mathcal{L}_2$, we have $\text{out}_1(\pi, x) \neq \emptyset$. Hence $\pi \in \mathcal{L}_1 \cap \mathcal{L}_2$. This leads to a contradiction to $\pi \in D(\mathcal{L}_1) \cap D(\mathcal{L}_2) \setminus (\mathcal{L}_1 \cap \mathcal{L}_2)$.

Then by definition, the above, and (25),

$$D(\mathcal{L}_1) \preceq_{red} D(\mathcal{L}_2)$$
$$\iff \forall \pi \in D(\mathcal{L}_1) \cap D(\mathcal{L}_2), \forall x \in \Sigma_I : \text{out}_{D_1}(\pi, x) \subseteq \text{out}_{D_2}(\pi, x)$$
$$\iff \forall \pi \in D(\mathcal{L}_1) \cap D(\mathcal{L}_2), \forall x \in \Sigma_I : \text{out}_{D_2}(\pi, x) = \Sigma_O^\perp$$
$$\vee \emptyset \neq \text{out}_1(\pi, x) \subseteq \text{out}_2(\pi, x)$$
$$\iff \forall \pi \in D(\mathcal{L}_1) \cap D(\mathcal{L}_2) \setminus (\mathcal{L}_1 \cap \mathcal{L}_2), \forall x \in \Sigma_I : \text{out}_{D_2}(\pi, x) = \Sigma_O^\perp$$
$$\wedge \forall \pi \in \mathcal{L}_1 \cap \mathcal{L}_2, \forall x \in \Sigma_I : \text{out}_2(\pi, x) = \emptyset \vee \emptyset \neq \text{out}_1(\pi, x) \subseteq \text{out}_2(\pi, x)$$
$$\iff \forall \pi \in D(\mathcal{L}_1) \cap D(\mathcal{L}_2) \setminus (\mathcal{L}_1 \cap \mathcal{L}_2), \forall x \in \Sigma_I : \text{out}_2(\pi, x) = \emptyset$$
$$\wedge \forall \pi \in \mathcal{L}_1 \cap \mathcal{L}_2, \forall x \in \Sigma_I : \text{out}_2(\pi, x) = \emptyset \vee \emptyset \neq \text{out}_1(\pi, x) \subseteq \text{out}_2(\pi, x)$$
$$\iff \forall \pi \in \mathcal{L}_1 \cap \mathcal{L}_2, \forall x \in \Sigma_I : \text{out}_2(\pi, x) = \emptyset \vee \emptyset \neq \text{out}_1(\pi, x) \subseteq \text{out}_2(\pi, x)$$
$$\iff \mathcal{L}_1 \preceq_{quasired} \mathcal{L}_2. \qquad \qquad \square$$

Theorem 7. $\mathcal{L}_1 \preceq_{strongred} \mathcal{L}_2 \iff \mathcal{L}_1^\perp \preceq_{red} \mathcal{L}_2^\perp$.

Proof. By definition we have

$$\mathcal{L}_1 \preceq_{strongred} \mathcal{L}_2$$
$$\Longleftrightarrow \forall \pi \in \mathcal{L}_1 \cap \mathcal{L}_2, \forall x \in \Sigma_I : \emptyset \neq \mathrm{out}_1(\pi, x) \subseteq \mathrm{out}_2(\pi, x)$$
$$\vee \, \mathrm{out}_1(\pi, x) = \emptyset = \mathrm{out}_2(\pi, x)$$
$$\Longleftrightarrow \forall \pi \in \mathcal{L}_1^{\perp} \cap \mathcal{L}_2^{\perp}, \forall x \in \Sigma_I : \emptyset \neq \mathrm{out}_1(\pi|_{\Sigma}, x) \subseteq \mathrm{out}_2(\pi|_{\Sigma}, x)$$
$$\vee \, \mathrm{out}_1(\pi|_{\Sigma}, x) = \emptyset = \mathrm{out}_2(\pi|_{\Sigma}, x)$$
$$\Longleftrightarrow \forall \pi \in \mathcal{L}_1^{\perp} \cap \mathcal{L}_2^{\perp}, \forall x \in \Sigma_I : \{\perp\} \neq \mathrm{out}_{1\perp}(\pi, x) \subseteq \mathrm{out}_{2\perp}(\pi, x)$$
$$\vee \, \mathrm{out}_{1\perp}(\pi, x) = \{\perp\} = \mathrm{out}_{2\perp}(\pi, x)$$
$$\Longleftrightarrow \forall \pi \in \mathcal{L}_1^{\perp} \cap \mathcal{L}_2^{\perp}, \forall x \in \Sigma_I : \mathrm{out}_{1\perp}(\pi, x) \subseteq \mathrm{out}_{2\perp}(\pi, x)$$
$$\Longleftrightarrow \mathcal{L}_1^{\perp} \preceq_{red} \mathcal{L}_2^{\perp}. \qquad \square$$

References

1. Chow, T.S.: Testing software design modeled by finite-state machines. IEEE Trans. Software Eng. **4**(3), 178–187 (1978)
2. Dorofeeva, R., El-Fakih, K., Yevtushenko, N.: An improved conformance testing method. In: Wang, F. (ed.) FORTE 2005. LNCS, vol. 3731, pp. 204–218. Springer, Heidelberg (2005). https://doi.org/10.1007/11562436_16
3. Hierons, R.M.: Testing from a nondeterministic finite state machine using adaptive state counting. IEEE Trans. Comput. **53**(10), 1330–1342 (2004)
4. Hierons, R.M.: Testing from partial finite state machines without harmonised traces. IEEE Trans. Software Eng. **43**(11), 1033–1043 (2017)
5. Hierons, R.M.: FSM quasi-equivalence testing via reduction and observing absences. Sci. Comput. Program. **177**, 1–18 (2019)
6. Huang, W., Özoguz, S., Peleska, J.: Safety-complete test suites. Software Qual. J. **27**(2), 589–613 (2019)
7. Huang, W., Peleska, J.: Complete model-based equivalence class testing for nondeterministic systems. Formal Aspects Comput. **29**(2), 335–364 (2017)
8. Huang, W., Peleska, J.: Model-based testing strategies and their (in)dependence on syntactic model representations. STTT **20**(4), 441–465 (2018)
9. Nerode, A.: Linear automaton transformations. Proc. Am. Mathem. Soc. **9**(4), 541–544 (1958)
10. Peleska, J., Huang, W.: Test Automation - Foundations and Applications of Model-based Testing. University of Bremen (2021), https://www.informatik.uni-bremen.de/agbs/jp/papers/test-automation-huang-peleska.pdf
11. Petrenko, A., Yevtushenko, N.: Conformance tests as checking experiments for partial nondeterministic FSM. In: Grieskamp, W., Weise, C. (eds.) FATES 2005. LNCS, vol. 3997, pp. 118–133. Springer, Heidelberg (2006). https://doi.org/10.1007/11759744_9
12. Petrenko, A., Yevtushenko, N.: Adaptive testing of deterministic implementations specified by nondeterministic FSMs. In: Wolff, B., Zaïdi, F. (eds.) ICTSS 2011. LNCS, vol. 7019, pp. 162–178. Springer, Heidelberg (2011). https://doi.org/10.1007/978-3-642-24580-0_12

13. Petrenko, A., Yevtushenko, N.: Adaptive testing of nondeterministic systems with FSM. In: 15th International IEEE Symposium on High-Assurance Systems Engineering, HASE 2014, Miami Beach, FL, USA, 9–11 January 2014. pp. 224–228. IEEE Computer Society (2014). https://doi.org/10.1109/HASE.2014.39,

14. Petrenko, A., Yevtushenko, N., v. Bochmann, G.: Testing deterministic implementations from nondeterministic FSM specifications. In: Baumgarten, B., Burkhardt, H.-J., Giessler, A. (eds.) Testing of Communicating Systems. ITIFIP, pp. 125–140. Springer, Boston, MA (1996). https://doi.org/10.1007/978-0-387-35062-2_10

15. Sachtleben, R., Peleska, J.: Effective grey-box testing with partial fsm models. Softw. Testing Verificat. Reliab. **32**(2), e1806 (2022). https://doi.org/10.1002/stvr.1806

16. da Silva Simão, A., Petrenko, A., Yevtushenko, N.: On reducing test length for fsms with extra states. Softw. Testing Verificat. Reliab. **22**(6), 435–454 (2012)

17. Tretmans, J.: Model based testing with labelled transition systems. In: Hierons, R.M., Bowen, J.P., Harman, M. (eds.) Formal Methods and Testing. LNCS, vol. 4949, pp. 1–38. Springer, Heidelberg (2008). https://doi.org/10.1007/978-3-540-78917-8_1

18. Vasilevskii, M.P.: Failure diagnosis of automata. Kibernetika (Transl.) **4**, 98–108 (1973)

On Scenario-Based Testing
of Cyber-Physical Systems

Alexander Pretschner[(⊠)], Florian Hauer, and Tabea Schmidt

Technical University of Munich, Munich, Germany
{alexander.pretschner,florian.hauer,tabea.schmidt}@tum.de

Abstract. We present several results on scenario-based testing, an equivalence class testing method typically applied to cyber-physical systems. We show that randomly sampling as well as re-using tests in general is problematic and that instead, new tests need to be generated for each new version of the systems. We discuss empirical results on the power of heuristic search and show that different algorithms lead to largely different results—with some generated test suites finding safety-critical behavior and some failing to do so. Finally, we present different dimensions of and criteria for completeness of scenario-based test suites.

1 Introduction

Automated tests of increasingly autonomous vehicles play a large role in assessing the safety of such systems. One suggestion is to choose single test drives from a large set of recorded test drives, randomly or on the grounds of specific selection criteria, and to subsequently use this subset of recorded test drives as test cases [3,20,23,29,30]. Unfortunately, if we aim to test these systems with "good" test cases and, thus, go beyond merely using random tests, this approach cannot be justified convincingly [15]. Instead, new system-specific test cases have to be generated for each version of the system. Such "good" test cases can be created through the intelligent instantiation of so-called scenario types and by performing a heuristic search.

In this paper, we center our treatise of scenario-based testing around the argument to generally not re-use tests for automated vehicles in three steps [15]. First, we recap the two-fold function of testing, which is used both to check functionality and to detect defects; and show that a meaningful notion of "good" test cases is based on a defect-based definition. Since approaches that are *not* defect-based do not allow to discriminate between test cases, no test case is, consequently, "better" than another with these approaches. Secondly, we explain the idea of recording test drives and replaying them as test cases - and argue why this is problematic: One such recorded test drive may provoke a lane change assistant to change the lane—or not. If no lane change happens, is this test case useful? And if a lane change does happen, is the corresponding situation in any way superior to other lane changes and in this sense "better" than these other situations/test cases? Our answer is "no:" roughly speaking, a good test case

A. E. Haxthausen et al. (Eds.): Peleska Festschrift 2023, LNCS 14165, pp. 68–82, 2023.
https://doi.org/10.1007/978-3-031-40132-9_5

for a Volkswagen beetle is not automatically a good test case for a Ferrari. This means that recorded test drives, or test cases respectively, should not be reused "blindly" if the dynamics of the two vehicles under test differ. Thirdly, we show how the problem can be solved with system-specific test case generation from scenario types that present typical situations that the autonomously operating system should be able to handle.

This test case generation procedure is based on encoding the definition of good test cases as an optimization problem where we typically try to minimize the distance to obstacles or other vehicles. The optimization problems are commonly solved by using heuristic search algorithms. By definition, heuristic search in general cannot guarantee optimality of the solutions it finds. We discuss recent results [27] that show that for testing the autopilot software of drones, different heuristic search algorithms, applied in different order, lead to results that differ by as much as 20% in terms of the minimum distance to obstacles. Some combinations of search algorithms do lead to scenario instances that cause crashes, and some do not. This unfortunately seems to suggest that it is not sufficient to just use one search algorithm, but rather multiple algorithms (and even this will not guarantee optimal solutions). This makes test case generation with heuristic search possibly a prohibitively expensive endeavor.

Scenario-based test case generation depends on the existence of abstract scenario types. These can be derived by experts or mined from recorded drives by means of clustering. We argue that redundancy between the two approaches is a promising way of arguing about completeness. Several approaches to clustering have been suggested in the literature. Unfortunately, it is hard to judge how "good" the resulting clusters are. Moreover, these clusters represent point clouds. If they are to be turned into scenario types that can subsequently be used for test case generation, we need to transform the clusters into a format that has clear semantics and that can be used for test case generation. This in turn, is not too hard a problem in itself. However, it is difficult to argue about the quality and accuracy of these semantic descriptions. We discuss recent work that helps provide respective arguments.

We conclude with a discussion of different facets of completeness for scenario-based testing.

2 Defect Hypotheses for "Good" Test Cases

Testing is an expensive process that is necessarily restricted to a few selected executions of the system. Testing has the double purpose of increasing confidence in the compliance of a system with its specification and of detecting defects. Regarding these two goals, "good" test cases reveal potential defects with good cost-effectiveness. Defects must be *potential* in this definition: When assuming *actual* defects instead, no good test cases could be created for a hypothetical defect-free system. The cost-effectiveness refers to the severity and occurrence probability of the failures as well as the effort of test generation and test execution [26]. These two perspectives are the foundations of risk-based and requirement-based testing: Risk-based testing is driven by the occurrence probability and severity of potential failures. While requirements-based testing does not explicitly consider the severity of potential failures, it implicitly emphasizes the functionality that is assumed to be executed more commonly or is more critical: those functions for which requirements are explicitly formulated.

While the idea of explicit potential defects is not present in test selection strategies based on code coverage, it is a constituent of many other test selection criteria. These include limit testing or combinatorial testing; potential defects are also encoded in many static analysers or when fuzzing for array overflows, null-pointer exceptions or divisions by zero; and they are also reflected in the idea of fault injection for measuring the quality of test cases. In practice, probably the most widespread variant is limit testing. Here, engineers assign "empirically interesting" values to input variables or internal variables; values which often proved incorrect in the past. If the corresponding variable types are ordered, these interesting values often are at the ends of the regarded intervals: MININT or MAXINT; NEGINFTY or POSINFTY; empty list or NULL; etc.

From a practical tester's perspective, these defect-based testing approaches by definition strongly limit the possible (input) values, namely to the mentioned few extreme values. Such a filter is missing in both purely requirements-based and coverage-based testing: all tests of one type are initially regarded as equivalent. These equivalence classes, or blocks of a partition of the input space, often result from the decomposition of the input space into categories that are meaningful from an application's requirements point of view, such as implemented scenarios or user stories. Sometimes they are created implicitly, namely when code coverage criteria are applied to select test cases. In many cases, it is possible to arrange (order) the values in the corresponding equivalence classes and to select test cases at the "corners" of these classes. If this type of test selection is applied, the underlying tests are based on a defect hypothesis.

If no defect hypothesis justifies the choice of the equivalence classes or the choice of elements from one class, all elements of a class or even the whole input space are, in fact, equivalent concerning their a-priori failure probability [31]. Then, test cases can be randomly selected from the equivalence classes or the whole input space. However, it is not clear how "good" these test cases are. This is in contrast to the test cases derived by test procedures based on defect hypotheses, which select input data with a-priori increased probabilities of revealing potential failures, e.g., input data at the edges of intervals. This argumentation also applies when testing autonomous driving systems: If we aim to justify why one test case is "better" than another, an assumption about potential defects is necessary [26].

3   (Regression) Testing with Recorded Drives

From the perspective of the system under test (SUT), the ego vehicle, recorded test drives are descriptions of its environment. For a lane change assistant, these descriptions include the vehicles that surround the ego vehicle and that are

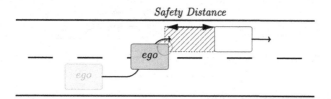

Fig. 1. Lane change of the SUT (ego) and the safety distance to the vehicle in front, undercut by the SUT.

relevant for the lane change decision. A typical goal for testing a lane change assistant is to test whether it keeps sufficient distance to the vehicles in its environment when changing lanes. For this purpose, the actually maintained distance to these vehicles is compared with a given safety distance.

Let us assume that our underlying test objective is the minimization of the distance that the ego vehicle keeps to the vehicle in front when changing lanes. It is reasonable to assume the existence of such a test objective because otherwise, our testing process would not be able to distinguish between the many situations in which a lane change occurs, most of which are uncritical anyway because, for instance, there are no cars in the vicinity. Let us further assume that during the execution of a test case we discover that the lane change assistant undercuts the safety distance when changing lanes, e.g., to a vehicle in the target lane in front of it (Fig. 1). Intuitively, this test case is useful because it reveals actually defective system behavior. Additionally, let us assume that the underlying problem in the system is subsequently solved by configuring the planner of the lane change assistant to be more "defensive," i.e., to only change lanes when the distance to the vehicle in front is sufficiently large. When testing the new system version of the lane change assistant, we may be tempted to reuse the same test case that has previously shown misbehavior. This exactly is what happens when once recorded test drives are used independently of the system for testing.

If we use the same test case in our example to test the new system version, the ego vehicle now does not change lanes when performing this test case (see Fig. 2), a consequence of the planner being more defensive. For the new system version, the previously useful test case no longer fulfills our test goal of minimizing the distance to the front vehicle when changing lanes because the lane change does not occur in the first place! And even if a lane change did take place, we would not know whether the second criterion of a minimum distance is fulfilled and whether the test case would be "good" in the sense that it provokes a lane change with minimum distance to the front vehicle. Since the test for the new system no longer meets its test objective, we cannot assume that it is "good."

This example suggests that the quality of test cases in general is system-specific: They can be "good" for one version of the system and "bad" for another version. In this sense, reused test cases are generally indistinguishable from randomly selected test cases. Therefore, they should generally not be executed "blindly," as spelt out in [15], if one shares the opinion that random tests

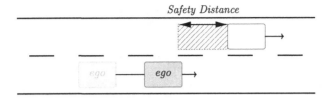

Fig. 2. SUT (ego vehicle) and safety distance to the vehicle in front. Here, the SUT does not change lanes anymore.

should perhaps complement, but not entirely replace, systematically generated test cases for the considered safety-critical systems. In this process, it does not matter where a reused test case originates, i.e., whether it was created by hand, generated by automatic test case generation, or extracted from recorded driving data. This essentially questions the very idea of system-level regression tests when the dynamics of the vehicle, or parameters relevant for the vehicle dynamics, have been altered. Without further knowledge, re-playing test drives as test cases is no better than random testing and - as far as the goal is to be verifiably better than random testing - cannot be conclusively justified.

One might argue that the test case T that does not provoke a lane change anymore is nevertheless "good" because it also tests a requirement, namely *not* to perform a lane change in precisely this situation. However, there is no evident reason to prefer this test case T over any other test case that does not provoke a lane change either. In this sense, T is no longer "good," or rather "better," than any random test. The selection of T is neither defect-based, nor risk-based, nor requirement-based since there is usually no specific requirement that describes precisely this one situation (and as an additional complication, in this case, there is no explicit specification of the lane change assistant in practice anyway).

In sum, if we modify the vehicle dynamics of the SUT, *test cases generally need to be recreated system-specifically.* In the field of regression testing, this is self-evident: tests that refer to the modified functionality of the system need to be created *anew.* Regression tests are meant to test *unmodified* behavior. When testing driving systems, the use of recorded drives as a reference test suite for all systems is not only problematic because of our theoretical derivation, but also directly contradicts the practice of regression tests.

4   Generating Test Cases

4.1   Levels of Abstraction

A promising approach for generating test cases [1,2,5,13] is based on the idea of instantiating abstract scenario types into concrete scenarios [21] by optimizing an objective function that encodes the quality of the test case, e.g., minimizing the distance to surrounding vehicles. Three levels of abstraction are methodologically relevant: scenario types, parameterized scenarios, and scenario instances (Fig. 3).

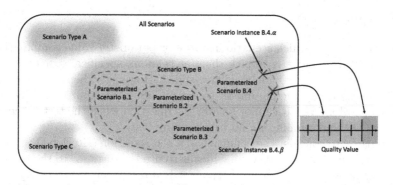

Fig. 3. Different kinds of scenarios [21]: Abstract scenario types are formalized as parameterized scenarios. Single parameter combinations of one parameterized scenario are scenario instances, which are the executable test cases. Their quality is determined by an objective function. Especially interesting are the "good" test cases in the limit region. Shape and location of the limit region are system-specific.

Scenario types are typical situations, e.g., a "lane change on the highway while a car is approaching on the left lane from behind." Scenario types are often depicted as pictures that describe a traffic situation using boxes representing vehicles and arrows that represent their movement in the scenario type, as in Fig. 2. These pictures do not come with a precise semantics but are very easily understood by humans both in terms of the spatial and temporal setup.

In order to be operational, scenario types need to be characterized by essential parameters and their value ranges, e.g., the number and width of lanes, the curvature of the road, or the number and position of surrounding vehicles. Determining the parameters and their ranges is crucial, as the completeness of the derived test suite critically depends on whether all relevant parameters have been accounted for. For instance, the friction coefficient of the road may or may not matter; and so do light and weather conditions. A *parameterized scenario* describes relevant parameters and their ranges as well as the maneuvers that the SUT (the ego car) and the other traffic participants are performing, i.e., the temporal and geometric constraints of a traffic situation.

Each concrete vector of parameter values constitutes one concrete *scenario instance*. Both scenario types and parameterized scenarios hence describe sets of scenario instances. Projecting a scenario instance to the behavior of the other traffic participants yields one concrete test case for the ego vehicle under test.

Note that both scenario types and parameterized scenarios constitute a partitioning of the input domain of the system under test. Scenario-based testing hence is an instance of partition-based testing. Both scenario types and parameterized scenarios as such usually are *not* defect-based but rather requirements-based. Defect-based testing is done within each scenario type. (If a history of real traffic accidents is used to derive scenario types, one needs to consider why automated vehicles should end up in the same accidents as human drivers.)

4.2 Big Picture

The question then is which scenario instance or parameter value combination to choose. One obvious idea is to pick them at random, specifically given that the power of random tests is widely acknowledged. However, when considering the high dimensionality of the parameter space, pursuing this approach alone seems questionable. Moreover, it cannot answer the question when the test process can be stopped without running prohibitively many tests.

It is natural to consider the definition of a test selection criterion that encodes some intuitive notion of quality. One idea is to use the distance to the surrounding vehicles as a quality measure because it is directly related to safety-critical behavior of the SUT. We assume that we consider only those situations where the ego vehicle can effectively avoid a crash. This is not always possible, e.g., when deer jump directly in front of the car. Now, if the distance to other traffic participants becomes negative in these "reasonable" situations, the SUT certainly is defective as this negative distance indicates a crash. If the distance is not negative but below an acceptable safety margin, this behavior is likely to constitute a defective situation and needs to be checked by an expert.

The idea of scenario-based test case generation now is to generate scenario instances where the distance to surrounding vehicles is minimized. The result, a scenario instance in Fig. 3, represents a test case that is "good" according to our definition above: If a scenario instance is found in which a minimum safety distance to a surrounding vehicle is undercut, possibly defective behavior of the system has been found. Remarkably, also if *no such undercut is found*, the test case is still "good" in the sense of limit testing since it approaches a *potential* undercut. Thus, it tests for a *potential* defect. And in contrast to a re-used test case, whose effectiveness cannot be measured, there is a clear argumentation for the purpose and necessity of this generated test case, which is desirable from the perspective of a safety argument.

Technically, this is done in a XiL simulation [12] where different values for the parameters of the scenario type are iteratively generated with heuristic search to optimize the value of a target function with the goal of reaching a limit value (Fig. 3). In our example, the objective function to minimize is the distance to at least one surrounding vehicle.

4.3 Scenario Types Derived by Experts and by Clustering

We have sketched *why* heuristic search should be used: because "good" test cases can and need to be generated in a defect-based manner. We now consider the overall process of *how* to do this in more detail, sketched in Fig. 4.

Scenario types built by experts. Intuitively, scenario-based testing starts with a sound and complete list of scenario types. Thus, initially, we need to gather these scenario types ①. One way is the manual derivation ② by experts, who use vehicle specifications, requirements and sometimes information about accidents ③ as well as their mental models ④ based on experience for this task. Structured

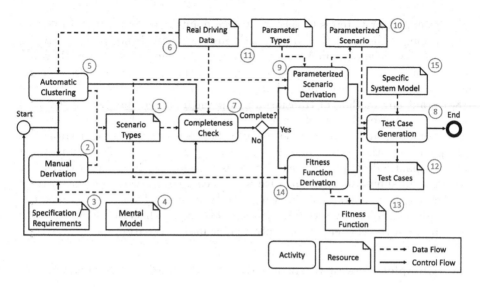

Fig. 4. Test case generation for scenario-based testing with search-based techniques.

approaches, e.g., ontologies [4,10], turn out to be convenient in this process. The determination of both granularity and structure of the scenario types is part of this process. Whether or not these are appropriate and suitable is generally hard to argue. Thus, validation is required, for which we suggest redundancy.

Scenario types built by clustering recorded drives. One way to achieve such redundancy is by automated clustering ⑤, which takes scenario instances recorded in real traffic ⑥ as input and yields clusters of these scenario instances [16,28] as output. This requires the choice of appropriate distance measures in-between scenario instances and, more difficult, adequate thresholds for determining the number of clusters. In practice, this is usually done using criteria such as the silhouette score or the elbow criterion.[1] However, these may or may not lead to an adequate set or size of the clusters. In any case, it is desirable that the clustering be as independent of the experts' mental model as possible [16]. Only then can true redundancy be achieved. Note that it is not the goal to replace the experts but to complement their efforts. Ideally, the automated derivation of scenario types will yield some scenario types that the experts did not come up with, and vice versa.

4.4 From Clusters to Descriptions of Scenario Types

The clusters are mere point clouds and therefore cannot directly be used for the generation of test cases. We hence need to transform them into scenario type

---

[1] https://en.wikipedia.org/wiki/Elbow_method_(clustering)
https://en.wikipedia.org/wiki/Silhouette_(clustering).

descriptions. A first step is to take individual points and turn them into textual descriptions of the corresponding scenario instance. This is not particularly difficult and has been done in a variety of ways, see [18] for an overview. However, it is less obvious how to verify the correctness of the resulting semantic scenario instance descriptions. Any manual approach is cumbersome. We have suggested [18] to take any method of transforming a point from the cluster to a semantic description, e.g. in the OpenScenario format, then replay this scenario instance in a simulator, and compute the distance between (1) the original trajectory (the point from the cluster) and (2) the result of transforming the original point into a semantic description which in turn is transformed back into a trajectory by means of simulation. An intuitive way of comparing two trajectories is the Fréchet distance,[2] colloquially known as the "walking dog" distance between two time series. A necessary second step then is the generalization of the semantic description of the cluster's most central point into a scenario type.

4.5   Completeness of Recorded Drives W.r.t. Relevant Scenario Types

In addition to improving and validating the completeness of the scenario types using redundancy, we suggest to perform a statistical completeness check ⑦. Intuitively, one can always come up with an additional scenario type, e.g., by simply adding another lane. However, not all scenario types are equally likely to occur in reality. This fact can be used to statistically assess that a given list of scenario types at least contains all scenario types that take place in real traffic up to a certain likelihood [14]. Similarly, it is important to statistically assess whether there is sufficient knowledge about the variety of different instances of a scenario type in real traffic [9]. If the statistical assessment suggests incompleteness, further manual effort needs to be undertaken and further data for automated clustering has to be collected. Conversely, if statistical completeness is achieved, the scenario types are ready for test case generation ⑧.

4.6   Test Case Generation with Heuristic Search

Recall that scenario types are not operational as they abstractly represent traffic situations and do not provide details about parameter types, ranges, and the precise trajectories of the traffic participants. Before test cases can be generated, we hence need to derive ⑨ parameterized scenarios ⑩ with their parameter types ⑪ [21,22]. The parameters and their ranges [19] are either determined by experts or are a result of the clustering process and hence the initial data collection process; see the comment on mental models above.

By definition, a parameterized scenario describes a multitude of different scenario instances: Each combination of concrete parameter values defines one such scenario instance. We have sketched above that the goal of the test case generation procedure is to identify the most challenging and interesting scenario

---

[2] https://en.wikipedia.org/wiki/Fr%C3%A9chet_distance.

instances. These are the desired test cases ⑫. It is not surprising that many approaches in the literature, e.g., [1,6,7], and industry, e.g., [11], suggest the use of search-based techniques. Those techniques iteratively create candidate scenario instances. The search is guided by evaluating the quality of the current candidates. This quality is determined by a so-called fitness function ⑬ that encodes the test objective and hence is identical to the optimization criterion mentioned above. The quality of a test case thus represents the quality of the system's performance in this test case [13]. In this way, "interesting" test cases are searched for and based on the quantitative measurement, it can be automatically decided in which of the many test cases the driving system passed or failed.

When using heuristic search, it does not suffice to encode the quality of a test case, i.e., the optimization criterion, as a fitness function ⑭. In addition, we need to encode the parameterized scenario itself, that is, the temporal and spatial relationships in-between the different traffic participants, e.g., "when the lane change occurs, another car is approaching with high speed from behind on the left lane." Intuitively, this appears to be a complex task, but it turns out that at least typical scenarios on highways and urban intersections can conveniently be composed by a set of only very few atomic fitness functions [13,17].

Test case generation is performed with the help of simulated scenarios and a model of the SUT, its software, or hardware ⑮ embedded into the XiL simulation. By thoroughly testing the system, some defective behavior might be revealed. After the development team has resolved the underlying issues, testing is performed again. Intuitively, failed test cases from the past could be reused, as they were proven to be "good" test cases. However, as previously discussed, these test cases should not be reused. Instead, we suggest to re-execute the test case generation procedure for each new system version.

Assuming that the heuristic search identifies the most challenging test case and that the driving system still behaves safely in this most challenging scenario, one can argue that it is also safe in any other scenario instance of the same scenario type. Repeating this argument for all scenario types ideally yields an overall safety argument.

5   Non-optimality of Tests Generated by Heuristic Search

The above approach relies on the idea that the optimal scenario instances generated by heuristic search indeed represent the worst possible behavior of the SUT in that they minimize, for instance, the distance to other vehicles and thus constitute limit tests. We have seen that the resulting test case is "good" in any case: if the minimum distance is negative, a crash has been detected; if it is smaller than some relevant safety distance, this may or may not constitute defective behavior but needs to be checked by an expert; and if it is larger than the safety distance, safe behavior can be assumed.

Unfortunately, the assumption that optimal test cases are derived is not necessarily true in practice. On the one hand, this does not come as a surprise because heuristic search is incomplete by design. On the other hand, this simple fact seems to be neglected in the current literature, even though it does have a profound impact on the feasibility and practicability of the approach.

To see why, we have used scenario-based testing for assessing the quality of an open-source autopilot for drones, the PX4 autopilot with obstacle avoidance [27]. Similar to the automotive case, the goal of scenario-based testing for drones is to create scenario instances, consisting of both static and dynamic obstacles, that are maximally challenging for the autopilot in that they minimize the distance in-between the drone and obstacles. To assess the quality of the generated scenario instances, we use multiple commonly used heuristic search algorithms both individually and in combination, including the popular Non-dominated Sorting Genetic Algorithm II (NSGA-II) [8], Particle Swarm Optimization [24], and Bayesian Optimization [25]. NSGA-II turns out to be the best individual algorithm in terms of the minimum distance between the drone and obstacles that it can be provoke: The minimum distance it finds in the scenarios under scrutiny is, on average, 21% smaller than that found by Bayesian Optimization. This is consistent with the literature on the performance of heuristic search algorithms.

As a next step, we sequentially apply the algorithms in the sense that the best solution found by one algorithm is used as a seed value for the next one, and do so for different permutations. It turns out that specific sequential combinations of algorithms outperform the individually best performing NSGA-II by a further 10% to 20%. More strikingly, sequentially composed algorithms do identify situations where the drone violates the safety distance, whereas the individual algorithms do not detect such unsafe behavior. Using the "wrong" algorithms would hence incorrectly suggest that the autopilot is operating correctly.

Once again, from a theoretical perspective it is not surprising that heuristic search does not necessarily find optimal solutions. However, the practical consequences seem severe: If we cannot know in advance which algorithm performs best, and if we cannot know in advance which combination of algorithms in which order performs best, we need to subject our optimization problem to all possible combinations, which requires the execution of 3*2=6 (or 4*3*2=24 in the case of four algorithms) differently ordered optimizations rather than just one, which increases the necessary computation power by about one order of magnitude. And even then, also a combination of algorithms cannot guarantee that the optimum solution will be found.

Given that the optimization of the simulation runs is very costly *and* given our argument that test cases need to be re-generated whenever the vehicle dynamics change, this means that it is economically mandatory to look into clever ways of how to combine optimizations—maybe not just at the level of entire optimization results but also at the level of the individual iterations within each algorithm. Anyway, this finding shows that it is not obvious how to directly construct convincing safety arguments from the results of scenario-based testing.

6   Completeness

Once crucial concern with testing always is completeness. Throughout our considerations, we have come across different forms of completeness, both implicitly and explicitly. Given that the current public debate often does not differentiate between different forms of completeness, we consider it worthwhile to conclude this article with a sketch of these different forms.

The first kind of completeness refers to completeness of scenario types: are all relevant traffic situations in the real world covered? As there is no ground truth w.r.t. which completeness could possibly be measured, we suggest to apply a redundancy argument here: Experts come up with a catalog of scenario types E, and clustering recorded drives leads to a catalog of scenario types C. The sets $E \setminus C$ and $C \setminus E$ provide interesting hints at scenario types that experts may have forgotten and that have not been detected by means of clustering. This consideration alone does, of course, not guarantee completeness, but it may increase confidence that the catalogs converge over time (and it can be expected that they do evolve over time). Note that it is not necessarily the case that those scenario types that are the result of a clustering procedure are easily understandable by humans. In practice, this tends to be the case, but this possibly is a result of the mental model encoded in the clustering procedure.

The second kind of completeness then refers to the parameters that define parameterized scenarios. These parameters are either provided explicitly by experts or implicitly by the parameters that have been used for recording actual drives (or are a result of a subsequent principal component analysis which usually is not interpretable by humans). Either way, these parameters define the granularity with which scenario types (or clusters) are described: Do lighting conditions matter? Does steepness of the road matter? Does friction of the road matter? Does the number of lanes matter? Does the temperature matter? Do wind conditions matter? Theoretically speaking, it seems hard to provide convincing completeness arguments in this context. Pragmatically speaking, it is likely that engineers will gain an increasingly complete understanding of what influences the behavior of ther vehicles under test.

Two further kinds of completeness relate to recorded drives. The third notion refers to the relative completeness of recorded drives w.r.t. a predefined catalog of scenarios. This completeness can be assessed in a statistical manner [14]. The fourth notion of completeness relates recorded drives to scenario types in the real world: If drives are exclusively recorded in the flatlands close to a coast, it seems unlikely that hairneedle pins will be covered. Abstractly speaking, this notion can be reduced to a combination of the first and fourth kind of completeness.

A fifth kind of completeness also has been discussed above: Does the test case generation algorithm provide optimal results? As we have seen, this is generally not the case. As of today, it is not obvious how to overcome this challenge.

Then, it seems practical to use the extreme candidates as limit tests and maybe a few tests from the "interior" of the scenario, as provided by early iterations of the optimization. Whether these are representative of all (defective) behaviors is an assumption that may be justified by the empirical practice of requirements-based and limit testing. It constitutes a sixth form of completeness.

Finally, we have only used one optimization goal, namely that of the distance to other traffic participants. Of course, there can be different goals that optimize, for instance, energy consumption or well-being of passenger and that are thus likely to yield different test cases.

7   Summary and Outlook

We have argued that test cases should be justifiably "good," especially in the context of safety-critical systems. Good test cases address potential defects. Scenario-based testing is one methodology to derive good test cases: scenario types that abstractly describe typical traffic situations are refined into operational parameterized scenarios that describe a set of concrete scenario instances. Heuristic search is then used to find the best instances. We have shown how the notion of "good" tests can be captured by the distance to surrounding vehicles. Heuristically searching for traffic scenarios with minimum distance turns scenario-based testing into a special form of limit testing.

If one wants to go beyond random tests, good test cases for cyber-physical systems cannot be reused for (regression) testing arbitrary variants or revisions of a system. If the system dynamics change, reused test cases are either no longer good, or there is no obvious argument for their quality. This is independent of whether the test cases were extracted from recorded drives, created manually, or generated automatically. Our argument is based on the example of autonomous and automated driving systems, but the considerations apply to CPS in general.

Accordingly, test cases must, in general, be re-generated for each system variant and version if changes to the system impact the functionality that is addressed by a test, or if we do not know if there is such an impact. This is theoretically and practically possible with scenario-based test case generation. Unfortunately, heuristic search cannot guarantee optimal results, an obvious fact that nonetheless seems overlooked in the current literature. We have provided an example from the context of drones where different search algorithms individually and in combination yield largely differing results, to the extent that one algorithm (combination) suggests the drone to be safe whereas another generates scenario instances that lead to unsafe behavior. This shows that safety arguments cannot directly be constructed from the results of scenario-based testing alone.

Relevant questions now refer (1) to the completeness and granularity of the catalogs of scenario types to be tested, (2) to the completeness of the relevant parameter sets of these scenario types, (3) to the impossibility of the heuristic search to guarantee global optima and (4) to the practical necessity of defining system and environment models for the simulation. (1) and (2) ultimately concern the question of well-founded test ending criteria, which are relevant in all areas of testing. Scenario types are usually defined by experts; obvious criteria for their completeness do not exist. We believe that this is where the true benefits of large amounts of recorded drives materialize. On the one hand, it is possible to calculate how many recorded trips would be necessary to prove the completeness of a list of scenario types [14]. On the other hand, scenario types can be derived automatically from existing trips by automated clustering [16]. A comparison with manually created catalogs may indicate incomplete data and missing scenario types in the manually created catalogs; and recorded test drives may also help to identify relevant parameters, such as whether the humidity of the road plays a role when testing the system.

While we have hinted at several open questions, overall we see good indications that scenario-based test case generation provides a sound and certification-relevant basis for arguing about the quality and completeness of tests that are performed on safety-critical systems.

References

1. Abdessalem, R.B., Nejati, S., Briand, L., Stifter, T.: Testing advanced driver assistance systems using multi-objective search and neural networks. In: 31st IEEE/ACM International Conference on Automated Software Engineering, pp. 63–74 (2016)
2. Althoff, M., Lutz, S.: Automatic generation of safety-critical test scenarios for collision avoidance of road vehicles. In: IEEE Intelligent Vehicles Symposium, pp. 1326–1333 (2018)
3. Bach, J., Holzäpfel, M., Otten, S., Sax, E.: Reactive-replay approach for verification and validation of closed-loop control systems in early development. SAE Technical Paper (2017)
4. Bagschik, G., Menzel, T., Maurer, M.: Ontology based scene creation for the development of automated vehicles. IEEE Intelligent Vehicles Symposium, pp. 1813–1820 (2018)
5. Bühler, O., Wegener, J.: Evolutionary functional testing of an automated parking system. In: Proceedings of the International Conference on Computer, Communication and Control Technologies (CCCT) and the 9th International Conference on Information Systems Analysis and Synthesis (ISAS) (2003)
6. Calò, A., Arcaini, P., Ali, S., Hauer, F., Ishikawa, F.: Generating avoidable collision scenarios for testing autonomous driving systems. In: IEEE International Conference on Software Testing, Validation and Verification (ICST), pp. 375–386 (2020)
7. Calò, A., Arcaini, P., Ali, S., Hauer, F., Ishikawa, F.: Simultaneously searching and solving multiple avoidable collisions for testing autonomous driving systems. In: Genetic and Evolutionary Computation Conference, pp. 1055–1063 (2020)
8. Deb, K., Pratap, A., Agarwal, S., Meyarivan, T.: A fast and elitist multi objective genetic algorithm: NSGA-II. IEEE Trans. Evol. Comput. $6(2)$, 182–197 (2002)
9. de Gelder, E., Paardekooper, J.-P., Op den Camp, O., De Schutter, B.: Safety assessment of automated vehicles: how to determine whether we have collected enough field data? Traffic injury prevention 20.sup1 (2019)
10. De Gelder, E., et al.: Ontology for scenarios for the assessment of automated vehicles (2020). arXiv preprint arXiv:2001.11507
11. Gladisch, C., Heinz, T., Heinzemann, C., Oehlerking, J., von Vietinghoff, A., Pfitzer, T.: Experience paper: search-based testing in automated driving control applications. IEEE/ACM International Conference on Automated SW Engineering, pp. 26–37 (2019)
12. Großmann, J., et al.: Model-Based X-in-the-Loop Testing. In: Model-Based Testing for Embedded Systems, pp. 299–337. Taylor & Francis (2012)

13. Hauer, F., Pretschner, A., Holzmüller, B.: Fitness functions for testing automated and autonomous driving systems. In: International Conference on Computer Safety, Reliability, and Security, pp. 69–84 (2019)
14. Hauer, F., Schmidt, T., Holzmüller, B., Pretschner, A.: Did we test all scenarios for automated and autonomous driving systems? In: IEEE Intelligent Transportation Systems Conference (ITSC), pp. 2950–2955 (2019)
15. Hauer, F., Pretschner, A., Holzmüller, B.: Re-using concrete test scenarios generally is a bad idea. In: IEEE Intelligent Vehicle Symposium (IV) (2020)
16. Hauer, F., Gerostathopoulos, I., Schmidt, T., Pretschner, A.: Clustering traffic scenarios using mental models as little as possible. In: IEEE Intelligent Vehicles Symposium (IV) (2020)
17. Kolb, N., Hauer, F., Pretschner, A.: Fitness function templates for testing automated and autonomous driving systems in intersection scenarios. In: 24th IEEE International Intelligent Transportation Systems Conference, pp. 217–222 (2021)
18. Kolb, N., Jordan, C., Huber, F., Pretschner, A.: Automatic evaluation of automatically derived semantic scenario instance descriptions. In: IEEE 25th International Conference on Intelligent Transportation Systems, pp. 1565–1571 (2022)
19. Kolb, N., Hauer, F., Golagha, M., Pretschner, A.: Data-driven assessment of parameterized scenarios for autonomous vehicles. In: 41st International Conference on Computer Safety, Reliability, and Security, pp. 350–364 (2022)
20. Lages, U., Spencer, M., Katz, R.: Automatic scenario generation based on laser scanner reference data and advanced offline processing. In: IEEE Intelligent Vehicles Symposium Workshops, pp. 146–148 (2013)
21. Menzel, T., Bagschik, G., Maurer, M.: Scenarios for development, test and validation of automated vehicles. In: IEEE Intelligent Vehicles Symposium, pp. 1821–1827 (2018)
22. Menzel, T., Bagschik, G., Isensee, L., Schomburg, A., Maurer, M.: From functional to logical scenarios: detailing a keyword-based scenario description for execution in a simulation environment. IEEE Intelligent Vehicles Symposium (IV), pp. 2383–2390 (2019)
23. Minnerup, P., Kessler, T., Knoll, A.: Collecting simulation scenarios by analyzing physical test drives. In: IEEE Intelligent Transportation Systems Conference (ITSC), pp. 2915–2920 (2015)
24. Moradi, M., Abedini, M.: A combination of genetic algorithm and particle swarm optimization for optimal dg location and sizing in distribution systems. Int. J. Electr. Power Energy Syst. **34**(1), 66–74 (2012)
25. Nogueira, F.: Bayesian Optimization: open source constrained global optimization tool for Python. https://github.com/fmfn/BayesianOptimization (2014)
26. Pretschner, A.: Defect-Based testing. In: Dependable Software Engineering (2015)
27. Schmidt, T., Pretschner, A.: StellaUAV: a tool for testing the safe behavior of UAVs with scenario-based testing (Tools and Artifact Track). In: IEEE 33rd International Symposium on Software Reliability Engineering, pp. 37–48 (2022)
28. Tkachenko, P., Zhou, J., del Re, L.: Unsupervised clustering of highway motion patterns. IEEE Intelligent Transportation Systems Conference, pp. 2337–2342 (2019)
29. Wachenfeld, W., Junietz, P., Wenzel, R., Winner, H.: The worst-time-to-collision metric for situation identification. In: IEEE Intelligent Vehicles Symposium (2016)
30. Wagner, S., Groh, K., Kuhbeck, T., Dorfel, M., Knoll, A.: Using time-to-react based on naturalistic traffic object behavior for scenario-based risk assessment of automated driving. In: IEEE Intelligent Vehicles Symposium (2018)
31. Weyuker, E., Jeng, B.: Analyzing partition testing strategies. IEEE Trans. Software Eng. **17**(7), 703–711 (1991)

Railway Verification and Safety and Security

Safety vs. Security – Why Separation of Concerns is a Good Strategy for Safety-Critical Systems

Jens Braband[(✉)]

Siemens Mobility GmbH, Ackerstr. 22, 38023 Braunschweig, Germany
jens.braband@siemens.com

Abstract. Cybersecurity plays an increasing role in critical infrastructure, in particular safety systems. Hence, it is necessary to compose systems that fulfill security and safety requirements, which are partially conflicting. Safety related software will rarely be changed after approval, whereas security related software needs almost permanently updates. This leads to problems that are hard to solve. Recently CENELEC TS 50701 "Cybersecurity for Railways" has been released that proposes separation concepts. In this paper we will discuss this approach and show, how a suitable architecture can help to satisfy the security as well as the safety requirements. We consider some examples of such architectures and show, how systems can be constructed that on the one hand side contain a safety code that is not changed and on the other hand side security software that can easily be patched.

Keywords: Railways · Safety Case · Cybersecurity Case

1 Introduction

1.1 Standardization Background

The discussion on the relationship between cybersecurity and safety has produced many different recommendations. In IEC TR 63069 [1] some general guidance for standardization has been worked out, but this paper aims at a more specific derivation and justification of basic principles for safety critical systems, in particular for railways.

Concerning terminology, 'security' is used in this paper often synonymously for cybersecurity unless physical security or other issues are explicitly meant. In the same way, 'safety' is used for functional safety. It is assumed that the reader is familiar with the basic safety and security concepts as stated, e.g., in standards such as EN 50126 [2], EN 50129 [3] the IEC/EN IEC 62443 series [4] and CENELEC TS 50701 [5].

A. E. Haxthausen et al. (Eds.): Peleska Festschrift 2023, LNCS 14165, pp. 85–95, 2023.
https://doi.org/10.1007/978-3-031-40132-9_6

1.2 Differences Between Safety and Security

Safety and security have.

- complementary goals: safety mainly protects people or the environment from malfunctions of automation systems, while security protects the technical systems from attacks from the environment
- different regulatory authorities, e. g. the Federal Railway Authority (EBA) and Federal Office for Information Security (BSI) in Germany, the National Cybersecurity Agency (ANSSI) and the national railways safety agencies in France, the European Union Agency for Railways (ERA) and the European Union Agency for Network and Information Security (ENISA) in Europe, etc.
- different concepts e.g., hazards are considered in safety and threats are considered in cybersecurity
- different communities, e.g., journals, conferences and standardization committees are mostly separated
- different standards, e.g., the EN 50126 and EN 50129 series for RAMS (including safety) and the ISO 27000 or IEC/EN IEC 62443 series for security.

In safety, frequent changes should be avoided because of the cost of safety approval renewal. In security, updates should be easy to be applied in order to be able to patch the system in a timely manner, as frequently as needed, e. g. when vulnerabilities are discovered. This is in particular important, if commercial-off-the-shelf (COTS) components are used. Thus, this provides a strong rationale to segregate security from safety as far as possible.

Methods and solutions are also different, as are requirements, which are often conflicting. A simple example is an emergency message (e.g., to immediately shut down or stop a system). From the safety view the message should be transmitted as fast as possible and the reaction should be executed immediately. From a security perspective the message should be authenticated to prevent masquerade which might lead at least to denial of service if an attacker could send emergency messages. But the coding and decoding of cryptographic algorithms consumes time and leads to a delay of the emergency message and the reaction. Alternatively, emergency messages could be pre-calculated at the sender side to save some time, but this may open the door for replay attacks. Another possibility might be the cyclic sending of heartbeat messages, which would trigger an emergency reaction if these were not received in time. So, the sender would stop sending heartbeats, but the delay would depend on the cycle time. In summary the trade-off in safe and secure system design is not easy and it can be sometimes hard to find an optimal solution.

So, we should conclude that safety and security are different and that they cannot easily be merged. Furthermore, security cannot simply be regarded as an add-on to safety or vice versa.

2 Co-engineering of Safety and Security

2.1 Security from a Safety Perspective, and Vice Versa

Safety relies on several environmental conditions or influences that need to be controlled in order to guarantee safety. These are listed in chapter 7.2 of EN 50129 and form a mandatory subclause, "assurance of safety with adverse external influences", in the technical safety case. One of these aspects to be covered is access protection and this is where security has its interface with safety.

Furthermore, it is required that the safety management process aims at minimizing the residual risk of safety-related systematic faults and security threats, which shall be managed during the risk assessment and hazard control. Finally, Measures addressing security shall be recorded or referenced in the Safety Case, that may be understood as a "security-informed safety case".

The view from a security perspective, e.g., IEC 62443, is similar. Here safety is viewed as an essential function that needs to be protected. Other essential functions are operational functions or availability. This means that safety functions can only fulfil their intended use in an appropriate secure environment. And this also explains why the UK Department of Transport is promoting "If it is not secure, it is probably not safe." Thus, the security environment should protect essential functions, incl. Safety.

In addition to safety, the availability of railway applications needs to be ensured at the same level of priority when considering security functions. While losses of availability for trains or railway networks might be considered safe in the scope of functional safety, continuous operation is one of the primary goals of security.

2.2 Process Interfaces

Because of the many differences it is not reasonable to integrate safety and security. However, the processes and lifecycles need to be coordinated and appropriate interfaces need to be established.

In particular, hazards resulting from security problems need to be identified, and they are then treated as threats in the security threat and risk assessment. The safety engineer needs to support the assessment to provide the safety implications (impact). The definition of the appropriate security countermeasures is the responsibility of security engineers in accordance with security standards. This means that security threat and risk assessment is the main interface with safety analysis on system level.

Conflicts between the identified safety and security measures must be resolved. During the safety risk assessment, the safety assessor evaluates the safety implications of the system design which includes the implementation of its security requirements. Here it can be helpful if the security management supplies evidence in a manner compatible with safety management, e.g., trusted verification documents with clearly stated assumptions and application rules, so that safety and security assessments can be decoupled.

The conclusion is to separate security and safety as far as possible but coordinate them effectively. This is also recommended by EN 50129, which recommends referencing security analyses in the safety case only. In order to ease the integration, as well as compatibility, it is recommended to base security considerations on established international standards such as ISO 27000 or IEC 62443, which may be adapted by sector specific guidelines such as CENELEC TS 50701.

2.3 Responsibility for Security

As in safety, there is usually no single individual or body fully responsible for all security aspects. It is a joint effort of the operators (often called asset owners in security), the system integrators (who supply complete systems) and the suppliers (implementing subsystems) and manufacturers (who sell components). But unlike safety, the monitoring processes operate at a higher frequency in security. Even without any incident it is good practice to update threat and risk assessments at least once per year and to feed the results forward and backward to the stakeholders at the interfaces. So, security is a collaborative continuous effort.

And similarly, to safety, effective security protection relies heavily on the company culture. Many successful attacks show a similar pattern:

- first, the attacker gains access to the system (network),
- then the attacker explores the system, often trying to gain higher privileges, until
- finally, the attacker carries out the attack.

Access or higher privileges can be obtained by exploiting vulnerabilities (e.g., weak passwords) or by social means such as phishing. Often, the attacker cannot achieve hisher goals without operators or employees who breach security rules or are complacent. So, it is very important that security awareness is promoted and trained as part of the company culture.

3 The Cybersecurity Case

3.1 Principles

To ensure the necessary stability of safety-related documentation and approval, it is recommended to separate cybersecurity and safety issues as far as possible and coordinate them adequately in order to decouple the different lifecycles and the approval processes. Otherwise, each change affecting the security of the system may trigger a new safety approval.

One possible solution to achieve separation and coordination between cybersecurity and safety processes is to define only a limited number of coordinated cybersecurity objectives on a high level. These objectives need to be fulfilled through security requirements or if not feasible, by security-related application conditions (SecRAC).

The fulfilment of the high-level cybersecurity objectives is the main part of the cybersecurity case. Either they are fulfilled by the cybersecurity functions or under certain security conditions and assumptions.

The cybersecurity case shall be maintained and updated. If the cybersecurity functions are changed, it shall be demonstrated that the safety-related cybersecurity objectives still hold (including the exported SecRAC). The cybersecurity case can be assessed according to the relevant cybersecurity standards.

Example: In the first release Safety Case 1.0 refers to Cybersecurity Case 1.0. Then Cybersecurity Case is changed to 1.1 but safety-related security requirements and safety-related security application condition remain unchanged. Then a Change report (confirming that requirements and application conditions have not changed) is submitted to the Safety Manager, and after approval Safety Case 1.0 remains valid with Cybersecurity Case 1.1. This principle of encapsulation can be iterated, to Cybersecurity Case 1.2 etc. In case of a major change, Cybersecurity Case is changed to 1.1 but safety-related security requirements or safety-related security application condition have to be changed. Then the safety case has to be updated to 1.1 as well and a new approval has to be granted.

As a result of this documentation structure, the documentation regarding functional safety can be considered stable as long as the cybersecurity process is properly adapted to changing threat scenarios. Hence, while the security documentation may be subject to frequent updates as a result of the volatile threat landscape, the safety approval can remain valid.

3.2 Contents

The cybersecurity case and its contents are introduced in CENELEC TS 50701. The structure it quite similar to a safety case (Table 1).

Table 1. Table of Contents of the Cybersecurity Case

Chapter	Title	Content
1	Introduction	System Definition (incl. Zoning Model), Risk Assessment
2	Cybersecurity Requirements	Assumptions, High-level objectives and derived requirements
3	Cybersecurity Management	Cybersecurity Policy, Plans, Processes incl. Vulnerability Management
4	Cybersecurity Fulfilment	Evidence e. g. of Implementation of Security Measures, V&V results
5	Security-related application conditions	Related e. g. to Installation, Maintenance and Operation
6	Conclusion	Incl. Residual Risks

3.3 Modularization

For several reasons it is inadequate to collect the evidence necessary for a Cybersecurity Case in a single document or folder, e. g. due to the fact that some information is confidential and is not disclosed to all stakeholders. Also, the evidence can be collected continuously during the lifecycle by the different stakeholders.

Table 2 shows a possibility to modularize the cybersecurity case based on system level and stakeholder. Each level contains a kind of specification, that is assessed and for which an assessment report or similar is provided, that clearly identifies the rules that are exported from the phase.

Table 2. Modular Cybersecurity Case

Level	Stakeholder	Specification	Assessment	Rules
System	Asset Owner	Threat & Risk Assessment	Assessment Report	Application Rules
Security Subsystem	System Integrator	Cybersecurity Case	Inspection Report	SecRAC
Generic Product	Supplier	(Technical) Cybersecurity Case	Inspection Report	SecRAC
Component	Manufacturer	Security Evidence	Certificate or similar	Application Manual

The assessment or inspection report should be written by an accredited assessor, so that the next level can rely on the results and there is no need for double-checking. By this way also the safety assessor does not need to check the cybersecurity case, but just needs to make sure that the requirements are adequate and that the exported rules are handled correctly.

4 Implementation Examples

4.1 The Importance of Architecture

While it is important that standards support separation and modularization, the real success factor to achieve a good implementation of safety and security requirements is the architecture. Safety and security architecture really makes the difference. It is hard to generalize the good practices that are known, but this paper tries to give a few example patterns.

4.2 The "Detect Single Faults" Pattern

The first example is a straightforward solution. We start with a well-known qualitative design pattern, which works for many safety-related systems. This is the so-called "fail-safe" system, see EN 50129. This pattern has also its merits for safety vs. security.

Assume, a single component K is added to the edge of a class 2 system S (or zone) according to EN 50159 [6], see Fig. 1. It could be a gateway or similar to protect the zone boarder.

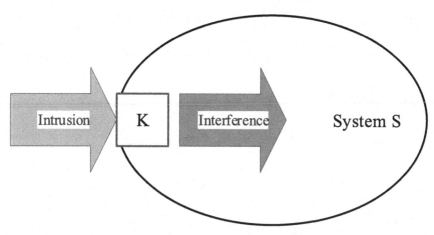

Fig. 1. Adding a security component K to a safety system S

Even if one just adds K to S, some safety homework still needs to be done, as K may have impact on S even if K does not implement a function for S. For example K may increase latency, decrease reliability etc. So, non-interference with S needs to be proven. The situation gets worse when K is connected to some outside network. Then, in addition a security risk assessment must be carried out, as intrusion may now be possible. Let us assume that this has been managed. However, the solution is not yet complete. One has still to make sure that the security functions implemented in K are fulfilling to their specification and that they persist doing this.

Normally the safety standards require that the security mechanisms of K are monitored by S. But the detailed requirements depend on the function that K implements and its architecture.

Example 1: Single-Component-Architecture. Assume K is a filter or firewall just as a kind of gatekeeper that lets only permitted traffic pass (simple whitelisting). If there is a reasonable single failure mode, e. g. bypass, that (partially) deactivates the function, then it is quite likely that monitoring has to be included to make sure that K continues to work as intended. The results need to be checked by a safe procedure as required by EN 50159 [6]. However, the monitoring needs not necessarily be performed by a technical function, it could also be done by an operator.

Example 2: Two-Component-Architecture: Assume K encrypts transparently all traffic from S to a neighboring zone S*, which has a counterpart K*. If now K fails to decrypt or encrypt any messages, then this will be immediately noticed at the other zone when messages start missing. So given a sufficient traffic flow, it is highly unlikely that both components suffer from similar faults with the same effect within a few milliseconds. One can neglect this risk and there is no need to implement any additional monitoring on the safety level. However, it is necessary to ensure that there are no common causes in the two components or in supporting processes as e. g. maintenance that may lead to the same failure on both sides. Examples are the deactivation of encryption on both sides, use of default keys outdated algorithms etc.

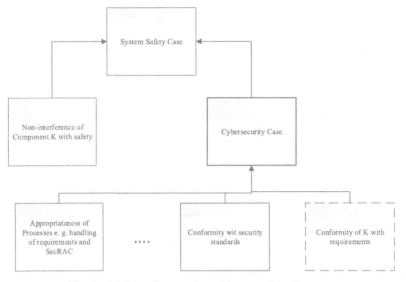

Fig. 2. Adding cybersecurity evidence to the safety case

Figure 2 shows how the necessary evidence can be incorporated into the system safety case. Already on system level the architecture can be evaluated, and it can be assured that the correct requirements are added into the cybersecurity requirements specification (CRS). This can generically be assessed by the safety assessor, who also needs to assess the non-interference of the additional component with the safety system, but this holds for any COTS component. For security aspects the safety case may point to the cybersecurity case. Also, in the cybersecurity case some aspects like appropriateness of processes and conformance with standards can be evaluated on a high level. Only the conformity of a particular component K needs to be evaluated on a low level. And, if the requirements do not change and the SecRAC stay the same for another component, then the components may be exchanged without changing the safety case.

4.3 The "Safety Channel" Pattern

Patching is a particularly hot topic when considering systems that need to fulfil safety and requirements. In safety applications, there is reluctance to change the certified "golden code", while in security some applications shall be updated or patched almost every day. This seems to be a contradiction. But it can be solved using an appropriate architecture.

Example 3: Assume a safety application, which needs to be protected by a virus checker (VC). A more general situation is, where 3rd party SW needs to be run on the same entity, be it a computer, a kernel or a virtual machine. Assume a majority of votes of different entities is needed for a safety critical decision, e.g., moving a switch.

The basic idea is to split the population of entities into two tribes: the entities labeled N are never changed - or only when the safety application needs to be updated, the entities labeled P can be patched as often as necessary. Of course, some integration tests need to be carried out before patching. Additionally, the architecture contains voters V that check the outputs. All components must be type checked before first operation.

Figure 3 shows this architecture for a 2oo2 configuration with one N and one P entity. Both run the same safety application, but entity P has another software implemented that needs regular updates. Entity N is sealed, physically and logically protected, e. g. tamper-proof. It is never touched (unless you want to change the safety application). In P the safety application is also never changed. On both channels this shall be checked, e.g., by using a hash code on the application or other means as a command from the voter requiring a specific response from both channels, which must coincide. Functional differences in both channels can be detected by the voter. Now whenever a safety decision needs to be taken, both N and P must agree, which is checked by the voter. So, a final decision of the system is only possible, if the unchanged safety application of N agrees with the decision of the application in P. And thus, it does not matter what other SW runs on P or if it is patched or not. If P was hacked or tampered with or the safety application influenced by the other applications, then P could not change the decision of N. But also, N cannot take any decisions of its own, it always needs an agreement of P, the channel that is virus protected etc.

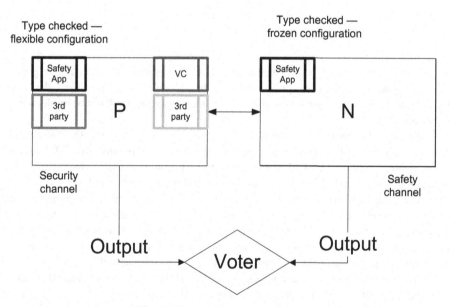

Fig. 3. Update-friendly architecture

This may now be generalized for example to 2 N and 2 P channels demanding that always a majority agrees etc. Note that some architecture elements have been left out for the clarity of the argument for example the inputs, power supply, communication as well as separation between the channels.

4.4 The "Mixed Architecture" or "EN 50159" Pattern

In some cases, it is not possible or not wanted to strictly separate the safety and the security components. Assume that in the safety part some security functions are integrated, i.e., because on the application level some encryption or message authentication is running. This type of function is implemented since measures described in EN 50159 are required. One must note that EN 50159 is not a cybersecurity standard, it is for safety related communications. So, the measures, although partially the same as in cybersecurity, are dedicated against technical processes that might influence or degrade communication. The failure mechanisms are different in cybersecurity, see Braband and Schäbe [7]. Nevertheless, we can derive the architecture in Fig. 4.

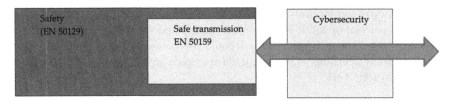

Fig. 4. Mixed Architecture

Assume that such a system is connected to a similar one. This means, that the safe transmission part of the system as well as the safety parts should not be changed (golden code). All patches should be applied in the cybersecurity part, which then also must compensate for those measures for cybersecurity that cannot and will not be implemented in the safety block.

Example 4: Let us consider the following example. In the safe transmission block, there is a cryptographic algorithm to protect the data with regards to confidentiality and authenticity (like ETCS). Of course, this protection would not be complete since a hacker might attack the safety part of the system and get access to the data and the code. Therefore, an additional security module is necessary to ensure complete cybersecurity protection. In this example, the security part is split: a never change tribe consisting of the safety part – including the safe transmission part and a patch tribe consisting of the security part. This is a bit similar to example 2 described above. In order to cope with the increasing possibilities of hackers, the security parts are patched.

From example 4, we see that it is only partially possible to design combined systems. Only methods that would not require permanent patching can be implemented in the safety part. Regarding the algorithms, they must work with a certain reserve, i.e., not only provide the simplest and most basic solutions to the problems. In the safety part, encryption can be used, where a method needs to be chosen that cannot be broken within the next years. Here, one must also not only look for the time that the method can withstand brute force attacks, but backdoors and exploits need to be absent. But of course, these basis security measures in the safety part do not need to be perfect. The main security protection is implemented in the cybersecurity part. Other components as interface drivers, firewalls etc. should not be contained in the safety part since they are candidates for permanent patching.

5 Discussion and Conclusion

In this paper, we have presented the cybersecurity case concept and example system architectures that allow to fulfill the requirements arising from security as well as from safety, while decoupling the approvals as far as possible. This allows in particular patching security or COTS components without renewing the system approval.

The solution has been found in parallel also in other contexts. For example, in the Technical Specification for Interoperability (TSI) for the Control-Command System of European Train Control System similar problems exist, e. g. when SW must be patched for bug-fixing [8]. The major difference is that the TSI procedure is for a particular fixed functionality describe in the TSI, so the requirements and the interfaces are fixed. The result is then, that (safety-related) application conditions may not be changed.

We have shown by examples, that with the help of an appropriate architecture, the dilemma of conflicting requirements can be solved in an efficient manner. Surely, not each architecture is applicable for each situation.

References

1. IEC: Industrial-process measurement, control and automation - Framework for functional safety and security, TR 63069 (2019)
2. CENELEC: Railway Applications - The Specification and Demonstration of Reliability, Availability, Maintainability and Safety (RAMS), EN 50126, part 1 & 2 (2017)
3. CENELEC: Railway applications - Communication, signalling and processing systems - Safety related electronic systems for signaling, EN 50129 (2018)
4. IEC: Industrial communication networks – Network and system security, multiple parts, IEC 62443
5. CENELEC: Railway applications – Cybersecurity, TS 50701 (2021)
6. CENELEC: Railway applications Communication, signalling and processing systems Safety-related communication in transmission systems, EN 50159 (2010)
7. Braband, J., Schäbe, H.: Probability and security – pitfalls and chances. Safety and reliability **36**, 3–12 (2016)
8. Schuster, H.: s, Global Railway Review. (2019)

Decomposing the Verification of Interlocking Systems

Anne E. Haxthausen[1]([✉]) [iD], Alessandro Fantechi[2] [iD], and Gloria Gori[2] [iD]

[1] DTU Compute, Technical University of Denmark, Lyngby, Denmark
`aeha@dtu.dk`
[2] University of Florence, Firenze, Italy
`{alessandro.fantechi,gloria.gori}@unifi.it`

Abstract. This paper considers model checking the safety for members of a product line of railway interlocking systems, where an actual interlocking system is modelled as an instance of a generic model configured over the network under its control. For models over large networks it is a well-known problem that model checking may fail due to state space explosion. The RobustRailS tools that combine inductive reasoning with SMT solving using Jan Peleska's powerful RT-Tester tool suite have pushed considerably the limits of the size of networks that can be handled. To further push these limits, we have proposed a compositional method that can be combined with RobustRailS to reduce the size of networks to be model checked: the idea is to divide the network of the system to be verified into two sub-networks and then model check the model instances for these sub-networks instead of that for the full network. In this paper we propose a strategy for applying such network divisions repeatedly to achieve a fine granularity decomposition of a given network into a number of small sub-networks. Under certain conditions, these sub-networks all belong to a library of pre-verified elementary networks, so model checking of the sub-networks is no longer needed.

Keywords: Formal Methods · Model Checking · Compositional Verification · Interlocking Systems

1 Introduction

Formal methods have successfully been applied to development and verification of railway systems [3,5,6]. In particular, it has been popular to use model checking techniques for formal verification of *interlocking systems* (controlling train movements inside a railway network) as these are fully automated. Interlocking systems are configured with *application data* that reflect the elements and topology of the railway network layout. Hence, formal verification aims to verify both the *generic application* with its algorithms for safe allocation of routes to trains, and the *specific application* produced by the configuration with application data for the network under control.

© The Author(s), under exclusive license to Springer Nature Switzerland AG 2023
A. E. Haxthausen et al. (Eds.): Peleska Festschrift 2023, LNCS 14165, pp. 96–113, 2023.
https://doi.org/10.1007/978-3-031-40132-9_7

Model checking is subject to *state space explosion*, which limits scalability of the approach so that automatic verification of interlocking systems for large networks is demanding in terms of computing resources, and may even fail [4].

Abstraction techniques have typically been adopted to limit state space explosion in model checking: abstraction should preserve the desired properties, hence the adopted abstraction technique should be defined specifically for the kind of system and properties under examination. For interlocking systems, a convenient abstraction can be based on the *locality* principle: properties concerning the allocation of a route to a train are typically not influenced by train movements over networks elements that are distant from, and not interfering with, the considered route. Locality of a safety property can be used to limit the state space by abstracting away such "distant movements". In [26] this principle supports domain-oriented optimisation of the variable ordering in a BDD-based verification; it also enables property-directed *model slicing*, ([4,10,11]), in which verification is performed only over the portion of the model that concerns the property of interest (*cone of influence*), allowing for an efficient verification of a property, but requiring to perform slicing and verification for every property (plus checking that that slicing preserves the related property).

It has also been suggested to use *bounded model checking* to perform *k-induction* proofs of safety properties expressed as state invariants to avoid exploring the whole state space. In the RobustRailS verification tools [25] for interlocking systems this technique was implemented using the powerful SMT-based bounded model checker of Jan Peleska's RT-Tester tool[1]; this made it possible to considerably push the bounds of the size of networks that can be verified without state space explosion [25].

Locality has also enabled our proposal of a *compositional* approach for addressing verification for very large networks: the idea is to divide the network to be verified into two (or more) sub-networks and then model check the model instances for these sub-networks instead of model checking the model instance of the full network [2,8,15,16]. For model checking, we use the RobustRailS verification tools. The soundness result for compositional safety verification given in [8] guarantees that, when properly cutting a network, proving safety for the sub-networks suffices to prove safety for the full network. In this way, the task of proving safety for a large network can be reduced to the task of verifying safety for sub-networks of a size manageable by the model checker.

The idea of compositional verification is also shared by the approach described in [12–14]. This approach that is based on the criteria of functional decomposition of interlocking systems defined by the Belgian railways in order to deal with the control of large networks by dividing the network into sub-networks, each possibly controlled by separate interlocking systems. A comparison of this approach with ours is presented in [1]. Indeed, it appears that decomposition of a network in this approach is grounded on pragmatic domain-related criteria, while our approach is more general. Furthermore, this approach uses an

---

[1] https://www.verified.de/products/rt-tester/.

assume-guarantee approach for verification which requires not only verification for the sub-networks as in our approach, but also verification of contracts.

The question of where to divide a network during compositional verification has triggered the contribution of this paper: an iterative decomposition strategy to achieve a fine granularity decomposition of a network into a number of small sub-networks, that under certain conditions belong to a library of pre-verified elementary networks. The soundness result for compositional safety verification guarantees that safety for the full network is given by the pre-verified safety of sub-networks. Therefore, to verify a network, it is in principle no more needed to run a model checker, independently of the size of the network, if specific network conditions are met.

The paper is structured as follows: First, in Sects. 2 and 3, short descriptions of the RT-Tester tool suite and of the RobustRailS verification method, built on top of RT-Tester, are given. Then, in Sect. 4, our compositional method using the RobustRailS tools is presented and a strategy for performing decomposition is discussed. The latter is the main, novel contribution of this paper. Section 5 draws some conclusions and ideas for future work.

2   The RT-Tester Tool Suite

In 1998 Jan Peleska and Cornelia Zahlten founded the company *Verified Systems International GmbH*, and Jan has been head of Research & Development in the company since then. The company provides tools and services in the field of safety-critical system development, verification, validation and test, and has a wide variety of customers including Siemens, Airbus and its suppliers. Verified's flagship product is *RT-Tester*[2], a very comprehensive model-based test automation tool suite for automatic test generation, test execution and real-time test evaluation. RT-Tester can not only be used for testing (see e.g. [19]), but also for bounded model checking (BMC) of which we will give an example in next section. RT-Tester's automation capabilities are discussed in [18], and special test case generation strategies implemented in RT-Tester are described in [9]. In 2015, the company was awarded the runner-up trophy of the EU Innovation Radar Prize due to the special testing strategy that was developed by Jan Peleska and Wen-ling Huang.

3   The RobustRailS Verification Method and Tools

In the RobustRailS research project[3] that was accompanying the Danish resignalling programme on a scientific level in 2012–2017, a formal method with tools support for automated, formal verification of railway interlocking systems was developed [22–25] by Linh Hong Vu under supervision of Jan Peleska and Anne Haxthausen. This section gives a short description of the RobustRailS method and tools.

---

[2] https://www.verified.de/products/rt-tester/.
[3] http://robustrails.man.dtu.dk.

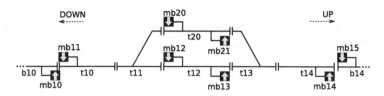

Fig. 1. A railway network layout example. From [23].

The Considered Interlocking Systems. An interlocking system is a signalling system component that is responsible for safe routing of trains through (a fraction of) a railway network under its control. An interlocking system is traditionally specified by a layout of the railway network that it controls and a so-called *interlocking table* that specifies allowed routes through the network and conditions for these routes to be exclusively reserved by a train. In Fig. 1 an example of a railway network layout for a small station is given. As it can be seen it consists of (1) train detection sections that are either linear sections (like t10) or switchable points (like t11) having a stem side and two branching sides (e.g. t11 has its stem next to t10 and its branches next to t20 and t12, respectively) and (2) markerboards[4] (like mb10) placed at the ends of linear sections and only visible in one direction (e.g. mb10 is visible in direction UP). As a general rule for the networks considered in this paper, there is at most one markerboard in each end of a linear section and it can only be seen when leaving the section. Furthermore, at the borders of a network, there are always two linear sections (like b10 and t10) with a signal configuration having an *entry signal* on the border section and an *exit signal* on the section next to the border section. Furthermore, networks are assumed to be *loop-free*[5].

The Tools and Method. The RobustRailS tools are centred around two inter-related DSLs (domain-specific languages):

- IDL: a DSL [23] for specifying (1) a generic, behavioural, formal model of a product line of interlocking systems and their environment and (2) generic safety properties in the form of state invariants, and
- ICL: a DSL [22] for specifying configuration data (a railway network layout and an interlocking table) that can be used to instantiate generic models and properties.

The RobustRailS tools can be used to formally verify the design of an interlocking system in the following steps, summarized in Fig. 2:

1. A generic model and generic properties are specified in IDL.

---

[4] We are considering modern ERTMS level 2 based interlocking systems for which there are no physical signals. They are replaced by markerboards, and in the control system there are virtual signals associated with the markerboards. Throughout the paper we use the term *signal* as a synonym for *markerboard*.

[5] A network is *loop-free*, if there are no physically possible path through the network containing the same section more than once.

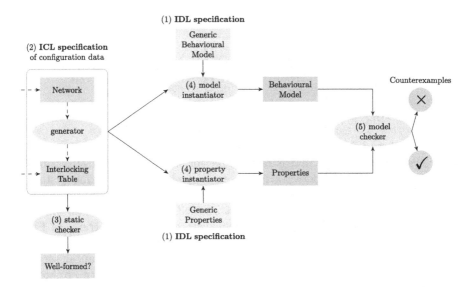

Fig. 2. The RobustRailS tool suite. From [23].

2. A railway network layout and its corresponding interlocking table are specified in ICL in the following order: first the network layout, and then the interlocking table. The creation of the latter is either done manually or generated automatically from the network layout.
3. A static checker verifies whether the configuration data is statically well-formed [7] according to the static semantics [24] of ICL.
4. Generators instantiate a generic behavioural model and generic safety properties with the well-formed configuration data to generate a model and safety properties for the network and routes described in the configuration data.
5. The generated model instance is then checked against the generated properties by a bounded model checker performing a k-induction proof.

The static checking in step (3) is intended to catch errors in the network layout and interlocking table, while the model checking in step (5) is intended to catch safety violations in the control algorithm of the instantiated model.

The tool chain associated with the method has been implemented using Jan Peleska's RT-Tester framework [18,21]. The bounded model checker in RT-Tester uses the SONOLAR SMT solver [20] to compute counterexamples showing the violations of the base case or induction step.

Applications. The RobustRailS method and tools have been used to successfully verify the safety of several interlocking systems. The first application was the Danish interlocking system for EDL, the first regional line in Denmark commissioned in the Danish Signalling Programme. First, the IDL language was used to specify a generic model for the novel family of Danish interlocking systems and generic safety conditions expressing that there are *no train collisions* (i.e. there must at most be one train on each section at the same time) and *no* *derailments* (i.e. when a train traverses a point, the point must be switched in the right direction for the train to pass). Then the network for the complete EDL line consisting of eight stations of various complexity was specified in the ICL language and an interlocking table was automatically generated from this. Then method steps 3–5 were performed. The verification metrics can be found in Table 1. For more details on this case study, see [25]. Other applications are mentioned in Sect. 4.2.

This achievement of model checking an interlocking system for such a big railway network was quite remarkable. A key reason for that was the use of RT-Tester's SMT based bounded model checker to perform an induction proof. That pushed considerably the limits of the size of networks for which interlocking systems can be verified.

4   Compositional Verification

However, networks of very large stations still exceed the model checking capacity. Therefore, to be able to perform verification for *any* size of networks, we have previously [2,8,15,16] suggested to use a compositional verification method on top of the RobustRailS verification method.

The idea of our compositional method is as follows: Assume given a generic model and generic safety properties for no collisions and no derailments. To verify an interlocking system instance for a specific network N, divide the network into two parts (sub-networks) N_1 and N_2, and then verify the interlocking system instances for these two networks using the RobustRailS method and tools. This division process can be applied repeatedly until all sub-networks are small enough to be verified.

In Sect. 4.1, we explain the compositional method in more detail, and in Sect. 4.2 we report on some case studies applying the method. Using our compositional method rises the question: which decomposition of a given network should be made? In Sect. 4.3 we explain an idea for that.

4.1   A Method for Compositional Verification

To introduce the compositional method, we first need to define what is a *cut* of a network, and how the sub-networks should be generated by the cut.

Cut Specifications. A *single cut* is a cut that can be performed between any two neighbouring, non-border sections $t1$ and $t2$ in a network N. An example of a single cut is shown in Fig. 3. The *specification* of that single cut is the pair $(t1, t2)$. To divide a network into two parts, it is not always enough to perform a single cut, but a *cluster cut* consisting of several single cuts may be needed. An example of a cluster cut is shown in Fig. 4. The *specification* of a *cluster cut* is the set of specifications of each of its single cuts. A cut is *legal*, if it divides the network into exactly two parts, no route is cut by more than one single cut, and no flank/front protecting elements[6] are separated by the cut from the sections they protect. In this paper we assume that flank/front protecting is not adopted.

---

[6] In the end of Sect. 4.3 the notion of flank protection is explained.

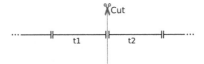

Fig. 3. An example of a single cut. From [8].

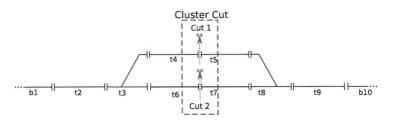

Fig. 4. An example of a cluster cut. From [8].

Decomposing a Network According to a Cut Specification. Given a net N and a legal cut specification, the network is decomposed into two networks as follows:

– if a single cut is between linear sections $t1$ and $t2$, first divide the network N between $t1$ and $t2$, obtaining two sub-networks N_{-1} and N_{-2}, and then add to N_{-1} and N_{-2} at the respective cut a border section and also an entry and an exit signal at that border, if there were not already signals placed around the cut. By doing so, two well-formed networks are obtained: N_1 and N_2. Figure 5 shows how a network is decomposed into two networks by a single cut $(t1, t2)$. It can be seen how N_1 is obtained from the sub-network N_{-1} on the left-hand side of the cut by adding a border section $b1$ and border signals s_{entry_1} and s_{exit_1}. N_2 is obtained in a similar way. When it is clear from the context, sometimes we also call the resulting networks N_1 and N_2 *sub-networks*;
– if a single cut is between a linear section $t1$ and a point p, the decomposition is treated as if there was an additional linear section $t2$ between $t1$ and p, and the cut specification was $(t1, t2)$;
– if a single cut is between two points $p1$ and $p2$, the decomposition is treated as if there were two additional linear sections $t1$ and $t2$ between $p1$ and $p2$, and the cut specification was $(t1, t2)$.
– if the cut is a cluster cut, the above rules are simultaneously applied to each of its single cuts.

A tool that takes a network and a cut specification as arguments and returns the two networks obtained by decomposing the network according to the cut specification has been developed [17]. This tool is called the *RobustRailS Network Cutter*.

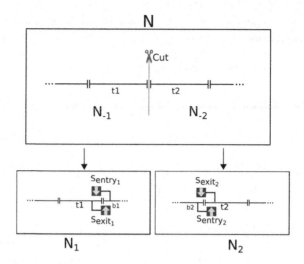

Fig. 5. An example of a decomposition of a network into two networks. From [8].

Method Steps. Using a legal cut allows to perform compositional verification in the following steps:

1. Decompose a network N according to a legal cut specification, achieving two networks N_1 and N_2.
2. For $i = 1, 2$, apply the interlocking table generator to N_i, check the resulting specification by the static checker, and generate a model m_i and properties ϕ_i from that.
3. For $i = 1, 2$, verify that m_i satisfies ϕ_i.

In [8] it is proved that this method is *sound*. This means that in order to prove safety of the model generated from the whole network, it is suffcient to verify safety for each of the models generated from the two sub-networks formed by a legal cut.

4.2   Case Studies

A number of case studies applying the presented compositional verification approach to different networks with different characteristics and layouts have been carried out. Table 1 shows the savings in verification time and needed memory obtained applying the compositional method to non-trivial cases. For each case, the statistics are shown first for each sub-network, then the global consumption of time and memory of the compositional approach and its reduction are shown in comparison with that of a monolithic verification for the full network. The first three examples have been presented at international conferences [1,2,16]; in particular the first one is the already mentioned EDL line, which has been decomposed in sub-networks related to each station of the line, among which the

Table 1. Verification statistics for the compositional verification method applied to some interlocking examples.

Example	Linears	Points	Signals	Routes	Time (s)	Memory (MB)
NFM2017 [16]						
Gadstrup	14	3	16	21	62	567
Havdrup	10	2	12	14	19	264
L. Skensved	15	3	16	21	72	616
Køge	58	23	62	75	5170	9243
Herfølge	6	2	10	14	13	210
Tureby	6	2	10	14	11	203
Haslev	10	2	12	14	14	256
Holme-Olstrup	12	2	16	20	22	352
Compositional					5383	9243
Full EDL	110	39	126	179	14352	22476
Reduction %					72.49%	68.88%
SEFM2017 [2]						
Low	28	13	26	56	12895.35	12176.6
High	25	10	24	66	8052.92	9517.9
Compositional					20948.27	12176.6
Full Fismn	49	23	46	124	51770.64	42483.7
Reduction %					59.54%	71.34%
RSSRail22 [1]						
LVR7A Left	20	7	31	30	670	2083
LVR7B Right	15	5	23	18	108	846
Compositional					778	2083
Full LVR7	26	12	42	48	2387	5467
Reduction %					67.41%	61.90%
Tramway line						
Down	12	5	12	12	81.42	462.8
Middle	9	4	8	12	55.77	392.2
Up	8	3	8	10	22.40	266.7
Compositional					159.59	462.8
Full line	22	12	20	62	28206.00	22762.7
Reduction %					99.43%	97.97%
Flying junction						
Each of 4 subnetworks	12	4	12	20	108.47 *max*	600.2 *max*
Compositional					369.69	600.2
Full junction	24	16	16	40	55853.76	23587.2
Reduction %					99.34%	97.45%

Køge station maintains its own high complexity. The second example is a single cut of a large network whose layout has been extracted from a portion of the main Florence station, while the third is a Belgian station on which a cluster cut has been applied, with the aim to compare the method with the decompositional approach of [14]. The remaining two have been purposely defined to explore different layout characteristics: one is inspired by a tramway network, that is, a single track tramway line with several branches and passing loops; the other is a complex flying junction, that allows grade-separated crossing of two double track lines, as well as full interconnection among the tracks of the two lines.

The highest savings are obtained when, in the full network, several routes do not conflict and therefore can be used concurrently, contributing to the state space explosion, due to interleaving of concurrent train movements over such routes: if the cut is made such that the number of independent routes inside a sub-network is low, the concurrency degree is dramatically decreased. This is the case of the tramway line example, divided into three sub-networks, and of the flying junction example, where the cut produces four almost isomorphic sub-networks of far lower complexity.

A deeper study on the correlation between full network topology, cut strategy, and verification savings by decomposition is planned as future work.

4.3   A Decomposition Strategy

Using the presented compositional verification method leaves the question: which cuts should be made in order to decompose a network into small networks that are fast to verify? In this section we will exploit the idea of providing a library of pre-verified, elementary networks and a strategy for dividing a given network into sub-networks of which as many as possible are elementary.

Elementary Networks. As elementary networks we allow one of the network patterns shown in Fig. 6: an elementary network can be a sequence of linear sections having only the required signals at the two borders (see a) and b)). It can alternatively (see c) and d)) be a network containing just one point surrounded by at least two linear sections on each of its three sides. There are only the required signals at the three borders and optionally zero, one, two or three of the signals shown directly facing the point. All patterns admit an unbounded number of linear elements at specific positions. In c) there is only one linear section between the the point and each of the three border sections, while in d), there are two (or more) linear sections between the point and the border section on the stem side. In a similar way it is allowed to have two (or more) linear sections between the point and the border sections on the branching sides of the point.

Model instances of the networks of Fig. 6 have been model checked to be safe, for all the admitted combinations of presence of markerboards, but without the presence of the admitted extra linear sections. Moreover, a result from [8] allows us to add an unbounded number of linear sections at the indicated specific

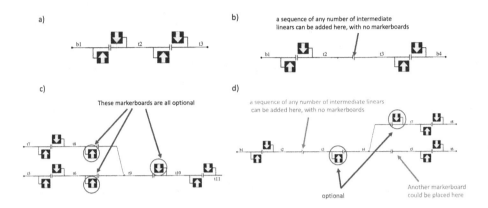

Fig. 6. Patterns for elementary networks.

positions without impacting safety. Hence, we can conclude that *model instances for all elementary networks are safe.*

Decomposing a Network. Given a network, now the idea is to search for places to make legal cuts, one by one, such that the network can be divided into parts that are either elementary networks or non decomposable networks (that is, they cannot be cut without breaking the rules for legal cuts). In the ideal case that the decomposition leads to networks that are all elementary, no model checking is needed.

As an example, consider the network shown in Fig. 7. By making the three cuts (two single cuts $(083, PM02U)$ and $(PM02U, PM03U)$ and the cluster cut $\{(802, PM04U), (801, PM04U)\}$) shown by green lines, one by one, one achieves the four elementary networks N_1^1, N_1^2, N_1^3, and N_2^3 shown in Fig. 8.

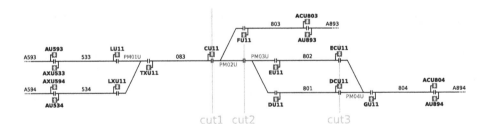

Fig. 7. Cuts shown on a network (LVR1).

In practice, a possible process of finding such cuts for a loop-free network N is as follows, provided that there are no flank/front protecting elements:

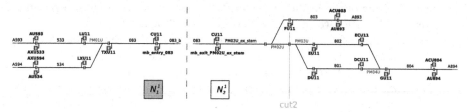

(a) Networks $N_1^1 + N_2^1$ resulting from decomposing the LVR1 network by *cut1*.

(b) Networks $N_1^2 + N_2^2$ resulting from decomposing N_2^1 by *cut2*.

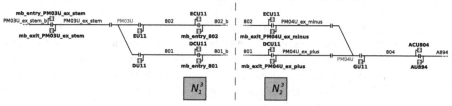

(c) Networks $N_1^3 + N_2^3$ resulting from decomposing N_2^2 by *cut3*.

Fig. 8. Decomposition of the LVR1 network in three steps according to the three cuts shown in Fig. 7. The four resulting green sub-networks N_1^1, N_1^2, N_1^3, and N_2^3 are elementary.

1. Start searching from the neighbour (linear section) l of some border section b of N. The search direction is from l towards the next adjacent element in the direction opposite to b.
2. Follow the sections from l one by one as long as they are linear and do not have any signals attached until one of the following happens:
   (a) If a linear section having an *exit signal* is found, we have reached a border and no cut should be made, as the considered network is an elementary linear network.
   (b) If two consecutive, linear sections $l1$ and $l2$ are found, and at least one of them has a signal facing the other, then a decomposition using the cut $(l1, l2)$ should be made. By this the generated sub-network containing $l1$ will by construction be an elementary linear network. The search for further cuts should then continue from $l2$ in the other sub-network.
   (c) If a point p is found, then we should continue to search for cuts on the two other sides of p. This search depends on from which side p was found: the

stem or one of the branching sides. In both cases the search also depends on whether the two other sides are connected or not.[7]

i. If coming from the stem of p, and the two branching sides are not connected, then we should search for cuts in each of the two branches. The search here is similar to the search starting from a border, except that if a second point is found, a single cut must be made just *before* that point. The two searches may hence lead to totally zero, one or two single cuts, dividing the network into (1) an elementary point network containing p and (2) zero, one or two additional sub-networks in which a search for cuts must be performed. For instance, when searching for a cut in network N_2^1 in Fig. 8 (a), starting from $PM02U\_ex\_stem$, a single cut, $cut2$: $(PM02U, PM03U)$, will be found in the lower branch, while no cuts are found in the upper branch (as a border is met before any further points or non-border signals), so it results in two sub-networks.

ii. If coming from the stem, and the two branching sides are connected, then a similar search is made in each of the branches. In this case two single cuts (one in each branch) will be found and these must be combined in a cluster cut (in order to divide the network into two parts) leading to an elementary point network containing p and one additional sub-network to which search for cuts must be recursively applied. That is e.g. the case when searching for a cut ($cut3$) in network N_2^2 in Fig. 8 (b), starting from $PM03U\_ex\_stem$.

iii. If coming from a branching side of p, and the stem and the other branching side are not connected, searches for cuts in the other branch and on the stem side must be performed in a similar way to case i) above. That happens e.g. when searching for the first cut in Fig. 7 starting from linear section 533.

iv. If coming from a branching side of p, and the stem and the other branching side are connected, the search to be performed is similar to case ii), except that in some cases it is not possible to find a legal cluster cut: that happens if a potential cluster cut divides a route into three parts[8], as shown in Fig. 9, where the cluster cut shown by a red, dotted line is found when searching from $L1$ on the upper branching side of point $P1$. In such a case we should then start a search from another border to see if a cut can be found from there. It is our conjecture that it is always possible to find a border from which it is possible to find a legal cluster cut through the connected sub-component, provided that the network is loop-free. For instance, in Fig. 9, the legal cluster cut $\{(P2, P1), (L24, P4)\}$ shown by a dashed, green line can be found when searching from $L2$. Figure 10 gives an

---

[7] By *connected* we mean that by navigating the graph of the not yet visited part of the network starting from the two sides we eventually reach a common point.

[8] Note that when coming from the stem, we do not have such a problem, as a route cannot pass through a point via its two branches.

example of a network that cannot be decomposed into elementary networks as the network is not loop-free.

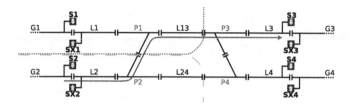

Fig. 9. The cluster cut $\{(P1, P2), (L13, P3)\}$ shown by a red, dotted line is illegal as it divides the route shown as a blue, solid arrow in three parts. The cluster cut $\{(P2, P1), (L24, P4)\}$ shown by a green, dashed line is legal. (Color figure online)

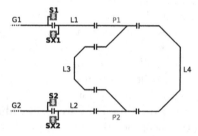

Fig. 10. An example of a non-loop-free, non-decomposable network.

In railway interlocking systems, specific additional mechanisms may be included to enforce safety also in the case in which trains do not strictly respect signals, due to a driver's misbehaviour or accidental inability to brake. In the *Flank Protection* mechanism points and signals not belonging to the route are properly set in order to avoid hostile train movements into the route at an incident point. In the example of Fig. 11 locking of route r requires the point $t20$ to be in the straight position in order to protect the flank of route r by a train accidentally missing the closed $mb20$ signal. If both point $t20$ and route r lie in the same sub-network when a cut is operated, the extra condition on the point position has no impact on compositionality: but this is not the case for the drawn cut, which separates the protecting and the protected points. As discussed in [8], in this case compositional verification results do not fully hold, so we consider such a cut as not legal: both elements should instead be in the same sub-network, which is therefore not elementary, since it contains two points. In the presentation of our approach, we have assumed that there is no flank protection. If flank protection was adopted, legal cuts would not be allowed to separate the protecting and the protected points. However, then we would no longer be able to decompose a loop-free network into networks that are all elementary.

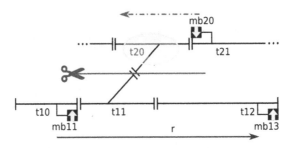

Fig. 11. Cut through a flank protection.

5   Conclusions and Future Work

In this paper we have presented a compositional method for model checking the safety of interlocking systems. The idea of the compositional method is to divide the network under control into some sub-networks and then model check the model instances for these networks instead of model checking the model instance of the full network. The paper suggests a novel strategy for decomposing a network into a number of small sub-networks that, under certain conditions, all belong to a library of pre-verified elementary networks, so no model checking is actually needed for the specific application.

This strategy will be the subject of further work, including its implementation in a tool for the automatic decomposition of a network: this will be accompanied by a deeper assessment of its soundness and completeness, as well as of its tractability, and on the other end will enable experimenting it on several complex layout examples. Also, this study will address a consolidated definition of the conditions under which the conjecture of full decomposition in elementary networks holds, and the impact of flank protection or other analogous protection mechanisms on the applicability of the decomposition algorithm.

Dedication and Acknowledgements

We dedicate this paper to Jan Peleska who we admire so much for his brilliant research in applicable formal methods for safe industrial products. The first author (Anne Haxthausen) would like to express her gratitude to Jan for more than 25 years of the most enjoyable, inspiring, and fruitful collaboration.

The RobustRailS tools used in the work presented in this paper were developed by her PhD student, Linh H. Vu, under co-supervision by Jan Peleska who came with brilliant ideas and generously provided the possibility of using RT-Tester as backend. All three authors are very indebted to Peleska and Vu. Furthermore, the authors would like to thank Hugo D. Macedo, who contributed to the initial work on the compositional method used in this paper, and to thank Anna Nam Anh Nguyen and Ole Eilgaard for their network cutter tool which we have also used in this paper.

References

1. Fantechi, A., Gori, G., Haxthausen, A.E., Limbrée, C.: Compositional verification of railway interlockings: comparison of two methods. In: Dutilleul, S.C., Haxthausen, A.E., Lecomte, T. (eds.) Reliability, Safety, and Security of Railway Systems. Modelling, Analysis, Verification, and Certification: Fifth International Conference, RSSRail 2022, Paris, France, June 1–2, 2022, Proceedings. Lecture Notes in Computer Science, vol. 13294, pp. 3–19. Springer Nature Switzerland AG (2022). https://doi.org/10.1007/978-3-031-05814-1_1

2. Fantechi, A., Haxthausen, A.E., Macedo, H.D.: Compositional verification of interlocking systems for large stations. In: Cimatti, A., Sirjani, M. (eds.) SEFM 2017. LNCS, vol. 10469, pp. 236–252. Springer, Cham (2017). https://doi.org/10.1007/978-3-319-66197-1_15

3. Ferrari, A., Ter Beek, M.H.: Formal methods in railways: a systematic mapping study. ACM Comput. Surv. **55**(4), 1–37 (2022)

4. Ferrari, A., Magnani, G., Grasso, D., Fantechi, A.: Model checking interlocking control tables. In: FORMS/FORMAT 2010 - Formal Methods for Automation and Safety in Railway and Automotive Systems. pp. 107–115. Springer (2010). https://doi.org/10.1007/978-3-642-14261-1_11

5. Ferrari, A., Mazzanti, F., Basile, D., ter Beek, M.H.: Systematic evaluation and usability analysis of formal methods tools for railway signaling system design. IEEE Trans. Softw. Eng. **48**(11), 4675–4691 (2022)

6. Ferrari, A., Mazzanti, F., Basile, D., Ter Beek, M.H., Fantechi, A.: Comparing formal tools for system design: a judgment study. In: Proceedings of the ACM/IEEE 42nd International Conference on Software Engineering, pp. 62–74. ICSE 2020, Association for Computing Machinery, New York, NY, USA (2020)

7. Haxthausen, A.E., Østergaard, P.H.: On the use of static checking in the verification of interlocking systems. In: Margaria, T., Steffen, B. (eds.) ISoLA 2016. LNCS, vol. 9953, pp. 266–278. Springer, Cham (2016). https://doi.org/10.1007/978-3-319-47169-3_19

8. Haxthausen, A.E., Fantechi, A.: Compositional verification of railway interlocking systems. Form. Asp. Comput. **35**(1) (2023). https://doi.org/10.1145/3549736

9. Huang, W., Peleska, J.: Complete model-based equivalence class testing. Int. J. Softw. Tools Technol. Transfer **18**(3), 265–383 (2016)

10. James, P., Möller, F., Nguyen, H.N., Roggenbach, M., Schneider, S., Treharne, H.: Decomposing scheme plans to manage verification complexity. In: Schnieder, E., Tarnai, G. (eds.) FORMS/FORMAT 2014–10th Symposium on Formal Methods for Automation and Safety in Railway and Automotive Systems, pp. 210–220. Institute for Traffic Safety and Automation Engineering Technische Univ., Braunschweig (2014)

11. James, P., et al.: Verification of solid state interlocking programs. In: Counsell, S., Núñez, M. (eds.) SEFM 2013. LNCS, vol. 8368, pp. 253–268. Springer, Cham (2014). https://doi.org/10.1007/978-3-319-05032-4_19

12. Limbrée, C., Cappart, Q., Pecheur, C., Tonetta, S.: Verification of Railway Interlocking - Compositional Approach with OCRA. In: Lecomte, T., Pinger, R., Romanovsky, A. (eds.) RSSRail 2016. LNCS, vol. 9707, pp. 134–149. Springer, Cham (2016). https://doi.org/10.1007/978-3-319-33951-1_10

13. Limbrée, C., Pecheur, C.: A framework for the formal verification of networks of railway interlockings - application to the Belgian railway. Electr. Commun. Eur. Assoc. Study Sci. Technol. **76** (2018)

14. Limbrée, C.: Formal verification of railway interlocking systems. Ph.D. thesis, UCL Louvain (2019)
15. Macedo, H.D., Fantechi, A., Haxthausen, A.E.: Compositional verification of multi-station interlocking systems. In: Margaria, T., Steffen, B. (eds.) ISoLA 2016. LNCS, vol. 9953, pp. 279–293. Springer, Cham (2016). https://doi.org/10.1007/978-3-319-47169-3_20
16. Macedo, H.D., Fantechi, A., Haxthausen, A.E.: Compositional model checking of interlocking systems for lines with multiple stations. In: Barrett, C., Davies, M., Kahsai, T. (eds.) NFM 2017. LNCS, vol. 10227, pp. 146–162. Springer, Cham (2017). https://doi.org/10.1007/978-3-319-57288-8_11
17. Nguyen, A.N.A., Eilgaard, O.B.: Development and use of a tool supporting compositional verification of railway interlocking systems. Master's thesis, Technical University of Denmark, DTU Compute (2020)
18. Peleska, J.: Industrial-strength model-based testing - state of the art and current challenges. In: Petrenko, A.K., Schlingloff, H. (eds.) 8th Workshop on Model-Based Testing, Rome, Italy. vol. 111, pp. 3–28. Open Publishing Association (2013)
19. Peleska, J., et al.: A real-world benchmark model for testing concurrent real-time systems in the automotive domain. In: Wolff, B., Zaïdi, F. (eds.) ICTSS 2011. LNCS, vol. 7019, pp. 146–161. Springer, Heidelberg (2011). https://doi.org/10.1007/978-3-642-24580-0_11
20. Peleska, J., Vorobev, E., Lapschies, F.: Automated test case generation with SMT-solving and abstract interpretation. In: Bobaru, M., Havelund, K., Holzmann, G.J., Joshi, R. (eds.) NFM 2011. LNCS, vol. 6617, pp. 298–312. Springer, Heidelberg (2011). https://doi.org/10.1007/978-3-642-20398-5_22
21. Verified systems international GmbH: RT-Tester model-based test case and test data generator - RTT-MBT - User Manual (2013). http://www.verified.de
22. Vu, L.H., Haxthausen, A.E., Peleska, J.: A domain-specific language for railway interlocking systems. In: Schnieder, E., Tarnai, G. (eds.) FORMS/FORMAT 2014–10th Symposium on Formal Methods for Automation and Safety in Railway and Automotive Systems, pp. 200–209. Institute for Traffic Safety and Automation Engineering Technische Universität, Braunschweig (2014)
23. Vu, L.H., Haxthausen, A.E., Peleska, J.: A domain-specific language for generic interlocking models and their properties. In: Fantechi, A., Lecomte, T., Romanovsky, A. (eds.) Reliability, Safety, and Security of Railway Systems. Modelling, Analysis, Verification, and Certification: Second International Conference, RSSRail 2017, Pistoia, Italy, November 14–16, 2017, Proceedings. Lecture Notes in Computer Science, vol. 10598, pp. 99–115. Springer Cham (2017). https://doi.org/10.1007/978-3-319-68499-4_7
24. Vu, L.H.: Formal development and verification of railway control systems - In the context of ERTMS/ETCS Level 2. Ph.D. thesis, Technical University of Denmark, DTU Compute (2015)

25. Vu, L.H., Haxthausen, A.E., Peleska, J.: Formal modelling and verification of inter-locking systems featuring sequential release. Sci. Comput. Programm. **133**, Part 2, 91–115 (2017)
26. Winter, K.: Optimising ordering strategies for symbolic model checking of railway interlockings. In: Margaria, T., Steffen, B. (eds.) ISoLA 2012. LNCS, vol. 7610, pp. 246–260. Springer, Heidelberg (2012). https://doi.org/10.1007/978-3-642-34032-1_24

Pattern-Based Risk Identification for Model-Based Risk Management

Maritta Heisel$^{(\boxtimes)}$ and Marvin Wagner

University of Duisburg-Essen, Duisburg, Germany
{maritta.heisel,marvin.wagner}@uni-due.de

Abstract. In a previous publication, we have introduced Risk Issue Questionnaires (RIQs) that serve to support risk identification for critical systems. The starting point of our risk identification method are architectural patterns contained in a system architecture, e.g., process control loops or interactive systems. A RIQ enumerates the typical risks associated with such a pattern. By assessing for each issue contained in a RIQ whether it is relevant or not, risks for the system under analysis are identified in a systematic way.

In this paper, we complement the RIQ method by a method to set up and validate CORAS threat models for documenting the identified risks. In this way, we provide a basis to perform the further steps of a model-based risk management process. We equip our RIQs with modeling hints that specify what kind of modeling element should be used to represent a given issue in a threat model. Furthermore, we define formal validation conditions (VCs) that allow the risk modeler to check the generated threat models for coherence and completeness, and present a modeling tool that is able to check the defined VCs.

1 Introduction

A thorough risk management process is of crucial importance for many IT-based systems that are used in modern society. Critical infrastructure has been subject to attacks in the past and will probably be so in the future. Autonomous systems can cause accidents that should be avoided. Our financial system would collapse if a longer outage of the underlying software occurred, and so on.

The ISO 31000 standard [1] defines the following steps that belong to a risk management process:

1. Context establishment: The objectives of the risk management process have to be stated, as well as the scope of the analysis. The external (e.g., legal) and internal (e.g., organizational) contexts have to be described. Moreover, the risk criteria must be defined, such as the definition of likelihoods and the level at which risk is acceptable or unacceptable. In particular, the assets that must be protected by the risk management process must be identified.

A. E. Haxthausen et al. (Eds.): Peleska Festschrift 2023, LNCS 14165, pp. 114–129, 2023.
https://doi.org/10.1007/978-3-031-40132-9_8

2. Risk identification: Sources of risk must be identified, as well as possible areas of impact, and events that may cause negative[1] consequences. In particular, for each asset, unwanted incidents that may harm the asset must be identified. Furthermore, it must be described how such unwanted incidents can happen.
3. Risk estimation: Risk involves unwanted incidents harming an asset. For each such unwanted incident, it has to be assessed how likely it is and how severe the consequences of the unwanted incident are. In model-based risk management, all elements of the risk model (such as the ones introduced in Sect. 2.1) are taken into account for risk estimation.
4. Risk evaluation: For each risk, it has to be determined whether it is acceptable or not. Often, this is performed using a risk matrix, where the lines are annotated with likelihoods and the columns are annotated with consequence levels. The cells of this matrix indicate whether the risk consisting of the given likelihood and the given consequence level is acceptable (green cells) or not (red cells). Is is also possible to have more cell colors, for example orange ones that indicate that the given risk must be monitored.
5. Risk treatment: For unacceptable risks, appropriate treatments must be chosen, e.g., encrypted communication. For the so changed system, the risk managements steps must be repeated, because the treatments can introduce new risks.

The risk management process terminates when all risks have been accepted or reduced to an acceptable level. In such a process, risk identification plays a crucial role, because missing a risk that is present in a system could lead to catastrophic consequences.

To support systematic risk identification, we have developed a method that uses the architecture of a given system to identify risks that come with a use of different architectural patterns, e.g., process control loops or interactive systems [2]. We have defined *risk issue questionnaires* (RIQs) for a number of architectural patterns that are frequently used in critical systems. Such a RIQ contains a list of issues that are related to specific properties of the system in question. Examples of issues are whether a sensor could be too slow or an operator could be malicious. For a given system, all architectural patterns that are contained in its architecture must be identified and instantiated. The corresponding RIQs are instantiated, too. For each issue contained in a RIQ, it must be decided whether it is relevant for the given system or not. The result of applying the RIQ method is a set of relevant issues for a given system that constitute risks and that has to be fed into the subsequent risk management process. These issues are expressed in natural language.

However, it is of advantage to use models for risk management. Models are often more concise than natural language text, and they can be equipped with formal semantics. They are machine-processable and can evolve during the risk

---

[1] Note that ISO 31000 also mentions positive consequences. However, such consequences do not require any treatment and are hence not taken into account in our work.

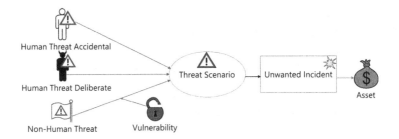

Fig. 1. CORAS notation for threat diagrams

management process. CORAS [3] is a prominent example of a model-based risk management method and notation.

In this paper, we connect the RIQ method to CORAS. In this way, we pave the way for performing steps 3) - 5) of the risk management process in a model-based manner. To this end, we equip the RIQs with modeling hints that propose a way how to model the relevant issues in a CORAS threat diagram. Besides preparing the later steps of risk management, the models allow us to define formal validation conditions (VCs) for the developed models and to check them with tool support. Such VCs are necessary conditions for the models to be sensible.

We present the necessary background in Sect. 2, followed by our risk modeling method in Sect. 3. The method is applied on an example in Sect. 4. Section 5 describes our support tool and how it can be used to check validation conditions. We discuss related work in Sect. 6 and conclude in Sect. 7.

2   Background

We briefly introduce CORAS threat models and summarize the RIQ method [2].

2.1   CORAS

CORAS [3] is a method for risk management that is equipped with a graphical notation to represent different aspects of risk modeling. We do not discuss the CORAS steps, which cover the entire risk management process. CORAS uses different kinds of diagrams, of which we only use *threat diagrams*. Figure 1 shows the notational elements that we will use in our modeling method, drawn with our tool (see Sect. 5). Table 1 explains these elements and introduces abbreviations for them that we will use in the modeling hints.

For further risk analysis, the links in a threat diagram can be annotated, e.g., with likelihoods. We will not use such annotations, however, in our method.

2.2   RIQ Method

We summarize the risk identification method introduced earlier [2]. It is based on architectural patterns such as the pattern for process monitoring given in Fig. 2.

Table 1. CORAS notational elements

Element	Abbr.	Definition taken from [3]
asset	—	something to which a party assigns value and hence for which the party requires protection
unwanted incident	UI	event that harms or reduces the value of an asset
threat	—	potential cause of an unwanted incident
threat scenario	TS	chain or series of events that is initiated by a threat and that may lead to an unwanted incident
vulnerability	V	weakness, flaw or deficiency that opens for, or may be exploited by, a threat to cause harm or to reduce the value of an asset
Element	**Abbr**	**Explanation** (not contained in [3])
human threat (deliberate)	HTD	person who attacks the system
human threat (accidental)	HTA	person who inadvertently causes harm
non-human threat	NHT	technical element that causes harm

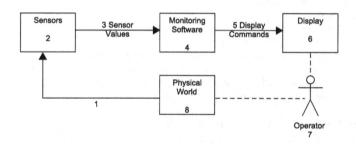

Fig. 2. Architectural Pattern: Process Monitoring

Process monitoring systems use sensors to monitor a part of the physical world to inform operators about its state, using a display. Based on the displayed information, the operator may take actions that are outside the scope of the system to be analyzed.

Each risk is associated with unwanted incidents that harm an asset, and a risk level, often expressed by the likelihood of that incident to happen, combined with the severity of its consequences. The issues in the RIQs describe conditions or scenarios that might lead to harm of an asset. We use the term "issue" because we do not want to distinguish between threats, vulnerabilities, attacks, etc. Everything that can lead to harm of an asset can be listed in a RIQ. This means that all kinds of risks can be identified using RIQs, in particular, security, safety, fault tolerance and even non-technical risks.

We have defined RIQs for a number of well-established architectural patterns used in the context of critical systems, in particular, process control systems, interactive systems, persistent storage systems, and communication channels. It is our goal to obtain a larger catalog of RIQs in the future.

RIQ for Process Monitoring. We present in RIQ 1 an excerpt of the RIQ for process monitoring systems. The complete RIQ can be found in [2]. The numbers of the RIQ items refer to the numbers used in Fig. 2. Each entry describes a possible risk, and the question to be answered is whether the described risk issue is relevant for the system under analysis or not. Each high-level issue (numbered 1–8) may contain sub-issues that further detail the high-level issue. If a high-level issue is assessed not to be relevant, its sub-issues are irrelevant, too. The RIQ also contains the modeling hints that will be explained in Sect. 3 (indicated by "→" and using the abbreviations introduced in Table 1). We completely present items 1,2, and 7 of the RIQ. The other items are grayed out, and their sub-items are not shown.

RIQ 1 Process Monitoring (PM), with modeling hints

1 Sensors cannot read entities from physical world properly (even though they function as intended) → TS
   1.1 Sensors not correctly installed→ V
   1.2 Inappropriate Sensors → V
      1.2.1 Sensors not fast enough → V
      1.2.2 Sensors do not measure what is needed → V
2 Sensor delivers wrong (HAZOP[2]) values → TS
   2.1 Sensor is single point of failure (insufficient redundancy) → V
   2.2 Sensor not sufficiently physically protected against environmental influences → V
   2.3 Sensor not sufficiently physically protected against attacks → V
   2.4 Sensor needs maintenance / repair → V
   2.5 Sensor is hacked → TS
   2.6 Sensor values do not reflect reality → V
3 Monitoring Software receives wrong (HAZOP) values from sensors → TS
4 Monitoring Software does not behave as intended, i.e., does not conform to its specification → TS
5 Display receives wrong (HAZOP) commands → TS
6 Display does not function correctly (HAZOP) → TS
7 Operator does not react as intended → TS
   7.1 Operator cannot correctly interpret displayed information → TS
      7.1.1 Too much information given → V
      7.1.2 Not enough information given → V
      7.1.3 Irrelevant information given → V
      7.1.4 Information incomprehensible → V
   7.2 Problems with Operator → TS
      7.2.1 Operator is malicious → HTD
      7.2.2 Operator is naive / careless / not concentrated → V
      7.2.3 Operator is mistaken about the situation / has wrong information → V
      7.2.4 Operator is not authentic → HTD
   7.3 Operator cannot act as intended → TS
8 Unexpected condition in physical world → TS

---

[2] When we use the term "HAZOP", we mean that the HAZOP guide-words [4] should be considered to determine what "wrong" values may be, e.g. *no*, *early*, *reverse*, etc.

Risk Identification Method. To perform risk identification using RIQs, the architectural patterns used in the system under analysis are identified. For each occurrence of such a pattern, the corresponding RIQ is instantiated accordingly. Each instantiated RIQ is then processed by determining for each issue whether it is relevant or not, and documenting the reasons for the answers. The resulting list of relevant issues is the final result of the risk identification method.

3 Modeling Method

The contribution of this paper is to enhance the RIQ method in such a way that the processed RIQs can be used to systematically set up CORAS threat diagrams. Thus, we achieve a seamless transition to model-based risk management. Furthermore, we equip threat diagrams with a rigorous semantics by defining a metamodel the developed models must adhere to. Based on this metamodel, formal validation conditions can be defined, which can be checked with tool support. This helps to assure the quality of the developed threat models and contributes to the overall quality of the risk management results.

To prepare for the modeling method, the RIQ method must be adjusted in two ways. First, when processing a RIQ, it must be specified what asset is harmed when an issue becomes relevant. Second, the RIQs must be equipped with modeling hints. These hints specify which model element should be chosen for incorporating a relevant issue in the developed threat model.

We first discuss the modeling hints and then describe the modeling method in more detail.

3.1 Defining Modeling Hints

The modeling hints are heuristics that have been validated by various examples. Our method is not automatic but gives guidelines that usually will lead to a meaningful threat model. If the modeler finds a situation where the modeling hint is not appropriate, a more appropriate way of modeling the given issue should be chosen.

The following modeling elements are at our disposition: unwanted incident, threat scenario, vulnerability, as well as three different kinds of threats (see Table 1. There are very few unwanted incidents used as modeling hints. This is because the possible assets are so diverse that unwanted incidents can hardly be identified on a pattern level. An exception is the RIQ for persistent storage. There, we have issues corresponding to the confidentiality, integrity, or availability of the persistent storage. Compromising one of the CIA properties is an issue for which an unwanted incident is proposed as a modeling element.

High-level issues of RIQs are often modeled as threat scenarios. For example, all issues 1 – 8 in RIQ 1 have "TS" as a modeling hint. This is because threat scenarios indicate that there is some behavior in the system that may lead to an unwanted incident harming an asset, and hence, a risk is present. For example, issue 2 of RIQ 1 "Sensor delivers wrong (HAZOP) values" describes a behavior that can constitute a risk.

Sometimes, however, a RIQ issue may correspond more to a condition than to a behavior. In this case, the modeling hint is a "V". For example, issue 2.1 of RIQ 1 "Sensor is single point of failure (insufficient redundancy)" is modeled as a vulnerability, because it points out a design flaw that in itself does not harm an asset, but that can enable a situation where fault tolerance is not given, which may lead to a failure of the system.

Still other issues are appropriately modeled as threats. For example, a malicious operator (see issue 7.2.1 of RIQ 1) should be modeled as a human threat (deliberate), and suitable vulnerabilities should be identified that enable the threat scenario "Problems with Operator" corresponding to issue 7.2 (see Sect. 3.2). Note that the cases of a careless and a malicious or fake operator are modeled differently. Whereas a careless operator constitutes a vulnerability to the system, a malicious or fake operator constitutes a threat for which vulnerabilities should be identified.

3.2   How to Set up Threat Models from RIQs with Modeling Hints

Starting point for constructing a threat model is an initial threat model consisting of all identified assets that are subject to risk and the unwanted incidents harming these assets. That information must be elicited before starting risk identification and hence is not subject of this paper. Furthermore, an instantiated RIQ must be given, together with the information which asset is harmed for each issue that is deemed relevant.

The model is constructed by incorporating all relevant issues and sub-issues one by one, using the modeling hints. Whenever a new model element is introduced following a modeling hint, the model must be completed in two ways: first, a path in the model must be constructed that starts from the new model element and ends in an unwanted incident, which in turn harms the asset that was specified when the issue was assessed as relevant. This means, we connect the model element "to the right". Second, a path must be constructed that starts from a threat and leads to the new model element. This means, we complete the model "to the left". If the new model element is itself a threat, then is does not need to be completed "to the left", but a vulnerability should be searched for – if not yet present – that allows the threat to cause a threat scenario.

The following detailed method describes how to introduce new model elements according to the modeling hints contained in a RIQ. To decide what elements should be introduced, pairs of modeling hints are considered, namely an issue i and one of its sub-issues $i.j$. Depending on different combinations of modeling hints for i and $i.j$, the method gives guidelines how to add new elements to the intermediate model. In particular:

1. For each relevant issue, collect the relevant sub-issues.
2. If an issue is relevant, but none of its sub-issues is, use the modeling hint to model the issue, complete it "to the left" and connect it "to the right".

3. For each relevant sub-issue:
   (a) If the modeling hint proposes a vulnerability, and the super-issue is a threat scenario, model the sub-issue as a vulnerability that leads to the threat scenario. Identify the threat that can exploit the vulnerability.
   (b) If the modeling hint proposes a vulnerability, and the higher-level issue is also a vulnerability, do not model the higher-level vulnerability. Instead, connect the new vulnerability to a suitable threat scenario as described in Step 4a.
   (c) If the modeling hint proposes a threat scenario, model the sub-issue as a threat scenario.
       i If the super-issue is a threat scenario, probably the super-issue does not have to be modeled at all. This is because the sub-issue is a special case of the super-issue and gives more information about the risk than the super-issue.
       ii If the super-issue is modeled as an unwanted incident, introduce the unwanted incident (if not yet present), and connect the threat scenario to the unwanted incident.
   (d) If the modeling hint proposes a threat, model the sub-issue as a threat, identify a vulnerability if possible, and connect it to a suitable threat scenario, which will often be representing the super-issue.
   (e) We have not yet found a situation where the modeling hint proposes an unwanted incident for a sub-issue, but only for top-level issues.
4. For each newly introduced threat scenario:
   (a) Connect the threat scenario to an unwanted incident, either directly, or indirectly. In the second case, the newly introduced threat scenario can lead to an already existing threat scenario, or one can identify one or more new threat scenarios to which the new one leads and that lead to an unwanted incident.[3].
   (b) Complete the model "to the left", i.e. identify a threat that may cause the threat scenario (new one or re-use existing one). If possible, identify a vulnerability that makes the threat scenario possible. Otherwise, not vulnerability will be given in the model.

Note that the method relies on the human understanding of the introduced modeling elements. It is possible that the threat scenario arising from the modeling hint does not sufficiently explain why the threat scenario can lead to harm for an asset. If this is the case, new threat scenarios must be introduced that clarify how the asset can be harmed in the context of the issue under consideration.

In performing the above method, we obtain separate models for each instantiated RIQ. When several RIQs need to be processed, they may have common elements, which must have the same name. Hence, it may be necessary to rename model elements[4]. With the help of our tool, different models obtained from different RIQs can be merged into one final threat model.

---

[3] The chain of threat scenarios must explain how the newly introduced threat scenario can harm the asset, which has been specified when marking the issue as relevant.

[4] It is not mandatory that the names of the modeling elements reflect the wording of the instantiated RIQs, but usually it is useful for traceability reasons.

3.3   Validation Conditions

We define various validation conditions (VCs) for the modeling method described in Sect. 3.2. Such validation conditions may refer to RIQs, threat models, or the relation between RIQs and threat models. In this paper, we present validation conditions that refer to the threat models developed with our method.

Since CORAS threat models can be regarded as directed graphs, formal validation conditions referring to paths in such a graph can be identified. Some examples are:

1. Each path in the final model starts from a threat and ends at an asset.
2. Each path not only ends in an asset, but there is an unwanted incident immediately before the asset in the path.
3. For each asset for which a risk was identified, there is a path that ends in it.

How the above VCs can be checked with tool support is discussed in Sect. 5.

4   Example

We now illustrate the modeling method explained in Sect. 3 by the same example as used in our previous paper [2]. We do not explain why we assessed some issues as relevant and others as non-relevant, but refer the interested reader to [2]. The example is a patient monitoring system in an intensive care unit (ICU) of a hospital, taken from [5]. The informal description is as follows:

> A patient monitoring program is required for the intensive-care unit of a hospital. Each patient is monitored by an analog device which measures factors such as pulse, temperature, blood pressure, and skin resistance. The program reads these factors on a periodic basis (specified for each patient) and stores the factors in a database. For each patient, safe ranges for each factor are also specified by medical staff. If a factor falls outside a patient's safe range, or if an analog device fails, then the nurses' station is notified.

The assets that are relevant for this system are the health of the patient, which is safety-related, and the confidentiality of the patients' data, which is security-related.

Figure 3 shows the part of the system architecture that is an instance of the *Process Monitoring* pattern. Instances of three other patterns are also contained in the architecture, see [2]. We apply our modeling method to selected issues of the RIQ for process monitoring in RIQ 2, using the instantiated RIQ 1. We again consider issues 1,2, and 7, as in Sect. 2.2. Issues that are assessed to be irrelevant or do not belong to issues items 1,2, or 7, are grayed out.

RIQ 2 Instantiated RIQ_PM for Patient Monitoring System, with modeling hints

1 Analog Devices cannot read factor values properly → TS

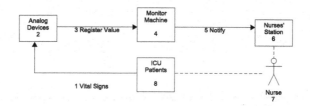

Fig. 3. Process Monitoring Part of Patient Monitoring System

1.1 Analog Devices not correctly installed → V
1.2 Inappropriate Analog Devices → V
2 Analog Devices deliver wrong or no values → TS
    2.1 Analog Devices are single point of failure (insufficient redundancy) → V
    2.2 Analog Devices not sufficiently physically protected against environmental influ-
        ences → V
    2.3 Analog Devices not sufficiently physically protected against attacks → V
3 Monitor Machine receives wrong (HAZOP) values from sensors → TS
4 Monitor Machine does not behave as intended, i.e., does not conform to its specification
    → TS
5 Nurses' Station receives wrong (HAZOP) commands → TS
6 Nurses' Station does not function correctly (HAZOP) → TS
7 Nurse does not react as intended → TS
    7.1 Nurse cannot correctly interpret displayed information → TS
    7.2 Problems with Nurse → TS
        7.2.1 Nurse is malicious → HTD
        7.2.2 Nurse is naive / careless / not concentrated → V
        7.2.3 Nurse is mistaken about the situation / has wrong information → V
        7.2.4 Nurse is not authentic → HTD

All issues are related to the asset *Patient Health* with the associated unwanted incident *Exceeded limits not noticed and not treated.* The model taking into account issues 1,2, and 7 is derived as follows. The final threat model is shown in Fig. 4.

Issue 1 Our method tells us to introduce a threat scenario *1. Analog Devices cannot read factor values properly*[5] with a vulnerability *1.1 Analog Devices not correctly installed.* The corresponding threat is a human threat (accidental) *Medical Staff.* However, the threat scenario *1. Analog Devices cannot read factor values properly* does not sufficiently explain why the *Patient Health* is harmed. Therefore, we introduce a new threat scenario *Alarm cannot be determined.*

Issue 2 Our method tells us to introduce a threat scenario *2. Analog Devices deliver wrong or no values* with a vulnerability *2.3 Analog Devices not sufficiently physically protected against attacks.* Here, the envisaged scenario is that

---

[5] To better map the model with the RIQ items, we include the number of the RIQ issue in the name of the modeling element.

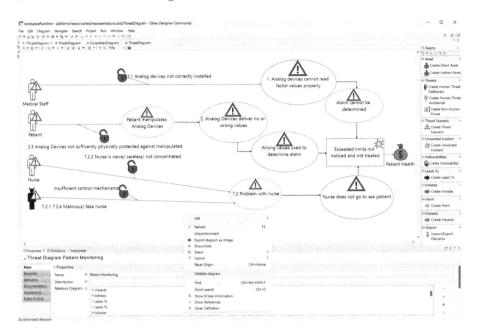

Fig. 4. Developed CORAS Tool, showing threat model for Patient Monitoring System

a patient in a confused mental state might want to get rid of the analog devices and manipulates them accordingly. Hence, we introduce an intermediate threat scenario *Patient manipulates Analog Devices*, and a human threat (accidental) *Patient*. To connect the new threat scenario "to the right", we introduce a threat scenario *Wrong values used to determine alarm* to clarify how wrong or no sensor values may harm the *Patient Health*.

Issue 7 According to the method Step 3(c)i, we do not introduce a threat scenario corresponding to the top-level issue but rather to the sub-issue 7.2. Sub-issues 7.2.1, 7.2.2, and 7.2.4 are treated as described in Steps 3a and 3d. To connect the new threat scenario *7.2 Problems with Nurse* "to the right", we introduce the threat scenario *Nurse does not go to see patient* (We do not consider a scenario where a malicious nurse actively harms a patient, because this would not be related to the operation of the monitor machine).

The final model, as shown in Fig. 4, has been developed systematically by following the modeling method of Section 3 and using the modeling hints of the instantiated RIQ 2. It fulfills all the validation conditions enumerated in Sect. 3.3 and can now be used as the basis for the further steps of a model-based risk management process.

5   Tool Support

In this section, we introduce the used CORAS metamodel [3] and our prototype tool. We implement the metamodel in the *Eclipse Modeling Framework (EMF)*[6]. The tool is implemented in *Sirius*[7] with *Java* Services. Both frameworks are open source. *EMF* provides an editor to create metamodels which are similar to *UML*. *EMF* automatically creates *Java* code based on the metamodel. *Sirius* builds on that *Java* code. *Sirius* uses the language *Acceleo Query Language (AQL)*[8], which is similar to the *Object Constraint Language(OCL)*[9]. *Sirius* makes it possible to easily create editors and provides default actions, such as creating, deleting, and editing elements. We use the *ObeoDesigner*[10] as an Integrated Development Environment (*IDE*). There are three levels in our tool:

- **Metamodel** The metamodel is realized in EMF. It defines the semantics for any CORAS model which can be created with our tool. It is part of the tools' backend. The metamodel is not relevant for the user of the tool.
- **Model Instance** Each model instance is an instance of the metamodel and describes a concrete CORAS model. The model instance can be created and edited with our graphical editor.
- **Graphical Representation** The model instance can be represented as a CORAS threat diagram. We specify different instruments to create and modify model elements based on the graphical representation.

5.1   Metamodel

The basis of our metamodel is the CORAS metamodel [3]. Since we focus on CORAS threat diagrams, we do not need the entire CORAS metamodel, but leave out some classes and associations. The main class of our metamodel shown in Fig. 5 is *CORASModel*, containing *Diagrams*, of which *ThreatDiagram* is an instance. We add two associations to the class *Diagram* to ensure that we can assign *Relation(s)* and *Element(s)*. For *ThreatDiagrams*, the association ends are named *relationsDiagram* and *elementsDiagram*, respectively. These additional associations are necessary because the result of our modeling method consists of multiple *ThreatDiagrams*, namely one for each RIQ that has been processed. However, not all diagrams share the same *Relations* and *Elements*.

5.2   Graphical Editor

The graphical representation of our tool builds on the *Sirius* framework. A screenshot of the tool is shown in Fig. 4. In the lower part, you can see the

---

[6] https://www.eclipse.org/modeling/emf/, accessed January 11, 2023.
[7] https://www.eclipse.org/sirius/, accessed January 11, 2023.
[8] https://www.eclipse.org/acceleo/documentation/, accessed January 11, 2023.
[9] https://www.omg.org/spec/OCL/, accessed January 11, 2023.
[10] https://www.obeodesigner.com/en/, accessed January 11, 2023.

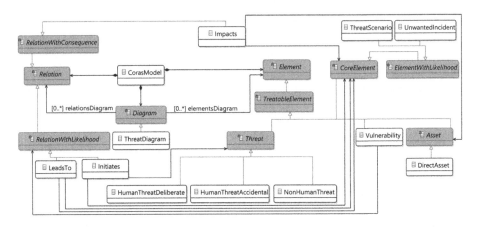

Fig. 5. Modified CORAS Metamodel; abstract classes shown in gray

property view. Each diagram element has a property view, where its attributes
are represented and editable.

The Palette, on the right-side of Fig. 4, consists of the instruments to create
new diagram elements. For each metamodel class except the main class and the
abstract classes, an instrument to create that element is available. The creation
involves a dialog, where the necessary information for an element can be entered,
e.g., the name of the element. If an element of the class *Relation* should be created then the user needs to click first on the source of the relation and then
on the target of the relation. The creation is semantically checked through the
metamodel. For example, the instrument for *Initiates* allows only diagram elements of the class *Threat* as source elements and diagram elements of the class
CoreElement as destinations.

A right-click in the diagram window opens a context menu, where the validation conditions can be checked using 'Validate diagram'.

5.3   Implemented Validation Conditions

All validation conditions of Sect. 3.3 are implemented in the tool. Here, we only
describe the implementation of the following validation condition:

For each asset, there is a path that ends in it.

That validation condition is formalized in *AQL* as follows:

```
Context :: ThreatDiagram
aql:   self.relationsDiagram ->filter(coras::Impacts).
       targetRelation ->includesAll(self.elementsDiagram ->filter(
       coras::Asset))
```

In this AQL predicate, 'self' is an instance of the class *ThreatDiagram*. We consider the *Relation*s assigned to the *ThreatDiagram* and filter them for instances
of the class class *Impacts*. This *Relation* is the only one which has as a target of
class *Asset*.

With 'targetRelation' we select all instances of the class *Asset* which have an input relation. After that, we check whether the following elements are in that set, expressed by 'includesAll'. We select all *Elements* which are assigned to the *ThreatDiagram* and filter them so that the set only contains *Elements* that are an instance of the class *Asset*. If all *Elements* of the second set are included in the first one, then we can conclude that all *Assets* are used in the *ThreatDiagram*.

6 Related Work

The earlier paper [2] contains an extensive discussion of related work on risk identification, which is also relevant for this paper. We discussed a number of vulnerability enumerations that are available on the Internet, e.g., the Common Vulnerability Scoring System (CVSS)[11]. These enumerations mostly focus on cyber-security, which is a narrower scope than the one we address. Security is also the focus of pattern-based approaches to risk analysis discussed in [2].

More approaches to security risk analysis are discussed in the literature review by Tuma et al. [6]. All of these are more specialized than ours. Mayer et al. [7] use a similar metamodel as we do and connect security risk analysis with enterprise architecture management. Their analysis is confined to security and rather takes a business process perspective than a system architecture perspective. It could complement our method.

The security risk assessment method proposed by Gol Mohammadi et al. [8] uses diagrams of the system architecture to exhibit security risks, but is focused on cloud systems. Maidl et al. [9] propose a metamodel for expressing system architectures that is specifically defined to support the security analysis of cyber-physical systems.

Shaked et al. [10] take a completely different approach than ours to cyber-risk identification, which is based on AI techniques as well as ontologies. They aim to automate cyber risk identification by integrating information from different resources. Our method does not strive for automation, but for systematization of risk identification.

As far as safety risks are concerned, established methods such as Hazard and Operability Study (HAZOP) [4], as well as the more recent approach System-Theoretic Process Analysis (STPA) [11] have been discussed in [2]. However, none of these methods is applicable to various kinds of risks, and none produces a model that can serve as a basis for the subsequent steps of risk management.

In contrast, Beckers et al. [12] have proposed a model-based method for Hazard Analysis and Risk Assessment (HARA) in the automotive sector, also using guide-words and taking ASILs (automotive safety integrity levels) into account. This method deals with risk identification, and it produces models, but is specialized on safety in the automotive sector. The risk analysis method presented by Neema et al. [13] is also focused on a specific domain, namely railway systems.

---

[11] https://www.first.org/cvss/, accessed January 6, 2023.

The CORAS method [3] contains a risk identification phase, but that phase is performed by brainstorming. Our method serves to replace the brainstorming process by a more systematic and repeatable method.

In summary, we can note that there are many risk analysis methods specialized to security. Safety-related methods, on the other hand, are often specialized to application domains, taking into account relevant safety standards. Even though CORAS publications mostly deal with security, CORAS is a general risk analysis method and notation, and therefore, is a good candidate to complement the RIQ method, which agnostic to the kind of risk that is identified with it.

7   Conclusion and Outlook

With the RIQ method [2] and the modeling method presented in this paper, we have established a solid basis to identify risks for critical systems, for which an architecture is given. That architecture must contain architectural patterns for which a RIQ is defined. The identified risks are not confined to security risks or any other kind of risk.

By developing risk models in a systematic way, we prepare the ground for the subsequent phases of a model-based risk management process. The approach does not depend on CORAS and its specific modeling notation. If a different notation should be used, the modeling hints and the metamodel of the tool, as well as the used icons, need to be adjusted. But the procedure would remain largely untouched, because the notions of risk management are shared among different risk management techniques.

Using models to represent the artifacts of a risk management process makes it possible to define formal validations conditions that can be checked with tool support. This can significantly improve the quality of the models and hence the entire risk management process.

In the future, we intend to enhance our catalog of available RIQs, and we want to identify and implement further validation conditions. As already mentioned, such validation conditions could also refer to RIQs without considering models, or to relations between RIQs and models. To this end, the metamodel needs to be extended to also cover RIQs and their relations to models.

Acknowledgments. We thank Jens Leicht, Thomas Santen and Roman Wirtz for their useful comments on this work.

References

1. International Organization for Standardization: ISO 31000:2018 Risk management - Principles and guidelines. Standard (2018)
2. Heisel, M., Omerovic, A.: Risk identification based on architectural patterns. In: Paiva, A.C.R., Cavalli, A.R., Ventura Martins, P., Pérez-Castillo, R. (eds.) QUATIC 2021. CCIS, vol. 1439, pp. 341–355. Springer, Cham (2021). https://doi.org/10.1007/978-3-030-85347-1_25

3. Lund, M.S., Solhaug, B., Stølen, K.: Model-Driven Risk Analysis, The CORAS Approach. Springer (2010). https://doi.org/10.1007/978-3-642-12323-8

4. IEC: Hazard and Operability Studies (HAZOP studies). IEC 61882, International Electrotechnical Commission (IEC) (2001)

5. Jackson, M.: Problem Frames: Analyzing and Structuring Software Development Problems. Addison-Wesley Longman Publishing Co., Inc. (2001)

6. Tuma, K., Çalikli, G., Scandariato, R.: Threat analysis of software systems: a systematic literature review. J. Syst. Softw. **144**, 275–294 (2018)

7. Mayer, N., Aubert, J., Grandry, E., Feltus, C., Goettelmann, E., Wieringa, R.J.: An integrated conceptual model for information system security risk management supported by enterprise architecture management. Softw. Syst. Model. **18**(3), 2285–2312 (2019)

8. Mohammadi, N.G., Goeke, L., Heisel, M., Surridge, M.: Systematic risk assessment of cloud computing systems using a combined model-based approach. In Filipe, J., Smialek, M., Brodsky, A., Hammoudi, S., eds.: Proceedings of the 22nd International Conference on Enterprise Information Systems, ICEIS 2020, Prague, Czech Republic, 5–7 May 2020, vol. 2, pp. 53–66. SCITEPRESS (2020)

9. Maidl, M., Wirtz, R., Zhao, T., Heisel, M., Wagner, M.: Pattern-based modeling of cyber-physical systems for analyzing security. In Sousa, T.B., ed.: Proceedings of the 24th European Conference on Pattern Languages of Programs, EuroPLoP 2019, Irsee, Germany, 3–7 July 2019, pp. 23:1–23:10. ACM (2019)

10. Shaked, A., Margalit, O.: Sustainable risk identification using formal ontologies. Algorithms **15**(9), 316 (2022)

11. Leveson, N.: Engineering a safer world : systems thinking applied to safety. MIT Press (2011)

12. Beckers, K., Frese, T., Hatebur, D., Heisel, M.: A structured and model-based hazard analysis and risk assessment method for automotive systems. In: Procs of the 24th IEEE International Symposium on Software Reliability Engineering, pp. 238–247. IEEE Computer Society (2013)

13. Neema, H., Wang, L., Koutsoukos, X.D., Tang, C.Y., Stouffer, K.: Model-based risk analysis approach for network vulnerability and security of the critical railway infrastructure. In David, D.P., Mermoud, A., Maillart, T. (eds.).: Critical Information Infrastructures Security - 16th International Conference, CRITIS 2021, Lausanne, Switzerland, 27–29 September 2021, Revised Selected Papers, vol. 13139. LNCS, pp. 79–98. Springer (2021). https://doi.org/10.1007/978-3-030-93200-8_5

Software Model Checking of Interlocking Programs

Phillip James[ID], Faron Moller[ID], and Markus Roggenbach[(✉)][ID]

Swansea University, Swansea, UK
{p.d.james,f.g.moller,m.roggenbach}@swansea.ac.uk

Abstract. In this paper, we report and reflect on successful technology transfer from Swansea University to Siemens Mobility over the years 2007–2022. This transfer concerns formal software verification technology for interlocking computers. It spans over Technology Readiness Levels TRL 1–7 and was reported on in two REF Impact Case Studies, in 2014 and 2021 [17,18].

To Jan

Who shows us that
excellence in research, both foundational and applied, and
technology transfer go hand in hand.

1   A Signalling Problem and Our Approach to Solving It

Interlockings are safety-critical systems which form an essential part of rail control systems. They are often realised as programmable logic controllers programmed in the language Ladder Logic, cf. IEC standard 61131 [8]. In the context of rail signalling systems, they provide a safety layer between a (human or automatic) controller and the physical track which guarantees safety principles such as: before a signal can show proceed, all train detection devices in the route indicate the line is clear. Rail authorities such as the UK Rail Safety and Standards Board as well as rail companies such as Siemens Mobility have defined such safety principles (currently, we work with about 350 principles) that shall guarantee safe rail operation. This poses the research question of how one can verify that a given program written in Ladder Logic fulfils a safety property, i.e., a logical representation of a safety principle.

Our journey to answer this question went, up to now, through three phases, cf. Fig. 1. A number of themes stayed invariant in all of them, though each phase shed its specific light on them: how to ensure faithful models of the software and its desired properties? what program size can be treated? who can use the produced artefacts? how can different components interact with each other?

The first phase concerns *Theoretical Foundations*, cf. Sect. 2. In terms of artefacts involved, all are paper-based documents, speaking about faithfully representing Ladder Logic programs and their properties in propositional logic and

A. E. Haxthausen et al. (Eds.): Peleska Festschrift 2023, LNCS 14165, pp. 130–146, 2023.
https://doi.org/10.1007/978-3-031-40132-9_9

Artefacts	Documents	1st Prototype	2nd Prototype
Theme	Theoretical Foundations	Academic Experiments	Technology Transfer
Faithful modelling	LL-programs as transition systems	Capturing rail-specific safety properties	'All' safety properties from standards
Scalability	'Small' theory only	Slicing	Optimised encoding
Usability	Mathematical reader	Tool programmer	Industry standard
Interoperability	Semantic preservation	'Whatever goes'	Bespoke Siemens formats

Fig. 1. The three phases of our journey.

first order logic. Only programs of a few lines length can be treated manually. Academics can work out examples. It is key to preserve semantics between the different artefacts (logics and automata), cf. Example 1 below.

The next phase was on building a 1st Prototype for carrying out *Academic Experiments*. As a proof of concept, selected rail-specific safety principles were modelled in first order logic and transformed into propositional formulae. Abstraction through program slicing turned out to be a necessity in order to verify interlocking programs of small railway stations with the SAT solvers and computing power available in 2010. The 1st Prototype could be operated mainly by the original tool developers. Its components were written in different languages with data exchange through text files.

The performance of the 1st Prototype was promising enough to support development of a 2nd Prototype, starting a process of *Technology Transfer*, i.e., for performing verification in the industrial setting of Siemens Mobility. Safety properties were systematically encoded in first order logic, their transformation to propositional logic was proven to be semantics-preserving using a temporal first order logic. In terms of scalability, optimised encodings of the safety properties were developed. The 2nd Prototype was developed with Rail Engineers as users in mind. All software was written in C♯ and bespoke Siemens Mobility interfaces were used to guarantee interoperability with existing Siemens Mobility tools.

Utilizing the notion of Technology Readiness Levels (TRLs)[1], the rest of the paper describes our journey through these three phases. The paper concludes with a perspective on the final phase: establishing an improved 2nd Prototype as a standard tool in interlocking design.

This paper can be read in different ways. The domain expert on Ladder Logic will find out about concrete, state-of-the-art steps of how to verify Ladder Logic programs of industrial size. The formal methods expert or industrial research manager will find a report on a successful technology transfer together with reflections on lessons learnt.

An early version of this paper appeared as an extended abstract in the proceeding of Isola'21 [3].

---

[1] Technology Readiness Levels, HORIZON 2020, Annex G.

2 Theoretical Foundations

We discuss the theoretical foundations of our first prototype. This includes basic principles (TRL1) and the formulation of a technology concept (TRL2).

2.1 Textbook Knowledge on Verifying Finite Transition Systems

The following definition is standard:

Definition 1. *Let $\bar{x} = (x_1, \ldots, x_n)$, $\bar{x}' = (x'_1, \ldots, x'_n)$, and $\bar{i} = (i_1, \ldots, i_m)$ be vectors of Boolean variables, for some $m, n \geq 0$. Given propositional formulae $I(\bar{x})$ (the initialisation condition) and $T(\bar{x}, \bar{i}, \bar{x}')$ (the transition condition), we define a* **labelled transition system** $\mathcal{S} = (S, \longrightarrow, Init)$ *as follows:*

- *The set of all Boolean vectors $S = \{0,1\}^n$ is the set of states;*
- *$\longrightarrow \subseteq S \times \{0,1\}^m \times S$ is the transition relation given by*

$$s \xrightarrow{\;i\;} s' :\Longleftrightarrow T(s, i, s') \text{ evaluates to } 1;$$

- *$Init = \{s \in S \mid I(s) \text{ evaluates to } 1\}$.*

We say that a state s is **reachable** *in $\mathcal{S}$, if there exists a (possibly empty) sequence of transitions from a state $init \in Init$ to s. We write $Reachable(\mathcal{S})$ for the set of reachable states of $\mathcal{S}$.*

Given a propositional formula $P(\bar{x})$, we say the transition system $\mathcal{S}$ **has safety property** P *if $P(s)$ evaluates to 1 for all $s \in Reachable(\mathcal{S})$.*

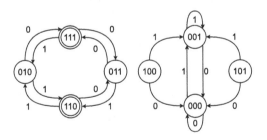

Fig. 2. A finite transition system

Example 1. Figure 2 shows the transition system defined by the initialisation condition $I = x \wedge y$ and the transition condition

$$T = \left(x' \longleftrightarrow (\neg x \wedge y)\right) \ \wedge \ \left(y' \longleftrightarrow y\right) \ \wedge \ \left(z' \longleftrightarrow a \oplus y'\right)$$

over the vectors (x, y, z), (x', y', z') and (a) of Boolean variables. The initial states are marked by double circles. Considering the property $P = x \lor y$, we can see that it holds for all reachable states; however, the property $Q = y \land z$ does not hold, as, e.g., the state 010 is reachable.

The following Theorem attests to the fact that various verification methods can be applied to such transition systems.

Theorem 1. *Let S be a transition system as in Definition 1, and let $P(\bar{x})$ be a propositional formula representing a safety property.*

Inductive Verification: *Provided*
- $I(\bar{x}) \longrightarrow P(\bar{x})$ *and*
- $P(\bar{x}) \land T(\bar{x}, \bar{i}, \bar{x}') \longrightarrow P(\bar{x}')$

hold, then S has safety property P.

Inductive Strengthening: *Let $Inv(\bar{x})$ be a propositional formula such that $Inv(s)$ evaluates to 1 for all $s \in Reachable(S)$. Provided*
- $I(\bar{x}) \longrightarrow P(\bar{x})$ *and*
- $P(\bar{x}) \land Inv(\bar{x}) \land T(\bar{x}, \bar{i}, \bar{x}') \longrightarrow P(\bar{x}')$

hold, then S has safety property P.

Bounded Model Checking: *If S has safety property P, then for all $k \geq 0$:*

$$I(\bar{x}) \land T(\bar{x}, \bar{i}, \bar{x}') \land T(\bar{x}', \bar{i}', \bar{x}'') \land \cdots \land T(\bar{x}^{(k-1)}, \bar{i}^{(k-1)}, \bar{x}^{(k)}) \longrightarrow P(\bar{x}^{(k)}).$$

(In the above, given a vector of boolean variables z, we denote by $\bar{z}^{(m)}$ a vector in which each variable has m prime symbols.)

Applying Theorem 1 to Fig. 2, we observe the following.

- *Inductive Verification* cannot be used to show that S has property P, as it considers all states rather than only reachable states; this over-approximation provides a false positive resulting from the unsafe state 001 being reachable from the safe but unreachable state 101.
- *Inductive Strengthening* can be used to show that S has property P, using the invariant $Inv = \neg((x \land \neg y \land z) \lor (x \land \neg y \land \neg z))$.
- *Bounded Model Checking* can be used to show that S does not have the property Q: $I(\bar{x}) \land T(\bar{x}, \bar{i}, \bar{x}') \rightarrow Q(\bar{x}')$ does not hold as $I(110)$ evaluates to 1, $T(110, 0, 010)$ evaluates to 1, but $Q(010)$ evaluates to 0.

The three verification methods listed in Theorem 1 can be decided utilising SAT solving. All conditions listed are of the form $\models \varphi$ for some propositional formula φ, i.e., we need to determine if a formula φ is valid. This is equivalent to determining if $\neg\varphi$ is satisfiable.

Definition 1 and Theorem 1 can be extended to cater for safety properties P that speak about several consecutive states and also take inputs into account.

2.2 Verifying Propositional Safety Properties of Ladder Logic Programs

The operation of an interlocking (IXL) can be described in terms of the following imperative program:

Algorithm 1: PLC Operation
input : Sequence of values
output: Sequence of values
initialisation
while (true) do
read (Input)   %% read
State' ← LadderLogicProgram(Input, State)   %% process
write (Output') & State ← State'   %% update

After initialisation of the system's state, the IXL runs in a non terminating loop. This loop consists of three steps: First, the IXL reads Input, a set of values; based on this Input and the IXL's current State, utilizing a Ladder Logic program, the IXL computes its next state State' which also includes some Output' values; finally, the PLC writes Output' and updates its state.

Ladder Logic, defined in the IEC standard 61131 [8], is a graphical programming language for PLCs. It gets its name from its ladder-like appearance for programs. We consider a sublanguage of Ladder Logic, which from a mathematical point of view is a subset of propositional logic.

Definition 2. *Let I and C be finite, disjoint sets of Boolean variables, where I represents input variables and $C = \{c_1, \ldots, c_n\}$ represents n distinct state/output variables, from which we define a set of* update *state/output variables $C' = \{c'_1, \ldots, c'_n\}$. A **Ladder Logic formula** ψ is a propositional formula of the form*

$$\psi \equiv (c'_1 \leftrightarrow \psi_1) \wedge (c'_2 \leftrightarrow \psi_2) \wedge \cdots \wedge (c'_n \leftrightarrow \psi_n)$$

*in which, for each $i \in \{1, \ldots, n\}$, $vars(\psi_i) \subseteq I \cup \{c'_1, \ldots, c'_{i-1}\} \cup \{c_i, \ldots, c_n\}$. The conjuncts of ψ are referred to as **rungs**; and the restriction on variables ensures that the update value c'_i of each rung depends only on input variables along with update values (c'_j with $j < i$) from earlier rungs and non-update values (c_k with $k \geq i$) from the previous cycle.*

Formula T from Example 1 is a Ladder Logic formula. Processing program T with Algorithm 1 runs it through the states as shown in Fig. 2, provided the initialisation step sets the initial states according to formula I.

This connection allows to apply the verification methods listed in Theorem 1 to prove that a propositional safety property holds for a Ladder Logic program.

2.3 Translating Generic Safety Principles to Track Plan Specific Ones

Safety principles, as stated by the UK Rail Safety and Standards Board or rail companies such as Siemens Mobility, are often formulated in tables, with one column providing preconditions for an effect such as "movement authority can be given", and further columns indicating the kind of route (main or shunting) to which a rule applies. The table entries are written in natural language. As such, the first step towards verification is to formalise such safety principles in, e.g., many-sorted first order logic (FOL) with variables ranging over entities such as points, signals, routes and track segments, resulting in predicates describing track layout and system state.

Example 2. The safety principle

> *For all pairs of distinct routes that share a track segment,*
> *at most one route is set to 'proceed'.*

can be formalised as

$$\forall rt, rt' \in \text{Route} \,.\, \forall ts \in \text{Segment} \,.\, rt \neq rt' \longrightarrow$$
$$((\text{part\_of}(ts, rt) \quad \wedge \quad \text{part\_of}(ts, rt')) \quad \longrightarrow \quad \neg(\text{route\_set}(rt) \quad \wedge$$
$$\text{route\_set}(rt'))$$

The following Theorem attests to the fact that, given a concrete track plan, formulae expressing safety principles in FOL can be translated to a logically equivalent formula in propositional logic (PL).

Theorem 2.

1. *Every formula in FOL is logically equivalent to a formula in prenex normal form (i.e., a formula is written as a string of quantifiers and bound variables, followed by a quantifier-free part).*
2. *Assuming that the carrier of a sort symbol s is freely generated by finitely many constant symbols $c_1, \ldots, c_k : s$,*
   - $\forall x \in s \,.\, \varphi(x) \leftrightarrow \varphi(c_1) \wedge \cdots \wedge \varphi(c_k)$ *and*
   - $\exists x \in s \,.\, \varphi(x) \leftrightarrow \varphi(c_1) \vee \cdots \vee \varphi(c_k).$

The formula in *Example 2* is in prenex normal form. Using quantifier replacement as formulated in Theorem 2, a typical resulting subformula looks like:

$$(\text{part\_of}(ts54, rt26) \wedge \text{part\_of}(ts54, rt27))$$
$$\longrightarrow \neg(\text{route\_set}(rt26) \wedge \text{route\_set}(rt27))$$

This subformula contains two different kinds of predicates. The first kind concerns the topology of a track plan: $\text{part\_of}(ts54, rt26)$. The property, if track segment 54 is part of route 26, can automatically be evaluated by analysing the track plan under discussion. The second kind concerns the state of the interlocking: $\text{route\_set}(rt26)$. This predicate, including its application to a constant, corresponds to a variable in the Ladder Logic program under discussion.

Outcomes:

General safety principles can be formalised within in FOL.
Then they are translated into track plan specific safety properties in PL.
Such properties in PL can be verified for Ladder Logic programs.

3   Technology Prototype

Having developed a sound formal basis, our work moved towards developing a verification process for Siemens Mobility. The main goal here was to provide an academically built, prototypical tool chain that allowed for experimental proof of concept (TRL3) and a technology that was validated in the controlled setting of an academic environment (TRL4). Many groups have worked on similar projects. As an example, we mention here Groote et al. who, as early as 1995, applied software verification to a real world interlocking [9].

3.1   Automatising Translations

The first aspect of our tooling concerns transformation between data formats. For our setting, the following data translations were required:

- Ladder Logic Programs L represented in Siemens Westrace format needed parsing and automatic translations to our defined transition system $\psi(L)$ (in a suitable formal format).
- Our first order logic safety principles needed translating into propositional logic instances specific to the given track plan T.
- A process for translating counterexamples from failed model checking attempts into a insightful format was needed.

We briefly explore initial tools that were developed, to overcome these challenges. For detailed reading we refer to [10–13].

The verification tool created by Kanso [12] and James [10] consisted of two underlying programs, one concerned with verification and the other concerned with safety properties. The general outline of these tools is shown in Fig. 3 and Fig. 4. The verification component of the tool was predominantly programmed using Haskell. As input, it takes a Ladder Logic program and a formal safety condition obtained from the safety condition generator. This program

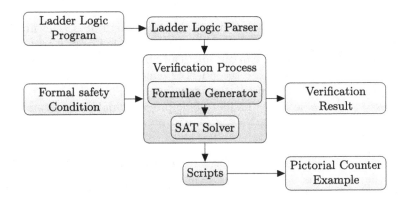

Fig. 3. Architecture of the verification tool.

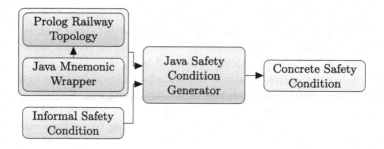

Fig. 4. Architecture of the Safety Condition Generator.

firstly uses a Ladder Logic parser to parse the Ladder Logic program into an internal abstract syntax for propositional formula. Using this propositional formula, and the safety condition (given by the process below), the program constructs either a pair of inductive formulae to be verified, or a bounded model checking problem. These formulae are then passed to a SAT solver to be verified. Depending on the result from the SAT solver, the program would then either report that the system was safe, or provide a counterexample showing the system to be unsafe; the counterexample would be run through a series of scripts to present it in pictorial form for the engineers at Siemens Mobility to study.

From Fig. 4, we can see that there are two inputs to the program for generating safety conditions to be used in the verification phase. One is an informal first order safety condition, given in a language defined by Kanso [12]. The other is a railway plan constructed out of two further parts: a railway topology describing the layout of the railway via an encoding in Prolog, and a Java mnemonic wrapper. The name space of the railway topology used for signals, points and other entities differs from the name space of the concrete Ladder Logic program. For this reason, a specific name space mnemonic wrapper was created in Java. This wrapper is responsible for converting names used in the railway topology into concrete names used within the Ladder Logic program.

Given these inputs, the safety condition generation program transforms the informal safety condition into a series of propositional formulae to be verified. The propositional formulae would contain concrete names instead of the abstract names that were given in the informal safety condition. For example the word "point" could be replaced by the actual point "TP101". These names are gained, as explained above, from the Prolog encoding and Java wrapper.

3.2   First Academic Experiments

Initial experiments conducted using the produced tool chain were based on two small interlocking programs (each around 300 rungs in size) and around five safety principles. The results [10,12] highlighted the following.

- Inductive verification can be successfully applied to verify properties of 'small' interlockings, although some properties could not be verified due to false-positives (see Theorem 1). Strengthening the approach to include k-induction [10] (also know as temporal induction [5]), which aims to avoid such false positives, was not feasible due to the size of the problems.

- The bounds that were practically explored using bounded model checking were fairly limited in size. However, applying bounded model checking allowed successful error detection (with run times stretching over hours).
- Presenting counterexamples that only included information on the final violating state were less useful in identifying underlying issues than studying (in a somewhat laborious manner) counterexample traces produced by bounded model checking.

3.3   Improving Verification Through Slicing

During the development of these results, it was clear that any potential abstractions that could be formulated to reduce the size of the state space for verification would greatly improve the applicability of the tool. The proposed approaches for the verification of Ladder Logic programs quickly give rise to large formulae to be verified. As the formula size increases, both the space and time requirements increase. This increase leads to a rather small bound (approximately 2 000) on the number of iterations of a Ladder Logic program that could be verified. Hence, in a somewhat hand-in-hand nature whilst running initial experiments, a program slicing abstraction was developed [10,11] following ideas presented in [6,9].

The intuition behind slicing is that the variables occurring in a safety condition often depend only on some part of the Ladder Logic program, and hence parts that have no effect on the safety condition can be removed. At a high level, the approach takes the following steps.

Step 1: Extract variables from safety conditions. Given a safety condition φ, we extract its variables $U = vars(\varphi)$.

Step 2: Calculate dependant variables. Calculate all the variables of the Ladder Logic formula that affect the variables in U. To do this, we begin at the last rung $R_i \equiv c'_i \leftrightarrow \psi_i$ of the Ladder Logic formula and compare its variable c'_i with the set of variables U. If $c'_i \in U$, then we add all the variables occurring in ψ_i to the set U. This step is repeated for each rung until a fixed point $\overline{U}$ is reached.

Step 3: Extract dependant rungs. Using the variable set $\overline{U}$, we remove all rungs that do not affect the safety condition. To do this, we construct the set

$$index = \{\, i \in \{1, \dots, n\} \mid c_i \in \overline{U} \ \text{ or } \ c'_i \in \overline{U} \,\}.$$

We then remove from the original program all rungs R_i whose indices do not appear in $index$. The result ψ_φ is the sliced version of program ψ.

Example 3. Considering the finite transition system in Example 1 and the safety property $P = x \vee y$, we can construct a sliced version of the propositional formulae. Here we can compute the variables in the formulae that affect the set $U = \{x, y\}$ of variables from our safety property. In particular, the formulae defining the values of x and y are both required, but the formula defining z is not. We can thus remove z from our transition system as it does not affect the values in U. This results in the transition system given in Fig. 5.

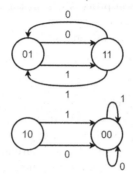

Fig. 5. The transition system from Example 1 after slicing

In [10] we proved the following theorem:

Theorem 3. *Let φ be a safety condition over a Ladder Logic formula ψ. The transition system induced by ψ has safety property φ iff the transition system induced by ψ_φ has safety property φ.*

Slicing proved effective in the two interlockings with which we experimented. For the first interlocking, the number of rungs was reduced, on average, from 331 rungs to 60 rungs. For the second interlocking, the number of rungs was reduced, on average, from 238 rungs to 25 rungs [11].

The novelty of our approach was that we gave the first proof that slicing is correct with respect to reachable states [10,11]. We also demonstrated that the above approach gave a significant reduction – a full order of magnitude on average – in the size of the state space required for verification of the five initial properties considered. For the first of the two interlockings with which we experimented. the number of rungs was reduced, on average, from 331 rungs to 60 rungs. For the second interlocking, the number of rungs was reduced, on average, from 238 rungs to 25 rungs. For full details and results we refer to [10,12].

Outcomes:

The 1st prototype fully automatically verifies Ladder Logic programs. With slicing, it can effectively handle small IXLs ($\sim$ 300 rungs). General safety properties are translated into location specific ones.

4 Technology Transfer

In the latest phase of development, a substantial effort has been put towards re-developing the technology stack. This has seen new formats developed for data along with a complete re-writing of the verification tool. This has allowed the demonstration of the verification process within the operational environment of signalling system design at Siemens Mobility (TRL 7). Here we highlight the main scientific and technological challenges.

4.1 Logic Rework

From a methodological point of view, in the logical approach developed in Sect. 2 one could see a number of weaknesses. The first concerns the nature of the safety properties under discussion. By their very nature, they are temporal properties relating consecutive states. However, we formulated them in FOL without mod-elling the temporal aspect. The second weakness is that, when translating a generic safety property in FOL to a track plan specific one in PL, for each track plan we are building a specialised logic. For instance, the truth of the formula $part\_of(ts54, rt26)$ depends on the track plan under discussion. Diaconescu dis-cusses how to build logics (institutions) with predefined types [4]. The final weakness concerns the application of a hybrid specification. Verification is car-ried out in PL, whilst the translation of generic safety properties to track plan specific properties is carried out in FOL with predefined types. These two logics are combined only by the sharing of signature elements rather than by a semantic integration.

Addressing the first and the last of these points, we sketch here a temporal logic based on ideas published in Gruner et al. [7]. *Signatures* are many sorted, first-order logic signatures. A *model* at a point of time is a pair (T, I) where T is a track plan and I is a propositional model for all propositional variables associated with T, e.g. $I(S106.G) \in \{true, false\}$. Sorts and functions are given a fixed interpretation according to the track plan, e.g.,

- $Signal_T = \{S100, ...\}$: iff T *has signals* $S100, ...$
- $routesOf_T(s) = \{r_1, ..., r_n\}$: iff *in* T, *signal* s *has routes* $r_1, ..., r_n$

Predicates obtain their interpretations usually from a combination of looking up information from both the track plan T and the propositional model I: $p\ isInCorrectPositionFor_{T,I}\ r\ \ holds$ iff

- **case 1:** in T, p needs to be in reverse for r and $I(p.RL)$ is true
- **case 2:** in T, p needs to be in normal for r and $I(p.NL)$ is true

Here, p is a point, r is a route, and $p.NL$ and $p.RL$ are variables in the Ladder Logic program representing point p being set to normal or reverse position respectively. The models of a signature are sequences of the form $(T, I_0), (T, I_1), ...$, i.e., the track plan in the first component stays constant, only the state of the propositional variables is changing.

Formulae are standard first order logic formulae, where predicate symbols can also appear with up to k primes, $k \geq 0$. The prime indicates that a predicate shall be evaluated in the k-th successor state.

Given $k+1$ models $(T, I_0), \ldots, (T, I_k)$, *satisfaction of a formula* is satisfaction as in first order logic, where l primed predicates are evaluated over (T, I_l). A formula φ holds in a sequence $\langle (T, I_0), (T, I_1), \ldots \rangle$, iff for all $i \geq 0$ the formula φ holds over $(T, I_i), \ldots, (T, I_{i+k})$.

4.2   Data Formats, Interoperability and Efficiency

A large focus of the redevelopment was on both expansion of the number of interlocking safety principles to cover the full standard (approximately 350 properties) and interoperability of the tool with existing Siemens Mobility formats. Here, the following core technology changes were made:

Systematic Documentation of Ladder Logic Variable Naming Schemes. Different interlockings use various naming schemes for variables. Typically these are dependant on the type of signalling scheme being deployed and the geographic location of the interlocking. Here, to allow for generalisability of the verification process, an XML schema was defined that allows for parameterisation of the verification process by a naming scheme.

Rewrite of the Verification Engine with a Focus on Efficiency. The underlying Haskell verification engine was rewritten in C#. Here, the main focus was on improvements in efficiency and ensuring Siemens Mobility development processes for developing safety critical software we followed.

Representation of Safety Properties. In order to provide a standardised language for Safety Properties, a new XML schema was defined that captured first order logic with predicates describing objects that occur within the railway domain. Rather than having an ad-hoc definition, these predicates were designed to align with an existing Siemens Object Model used internally to capture railway components. However, the language was also influenced by the earlier Prolog formats and included predicates to describe states of variables (such as in the next step). All 350 safety principles were then modelled within this language. To ease readability of the XML, an XSLT transformation was defined to produce HTML-viewable formulae. This also allowed for independent validation of the modelling. Finally, a C# module was developed to translate the XML properties down into the concrete condition format used by the verification engine which we developed. This translation included a mapping for variable names as defined by the given XML mapping presented above.

Professional UI Supporting Verification Work-flow. An extensive user interface was developed in C# allowing signalling engineers to interact with the verification process. Here, not only were obvious features implemented such as file interactions, but also strategies for verification were introduced that involved imposing order on proof attempts (for example inductive, then bounded model checking) along with parallelisation of proof attempts. Another feature that was heavily explored was dealing with particularly large and lengthy counterexamples. This led to a parser for counterexamples being developed along with features for filtering and the dynamic selection of variables based on the failing property. Here, earlier work on counterexample visualisation was used as a motivation [16].

4.3   Technicalities of Real World Constraints

During the redevelopment, the verification process was actively tested against a number of more complex interlockings (see Sect. 4.4). During this, several unexpected phenomena were observed that challenged the underlying theoretical foundations of the tool. There were also improvements made to the efficiency of the verification engine thanks to insights from domain knowledge.

Fleeting Outputs. Fleeting outputs are regarded as outputs that "flip" their value for a single cycle of the interlocking. Such outputs can cause counterexamples when model checking; however, in practice, this flip happens at a rate that is quicker than can be observed on the railway, and thus is not too concerning for signalling engineers. Here, a strategy was devised to allow checks that can ignore fleeting outputs if requested by the engineer during verification. Logically, 'Fleeting outputs' require more than two successive states to be encoded into a safety property, i.e., changing a formula from $\bar{x}$ and $\bar{x}'$ to $\bar{x}^1, \bar{x}^2, \ldots, \bar{x}^k$, $k = 3$ appears to be enough. This is, however, a check that should only be enabled after careful consideration of the original counterexample.

Boundary Based Properties. A number of interlocking safety principles concern the operation of the interlocking with respect to the boundary regions of the railway it controls. Here, verification of these particular principles became a challenge as it became apparent that the principles relied on assumptions made about a bordering interlocking controlling an adjacent region. Here, the decision was made that such assumptions would be documented, and an option provided within the use interface to verify with or without this assumption being included as an additional constraining formula when verifying.

Optimised Encoding of Safety Properties. During tests, it was observed that the underlying translation of safety properties was simpler/more efficient if properties were expressed in a particular manner. For example,

$$\forall x . \varphi(x) \rightarrow \big(\forall y . \psi(x, y) \rightarrow \xi(x, y)\big)$$

leads to faster verification than a property of the form

$$\forall x, y . \big(\varphi(x) \wedge \psi(x, y)\big) \rightarrow \xi(x, y)$$

We believe this is due to the falsified cases of the precondition being large when a condition is expressed for a concrete interlocking.

Invariants Based on Design Decisions. Finally, optimisations to the verification procedure were also devised thanks to extended discussions around variables within the Ladder Logic program. Inevitably, some variables exhibit inherent relationships thanks to design decisions. A typical example would be a classic SR latch where, if the reset bit is set, we know the output will be reset. This can allow for constraints on these variables to be added as invariant formulae to the model checking procedure, in turn constraining the state space. Here we have yet to systematically analyse the effect of this on verification.

4.4 Fully Functional Prototype at Siemens Mobility

As documented in our REF 2021 impact case study [18], there is now a fully functioning Ladder Logic Verifier running at Siemens Mobility. It has roughly 350 safety principles implemented, taken from various standards and developed from Siemens test objectives. This 2nd prototype is fully integrated into the Siemens Mobility ecosystem of IXL development tools and has been demonstrated in Siemens Mobility operational environment through the verification of about 10 interlockings with up to 12 000 rungs and 75 000 variables. Safety checking of one IXL takes about two hours. The verification approach has uncovered mistakes in IXLs that Siemens Mobility deems non-detectable by testing.

One unresolved challenge is that there are safety properties with can neither be decided by inductive verification nor by bounded model checking: inductive verification fails; and bounded model checking does not find a counterexample within reasonable bounds, meaning the property may or might not hold. In our verification practice, depending on the IXL under discussion, about 35–40% of all properties fall into this category.

Outcomes:

The 2nd prototype is fully integrated in the Siemens Mobility ecosystem. Large IXLs can now be verified against 350 properties within two hours. But 35–40% of an IXL's safety properties cannot be decided.

---

5 Future Development

Though our 2nd prototype is a big step towards the ultimate goal to automatically verify Ladder Logic programs, there are still a number of aspects to be addressed before it is complete and qualified (TRL 8) and is proven in the operational environment (TRL 9).

In terms of completeness, it is necessary to include decision procedures that allow to effectively prove or disprove *all* safety properties. Section 5.1 and Sect. 5.2 discuss ongoing work to address this. In terms of introducing the technology, key enablers and inhibitors to the acceptance and adoption of utilising the 2nd prototype within Siemens Mobility need to be identified, and, based on a data collection, it remains to be shown that overall it is beneficial to use this new technology. Our plans in this direction are discussed in Sect. 5.3.

5.1   IC3 Algorithm

In order to address the 35–40% of safety properties that cannot be decided with the verification technologies implemented in the 2nd prototype, the MRes project by Bryant [2] investigated if Bradley's IC3 algorithm [1] would offer a suitable solution. Bryant could show that with IC3, all properties can effectively be decided. Here, runtime per verification task was smaller than a second.

5.2   Invariant Finding via Reinforcement Learning

It is accepted that so-called invariants, properties which hold for all states under which a system operates, can help reduce occurrences of false positives. However, automated deduction of these invariants remains a challenge. We are currently exploring the use of reinforcement learning [19] where agents are used to build a dataset of observed states. These observations are then used to compute correlation coefficients between all variables composing a Ladder Logic program. This in turn allows proposals for candidate invariant properties [14,15].

5.3   Measuring Cost and Benefit

In an interdisciplinary project, spanning Business Management, Engineering and Computer Science we plan to identify key enablers and inhibitors to the acceptance and adoption of utilising the 2nd prototype within Siemens Mobility. To this end, we will embed a longitudinal comparative study to align data collection with Siemens Mobility (i.e., within each development and testing cycle, a parallel stream embedding the Ladder Logic Verification will be added in order to gather data enabling robust comparisons). As part of this data collection, insight will be gained through the interaction with the technical and management teams responsible for setting up and carrying out contracts to understand the complex dynamics at play and identify factors that may prevent the organisation from accepting and embracing the new methodology. Such interaction will be both of a formal and informal nature, spanning meeting observations, interviews, focus groups and semi-quantitative surveys. The multi-faceted nature of the data gathered will enable the development of a robust business case for the introduction and adoption of the novel methodology within Siemens Mobility.

Ideal Outcomes:

Our verifier is integral to any IXL development at Siemens Mobility.
It efficiently decides all properties under discussion.
Rail authorities accept its proofs as evidence within certification.

6 Summary

For us, one important learning outcome of this long-lasting technology transfer project is that it becomes only clear at the end of each phase what the next challenges will be. Having understood the theory (as given in Sect. 2), it was clear what transformations needed to be implemented and that counterexamples would need to be presented in a user friendly way, leading to the 1st prototype (as discussed in Sect. 3). Driven by the need to integrate with the Siemens Mobility ecosystem and follow Siemens practices, the 2nd prototype was created (as discussed in Sect. 4). Here, experience from the 1st prototype aided in system architecture and data type choices. In addition, a closer working relationship with Siemens Mobility allowed for extensive experimentation and brought in deeper domain knowledge. This led to a number of optimisations. The Siemens Mobility research team is now convinced by the technology. However, there is future work to be done (see Sect. 5). A formal business case remains to be made demonstrating the advantages of the process. Furthermore, experience gained whilst evaluating the second prototype towards verification coverage demonstrates that further verification methods are needed.

Overall, our journey turns out to be a far longer one than expected. Originally, perhaps as naive academics, we thought that the 1st prototype would be the end. When the decision came to build the 2nd prototype, we thought that this would then be the end. Having now implemented the 2nd prototype, we understand that there is still further to go towards a fully deployed technology. Overall, the journey up to now (excluding natural periods of inactivity) has taken about eight years and allowed us to gain expertise on the process of technology transfer.

Thanks to a long standing collaboration between industry and academia, it has been possible to explore the applicability of a set of formal methods to a challenge in the real world (with all its complexities). Though our endeavour continues, substantial progress has been made and there is honest belief by all involved that the above stated ideal outcomes will be achieved.

Acknowledgment. The authors would like to thank Siemens Mobility for the long-standing, fruitful and successful research collaboration, the students and colleagues in the Swansea Railway Verification Group for their support and helpful feedback and discussions, and Erwin R. Catesbeiana (Jr.) for pointing out that logic is not everything.

References

1. Bradley, A.R.: Understanding IC3. In: Cimatti, A., Sebastiani, R. (eds.) SAT 2012. LNCS, vol. 7317, pp. 1–14. Springer, Heidelberg (2012). https://doi.org/10.1007/978-3-642-31612-8_1
2. Bryant, H.: Exploring the IC3 algorithm to improve the Siemens-Swansea ladder logic verification tool. MRes Dissertation (under submission), Swansea University (2023)

3. Chadwick, S., James, P., Moller, F., Roggenbach, M., Werner, T.: A journey through software model checking of interlocking programs. In: Leveraging Applications of Formal Methods, Verification and Validation: 10th International Symposium on Leveraging Applications of Formal Methods, ISoLA 2021, Rhodes, Greece, October 17–29, 2021, Proceedings. vol. 13036, p. 495. Springer Nature (2021)

4. Diaconescu, R.: Institution-independent Model Theory. Birkhäuser (2008)

5. Eén, N., Sörensson, N.: Temporal induction by incremental sat solving. Electron. Notes Theoret. Comput. Sci. **89**(4), 543–560 (2003). bMC'2003, First International Workshop on Bounded Model Checking

6. Fokkink, W., Hollingshead, P.: Verification of interlockings: from control tables to ladder logic diagrams. In: FMICS 1998 (1998)

7. Gruner, S., Kumar, A., Maibaum, T., Roggenbach, M.: On the Construction of Engineering Handbooks - with an Illustration from the Railway Safety Domain. Springer, Cham (2020). https://doi.org/10.1007/978-3-030-44648-2

8. Programmable Controllers - Part 3: Programming languages. IEC Standard 61131–3 (2003)

9. J. Groote, S. v.Ṽlijmen, J.K.: The safety guaranteeing system at station hoorn-kersenboogerd. Technical report, Utrecht University (1995)

10. James, P.: Sat-based model checking and its applications to train control systems. MRes Dissertation, Swansea University (2010)

11. James, P., Roggenbach, M.: Automatically Verifying Railway Interlockings using SAT-based Model Checking. In: Proceedings of AVoCS 2010. Electronic Communications 35 of EASST (2010)

12. Kanso, K.: Formal verification of ladder logic, MRes dissertation, Swansea University (2008)

13. Lawrence, A.: Verification of railway interlockings in SCADE. MRes dissertation, Swansea University (2011)

14. Lloyd-Roberts, B., James, P., Edwards, M.: Mining Invariants from State Space Observations. Extended abstract at 33rd Nordic Workshop on Programming Theory, NWPT (2022)

15. Lloyd-Roberts, B., James, P., Edwards, M., Werner, T., Robinson, S.: Improving railway safety: human-in-the-loop invariant finding. In: Case Studies of HCI in Practice, CHI 2023. ACM (2023, to appear)

16. Pantekis, F., James, P., O'Reilly, L., Archambault, D., Moller, F.: Visualising railway safety verification. In: Hasan, O., Mallet, F. (eds.) FTSCS 2019. CCIS, vol. 1165, pp. 95–105. Springer, Cham (2020). https://doi.org/10.1007/978-3-030-46902-3_6

17. Improving processes and policies in the UK railway industry. https://results.ref.ac.uk/(S(ozgare1un34qrlg44nt3gsh3))/DownloadFile/ImpactCaseStudy/pdf?caseStudyId=5798

18. Improving performance, safety and software development of railway signalling. https://results2021.ref.ac.uk/impact/a117e4ed-a960-4dc6-8e13-8c98d8ea5aef?page=1

19. Sutton, R.S., Barto, A.G.: Reinforcement Learning: An Introduction. MIT Press, Cambridge (2018)

Formal Modelling to Improve Safety and Security

Thierry Lecomte[(✉)]

CLEARSY, 320 Avenue Archimède, Aix en Provence, France
thierry.lecomte@clearsy.com

Abstract. System safety is based on the implementation of technical and organisational principles to ensure that a feared event cannot occur more frequently than expected. Such a demonstration, so-called safety case, relies on domain specific standards which capitalise on experience gained after decades of development and operation. For more than a decade, the threat of human attacks aimed at disrupting the operation of such systems has become more acute. In the railways, communications between on board and track-side equipment are naturally subject to targeted attacks aimed at reducing the availability of the equipment or disrupting its operational safety to the point of creating accidents. This paper aims to sketch the range of logical and hardware attacks practised today that could be used in the future to attack railway systems to make them less available or less secure. It also presents a combination of techniques and technologies that, assisted by formal methods, can reduce the chances of success of such attacks.

Keywords: formal methods · cybersecurity · safety

1 Introduction

Railway signalling is a safety-critical system whose responsibility is to guarantee a safe and efficient operation of railway networks. Given the safety-critical nature of railway signalling and the complexity of novel distributed signalling solutions, their safety should be guaranteed. With the forthcoming progressive distribution of the signalling functions (sensing, making decision, controlling) based on network connectivity, it is also mandatory to ensure their security as well. The two worlds, namely safety and security, are quite orthogonal as they require to resist to "probabilistic failures" on one hand and to specifically crafted attacks that would timely target the existing vulnerabilities on the other hand. Their requirements are sometimes contradictory, as safety critical systems are usually expected to last decades without modification once certified, while secure systems are supposed to evolve often to take into account uncovered vulnerabilities.

System safety is a field with a long history of experience, effective standards and established industry practice. Formal methods have experienced a notable boom in many industrial fields where they are used in a reasoned manner. If the reliability of digital technologies is nowadays mastered, their security

A. E. Haxthausen et al. (Eds.): Peleska Festschrift 2023, LNCS 14165, pp. 147–159, 2023.
https://doi.org/10.1007/978-3-031-40132-9_10

is undermined by attackers using their human intelligence, technical knowledge and inventiveness to devise new means (including social engineering) capable of disrupting digital systems or taking control of them.

This article provides an overview of the use of formal methods to ensure rail transport safety. It also sketches the range of logical and hardware security attacks practised today that could be used in the future to attack railway systems to make them less available or less secure. It then presents a combination of formal techniques can reduce the chances of success of such attacks.

This paper is structured in 6 parts. Section 2 introduces the terminology. Section 3 describes how formal methods are used to improve the safety of railway systems. Section 4 presents the security attacks that are used today at software and hardware levels to either perturb the behaviour or take control of the target system. Section 5 provides an inventory of current formal techniques that could be used to improve the safety level of existing and future railway systems, before concluding in Sect. 6.

2 Terminology

This section contains specific definitions, concepts, and abbreviations used throughout this paper.

CCT refers to Constant Time Cryptography. It is related to cryptographic algorithms and protocols that take the same amount of time to execute regardless of the input data or key values. The goal of constant-time cryptography is to prevent timing attacks, which are a type of side-channel attack that can be used to extract sensitive information from a cryptographic implementation by analysing the time it takes to perform certain operations. This can be achieved by designing algorithms and protocols that avoid branching or other operations that depend on the input data or key values.

CRC refers to Cyclic Redundancy Check. It is a checksum used for error detection.

Cybersecurity refers to the protection of digital systems and related networks from information disclosure, theft of or damage to their hardware, software, or electronic data, as well as from the disruption or misdirection of the services they provide.

HSM refers to Hardware Security Module. It is a device that safeguards and manages digital keys, performs encryption and decryption functions for digital signatures, strong authentication and other cryptographic functions.

PKI refers to Public Key Infrastructure. It is a set of roles, policies, hardware, software and procedures needed to create, manage, distribute, use, store and revoke digital certificates and manage public-key encryption. It binds public keys with respective identities of entities. The binding is established through a process of registration and issuance of certificates at and by a certificate authority.

TEE refers to Trusted Execution Environment. It is a secure area of a main processor. It guarantees code and data loaded inside to be protected with respect to confidentiality and integrity.

TPM refers to Trusted Platform Module. It is a secure cryptoprocessor, a dedicated microcontroller designed to secure hardware through integrated cryptographic keys, compliant to the TPM international standard.

3 Ensuring Safety with Formal Methods

Safety in the railway industry refers to the measures and practices that are put in place to protect passengers, employees, and the general public from accidents and injuries. This includes both physical safety, such as preventing collisions or derailments, as well as the safety of passengers and employees while on or around trains and railway infrastructure. The safety measures that are commonly used in the railway industry include track maintenance and inspection to ensure that the rails and other infrastructure are in good condition and free of defects, automatic train control systems that help to prevent collisions by automatically slowing or stopping trains that are going too fast or are on a collision course, and positive train control systems, which use GNSS and other technologies to monitor train location and speed, and can automatically slow or stop a train if necessary. Railways safety on a number of standards such as EN 50128 and EN 50129 which provide guidelines for respectively the safety-related software-based and electronic systems used in railway signalling and control systems. These standards are intended to ensure the safety, reliability, and availability of these systems, which are critical for the safe operation of trains. They cover the entire life-cycle of safety-related software and electronic systems, from requirements gathering and design to installation, commissioning, operation, and maintenance. They include requirements for software development and system design, including the use of formal methods and hazard analysis, as well as guidelines for testing and validation.

A number of successful applications of formal methods to operational systems have been reported so far, in the railways as well as in other industries [16,24,25]. A large number of publications [15] cover the subject extensively. Only a few applications are listed below, addressing various safety-related activities (Fig. 1).

Software Development, Verification and Validation. A set of mathematical techniques and tools are used to formally specify, design, and verify the behaviour of software systems. They are used to ensure that software systems are correct, consistent, and secure, and that they meet their requirements and specifications. Target software are for example Automatic Train Protection for the computation of braking curves, or Boolean equations solver to compute interlocking states [5,9,13]. Formal methods are either part of the development process or implemented in the verification and validation phase. Software may be programmed with languages like C, Ada, assembly, one of the 5 standardised languages used to program PLC, or even DSL/diagrams used for relay-based and wired logic [1]. For the highest safety integrity levels, software safety is tightly linked with the safety computer [3,18,35] executing it.

Data Validation. Formal data validation [11,26,30] refers to the process of formally checking that data satisfies certain predefined constraints or rules (type-checking, range checking, logical constraints, complex constraints). These constraints and rules are expressed mathematically, and the process of validation typically involves using model checking, to check that the data meets these constraints. A model checker will either ensures that the data complies with the formal model or provides all the counterexamples [17,23]. This is particularly useful in the context of safety-critical systems, where even small errors or inconsistencies in the data can have serious consequences, when data is used by a safety function.

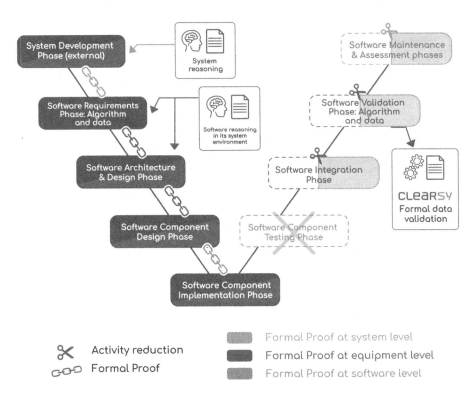

Fig. 1. Example of formal activities covering the V cycle.

System Validation. This is where the most errors are likely to be found when the different elements of a railway system are integrated. Because of the variety of elements involved and the complexity of their relationships, the use of formal methods at system level is less mature than the activities listed above. The large size and variety of models involved make modelling difficult to grasp for a human being [29] and model-checking impossible to complete once the model under consideration becomes significant [14,19,22,34]. Validation is then limited to small configurations or reduced scenarios [21]. Taking into account both continuous and discrete aspects [2], for describing physical laws and controller timed actions, is constrained at the moment to toy models and lacks proof tools able to handle resulting heterogeneous verification conditions. Modelling the safety reasoning rather than the structural and behavioural aspects of a system seems to overcome the constraints of size and complexity [10,31,32] at the cost of a greater effort to communicate with the architects of the system in order to find the reasons that led to its specification.

4   Software and Hardware Security Attacks

Railway systems are becoming vulnerable to cyber attack [6] due to the move away from bespoke stand-alone systems to open-platform, standardised equipment built using Commercial Off The Shelf (COTS) components, and increasing use of networked control and automation systems that can be accessed remotely via public and private networks. The connection of a safety-critical component to any network is not secure as this component has been designed to resist to "probabilistic failures", not to specifically crafted attacks that would timely target the existing vulnerabilities. In reaction, the Technical Specification CLC/TS 50701 'Railway applications - Cybersecurity' has been issued in 2021 to provide requirements and recommendations to handle cybersecurity in a unified way for the railway sector. This specification takes into consideration relevant safety related aspects (EN 50126) and takes inspiration from different sources (IEC 62443-3-3, CSM-RA), adapting them to the railway context. It covers numerous key topics such as railway system overview, cybersecurity during a railway application life cycle, risk assessment, security design, cybersecurity assurance and system acceptance, vulnerability management and security patch management.

Taking into account cybersecurity at equipment level requires to consider both logical and physical attacks.

Logical Attacks. They are certainly the most popular, following the multiplication of recent attacks against hospitals, websites and corporate computer networks. They allow to make computer systems non-responsive, to take control of them remotely, and to access sensitive data. Man-in-the-middle, eavesdropping are usual kind of attacks, requiring both technical knowledge (network architecture, communication protocol, programming, intrusion toolkit, vulnerabilities database) and social engineering to identify and exploit non-patched vulnerabilities. Some attacks may even target computer systems not connected to a computer network.

Physical Attacks. They refer to any type of offensive action that targets the physical components of a computer or network, such as the hardware or infrastructure. These types of attacks can be particularly difficult to defend against because they involve direct manipulation of the devices and systems that make up the network. They include tampering with or damaging equipment, reverse-engineering the device, injecting fault, performing side-channel attack[1].

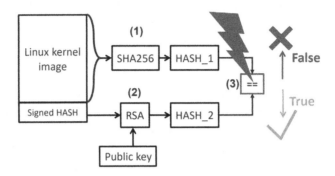

Fig. 2. Example of attack aimed at corrupting the result of the test with fault injection (power consumption analysis and clock glitch) and bypassing the Android Secure-Boot. In [12], 15 min are required to upload a malicious Linux kernel and take control of the device.

Railways connected equipment are potentially subject to both attacks, possibly in combination:

– *Logical attacks* are aimed at the communication between any equipment, installed on-board, on the tracks or in the technical rooms of stations, and supervision systems (SCADA). Topics of interest are logs exchanged, commands issued and received, and firmware updates. Accessing logs helps to better understand the behaviour of a device. With an attacker impersonating another device, valid commands can be issued to change the configuration or status of the equipment. Finally generating a valid firmware allows to fully reprogram the device and to implement any dangerous behaviour.

---

[1] It is a type of security exploit that aims to extract secret information from a system by analysing its physical characteristics, such as power consumption, electromagnetic emissions, or even the sound or vibration it produces, rather than by attempting to directly access the data stored on it. One of the most common forms of side-channel attacks is the power analysis attack, which relies on measuring the power consumed by a device as it performs cryptographic operations. By analysing the fluctuations in power consumption, an attacker can extract information about the secret key used in the encryption. Timing analysis is another popular side-channel attack which relies on measuring the time it takes a device to perform a specific operation, an attacker can extract information about the secret key and operations.

– *Physical attacks* are aimed either dumping the binary code of the firmware[2], uploading a malicious bootloader or firmware, degrading the service provided, or denying any action. The spectrum of attacks is very broad and constantly changing [33] as a reaction to the countermeasures put in place by the industry. A laser, an electromagnetic shock, X-rays, an extra and very short clock pulse (glitch), a supply current that is too low can all disrupt the behaviour of a processor or alter the content of the memory. Synchronising such disturbances (Fig. 2) can allow for example a firmware with an invalid signature to be successfully loaded by disturbing the result of the signature validity test [12].

None of the safety features implemented by EN 50128 and 50129-compliant safety computers protect against such attacks. In particular, the main integrity check is usually based on CRC that is not considered as a cryptographic primitive[3]. Messages received can only be checked well-formed, but not issued from a valid emitter.

Three principles need to be added to railways connected equipment:

– **confidentiality** (keeping data secure): ensures that sensitive information are accessed only by an authorised person and kept away from those not authorised to possess them;
– **integrity** (keeping data clean): ensures that information are in a format that is true and correct to its original purposes.
– **availability** (keeping data accessible): ensures that information and resources are available to those who need them.

Usually security design implements these three principles with public key cryptography and specific hardware to constitute a Root of Trust, a source that can always be trusted within a cryptographic system and is critical for PKI. Hardware could rely on a TPM[4], a HSM[5] or any Secure Enclave module. In addition, an isolated execution environment (a TEE, such as ARM TrustZone) provides security features such as isolated execution, integrity of applications executing with the TEE, and confidentiality of their assets.

The security standards do not impose any particular architecture, so the detailed design may vary depending on the hardware platform and associated security features, on the software architecture (bare-metal or OS-based application), and selected communication protocols. Demonstration of compliance with

---

[2] With reverse-engineering in mind for vulnerability analysis or with the idea of making copies.

[3] They are not robust to collision attacks, meaning that somebody can take a given CRC and easily find a second input that matches it.

[4] A TPM contains a hardware random number generator, facilities for the secure generation of cryptographic keys for limited uses, a generator of unforgeable hash key summary of a configuration, and a data encryptor/decryptor.

[5] A HSM is similar to a TPM. HSMs are focused on performance and key storage space, where as TPMs are only designed to keep a few values and a single key in memory and don't put much effort into performance.

security standards also depends: IEC 62443 covers the whole development cycle while Common Criteria-based CSPN[6] only requires a Security Target document, a user manual, and a third-party penetration testing.

Finally the embedding of cryptographic capabilities (algorithms, data storage) requires resources (computing, memory) that are not necessarily available on-board. Ciphering and deciphering, generating and managing keys[7], controlling correct protocol execution imply extra processing time that could prevent hard real-time compliance.

5   Formal Techniques for Security

Even if a secure system is not intended to be modified once certified (except for functional changes in the expected services or in the environment) whereas a safe system will have to evolve to take into account new threats, the formal methods apply in an similar way to both types of systems. However, the broad spectrum of attacks that have been (and will be) carried out makes it easier to formally demonstrate the safety of a system against known failures than to ensure its security against yet unknown vulnerabilities. A number of formal techniques are used to cover logical attacks.

Absence of Programming Errors. Formal development (à la B) and (assertion-based) verification techniques (see Sect. 3) are proven techniques that are frequently used in the development of software for SIL3 or SIL4 level systems. They allow to avoid programming errors and in particular, in a security context, buffer overflows or bad pointer management, sometimes for restricted use (pointer management in Windows device drivers [27]).

Security Policy Enforcement. The Common Criteria standard requires the production of a formal modelling of the security policy and the demonstration by mathematical proof that the specification of the product in charge of security enforces this policy. This evaluation is focused on the components that are directly involved in establishing and maintaining security. [7] exposes the modelling principles of a smart card Memory Protection Unit used to obtain an EAL6+ CC3.1 certificate[8].

Protocol Engineering. Using formal methods, the cryptographic protocols can be mathematically proven to provide a desired level of security, such as confidentiality, integrity, and authenticity. Tools such as ProVerif [8] are used for Protocol Engineering in order to prove secrecy and authenticity properties of

---

[6] Certification de Sécurité de Premier Niveau - https://www.ssi.gouv.fr/administration/produits-certifies/cspn/.

[7] A PKI has to implemented on the network. If not, security is degraded as it is only based on fixed pre-shared secrets on all equipment.

[8] See https://www.ssi.gouv.fr/administration/produits-certifies/cc/produits-certifies-cc to get access to the up-to-date list of certified products.

cryptographic protocols. The program ProVerif takes as input a description of a cryptographic protocol, and checks whether it satisfies secrecy, authenticity, or equivalence properties. Protocol analysis is considered with respect to an unbounded number of sessions and an unbounded message space. Moreover, the tool is capable of attack reconstruction: when a property cannot be proved, ProVerif tries to reconstruct an execution trace that falsifies the desired property. This kind of tool makes it possible to ensure the specification of a protocol and to determine the impact on security of disclosing one of the secrets implemented in the protocol (Fig. 3).

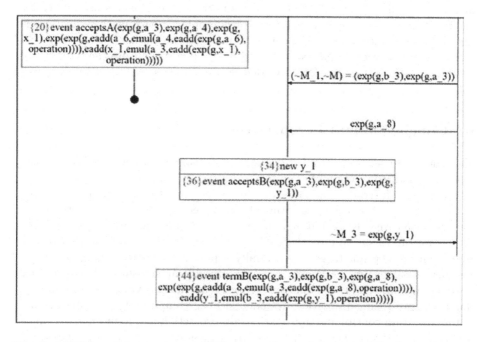

Fig. 3. MQV-based key exchange UKS protocol attack trace graph obtained with ProVerif.

Constant-Time Cryptography. The cryptographic constant-time (CCT) property is an effective counter-measure against practical side-channel attacks. It has been shown in practice that compilers do not always preserve this non-functional property and introduce vulnerabilities in otherwise secure programs. Formal methods may be used [4] to prove that a compiler is not subject to this issue: even though it transforms the control-flow and introduces memory accesses, it will neither remove counter-measures nor introduce sensitive information flows.

Inverted Test Redundant-Check Countermeasure. To counter fault injection based attacks, sensitive software use redundancy based countermeasure schemes. In particular, critical checks in the code are duplicated to ensure that an attacker cannot bypass such a check by flipping its result in order to get to a protected point[9] [28] exposes a source-codelevel verification technique of the correct implementation of such countermeasures, based on code instrumentation and deductive verification.

For physical and covert channel attacks, formal methods can be used a posteriori to show the effectiveness of a technical measure against a known attack, but they cannot provide definitive proof of its effectiveness against original attacks using new penetration vectors. Some technical measures used to verify the integrity of a processor's operation (by equipping it with markers, by encoding and redundantly storing the contents of certain memories) have recourse to techniques that were developed and used in the 1980s to ensure the integrity of the processing carried out (PSC - Coded Secure Processor[10], DIGISAFE protocol).

6 Conclusion and Perspectives

The safety and security of rail transport are nowadays closely linked due to the increasing interconnection of equipment and technical systems of various kinds. While good industrial practices have made it possible to build up a strong normative reference framework in terms of safety, security does not have the same degree of maturity. Repeated attacks on critical infrastructures (pipelines, hospitals, etc.) have shown that the security problem is global. Rail transport systems seem to be prime targets, potentially exposing the health or lives of a large number of passengers while offering a considerable attack surface[11] to (usually nation-state) attackers. [20] analysed recently threats and vulnerabilities of fundamental rail-road automation systems such as computer based interlocking, automatic train control and automatic train protection and found many vulnerabilities at all levels (incorrect protocol implementation, private keys embedded on distributed equipment, etc.). Such equipment subject to cyber attacks have to resist to reverse engineering, logical and physical attacks.

It appears that the formal techniques used to establish the safety of a railway system can be used to improve its security level. The combination of these analyses with physical penetration tests is successfully practised in the Common Criteria framework. However, given the wide variety and scalability of the attacks, the conclusions of formal analyses can only be ad hoc and partial. The

---

[9] Corresponding to a successful authentication or code integrity verification.

[10] https://www.atelierb.eu/wp-content/uploads/2021/03/Le-Rail-136-Methode-B.pdf.

[11] A major breakdown of Denmark's train network in October 2022 was the result of a malicious hacker attack on an IT subcontractor's software testing environment. The attack prompted subcontractor Supeo to shut down its servers, which in turn affected locomotive drivers' ability to operate the trains for several hours.

more intertwined combination of formal techniques used to model both safety and security seems to be the way forward. These are often used independently at different levels (specification, source code, binary, electronic circuit, silicon) and for different types of analysis (functional, temporal, dysfunctional). In any case, the consideration of safety and security requires very specialised knowledge and skills and it is perhaps this aspect that will limit the effective implementation of efficient technical means.

Acknowledgements. The work and results described in this article were partly funded by BPI-France (Banque Publique d'Investissement) as part of the project CASES (Calculateur Sûr et Sécuritaire) selected for the call "Stratégie Cyber 2021 - Développement de technologies innovantes critiques".

References

1. de Almeida Pereira, D.I., Deharbe, D., Perin, M., Bon, P.: B-specification of relay-based railway interlocking systems based on the propositional logic of the system state evolution. In: Collart-Dutilleul, S., Lecomte, T., Romanovsky, A. (eds.) RSS-Rail 2019. LNCS, vol. 11495, pp. 242–258. Springer, Cham (2019). https://doi.org/10.1007/978-3-030-18744-6_16

2. Banach, R.: Issues in automated urban train control: 'tackling' the rugby club problem. In: Butler, M., Raschke, A., Hoang, T.S., Reichl, K. (eds.) Abstract State Machines, Alloy, B, TLA, VDM, and Z, pp. 171–186. Springer, Cham (2018). https://doi.org/10.1007/978-3-319-91271-4_12

3. Baro, S.: A high availability vital computer for railway applications: architecture & safety principles. In: Embedded Real Time Software and Systems (ERTS2008), Toulouse, France, January 2008. https://hal.archives-ouvertes.fr/hal-02269811

4. Barthe, G., Grégoire, B., Laporte, V., Priya, S.: Structured leakage and applications to cryptographic constant-time and cost. In: Proceedings of the 2021 ACM SIGSAC Conference on Computer and Communications Security, CCS 2021, pp. 462–476. Association for Computing Machinery, New York, NY, USA (2021). https://doi.org/10.1145/3460120.3484761

5. Behm, P., Benoit, P., Faivre, A., Meynadier, J.-M.: Météor: a successful application of B in a large project. In: Wing, J.M., Woodcock, J., Davies, J. (eds.) FM 1999. LNCS, vol. 1708, pp. 369–387. Springer, Heidelberg (1999). https://doi.org/10.1007/3-540-48119-2_22

6. Bendovschi, A.: Cyber-attacks - trends, patterns and security countermeasures. Procedia Econ. Finance **28**, 24–31 (2015)

7. Benveniste, M.V.: On using B in the design of secure micro-controllers: an experience report. Electr. Notes Theor. Comput. Sci. **280**, 3–22 (2011)

8. Blanchet, B., Smyth, B., Cheval, V., Sylvestre, M.: ProVerif 2.04: automatic cryptographic protocol verifier, user manual and tutorial, November 2021

9. Burdy, L., Meynadier, J.M.: Experience on the use of a formal method in a railway company. IFAC Proc. Vol. **33**, 193–197 (2000)

10. Comptier, M., Leuschel, M., Mejia, L.F., Perez, J., Mutz, M.: Property-based modelling and validation of a CBTC zone controller in Event-B, pp. 202–212, January 2019

11. Falampin, J., Le-Dang, H., Leuschel, M., Mokrani, M., Plagge, D.: Improving railway data validation with ProB. In: Romanovsky, A., Thomas, M. (eds.) Industrial Deployment of System Engineering Methods, pp. 27–43. Springer, Cham (2013). https://doi.org/10.1007/978-3-642-33170-1_4

12. Fanjas, C., Gaine, C., Driss Aboulkassimi, D., Pontié, S., Potin, O.: Combined fault injection and real-time side-channel analysis for android secure-boot bypassing, November 2022

13. Fantechi, A.: The role of formal methods in software development for railway applications (2012)

14. Fantechi, A., Gnesi, S., Haxthausen, A.: Formal methods for distributed computing in future railway systems, pp. 389–392, October 2020

15. Ferrari, A., et al.: Survey on formal methods and tools in railways: the ASTRail approach. In: International Conference on Reliability, Safety, and Security of Railway Systems (2019)

16. Ferrari, A., et al.: Survey on formal methods and tools in railways: the ASTRail approach. In: Collart-Dutilleul, Simon, Lecomte, Thierry, Romanovsky, Alexander (eds.) RSSRail 2019. LNCS, vol. 11495, pp. 226–241. Springer, Cham (2019). https://doi.org/10.1007/978-3-030-18744-6_15

17. Ferrari, A., Magnani, G., Grasso, D., Fantechi, A.: Model checking interlocking control tables. In: Schnieder, E., Tarnai, G. (eds.) FORMS/FORMAT 2010, pp. 107–115. Springer, Heidelberg (2011). https://doi.org/10.1007/978-3-642-14261-1_11

18. Forin, P.: Vital coded microprocessor principles and application for various transit systems. IFAC Proc. Volumes **23**(2), 79–84 (1990). IFAC/IFIP/IFORS Symposium on Control, Computers, Communications in Transportation, Paris, France, 19–21 September. http://www.sciencedirect.com/science/article/pii/S1474667017526531

19. Geisler, S., Haxthausen, A.: Stepwise development and model checking of a distributed interlocking system using raise. Formal Aspects Comput. (2020)

20. Gordeychik, S., Timorin, A.: The great train cyber robbery, December 2015

21. Halchin, A., Feliachi, A., Singh, N.K., Aït-Ameur, Y., Ordioni, J.: B-PERFect - applying the PERF approach to B based system developments. In: International Conference Reliability, Safety, and Security of Railway Systems. Modelling, Analysis, Verification, and Certification (RSSRail 2017), vol. 10598, pp. 160–172, Pristoia, Italy, November 2017. https://hal.archives-ouvertes.fr/hal-02451007

22. Hansen, D., et al.: Validation and real-life demonstration of ETCS hybrid level 3 principles using a formal B model. Int. J. Softw. Tools Technol. Transfer **22**, 315–332 (2020)

23. Hansen, D., Schneider, D., Leuschel, M.: Using B and ProB for data validation projects. In: Butler, M., Schewe, K.-D., Mashkoor, A., Biro, M. (eds.) ABZ 2016. LNCS, vol. 9675, pp. 167–182. Springer, Cham (2016). https://doi.org/10.1007/978-3-319-33600-8_10

24. Lecomte, T.: Safe and reliable metro platform screen doors control/command systems. In: Cuellar, J., Maibaum, T., Sere, K. (eds.) FM 2008. LNCS, vol. 5014, pp. 430–434. Springer, Heidelberg (2008). https://doi.org/10.1007/978-3-540-68237-0_32

25. Lecomte, T.: Applying a formal method in industry: a 15-year trajectory. In: Alpuente, M., Cook, B., Joubert, C. (eds.) FMICS 2009. LNCS, vol. 5825, pp. 26–34. Springer, Heidelberg (2009). https://doi.org/10.1007/978-3-642-04570-7_3

26. Lecomte, T., Burdy, L., Leuschel, M.: Formally checking large data sets in the railways. CoRR abs/1210.6815 (2012)

27. Leino, K.R.M.: Developing verified programs with Dafny. In: Proceedings of the 2012 ACM Conference on High Integrity Language Technology, HILT 2012, pp. 9–10. Association for Computing Machinery, New York, NY, USA (2012). https://doi.org/10.1145/2402676.2402682

28. Martin, T., Kosmatov, N., Prevosto, V.: Verifying redundant-check based counter-measures: a case study, pp. 1849–1852, April 2022

29. Metayer, C., Clabaut, M.: DIR 41 case study. In: Börger, E., Butler, M., Bowen, J.P., Boca, P. (eds.) ABZ 2008. LNCS, vol. 5238, pp. 357–357. Springer, Heidelberg (2008). https://doi.org/10.1007/978-3-540-87603-8_44

30. Peleska, J., Krafczyk, N., Haxthausen, A.E., Pinger, R.: Efficient data validation for geographical interlocking systems. In: Collart-Dutilleul, S., Lecomte, T., Romanovsky, A. (eds.) RSSRail 2019. LNCS, vol. 11495, pp. 142–158. Springer, Cham (2019). https://doi.org/10.1007/978-3-030-18744-6_9

31. Sabatier, D.: Using formal proof and B method at system level for industrial projects. In: Lecomte, T., Pinger, R., Romanovsky, A. (eds.) RSSRail 2016. LNCS, vol. 9707, pp. 20–31. Springer, Cham (2016). https://doi.org/10.1007/978-3-319-33951-1_2

32. Sabatier, D., Burdy, L., Requet, A., Guéry, J.: Formal proofs for the NYCT line 7 (Flushing) modernization project. In: Derrick, J., et al. (eds.) ABZ 2012. LNCS, vol. 7316, pp. 369–372. Springer, Heidelberg (2012). https://doi.org/10.1007/978-3-642-30885-7_34

33. Shepherd, C., et al.: Physical fault injection and side-channel attacks on mobile devices: a comprehensive analysis. Comput. Secur. 111, 102471 (2021)

34. Stankaitis, P., Iliasov, A.: Theories, techniques and tools for engineering heterogeneous railway networks, In: Fantechi, A., Lecomte, T., Romanovsky, A. (eds.) Reliability, Safety, and Security of Railway Systems. Modelling, Analysis, Verification, and Certification, RSSRail 2017. LNCS, vol. 10598, pp. 241–250. Springer, Cham (2017). https://doi.org/10.1007/978-3-319-68499-4_16

35. Zheng, S., Cao, Y., Zhang, Y., Jing, H., Hu, H.: Design and verification of general train control system's safety computer 38, 128–134+145 (2014)

Intelligent Systems and Cyber-Physical Systems

Time for Traffic Manoeuvres

Christopher Bischopink$^{(\boxtimes)}$ and Ernst-Rüdiger Olderog

Carl von Ossietzky University Oldenburg, Oldenburg, Germany
{bischopink,olderog}@informatik.uni-oldenburg.de

Abstract. The use of driving assistance systems up to the level of autonomous cars asks for methods showing that cars equipped with such systems behave safely. In previous work, we realised that spatial reasoning is a key to prove collision freedom. Our method was based on a dedicated Multi-lane Spatial Logic (MLSL) for traffic on motorways [10].

In this paper, we extend this approach by taking into account the plans of cars in the near future up to a certain time bound. We employ runtime monitoring of car traffic on motorways using extended State Clock automata for State Clock Logic (SCL) as defined in [17]. The extensions are that the SC automata use MLSL formulae as propositional symbols as in Timed MLSL [2] and communication primitives as in Timed Automata of UPPAAL. The idea is that a car can perform a traffic manoeuvre like a lane change only if it successfully communicates with all surrounding cars that check their internal extended SC automata for compliance with their safety and time constraints in the near future.

Keywords: Multi-lane Spatial Logic · State Clock Automata · Bounded Runtime Enforcement

1 Introduction

With Jan Peleska we share the interest in safe traffic systems. The development and verification of railway control systems has been one of the major research topics of Jan Peleska [7,8,16]. Of traffic systems, trains have less freedom to move than cars and planes. This provides new challenges for the latter ones. Since some time our group in Oldenburg is working on formal specification methods for the safety of car traffic. In [10], we realised that safety in the sense of collision freedom is a spatial property and introduced an abstract model of traffic on multi-lane motorways and a dedicated logic called Multi-lane Spatial Logic (MLSL) that is well-suited to express safety-related properties of cars performing traffic manoeuvres. This approach has been extended to more demanding topologies of traffic like country roads [9] and intersections in urban traffic [19].

An overview of various results on MLSL is presented in [15]. A limiting factor has been the emphasis on safety. Currently, we are extending our approach to include timed liveness in the sense that we would like to show that certain traffic manoeuvres like a lane change can be performed within given time bounds. In [2], we introduced a timed version of MLSL called TMLSL that is able to specify such properties. This logic combines State Clock Logic (SCL) [17] with MLSL.

A. E. Haxthausen et al. (Eds.): Peleska Festschrift 2023, LNCS 14165, pp. 163–179, 2023.
https://doi.org/10.1007/978-3-031-40132-9_11

In this paper, we employ the concept of *runtime enforcement*. According to Y. Falconer, 'runtime enforcement is a techniques dedicated to ensure that a run of a system satisfies a given desired property' (see Definition 4 in [4]). We instantiate this concept by equipping each car with a monitor for TMLSL properties that it wishes to achieve. When some other car intends to perform a traffic manoeuvre, this will be communicated to its neighbouring cars asking for permission. These cars employ their monitors to check it for compliance with their safety and time constraints in the near future. If this is not the case, permission will be denied.

The notion of enforcing properties at runtime goes back to F.B. Schneider, who introduced the notion of security automata to enforce security policies [18]. The idea of enforcing properties is also pursued by Jan Peleska who studies safety supervisors for robotic and autonomous systems [6].

The remainder of this paper is structured as follows. Section 2 recalls the concepts of Multi-lane Spatial Logic with scopes, State Clock Logic as well as State Clock Automata with some basic properties, and Timed Multi-lane Spatial Logic. Section 3 illustrates our approach by an example and Sect. 4 provides the formalisation. Section 5 presents a conclusion.

Dedication. Ernst-Rüdiger Olderog dedicates this paper to Jan Peleska, who has the talent of understanding real-world applications in the area of distributed, real-time systems and being able to translate their challenges into problems in formal methods so that mathematically oriented researchers can contribute to their solutions. During the years 1995–98 this happened in the context of the project UniForM Workbench, where Jan Peleska and Bernd Krieg-Brückner of the University of Bremen collaborated with the second author in Oldenburg and Alexander Baer of the company Elpro LET in Berlin [11]. The application area was railway control for trams driving in Berlin. The engineers at Elpro used programming languages dedicated for Programmable Logic Controllers (PLCs). My group learned the essence of PLCs and was able to built an abstract formal model called PLC automata with formal semantics amenable for real-time model checking [3].

2   Preliminaries

2.1   Multi-lane Spatial Logic with Scopes

Multi-lane Spatial Logic (MLSL) was introduced in [10] to express spatial properties of cars driving along a multi-lane motorway. One can distinguish between spaces that a car has *reserved* for its exclusive use and spaces, called *claims*, that it wishes to reserve next in order to prepare for a lane change. Formulae of that logic are evaluated on an abstract model of the motorway built upon the notion of a *traffic snapshot*, which gives a static picture of the motorway. To model car dynamics, transitions are introduced that describe the evolution of a traffic snapshot. MLSL is well suited to express safety properties of car traffic like collision freedom, meaning the disjointness of reserved spaces. For full MLSL the satisfaction problem is undecidable [13]. To obtain decidability results, a variant of MLSL with *scopes* (MLSLS) has been introduced in [5]. A scope limits the cars to be considered to a finite set.

Abstract Model. In our model of multi-lane motorway traffic, cars have unique identifiers drawn from an infinite set $\mathbb{I} = \{A, B, \ldots\}$, the road is considered infinite in length, with positions represented by real numbers in $\mathbb{R}$, and finite in width, with lanes represented by a finite set $\mathbb{L} = \{0, \ldots, N\}$ of natural numbers. On a motorway, all traffic proceeds in one direction, with increasing position values, in pictures shown from left to right.

A *traffic snapshot* describes where currently cars are positioned on the road and what their speed and acceleration is. The speed determines how much space a car reserves or claims because the length of a reservation or claim is taken as the size of the car plus its (speed-dependent) braking distance. Formally, a traffic snapshot is a tuple $TS = (res, clm, pos, spd, acc)$ with functions

- $res/clm : \mathbb{I} \to \mathcal{P}(\mathbb{L})$, stating the lanes each car reserves/claims, and
- $pos/spd/acc : \mathbb{I} \to \mathbb{R}$, stating the position/speed/acceleration of each car.

Figure 1 shows the graphical representation of three traffic snapshots, where each of them has two lanes and two cars, both of them in lane one, with car A behind car B. The pentagon in front of the rectangle depicts the braking distance of the car. In the second and third traffic snapshot, car A is preparing for a lane change: it has set its turn signal to lane two, which is represented as a claim, shown as a dashed copy of its reserved space on lane one, to that lane.

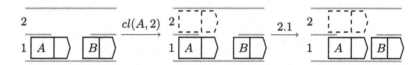

Fig. 1. A transition sequence including the graphical representation of three traffic snapshots and two transitions.

Evolution. While a traffic snapshot describes the static situation at one point in time, this situation may evolve when the cars in the traffic snapshot execute actions α, formalised by *transitions* between traffic snapshots: $TS \xrightarrow{\alpha} TS'$. We consider the following actions α for a car C: claiming a lane n ($\alpha = \mathsf{c}(C, n)$), withdrawing a claim ($\alpha = \mathsf{wd}\ \mathsf{c}(C)$), reserving a formerly claimed lane ($\alpha = \mathsf{r}(C)$), withdrawing all reservations except the one on lane n ($\alpha = \mathsf{wd}\ \mathsf{r}(C, n)$), and setting its acceleration to some value a ($\alpha = \mathsf{acc}(C, a)$). We usually assume that there is a bound on the acceleration values of the cars, without mentioning concrete values here. Additionally, the passing of t time units ($\alpha = t$) is possible. For a formal definition see [10]. We consider each labelled arrow $\xrightarrow{\alpha}$ as a relation on traffic snapshots. These relations can be combined by *relational composition*.

For example, $\xrightarrow{t} \circ \xrightarrow{\text{acc}(C,a)}$ expresses that first a delay of time t occurs and then the acceleration of car C is set to a.

By the set Act of *MLSL actions* we mean the transitions above, without the one where time passes. Figure 1 illustrates the evolution of a traffic snapshot along a transition sequence $(\langle \text{cl}(A, 2), 2.1 \rangle)$, where car A claims lane 2 and afterwards 2.1 time units pass, during which the two cars move along the lanes with their speeds and accelerations. We will consider timed words over Act:

Definition 1 (Timed words over MLSL actions). *A* timed word *or* timed sequence *over MLSL actions is an infinite or finite sequence* $\omega = \langle (\alpha_1, t_1), (\alpha_2, t_2), \ldots \rangle$ *with* $\alpha_i \in Act$ *and* $\langle t_1, t_2, \ldots \rangle$ *forming a real-time sequence, that is, a monotonically increasing sequence of time stamps.*

Although the road itself is considered as infinite, at each moment only a finite part of it is relevant for each car E, called its *view*. Formally, a view is a tuple $V = (L, X, E)$, with L being the set of lanes visible to the view's owner E, and X the finite extension (length of the road) visible to E. The view is also entering the definition of the semantics of MLSLS.

Spatial Logic. We consider MLSLS, the variant of the Multi-lane Spatial Logic MLSL *with scopes* proposed in [5]. It restricts quantification and free spaces in formulae to range over a finite set of car identifiers. This is done by prefixing a formula with a *scope*, a finite subset $cs \subseteq CVar$ of car variables. Given $c, \gamma, \gamma' \in CVar$, $k \in \mathbb{R}$ and finite $cs \subseteq CVar$, the syntax of MLSLS formulae φ is as follows:

$$\varphi ::= true \mid \gamma = \gamma' \mid free \mid re(\gamma) \mid cl(\gamma) \mid l = k \qquad \text{(atoms)}$$

$$\mid \neg\varphi_1 \mid \varphi_1 \wedge \varphi_2 \mid \exists c \colon \varphi_1 \qquad \text{(first-order logic)}$$

$$\mid \varphi_1 \frown \varphi_2 \mid \frac{\varphi_2}{\varphi_1} \mid cs \colon \varphi_1 \qquad \text{(chop and scope)}$$

Atomic formulae are *true*, checks for equality of two car variables, *free* denoting free space on a lane, $re(\gamma)$ and $cl(\gamma)$ denoting a reservation and a claim of a car γ, respectively, and a check for equality of the length of a segment against some value k. Formulae can be combined by Boolean operations, quantification over car variables, and two *chop* operators. The chop $\varphi_1 \frown \varphi_2$ expresses that the view can be *split horizontally* into a first part where φ_1 holds and a second part where φ_2 holds. The chop $\frac{\varphi_2}{\varphi_1}$ expresses that the view can be *split vertically* into a lower part where φ_1 holds and an upper part where φ_2 holds. Also, the evaluation of formulae can be restricted to a certain scope cs of cars. We denote the set of all MLSLS formulae by Φ_{MLSLS}.

Formulae are called *well-scoped* if every formula containing the atom *free* or existential quantification has a scope and every scoped formula is followed by an existential quantification or the atom *free*. For the moment, we require that the scope of all formulae is the same.

The *semantics* of a formula is evaluated in a model consisting of a traffic snapshot TS, a scope CS, the car's view V, and a valuation ν assigning values to variables. Instead of $CS, TS, V, \nu \vDash \varphi$ we usually write $TS \vDash \varphi$ and require a sufficiently large view V and scope CS and a proper valuation ν. For a detailed, formal semantics see [5].

An important abbreviation is the two-dimensional modality *somewhere* defined by $\langle \varphi \rangle \equiv true \frown \begin{pmatrix} true \\ \varphi \\ true \end{pmatrix} \frown true$, expressing that in some space within the considered view, φ holds. For example, the car *ego* has a *potential collision* if somewhere its claim overlaps with the reservation or claim of another car, formally:

$$pc(ego) \equiv \exists c : c \neq ego \wedge \langle cl(ego) \wedge (re(c) \vee cl(c)) \rangle .$$

The formula $\left\langle \begin{array}{c} cl(A) \frown free \\ re(A) \frown free \frown re(B) \end{array} \right\rangle$ specifies that car A has a claim on the lane next to its reservation, there is free space in front of both, and car B is in front of A. On the second traffic snapshot depicted in Fig. 1, this formula holds.

2.2   State Clock Logic

State Clock Logic (SCL) has been introduced in [17] to specify real-time properties. It comes with a corresponding operational model called state-clock automata (see Sect. 2.3). Unlike timed automata [1], they are complementable so that language inclusion is decidable. The syntax of SCL formulae ψ is as follows:

$$\psi ::= p \mid \neg \psi \mid \psi_1 \vee \psi_2 \mid \psi_1 \mathcal{U} \psi_2 \mid \psi_1 \mathcal{S} \psi_2 \mid \rhd_{\sim c} \psi \mid \psi \lhd_{\sim c},$$

where $\sim \in \{<, \leq, =, \geq, >\}$. Here p ranges over a set $\mathcal{P}_0$ of propositional symbols, which are used to describe the phases. Apart from Boolean combinations and the temporal operators $\mathcal{U}$ (until) and $\mathcal{S}$ (since), there are two real-time operators: the *state prophecy operator* $\rhd$ and the *state history operator* $\lhd$. The formula $\rhd_{\sim c} \psi$ describes that the time until ψ holds for the next time must satisfy the constraint $\sim c$, and $\psi \lhd_{\sim c}$ handles the analogous case for the past. We use also some abbreviations, for example $\rhd_{[l,r)} \psi$ stands for $\rhd_{\geq l} \psi \wedge \rhd_{<r} \psi$.

A *timed sequence of states* is an infinite sequence $m = \langle (s_0, I_0), (s_1, I_1), \ldots \rangle$, where $s_i \subseteq \mathcal{P}_0$ and I_i is a real–valued non–empty interval. It is required that any two neighbouring intervals are adjacent and there is no Zeno behaviour, i.e., that time progresses beyond any bounds. Each pair (s_i, I_i) is considered as a *state*.

Formulae of SCL are evaluated on timed sequences of states. The semantics of Boolean operators and $\mathcal{U}$ and $\mathcal{S}$ is as expected. The real-time operators $\rhd_{\sim c} \psi$ ($\psi \lhd_{\sim c}$) are true when the time until (since) ψ holds (held) for the next (last) time complies to $\sim c$. For $\rhd_{\sim c} \psi$, this means $t_j - t_i \vDash \sim c$, with t_j being the left border of the interval of the state where ψ holds for the next time and t_i the time point $\rhd_{\sim c} \psi$ is evaluated at. For a detailed, formal definition of the semantics, we refer to [17]. There it is defined when an SCL formula φ holds in a timed sequence of states m at position i and at time $t \in I_i$, abbreviated $(m, i, t) \vDash \varphi$. Further on, m is a *model* of φ, abbreviated $m \vDash \varphi$, iff $(m, 0, 0) \vDash \varphi$.

2.3 SC Automata

In [17], a corresponding model of automata that accepts timed sequences of states, called *State Clock automata (SC automata)*, is defined. An *SC automaton* $\mathcal{A} = (\mathcal{P}, C_{\mathcal{P}}, L, L_0, E, \mathcal{L}, \Delta, \mathcal{F})$ consists of a finite set $\mathcal{P} \subseteq \mathcal{P}_0$ of propositions, a finite set $C_{\mathcal{P}}$ of clocks, with two clocks for each proposition p, a *history clock* x_p and a *prophecy clock* y_p, a finite set L of locations with a non-empty set $L_0 \subseteq L$ of start locations, a set $E \subseteq L \times L$ of edges, a proposition labelling function $\mathcal{L} : L \to 2^{\mathcal{P}}$ representing for each location l the set of propositions that are true in l, a constraint labelling function $\Delta : L \to 2^{\mathbb{C}}$, where $\mathbb{C}$ is the a set of time constraints on the clocks in $C_{\mathcal{P}}$, and a family $\mathcal{F}$ of Büchi acceptance sets $F_i \subseteq L$.

In [17], the notion of a *run* of $\mathcal{A}$ *accepting* a timed sequence of states m is defined. In particular, one location of each of the Büchi acceptance sets F_i must be visited infinitely often, and the timing constraints on the clocks of each visited location must be respected. The idea of the clocks is that x_p records the time since p held the last time, whereas y_p records the time until p holds for the next time. The language $L(\mathcal{A})$ is a set of timed sequences of states accepted by $\mathcal{A}$. A main result of [17] is that for each SCL formula φ an SC automata $\mathcal{A}_\varphi$ can be constructed such that a timed sequence of states is a model of φ iff it is in $L(\mathcal{A}_\varphi)$.

We extend SC automata so that other automata can interact with them, allowing them to make decisions which actions to execute based on the state an SC automaton is in. For this purpose, we enable SC automata to *communicate* with each other by (a) broadcast communication on the edges of E, (b) evaluating guards, and (c) simple operations regarding lists and MLSL actions.

We do not introduce all of these concepts formally, but would like to give intuitions for each of them. For the broadcast communication (a) to occur on an edge, we can chose from two set of communication actions, input actions *In* and output actions *Out*. The latter one describes sending data $\overrightarrow{c}$ over a communication channel *com*, denoted by $com!\overrightarrow{c}$. A communication from *In* "listens" on a communication channel, say *com*, and synchronises when data $\overrightarrow{c}$ received via this channel satisfies its communication guard φ_c, denoted by $com?\overrightarrow{c} : \varphi_c$. In addition to communication guards, "normal" guards (b) can be used to restrict the usage of a transition. When taken, transitions can execute (c) certain actions, for which we allow MLSL actions and operations on lists. These concepts are as in timed automata of UPPAAL [12] and *Automotive-Controlling Timed Automata* [19], to which we refer for formal definitions.

Definition 2 (Communicating State Clock automata). *A communicating SC automaton is a tuple* $\mathcal{A} = (\mathcal{P}, C_{\mathcal{P}}, L, L_0, E', \mathcal{L}, \Delta, \mathcal{F})$, *where all components are the same as stated above, except for the set of edges* $E' = E \cup E_c$ *with* $E_c \subseteq L \times \varphi \times In/Out \times Act' \times L$, *where* Act' *is the set of MLSL actions* Act *plus the previously mentioned operations on lists.*

For an example of a communicating SC automaton see Fig. 6 in Sect. 4. The semantics of these automata and networks of them is as expected, it accepts runs that visit a location from each accepting set for each of the automata in the network infinitely often. In doing so, guards, communication and actions on communication edges need to be respected. In particular, communication edges with *Out* communication synchronise with each enabled communication edge with *In* communication over the same channel where all guards are satisfied. Also, edges with *In* communication cannot be taken if there is no corresponding *Out* communication. We denote a network of two communicating SC automata $\mathcal{A}$ and $\mathcal{B}$ as $\mathcal{A} \parallel \mathcal{B}$.

In this paper, we use SC automata as monitors of *finite* prefixes of their runs. After such a prefix, the values of the prophecy clocks can be unknown, and thus the monitor can be in several possible locations. We compute the set of reachable locations of an SC automaton $\mathcal{A} = (\mathcal{P}, C_{\mathcal{P}}, L, L_0, E, \mathcal{L}, \Delta, \mathcal{F})$.

Definition 3 (Reachable locations after a prefix). *For a prefix* $m = (s_0, I_0), \ldots, (s_n, I_n)$ *of a timed sequence of states of a run of* $\mathcal{A}$, *the set* $\mathcal{A}[m\rangle$ *of reachable locations after* m *is defined inductively:*

- *If* $|m| = 1$, $\mathcal{A}[m\rangle = \{l \mid l \in L_0 \wedge \mathcal{L}(l) = s_0 \wedge m \vDash \Delta_h(l)\}$
- *If* $|m| > 1$, $\mathcal{A}[m\rangle = \{l' \mid \exists l : l \in \mathcal{A}[m^-)\rangle \wedge (l, l') \in E \wedge m \vDash \Delta_h(l')\}$,

where $\Delta_h(l)$ *denotes the part of* $\Delta(l)$ *constraining the history clocks and, intuitively,* $m \vDash \Delta_h(l)$ *iff for each history clock* x_{φ_i} *the time since* φ_i *held for the last time satisfies the timing constraint for this clock, and* m^- *is* m *without the last state* (s_n, I_n),

Later we need the notion of "bad" locations. These are the locations from which it is impossible to find a suffix that leads to an accepting infinite run.

Definition 4 (Bad locations). *The set of* bad locations *of* $\mathcal{A}$ *is defined as* $\{s \in L \mid \exists F_i \in \mathcal{F} \; \forall f \in F_i : (s, f) \notin E^*\}$.

Lemma 1 (Extensions to timed sequences of states). *For a finite prefix* m *of a timed sequence of states of a run of* $\mathcal{A}$, *where* $\forall l \in \mathcal{A}[m\rangle : l \in$ bad, *there does not exist a continuation* m' *with* $m.m' \in L(\mathcal{A})$. *For a finite prefix* n, *where* $\exists l \in \mathcal{A}[n\rangle : l \notin$ bad, *there exists at least one continuation* n' *with* $n.n' \in L(\mathcal{A})$.

Proof. This follows immediately from Definition 3 and Definition 4. □

2.4   Timed Multi-lane Spatial Logic

In [2], we introduced Timed Multi-lane Spatial Logic (TMLSL) as a combination of SCL and MLSLS, where the uninterpreted propositions p of SCL are instantiated by MLSLS formulae $p \in \Phi_{MLSLS}$. This way MLSLS formulae express the static properties of traffic snapshots whereas the temporal and real-time operators of SCL enable us to express properties of the evolution of traffic snapshots.

For infinite sequences and the "strong" semantics, an infinite sequence of actions ω satisfies a formula φ iff it visits a location from each Büchi set infinitely often. We denote this as $TS, \omega \vDash \varphi$. In what follows, however, we focus on finite sequences. The reason is that we require the cars to plan ahead up to a given time bound only. Intuitively, a finite sequence of actions w and a traffic snapshot TS satisfy a formula if "nothing bad happened yet" $(TS, w \not\models \neg\varphi)$, sometimes called weak semantics. More formally, we require that the evolution of TS along w leads to a timed sequence of states m whose prefix up to the time bound t satisfies the TMLSL formula φ. We denote this as $TS, w \models_t \varphi$. We elaborate more on the connection between timed sequences of actions and timed sequences of states in Sect. 4.

3   Example

We illustrate our approach of collectively finding "good" actions for the cars to take. Consider three cars, A, B and E, with reservations, positions and speeds as shown in Fig. 2. The accelerations are assumed to be 0. Suppose that (1) the cars A and B do not change their behaviour by executing any actions, only time passes, (2) car E is required to change lanes soon, it needs to have two neighbouring reservations within 8 time units, and (3) the size of each car including its braking distance is 5.

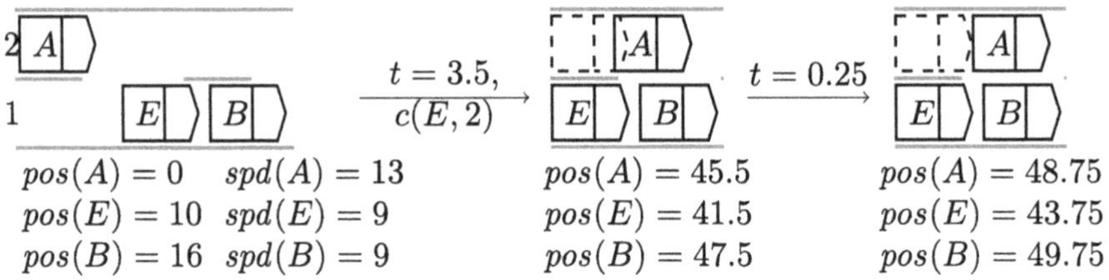

$pos(A) = 0 \quad spd(A) = 13$
$pos(E) = 10 \quad spd(E) = 9$
$pos(B) = 16 \quad spd(B) = 9$

$pos(A) = 45.5$
$pos(E) = 41.5$
$pos(B) = 47.5$

$pos(A) = 48.75$
$pos(E) = 43.75$
$pos(B) = 49.75$

Fig. 2. Prefix of the accepted sequence of actions w_2, where car E announces a claim on lane 2 at $t = 3.5$, with a potential collision that is resolved after 0.25 time units.

In this example, cars are allowed to change lanes if the claim of a car is stable for at least 4 time units and no potential collision was detected during that time, expressed by the TMLSL formula $\varphi_1 = (\langle pc(E) \rangle \vee \neg \langle cl(E) \rangle) \vartriangleleft_{\geq 4} \rightarrow \begin{pmatrix} re(E) \\ re(E) \end{pmatrix}$. Another formula that we want the cars to respect is $\varphi_2 = \langle pc(ego) \rangle \rightarrow \vartriangleright_{[0,2)} \neg \langle pc(ego) \rangle$. This formula means that an intersection of a car's claim and another car's reservation can take place, but needs to be resolved within 2 time units. The cars use monitors to represent the satisfaction of these formulae. An excerpt of the monitor representing formula φ_2 is shown in Fig. 3.

Car E now wants to change lanes, therefore it first announces the actions it wants to execute for this purpose, and then waits for answers from the other cars. To this end, each location of each monitor is equipped with an extra transition. These transitions check whether the announced behaviour leads to a "bad" location. In case of the monitor from Fig. 3, a bad location (and the ones that can be reached from there on) would be the ones coloured red, as in this case we arrived here with a potential collision and are not going to resolve it within 2 time units. A visualisation of the transitions that decide whether the announced actions are allowed is depicted in Fig. 5 of Sect. 4.

We now give two examples of timed sequences of MLSL actions that car E can announce. The first one is $\omega_1 = \langle (c(E,2), 1.25), (r(E), 6) \rangle$ and the second one is $\omega_2 = \langle (c(E,2), 3.5), (r(E), 8) \rangle$.

The first sequence is denied by car A. Assuming that its monitor (Fig. 3) is in location l_1, the announced action $c(E,2)$ at time $t = 1.25$ leads to an immediate potential collision (overlap starting in position 21.25). It would take 2.5 time units to resolve this, as we assumed that car A and B cannot change their acceleration and car E did not announce an acceleration change. Therefore the negotiating transition of the monitor computes that it would make it to the bad location l_5 with this sequence and thus the sequence is rejected.

The second sequence is allowed by car A. Assuming that the monitor is again in location l_1, the announced action $c(E,2)$ at time $t = 3.5$ leads again to an immediate potential collision. However, it would only take 0.25 time units until the potential collision is resolved. The monitor therefore computes that it would reach location l_4. Assuming that the second announced action $r(E)$ at time $t = 8$ also does not lead to a bad state, car A allows the actions and thus car E executes them. The part of the sequence ω_2 where the potential collision occurs and is resolved is shown in Fig. 2.

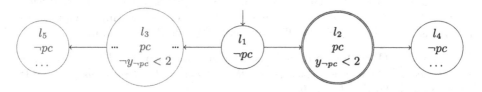

Fig. 3. Excerpt of the monitor for property φ_2 with the prophecy clock $y_{\neg pc}$. The red locations are bad ones because a path through these locations does not resolve a potential collision fast enough and thus cannot be accepting. (Color figure online)

4   Formalisation

We now formalise our approach of finding actions for the cars to take in a distributed manner such that these actions respect the cars' specification up to some time bound t. The idea is to utilise the monitors representing the satisfaction of the cars' specifications for this purpose. The monitors cooperate with the cars' controllers in a way that they first check whether the announced actions are going to violate its car's specification within the next t time units. If so, the announced actions are denied, and allowed otherwise.

Let us reconsider two terms introduced in Sect. 2: *timed sequences of states* and *timed sequences or words over MLSL actions*. The first one stems from

SC automata and is a sequence of propositions valid during intervals and is the semantic basis for SCL and TMLSL formulae. The second one stems from MLSL and describes what actions cars execute at which time points. Applying the actions to a traffic snapshot can change the propositions valid on it. Figure 4 illustrates the connection between these two concepts. Several sequences of states $\langle (s_0, I_0), \ldots, (s_n, I_n) \rangle$ hold when applying $\omega = \langle (\alpha_0, t_0), \ldots, (\alpha_{n-1}, t_{n-1}) \rangle$ to TS. We consider here a timed sequence of states $m(TS, \omega)$ that is complete and consistent, only using the MLSLS formulae as propositions that φ is built from.

$$TS_0 \xrightarrow{(\alpha_0, t_0)} TS_1 \xrightarrow{(\alpha_1, t_1)} TS_2 \xrightarrow{(\alpha_2, t_2)} \cdots \xrightarrow{(\alpha_{n-1}, t_{n-1})} TS_n$$

$$\begin{array}{cccc} \pi & \pi & \pi & \uparrow \\ s_0 & s_1 & s_2 & t \end{array}$$

Fig. 4. Illustration of the different sequences used in our approach. The pairs (α_i, t_i) form the timed sequence of actions that the cars want to find such that the traffic snapshot TS_0 evolves in a way that it successively satisfies the states of $m = (s_0, I_0), \ldots, (s_n, I_n)$, where t is the right end point of the interval I_n.

For all that follows, let a monitor $\mathcal{A}_\varphi = (\mathcal{P}, C_\mathcal{P}, L, L_0, E, \mathcal{L}, \Delta, \mathcal{F})$ representing the satisfaction of a TMLSL formula φ be given. This monitor $\mathcal{A}_\varphi$ is a normal (not communicating) SC automaton and some of its locations are labelled *bad*.

For $\mathcal{A}_\varphi$ we define now the set of reachable locations after a finite sequence of actions is applied to a given traffic snapshot TS_0, similar to Definition 3.

Definition 5 (Reachable locations after a timed word). *For a timed word of actions* $\omega = \langle (\alpha_1, t_1), \ldots, (\alpha_n, t_n) \rangle$, *the set* $locset(\mathcal{A}_\varphi, TS_0, \omega)$ *of reachable locations is defined inductively:*

- *If* $|\omega| = 0$, $locset(\mathcal{A}_\varphi, TS_0, \omega) = \{l \in L_0 \mid TS_0 \vDash \mathcal{L}(l)\}$.
- *If* $|\omega| \geq 1$, $locset(\mathcal{A}_\varphi, TS_0, \omega) = \{l' \mid l \in locset(\mathcal{A}_\varphi, TS_{n-1}, \omega^-) \wedge (l, l') \in E \wedge TS_{n-1} \xrightarrow{t_n - t_{n-1}} \circ \xrightarrow{\alpha_n} TS_n \wedge m(TS_0, \omega) \vDash \Delta_h(l') \wedge TS_n \vDash \mathcal{L}(l)\}$,

where $\circ$ *denotes relational composition,* $\Delta_h(l)$ *again denotes the constraints of* $\Delta(l)$ *over history variables, and* ω^- *is* ω *without the last pair* (α_n, t_n).

Later we consider runs that start from a set of locations L_0' that may be different from the initial one, in particular when L_0' is reached during a previous evolution along some timed word. We write $\mathcal{A}_{\varphi, L_0'}$ if the set of initial locations L_0 of $\mathcal{A}_\varphi$ is replaced by L_0'.

One could assume that there is a result corresponding to Lemma 1, expressing that one can find a sequence of actions that yields a satisfying run, as long as no bad location is visited. However, the possibility to extend a finite timed sequence of states into a satisfying one is not sufficient when asking for a corresponding timed sequence of actions:

Lemma 2 (Extensions to timed words of actions). *For an SC automaton $\mathcal{A}_\varphi$ over MLSLS propositions and a timed word of actions w, if there exists a location $l \in locset(\mathcal{A}_\varphi, TS_0, w)$ that is not bad, there does not necessarily exist a sequences of timed actions w' s.t. $TS, w.w' \models \varphi$.*

Proof. We describe the structure of a counterexample, showing that under the assumptions of the lemma, the property $TS, w.w' \models \varphi$ does not hold. Consider a traffic model with only one lane and only two cars A and B on it. We assume that a TMLSL formula φ is given such that the corresponding SC automaton $\mathcal{A}_\varphi$ accepts the infinite timed sequence

$$m' = \prod_{n \in \mathbb{N}} \langle (\varphi_A, 4n + [0, 1)), (\varphi_C, 4n + [1, 2), (\varphi_B, 4n + [2, 3), (\varphi_C, 4n + [3, 4)),$$

where $\prod_{n \in \mathbb{N}} seq_n$ denotes the iterated concatenation of the sequences seq_n and $\varphi_A = \langle re(A) \frown re(B) \rangle \wedge \varphi_C, \varphi_B = \langle re(B) \frown re(A) \rangle \wedge \varphi_C, \varphi_C = \neg \langle re(A) \wedge re(B) \rangle$. Consider the finite prefix $m = \langle (\varphi_A, [0, 1), (\varphi_C, [1, 2)) \rangle$ of m'. Suppose that m leads to a location $l \in \mathcal{A}_\varphi[m]$ with $l \notin bad$ and that for the continuation $m'' = \langle (\varphi_B, [2, 3), (\varphi_C, [3, 4) \rangle \cdot \prod_{n \in \mathbb{N} \setminus \{0\}} \langle (\varphi_A, 4n+[0, 1), (\varphi_C, 4n+[1, 2), (\varphi_B, 4n+[2, 3), (\varphi_C, 4n + [3, 4) \rangle$ of m the property $m.m'' = m' \models \varphi$ holds.

However, since our abstract model has only a single lane and φ_A is true in the beginning, no action sequence $w.w'$ corresponding to the timed sequence of states m' can lead to a traffic snapshot where φ_B is satisfied without violating φ_C in between. □

In this counterexample, no sequence of actions can exist that yields a satisfying timed sequence of states. In other cases, however, there could be a satisfying sequence of actions but with acceleration values for some of the cars that are beyond any reasonable bounds. In [2], we therefore considered constraints on the acceleration forces and speeds of the cars when answering the question whether a specification is satisfiable at all.

We already motivated in Sect. 2 that we enable SC automata to communicate with each other. The reason is that we want to enable the monitors to enforce the properties up to some time bound. For this purpose, we add transitions to the monitors that are used to check whether the announced actions of the cars violate the specification that this monitor represents.

Definition 6 (Negotiating Transitions). *Let $t(l) = (l, true, com?w, c_l)$, $(c_l, check(\cdot, l, w), allow!(ego, w), l), (c_l, \neg check(\cdot, l, w), deny!w, l)$ denote a negotiating transition for $\mathcal{A}_\varphi$ with $l \in L$, w is a timed word of MLSL actions and 'com', 'deny' and 'allow' are channels with corresponding input and output actions.*

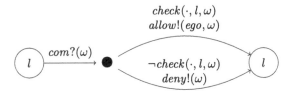

Fig. 5. Transition that we add to each location l of the monitors. After receiving a planned sequence of actions ω via a channel com, the predicate $check(TS, l, \omega)$ determines whether the sequence should be allowed or denied. The first parameter TS is not shown on the transition; it is implicitly forwarded to $check(TS, l, \omega)$ when the transition is triggered.

A graphical representation of these transitions is shown in Fig. 5. The predicate $check(TS, l, \omega)$ (with the first parameter hidden in the negotiating transitions) is used to determine whether the announced behaviour is allowed by the monitor. For this purpose, the monitor virtually applies the announced actions to the traffic snapshot and computes the set of locations that it would reach in an evolution caused by the announced actions:

Definition 7 ($check(TS, l, \omega)$). *Triggered in a location l of $\mathcal{A}_\varphi$, we define for a traffic snapshot TS and a sequence of actions ω*

$$check(TS, l, \omega) = true \text{ iff } \exists l' \in locset(\mathcal{A}_{\varphi, \{l\}}, TS, \omega) \wedge l' \notin bad.$$

One can check the satisfaction of this predicate in traffic snapshots TS different from the initial one. We incorporated this in Definition 7 by considering a location l, where the predicate $check$ is evaluated, which might be different from the initial location of $\mathcal{A}_\varphi$. This location might be reached by the evolution along some timed word.

Lemma 3 (Guarded execution of actions). *Given two traffic snapshots TS_0 and TS with $TS_0 \xrightarrow{\omega'} TS$, a location $l \in locset(\mathcal{A}_\varphi, TS_0, \omega')$ reached by the evolution along ω', a time bound t, a sequence of actions ω up to t, we have $check(TS, l, \omega) = true$ iff $TS_0, \omega'.\omega \models_t \varphi$.*

Proof. Consider $check(TS, l, \omega)$ being true in a location $l \in locset(\mathcal{A}_\varphi, TS_0, \omega')$ reached in $\mathcal{A}_\varphi$ by a timed sequence of actions ω' with $TS_0 \xrightarrow{\omega'} TS$. By Definition 7, $\exists l' \in locset(\mathcal{A}_{\varphi, l}, TS, \omega) \wedge l' \notin bad$. Therefore there exists a timed sequence of states $m(TS_0, \omega'.\omega) = \langle (s_0, I_0), \ldots, (s_n, I_n) \rangle$ with $TS_0 \models s_0 \wedge TS' \models s_n \wedge t \in I_n$. Since $l' \notin bad$, $m(TS, \omega'.\omega) \nvDash \neg\varphi$. Therefore $TS_0, \omega'.\omega \models_t \varphi$. ☐

In what follows, we do not employ that we can start in traffic snapshots different from the initial one and instead always start the planning there. A benefit, however, is that one could use the evolution from TS_0 to TS to model that the planning and communication of controllers and monitors needs time and thus the traffic situation evolves. A further utilisation could be possible when this procedure is executed iteratively to achieve a satisfaction beyond t, cf. Sect. 5. We now add the transitions of Definition 6 to every location $l \in L$ of $\mathcal{A}_\varphi$:

Definition 8 (Supervisor).   *Given a monitor $\mathcal{A}_\varphi$ for a specification φ and negotiating transitions according to Definition 6, $A'_\varphi = (\mathcal{P}, C_\mathcal{P}, L, L_0, E', \mathcal{L}, \Delta, \mathcal{F})$, where $E' = E \cup \{t(l) \mid \forall l \in L\}$ is a supervisor or an enforcer for φ up to time t.*

The communicating SC automaton $\mathcal{A}'_\varphi$ can now check for announced sequences of actions whether they conform to the φ that it is build from. This feature can be used in various ways. Every single controller that conforms to the simple protocol: (1) it announces all actions that it wants to execute up to time bound t and (2) only executes them when the supervisors allow it, now satisfying φ up to t.

In the Example of Sect. 3, only a single car participated. In case that there is more than one controller present, the controllers first need to cooperate and build the sequence of actions to announce collectively before starting the request to the supervisors. A detailed interplay between the controllers and enforcers could be possible here, with strategies and heuristics about finding optimal actions to announce. Yet, for the moment, we only propose a simple nondeterministic controller $\mathcal{C}$, where the cars simply guess their actions, communicate them via a channel a and append them to the sequence of actions to execute and re-do this in the case the sequence was rejected until an allowed one is found. A (simplified) graphical representation of this controller is depicted in Fig. 6.

In the initial location l_0, the controllers successively guess actions α that they wish to execute at time t, communicate them via the channel a and append these actions to the sequence of actions ω. We silently assume that each controller only guesses actions for its own car. At any point, the controller, if the time stamps of ω form a real-time sequence, can proceed to the intermediate location (denoted by •), announcing the sequence ω to the supervisors and the other controllers via the channel *com*. The controller then waits for the supervisors to allow the sequence. Positive answers to this are stored in the list β of cars that already allowed for the sequence. If all supervisors allow the sequence, the controller proceeds to l_1 and executes the actions it itself appended to β, until there are no further actions to execute. In case a supervisor denies the sequence of actions, both the sequence of actions ω and the list β of cars that already allowed for the sequence are deleted and the location is changed to l_0 again.

Using the controller $\mathcal{C}$, we can now state that every sequence found indeed respects the cars' specification:

Theorem 1 (Every sequence in the semantics is a solution). *For every sequence $m \in L(\mathcal{A}'_\varphi \parallel \mathcal{C})$ there is a timed word of actions ω that is the outcome of the negotiating transitions of the enforcer $\mathcal{A}'_\varphi$ such that (1) the states in m describe the evolution of TS along ω, and (2) ω and TS are a model of φ up to time t, $TS, \omega \vDash_t \varphi$.*

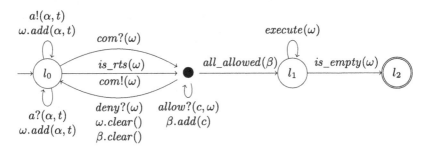

Fig. 6. A nondeterministic controller $\mathcal{C}$. Multiple of these controllers collectively "guess" a sequence of actions to announce and execute their actions if the sequence is accepted. In the case of a reject, the controllers start the procedure again. We omitted propositions and clock constraints forcing the controller to actually take the transitions and reach the final location.

Proof. A satisfying sequence m needs to visit the final location of the controller $\mathcal{C}$. Therefore, the $all\_allowed(\beta)$ transition was taken and $\mathcal{A}'_\varphi$ avoided its bad locations. Thus, there is an initial location l_0 in $\mathcal{A}'_\varphi$ and a sequence ω such that $check(TS_0, l_0, \omega)$ was successful. Due to Lemma 3, $TS_0, \omega \vDash_t \varphi$ holds.   □

Please note that we do not distinguish between $\mathcal{A}'_\varphi$ being the supervisor for a single or for all cars in the theorem. In the case of multiple cars, $\mathcal{A}'_\varphi$ is the network $\mathcal{A}'_{\varphi_A} \parallel \mathcal{A}'_{\varphi_B} \parallel \ldots$ of the supervisors for the single cars $A, B, \ldots$. The same applies for the controller $\mathcal{C}$.

Even though no one would want this non-deterministic controller in practice in her/his car, we can use it to show that the supervisor $\mathcal{A}'_\varphi$ does not hinder the execution of any satisfying sequence of actions and if there exists a satisfying sequence of actions, it can actually be found:

Theorem 2 (Existence of a solution). *Every timed word of actions ω with $TS_0, \omega \vDash \varphi$ satisfies $m(TS_0, \omega) \in L(\mathcal{A}'_{\varphi, L'_0} \parallel \mathcal{C})$ with $L'_0 = \{l \in L_0 \mid TS_0 \vDash \mathcal{L}(l)\}$.*

This theorem follows immediately from Theorem 1 and the nondeterminism in the controllers.

5   Conclusion

We presented and demonstrated an approach for autonomous vehicles in motorway traffic for finding actions that respect the specifications of all participating cars up to a time bound. In doing so, the cars utilise internal monitors representing the satisfaction of their specification. Enabling the monitors to communicate, they act as supervisors for their specification and allow announced actions only if these actions do not violate the specification up to a given time bound. Using a nondeterministic controller, we showed that the supervisors do not forbid any actions that respect the satisfaction of the specification.

Future Work. A topic for future work is enforcing the satisfaction of a TMLSL property not only up to a certain time bound, but along a possibly infinite evolution. There are different possibilities to achieve this. In [2], we employed *equivalent* traffic snapshots for determining if, given an initial traffic snapshot TS_0, a specification is satisfiable at all, along some infinite evolution starting in TS_0. The idea is that a sequence entering a loop, where a traffic snapshot TS' is equivalent to a previous traffic snapshot TS (in symbols $TS \equiv TS'$), can be extended by executing the loop infinitely often, with all MLSL formulae valid during the first loop execution would also be valid during any further execution of the loop. Figure 7 illustrates the mentioned behaviour. Utilising these equivalent traffic snapshots, one could extend our enforcement approach to allow a sequence of actions only if each accepting set is visited along a sequence of actions and equivalent traffic snapshots are reached, so that the found sequence could be executed infinitely often. In this case, one would need to plan ahead such that a desired behaviour (for all cars) is part of the loop.

$$TS_0 \longrightarrow TS \quad\overset{\frown}{\underset{\smile}{}}\quad TS' \qquad \text{with } TS \equiv TS'$$

Fig. 7. Illustration of behaviour that can be executed infinitely often.

Another option would be to plan *sufficiently* ahead and trigger a re-planning of the sequence. For this, it is of interest what a sufficient time bound is. In this case, one would need to plan so far ahead such that the sequences do not necessarily lead to any undesired behaviour. Even without the knowledge of the exact boundaries to plan ahead, re-planning should lead to a satisfaction of a property along a longer run.

For both extensions just mentioned as well as the approach introduced in this paper, an implementation is desirable and ongoing work. For this, a visualisation of the behaviour of the monitors and the cars movement in SuMo [14] is the goal.

The model of MLSL presented in this paper only considers motorway traffic. Over the years, different extensions were proposed, e.g. for country roads [9] and urban traffic [19]. The extension of TMLSL and the runtime monitoring approach to also cover these traffic scenarios is thus a further desirable extension.

References

1. Alur, R., Dill, D.L.: A theory of timed automata. Theor. Comput. Sci. **126**(2), 183–235 (1994). https://doi.org/10.1016/0304-3975(94)90010-8
2. Bischopink, C., Olderog, E.R.: Spatial and timing properties in highway traffic. In: Seidl, H., Liu, Z., Pasareanu, C.S. (eds.) Theoretical Aspects of Computing, ICTAC 2022, Proceedings. LNCS, vol. 13572, pp. 114–131. Springer, Cham (2022). https://doi.org/10.1007/978-3-031-17715-6
3. Dierks, H.: PLC-automata: a new class of implementable real-time automata. Theor. Comput. Sci. **253**(1), 61–93 (2001). https://doi.org/10.1016/S0304-3975(00)00089-X

4. Falcone, Y.: You should better enforce than verify. In: Barringer, H., et al. (eds.) Runtime Verification, pp. 89–105. Springer, Cham (2010). https://doi.org/10.1007/978-3-642-16612-9

5. Fränzle, M., Hansen, M.R., Ody, H.: No need knowing numerous neighbours - towards a realizable interpretation of MLSL. In: Meyer, R., Platzer, A., Wehrheim, H. (eds.) Correct System Design. LNCS, vol. 9360, pp. 152–171. Springer, Cham (2015). https://doi.org/10.1007/978-3-319-23506-6_11

6. Gleirscher, M., Peleska, J.: Complete test of synthesised safety supervisors for robots and autonomous systems. In: Farrell, M., Luckcuck, M. (eds.) Proceedings Third Workshop on Formal Methods for Autonomous Systems, FMAS 2021, Virtual. EPTCS, vol. 348, pp. 101–109 (2021). https://doi.org/10.4204/EPTCS.348.7

7. Haxthausen, A.E., Peleska, J.: Formal development and verification of a distributed railway control system. IEEE Trans. Software Eng. **26**(8), 687–701 (2000). https://doi.org/10.1109/32.879808

8. Haxthausen, A.E., Peleska, J., Kinder, S.: A formal approach for the construction and verification of railway control systems. Formal Aspects Comput. **23**(2), 191–219 (2011). https://doi.org/10.1007/s00165-009-0143-6

9. Hilscher, M., Linker, S., Olderog, E.R.: Proving safety of traffic manoeuvres on country roads. In: Liu, Z., Woodcock, J., Zhu, H. (eds.) Theories of Programming and Formal Methods. LNCS, vol. 8051, pp. 196–212. Springer, Cham (2013). https://doi.org/10.1007/978-3-642-39698-4_12

10. Hilscher, M., Linker, S., Olderog, E.-R., Ravn, A.P.: An abstract model for proving safety of multi-lane traffic manoeuvres. In: Qin, S., Qiu, Z. (eds.) ICFEM 2011. LNCS, vol. 6991, pp. 404–419. Springer, Heidelberg (2011). https://doi.org/10.1007/978-3-642-24559-6_28

11. Krieg-Brückner, B., Peleska, J., Olderog, E.R., Baer, A.: The UniForM workbench, a universal development environment for formal methods. In: Wing, J.M., Woodcock, J., Davies, J. (eds.) FM 1999 - Formal Methods, World Congress on Formal Methods in the Development of Computing Systems, Proceedings, Volume II. LNCS, vol. 1709, pp. 1186–1205. Springer, Cham (1999). https://doi.org/10.1007/3-540-48118-4

12. Larsen, K., Petterson, P., Yi, W.: UPPAAL in a nutshell. Int. J. Softw. Tools Technol. Transf. **1**(1+2), 134–152 (1997). https://doi.org/10.1007/s100090050010

13. Linker, S., Hilscher, M.: Proof theory of a multi-lane spatial logic. Log. Methods Comput. Sci. **11**(3) (2015). https://doi.org/10.2168/LMCS-11(3:4)2015

14. Lopez, P.A., et al.: Microscopic traffic simulation using SUMO. In: The 21st IEEE International Conference on Intelligent Transportation Systems, pp. 2575–2582. IEEE, November 2018. https://elib.dlr.de/127994/

15. Olderog, E.R.: Space for traffic manoeuvres: an overview. In: Jones, C.B., Wang, J., Zhan, N. (eds.) Symposium on Real-Time and Hybrid Systems. LNCS, vol. 11180, pp. 211–230. Springer, Cham (2018). https://doi.org/10.1007/978-3-030-01461-2

16. Peleska, J.: New distribution paradigms for railway interlocking. In: Margaria, T., Steffen, B. (eds.) Leveraging Applications of Formal Methods, Verification and Validation: Applications, ISoLA 2020, Proceedings, Part III. LNCS, vol. 12478, pp. 434–448. Springer, Cham (2020). https://doi.org/10.1007/978-3-030-61467-6

17. Raskin, J.-F., Schobbens, P.-Y.: State clock logic: a decidable real-time logic. In: Maler, O. (ed.) HART 1997. LNCS, vol. 1201, pp. 33–47. Springer, Heidelberg (1997). https://doi.org/10.1007/BFb0014711

18. Schneider, F.B.: Enforceable security policies. ACM Trans. Inf. Syst. Secur. **3**(1), 30–50 (2000). https://doi.org/10.1145/353323.353382
19. Schwammberger, M.: An abstract model for proving safety of autonomous urban traffic. Theor. Comput. Sci. **744**, 143–169 (2018). https://doi.org/10.1016/j.tcs.2018.05.028

Safer Than Perception: Assuring Confidence in Safety-Critical Decisions of Automated Vehicles

Martin Fränzle[1], Willem Hagemann[2(✉)], Werner Damm[1], Astrid Rakow[1], and Mani Swaminathan[3]

[1] Carl von Ossietzky Universität Oldenburg, Oldenburg, Germany
{fraenzle,damm,rakow}@informatik.uni-oldenburg.de
[2] German Aerospace Center, Oldenburg, Germany
willem.hagemann@dlr.de
[3] Federal Office for Information Security, Bonn, Germany

Abstract. We address one of the key challenges in assuring safety of autonomous cyber-physical systems that rely on learning-enabled classification within their environmental perception: How can we achieve confidence in the perception chain, especially when dealing with percepts safeguarding critical manoeuvres? We present a methodology which allows to mathematically prove that the risk of misevaluating a safety-critical guard conditions referring to environmental artefacts can be bounded to a considerably lower frequency than the risk of individual misclassifications, and can thereby be adjusted to a value less than a given level of societally accepted risk.

Keywords: Highly Automated Vehicles · Learning-enabled cyber physical systems · Learning Algorithms · Safety Assurance · Perception Chain

1 Introduction

Inspired by our joint interest with Jan Peleska in rigorously assuring safety of highly automated transportation systems, we present a methodology and architecture for assuring the safety of highly automated vehicles (HAV), which guarantees that what the ego car, i.e. the own car, believes to be true about its environment, and the actual ground truth, rarely differ for all aspects which are relevant for ensuring the safety of the ego vehicle. How rare is rare enough is a matter of societal debates—e.g. the German Department of Transportation requires HAV to reduce the overall rate of fatalities compared to human-operated

M. Fränzle—Supported by the State of Lower Saxony within the Zukunftslabor Mobilität as well as by Deutsche Forschungsgemeinschaft under grant no. DFG FR 2715/5-1.
M. Swaminathan—Contribution while employed at the University of Oldenburg.

A. E. Haxthausen et al. (Eds.): Peleska Festschrift 2023, LNCS 14165, pp. 180–201, 2023.
https://doi.org/10.1007/978-3-031-40132-9_12

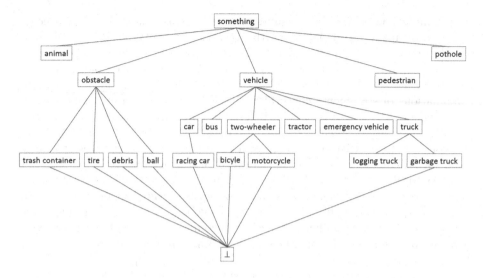

Fig. 1. An ontology for labelling occupancies in an occupancy grid.

vehicles. No matter what order of magnitude these debates will converge to, they will formally result in acceptance thresholds r and s bounding the likelihood of false adoption and of false omission, resp., of safety-critical manoeuvres, where a false positive decision for a safety-critical manoeuvre potentially leads to a risk while a false negative decision against such a manoeuvre potentially incurs a performance penalty. The respective bounds r and s will inevitably be orders of magnitude tighter than what machine-learning-based perception and classification systems can guarantee currently and in the foreseeable future.

This paper sets out to bridge this gap between actual perception performance and expected societal acceptance thresholds by answering the following question: if r, s are the level of societally accepted risk (performance penalty, resp.) budgeted for *relevant* misperceptions induced by false positives (false negatives, resp.), then (1) what renders a misperception "relevant", (2) how can we mathematically prove that perception of relevant environmental artefacts errs with false-positive rate of at most r while guaranteeing a true-positive rate of at least $1 - s$, and (3) what requirements do these false-positive and true-positive rates of relevant, in general compound, percepts imply for the permissible misperception rates of atomic percepts?

We provide a mathematical setting for addressing this challenge, which is based on a reference architecture for the key functional ingredients of the perception chain. While each Original Equipment Manufacturer (OEM) has highly proprietary implementations, there seems to be an emerging consensus that an agreement on a functional reference architecture is both desirable and achievable. Our proposal for the reference architecture uses labelled occupancy grids for fusion of sensor data from radar, lidar, video, etc., and as interface to learning-algorithms based components for classifying objects in the environment of the ego-vehicle according to a (generally partially ordered, e.g., collecting cars, trucks, motor-cycles, etc. into a super-class of vehicles, like in Fig. 1) ontology. Such an occupancy grid partitions the geometric vicinity of the ego car into finitely many grid elements and records an occupancy information label from the ontology for each of these. Typical conditions enabling or blocking—and thereby meant to safeguard—critical manoeuvres then take the form of Boolean combinations of statements concerning the occupancy of certain traffic spaces, i.e. elements of the occupancy grid, by certain object types named in the ontology, plus maybe additional environmental ones, e.g., visibility conditions. As an example take an evasive manoeuvre of a car to the sidewalk in order to make room for an emergency vehicle: initiation of such a manoeuvre by the ego car would naturally be safeguarded by a Boolean condition requiring (1) presence of an emergency vehicle somewhere in the occupancy grid elements belonging to the traffic space reasonably close behind the ego car, (2) absence of vulnerable road users within some sufficiently large and connected group of occupancy grid elements belonging to the bike lane and sidewalks just ahead of the ego vehicle, (3) absence of any obstacles, including parked or stopped cars, on the line between the current ego position and the space for evasion identified via the previous condition, and finally (4) general (like absence of dense mist, presence of light) and geometric (like absence of occlusions) visibility conditions pertaining to the critical objects mentioned throughout the previous conditions.

While all the sub-conditions of the above guard condition intuitively make sense as being necessary conditions for safe execution of the safety-critical evasive manoeuvre, a safety risk due to misperception of some of the atomic statements occurring in the guard condition prevails, as no technical (nor a biological) perception system is perfect. In complex road scenes, we can neither expect to detect all potentially relevant objects nor are safe from misclassification of harmful objects as harmless and irrelevant. With absolute object detection rates often dropping below $\frac{2}{3}$ and classification accuracy easily falling below 90% in non-ideal visibility conditions [6], would our reliance into the evaluation of the guard condition drop into similar ranges due to the weakest link principle?

Intuitively, it might not have to, being a massive Boolean combination of atomic percepts such that individual misperceptions might mask each other: not every pedestrian needs to be detected, as allowing oneself to cross a strip of pedestrian lane certainly does not depend on whether it hosts a single or a number of pedestrians. Likewise, slight misplacements of perceived objects would not affect evaluation of the guard condition, as given small enough cells of the occupancy grid, a slight offset in locating a cyclist will not change drivability of the manoeuvre. Neither will mistaking a pedestrian for a cyclist do. The weakest link principle thus does not seem to apply here. The very nature of reasonable safeguarding conditions for safety-critical manoeuvres intuitively seems to induce a considerably lower misevaluation rate for the overall condition than for its constituents, i.e., than for the atomic percepts dealing with detecting, locating, and classifying objects. Within this note, we are trying to make this intuitive argument rigorous and formal, thus lifting reliability levels of combinatorial critical environmental perception well beyond the figures for atomic percepts achieved by state-of-the-art perception [6] paired with fusion techniques [11].

The main result of this paper is a methodology for formally establishing refined bounds on the risks of misperception for guard conditions concerning safety-critical manoeuvres based on the rates of misperception of atomic environmental artefacts. It complements both formal synthesis-based approaches towards achieving safe controllers as well as engineered control architectures, as our reference architecture does not restrict the typically highly proprietary planning and manoeuvre control of HAV, and instead provides a generic interface between any such proprietary solutions and the perception chain. It does so by allowing to tune the confidence level of individual percepts to their current criticality, allowing to optimise the trade-off between availability (induced from "don't knows") and safety (bounding the error of misconception to societally accepted risk).

This paper is organised as follows: Sect. 2 provides a simple example showcasing the effect of why and how the evaluation of a complex guard condition safeguarding a safety-critical manoeuvre can be "safer than perception". The subsequent Sect. 3 develops the mathematical framework facilitating quantitative analysis of this effect and proving its existence. Sections 4 and 5, finally, refer related work and provide a summary and pointers to future work.

2   A Simple Example

Let us assume the ego car is in a situation as the blue car in Fig. 2a. As the ego car wants to make progress, detecting the obstacle A1 would prompt it to consider circumventing the obstacle by temporarily moving across the dividing line into the oncoming lane. This manoeuvre would, however, only be selected iff it (1) is necessary to avoid collision on the originally planned track and (2) it is considered safe w.r.t. the available information about the environmental state.

The manoeuvre would thus be (safe-)guarded by a guard condition g defined as $g \equiv necessary \wedge safe$, where

$$necessary \equiv \bigvee_{x=6}^{7} \bigvee_{y=1}^{5} obstacle@(x_{ego} + x, y)$$

denotes that some type of obstacle is detected as being present on the own lane, i.e. between 1 and 5 in y position, within relevant x distance (here, for the sake of a depictable example, shown as just 6 to 7 grid elements away in the x direction — the real figure would be considerably larger). Within the ontology, *obstacle* denotes an arbitrary type of road-blocking object and is defined as a

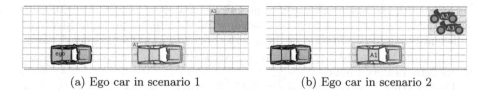

(a) Ego car in scenario 1   (b) Ego car in scenario 2

Fig. 2. Example Scenarios

disjunction about different basic object classification labels, like *trash container*, *tire*, *debris*, or *ball* (cf. Fig. 1). Note that this very definition already induces perceptive fault-tolerance: identifying the necessity for circumvention neither requires identifying the full back frontier of the obstacle, as the disjunction across y positions would evaluate to true already if only a fraction of the frontier is detected, nor identifying correctly the exact type of obstacle, as *obstacle* is a disjunction across numerous obstacle types. Even identification of the x position of the obstacle would permit for tolerances if circumvention manoeuvres are dimensioned with a safety margin: locating A1 further left than it actually is would not cause risk (yet extend the circumvention), while locating it too far right stays collision-free if the misplacement remains within the safety margin. Note the combinatorially vast number of distorted perceptions of A1 that would thus still lead to the same truth value as the ground truth does. The likelihood of failing to detect the necessity of a circumvention consequently remains very low compared to the reliability of atomic percepts. This implies that the rate of false negative verdicts in the evaluation of *necessary* remains low. We will later see that by just some rewriting to the way *necessary* is expressed, we will also be able to reduce the false-positive rate of the evaluation of *necessary* to a frequency well below the false-positive rate of the atomic percepts.

We now turn to the safety condition, yet do in this note simplify its exposition slightly by omitting some additional conditions that are structurally perfectly similar to the ones shown. These omissions deal with occluded areas and are perfectly symmetric to the conditions on oncoming traffic explicated in the sequel. With these simplifications, the safety condition reads

$$safe \equiv \neg \bigvee_{y=6}^{10} \left(\begin{array}{c} \bigvee_{x=1}^{20} pedestrian@(x_{\text{ego}} + x, y) \quad \vee \\ \bigvee_{x=-4}^{40} car@(x_{\text{ego}} + x, y) \quad \vee \\ \bigvee_{x=-1}^{60} motorcycle@(x_{\text{ego}} + x, y) \end{array} \right) .$$

It determines presence of critical objects on the oncoming lane within the ego car's vicinity, constituting the safety condition that may block the circumvention manoeuvre when its execution may become hazardous. As this condition *safe* structurally resembles *necessary* with an outermost negation added, its fault-tolerance properties concerning misperception might at first glance seem dual: where *necessary* is massively disjunctive and therefore tolerant against some or even numerous lacking or inaccurate percepts, *safe* as a negation over a disjunction essentially is conjunctive and consequently seems to require completeness of all percepts across the large set of atomic observations it mentions. This would, however, be devastating! If true and insurmountable, it would imply that the very safety condition *safe* were not only as, but even orders of magnitude more fragile against misperception than any of the atomic percepts involved. Sufficiently reliable evaluation of the safety condition would consequently seem elusive, given that reliability of atomic percepts already falls considerably short of our actual safety targets.

Luckily, this problem can be alleviated by careful analysis of the Boolean problem structure of the safety condition *safe* or more generally the guard condition g, which we pursue via the general mathematical framework provided in the next section. An idea of how the problem is resolved by careful mathematical and logical analysis can readily be obtained from the situation depicted in Fig. 2b. The choice whether ego actually circumvents A_1 given (perceived) validity of *necessary* now depends on detecting A_2 *or* A_3. It neither is necessary to detect both of them nor to locate them exactly or to see their full frontier nor even to classify them accurately! Ego will not choose to circumvent A_1 even when recognizing only one (or part of one) of the oncoming motorbikes and even when it only detects some vehicle without being able to determine exact vehicle type. Again, and not withstanding the logical complementarity between the conditions *necessary* and *safe*, there is a combinatorially vast set of misperceptions that do not alter perceived truth of *safe* compared to its ground truth.

Consequently, both *necessary* and *safe* and therefore also their combination in the guard condition g enabling the safety-critical manoeuvre seem rather safe against misevaluation due to misperception. Intuitively this is the case as they are or can be rephrased, as we will see, in a form that is both highly symmetric and not over-specific. Highly symmetric here means that they feature multiple large groups of atoms that have the same effect on the overall truth value of g, like e.g. the detection of obstacles at different occupancy grid points. This also implies that they are not over-specific in that they neither have a particularly small nor a particularly large set of models, i.e. of satisfying grid valuations, but that models rather come in large combinatorial groups. The consequential cardinality and topology of the set of models renders them relatively robust against misperceptions as we will see.

3   Boolean Formulae as Classifiers

Let Φ be a formula that guards a safety-critical manoeuvre in the sense that the driving function will only adopt the manoeuvre when it has positive evidence of the validity of Φ in the current situation, implying that the manoeuvre would be avoided (and a safer substitute adopted) whenever Φ is violated *or* evaluation of Φ remains inconclusive. Such formulae Φ are generated by the prediction component on the fly. They comprise massive Boolean combinations of conditions on individual cells of the occupancy grid, where both the particular cells referenced and the individual conditions vary situationally, i.e. the universe of such queries Φ is far too large to compute optimised detectors in advance. E.g. Φ may safeguard a fast transit of a critical passage by ensuring that there are no humans on the sidewalk, where the geometric position of the sidewalk will depend on street geometry and position of the car in the lane, while the lookahead and thus number and distance of the cells referenced depends on current speed, road conditions, etc. In this particular setting $\Phi = \mathrm{lit}_1 \wedge \mathrm{lit}_2 \wedge \cdots \wedge \mathrm{lit}_n$ is a conjunction of literals $\mathrm{lit}_i = \neg A_i$ of the form "it is false that there is a human at cell c_i". The truth value of each atom A_i directly depends on a classifier output, which is, in this particular example, a classifier for the object class "human".

Our ultimate goal is to find an optimal combination of threshold values for the related classifiers, separately for each cell, such that the risk of misperception, i.e.

the false-positive rate for evaluation of Φ, is restricted to a given safety bound ϵ while the availability, i.e. the true-positive rate for evaluation of Φ, is maximised. In the following we show that both the true-positive and the false-positive rate of a compound observation predicate ca be bounded by polynomials over the respective rates of atomic percepts such that the aforementioned optimization problem can be translated into a polynomial optimisation problem. While we will not solve the optimisation problem in this note, we will subsequently show the translation and discuss some of its properties. We first summarise the main results here and give brief notes on the evidence. The reader will find a detailed version of the proofs in the appendix.

3.1 Probabilistic Preliminaries and Assumptions

Let $\{A_1, \ldots, A_n\}$ be the set of atoms. Each atom A_i corresponds to a classifier whose sensitivity and specificity can be adjusted by parameters. Thus, for fixed parameters, any atom A_i is a discrete random variable that maps any possible outcome $\omega \in \Omega$ to a pair $A_i(\omega) = (A_i^\lambda(\omega), A_i^\pi(\omega))$ consisting of its label $A_i^\lambda(\omega) = \lambda_i \in \{-, +, ?\}$ assigned by the perception component and its actual ground-truth value $A_i^\pi(\omega) = \pi_i \in \{\bot, \top\}$. The label values $-, +, ?$ denote respectively negative, positive, or inconclusive evidence for validity of the atom under consideration. The truth values $\bot, \top$ denote respectively that A_i is actually invalid or valid. Instead of $A_i^\lambda(\omega) = \lambda_i$ with $\lambda_i \in \{-, +, ?\}$ we often use the short notation $A_i^{\lambda_i}$ and likewise we often use $A_i^{\pi_i}$ with $\pi_i \in \{\bot, \top\}$ instead of $A_i^\pi(\omega) = \pi_i$.

A formula is a Boolean combination of atoms. By the following inductive definition any formula also is a discrete random variable.

Definition 1. *We extend the set of discrete random variables to formulae.*

(i) Any atom is a discrete random variable.
(ii) Let ϕ be a random variable. Then $\neg\phi$ also is a random variable, where the truth value $(\neg\phi)^\pi$ is given as usual and $(\neg\phi)^+ :\Leftrightarrow \phi^-$, $(\neg\phi)^- :\Leftrightarrow \phi^+$, and $(\neg\phi)^? :\Leftrightarrow \phi^?$.
(iii) Let ϕ, ψ be two random variables. Then $\phi \wedge \psi$ is a random variable too, where the truth value $(\phi \wedge \psi)^\pi$ is given as usual and $(\phi \wedge \psi)^+ :\Leftrightarrow \phi^+$ and ψ^+, $(\phi \wedge \psi)^- :\Leftrightarrow \phi^-$ or ψ^-, and $(\phi \wedge \psi)^?$ otherwise.
(iv) Let ϕ, ψ be two random variables. Then $\phi \vee \psi$ is a random variable, and is defined using the classical equivalence $\phi \vee \psi \leftrightarrow \neg(\neg\phi \wedge \neg\psi)$ that induces appropriate two- and three-valued interpretations.

Let ϕ be an arbitrary formula, let $m = (A_1^{\pi_1}, \ldots, A_n^{\pi_n})$ be a truth assignment that assigns a truth value to each atom A_i, and $l = (A_1^{\lambda_1}, \ldots, A_n^{\lambda_n})$ be a label assignment that assigns a label to each atom A_i. We write $m \models \phi^{\pi_\phi}$ if and only if ϕ evaluates to π_ϕ under the assignment m. Similarly, we write $l \models \phi^{\lambda_\phi}$ if and only if l yields the label λ_ϕ for ϕ. We will occasionally consider domain models for the ground truth. A domain model $\mathcal{M}$ further restricts the admissible truth assignments of atoms, in general by enforcing domain invariants. For example, $\mathcal{M}$ could restrict the minimum number of (adjacent) grid occupancies for large *vehicles or define non-occupiable cells due to buildings, etc. Note that domain models do not restrict the admissible label assignments.*

We extend the usual true positive (TP), false negative (FN), true negative (TN), and false positive (FP) rates to formulae as expected:

Definition 2. *For any formula ϕ we define the following performance rates:*

$$\mathrm{TPR}_\phi := P(\phi^+ \mid \phi^\top), \qquad\qquad \mathrm{FNR}_\phi := P(\phi^- \mid \phi^\top),$$
$$\mathrm{TNR}_\phi := P(\phi^- \mid \phi^\perp), \qquad\qquad \mathrm{FPR}_\phi := P(\phi^+ \mid \phi^\perp),$$

where $P(\phi^{\lambda_\phi} \mid \phi^{\pi_\phi})$ denotes the conditional probability that ϕ is labelled with $\lambda_\phi \in \{+, -, ?\}$ given that the truth value of ϕ is $\pi_\phi \in \{\top, \perp\}$.

Let ϕ be an arbitrary formula with label ϕ^{λ_ϕ} and truth value ϕ^{π_ϕ}. Our goal is to relate the respective performance rates of the complex Boolean formula ϕ to performance rates of its atoms. The main device of such a reduction is an explicit enumeration of all label and truth assignments l and m that yield ϕ^{λ_ϕ} and ϕ^{π_ϕ}. As all these assignments are disjoint sets, a first option is to exploit the σ-additivity $P(A \uplus B) = P(A) + P(B)$. However, since the rates under consideration are conditional probabilities where the event set is determined by the label and the conditional event is determined by the truth value, we need to decompose the event as well as the conditional event set. Let us first consider a decomposition for the conditional event.

Lemma 1. *Let $\frac{a_1}{b_1}, \ldots, \frac{a_n}{b_n}$ be fractions with real numbers $a_1, \ldots, a_n$ and positive real numbers $b_1, \ldots, b_n$. Then the following bounds hold:*

$$\min_{i=1,\ldots,n}\left\{\frac{a_i}{b_i}\right\} \leq \frac{\sum_{i=1}^n a_i}{\sum_{i=1}^n b_i} \leq \max_{i=1,\ldots,n}\left\{\frac{a_i}{b_i}\right\}.$$

Proof. The inequality can be proved by induction over n using the mediant inequality $\frac{a}{b} \leq \frac{c}{d} \implies \frac{a}{b} \leq \frac{a+c}{b+d} \leq \frac{c}{d}$ for real numbers a, b and positive real numbers b, d. Details can be found in the appendix. □

This generalised median inequality permits decomposition for the conditional event as follows.

Lemma 2. *Let $B_1, \ldots, B_n$ be disjoint events. For the conditional probability $P(A \mid \biguplus_{i=1}^n B_i)$ the following inequalities hold:*

$$\min_{i=1,\ldots,n}\{P(A \mid B_i)\} \leq P(A \mid \biguplus_{i=1}^n B_i) \leq \max_{i=1,\ldots,n}\{P(A \mid B_i)\}.$$

Proof. The inequalities follow by exploiting the σ-additivity and rewriting. Details can be found in the appendix. □

Thus, using the preceding lemma, we can decompose the truth condition of rates and estimate the rate as follows, where $m = (A_1^{\pi_1}, \ldots, A_n^{\pi_n})$.

$$\min_{m \models \phi^{\pi_\phi}} P(\phi^{\lambda_\phi} \mid m) \leq P(\phi^{\lambda_\phi} \mid \phi^{\pi_\phi}) \leq \max_{m \models \phi^{\pi_\phi}} P(\phi^{\lambda_\phi} \mid m).$$

We can even step further and decompose the event ϕ^{λ_ϕ} into proper assignments $l = (A_1^{\lambda_1}, \ldots, A_n^{\lambda_n})$.

$$\min_{m \models \phi^{\pi_\phi}} \sum_{l \models \phi^{\lambda_\phi}} P(l \mid m) \leq P(\phi^{\lambda_\phi} \mid \phi^{\pi_\phi}) \leq \max_{m \models \phi^{\pi_\phi}} \sum_{l \models \phi^{\lambda_\phi}} P(l \mid m). \tag{1}$$

The following plausible assumption allows a further decomposition of the labelling event into atomic labelling events.

Assumption 1 (Independent Labelling). *We assume that labelling $A_i^{\lambda_i}$ of an atom A_i depends on a given truth assignment $A_1^{\pi_1}, \ldots, A_n^{\pi_n}$ but not on the label assignment of other atoms, i.e., for any $i \neq j$ the independent labelling property $P(A_i^{\lambda_i} \mid A_1^{\pi_1}, \ldots, A_n^{\pi_n}, A_j^{\lambda_j}) = P(A_i^{\lambda_i} \mid A_1^{\pi_1}, \ldots, A_n^{\pi_n})$ holds.*

The independent labelling assumption allows us to decompose simultaneous labelling of different atoms.

Lemma 3. *The independent labelling property is equivalent to for all $i \neq j$:*

$$P(A_i^{\lambda_i}, A_j^{\lambda_i} \mid A_1^{\pi_1}, \ldots, A_n^{\pi_n}) = P(A_i^{\lambda_i} \mid A_1^{\pi_1}, \ldots, A_n^{\pi_n}) P(A_j^{\lambda_j} \mid A_1^{\pi_1}, \ldots, A_n^{\pi_n}).$$

Proof. The reader is referred to the appendix. ☐

The Independent Labelling Assumption 1 allows us to decompose any labelling event l of the form $l = (A_1^{\lambda_1}, \ldots, A_n^{\lambda_n})$ into products over its atoms.

$$\min_{m \models \phi^{\pi_\phi}} \sum_{l \models \phi^{\lambda_\phi}} \prod_{i=1}^{n} P(A_i^{\lambda_i} \mid m) \leq P(\phi^{\lambda_\phi} \mid \phi^{\pi_\phi}) \leq \max_{m \models \phi^{\pi_\phi}} \sum_{l \models \phi^{\lambda_\phi}} \prod_{i=1}^{n} P(A_i^{\lambda_i} \mid m). \tag{2}$$

As the pertinent recommendations concerning operational domains [21] suggest that true positive rates, false negative rates, etc., ought maintain their accepted lower or upper, resp., bounds across all operational domain, i.e. no operational domain gets "discriminated" by having to accept excessive FNR for example, we adopt the following additional assumption.

Assumption 2. *Let A_i be an arbitrary atom (in our case reflecting an element of the occupancy grid). We assume that the following lower and upper bounds on the conditional probability $P(A_i^{\lambda_i} \mid A_1^{\pi_1}, \ldots, A_n^{\pi_n})$ exist depending on the labelling $A_i^{\lambda_i}$ and the truth value $A_i^{\pi_i}$ and are valid for all truth assignment $A_1^{\pi_1}, \ldots, A_n^{\pi_n}$.*

$$\underline{\mathrm{TPR}}_{A_i} \leq P(A_i^+ \mid A_1^{\pi_1}, \ldots, A_i^\top, \ldots, A_n^{\pi_n}) \leq \overline{\mathrm{TPR}}_{A_i},$$
$$\underline{\mathrm{FNR}}_{A_i} \leq P(A_i^- \mid A_1^{\pi_1}, \ldots, A_i^\top, \ldots, A_n^{\pi_n}) \leq \overline{\mathrm{FNR}}_{A_i},$$
$$\underline{\mathrm{TNR}}_{A_i} \leq P(A_i^- \mid A_1^{\pi_1}, \ldots, A_i^\bot, \ldots, A_n^{\pi_n}) \leq \overline{\mathrm{TNR}}_{A_i},$$
$$\underline{\mathrm{FPR}}_{A_i} \leq P(A_i^+ \mid A_1^{\pi_1}, \ldots, A_i^\bot, \ldots, A_n^{\pi_n}) \leq \overline{\mathrm{FPR}}_{A_i}.$$

Note that the bounds only depend on the label and the truth value of A_i and are independent from the truth value of other atoms. I.e., we assume that for all atoms A_i and their given truth values $A_i^{\pi_i}$ the limit probabilities $\underline{P}$ and $\overline{P}$ with

$$\underline{P}(A_i^{\lambda_i} \mid A_i^{\pi_i}) \le P(A_i^{\lambda_i} \mid A_1^{\pi_1}, \ldots, A_i^{\pi_i}, \ldots, A_n^{\pi_n}) \le \overline{P}(A_i^{\lambda_i} \mid A_i^{\pi_i})$$

exists for all truth assignments $m = (A_1^{\pi_1}, \ldots, A_n^{\pi_n})$ with $m \models A_i^{\pi_i}$, such that

$$
\begin{aligned}
\underline{\text{TPR}}_{A_i} &= \underline{P}(A_i^+ \mid A_i^\top), & \overline{\text{TPR}}_{A_i} &= \overline{P}(A_i^+ \mid A_i^\top), \\
\underline{\text{FNR}}_{A_i} &= \underline{P}(A_i^- \mid A_i^\top), & \overline{\text{FNR}}_{A_i} &= \overline{P}(A_i^- \mid A_i^\top), \\
\underline{\text{TNR}}_{A_i} &= \underline{P}(A_i^- \mid A_i^\perp), & \overline{\text{TNR}}_{A_i} &= \overline{P}(A_i^- \mid A_i^\perp), \\
\underline{\text{FPR}}_{A_i} &= \underline{P}(A_i^+ \mid A_i^\perp), & \overline{\text{FPR}}_{A_i} &= \overline{P}(A_i^+ \mid A_i^\perp).
\end{aligned}
$$

Lemma 4. *The following identities hold for all $\underline{P}$, $\overline{P}$ and $i \ne j$:*

$$\underline{P}(A_i^{\lambda_i}, A_j^{\lambda_j} \mid A_i^{\pi_i}, A_j^{\pi_j}) = \underline{P}(A_i^{\lambda_i} \mid A_i^{\pi_i})\underline{P}(A_j^{\lambda_j} \mid A_j^{\pi_j}),$$
$$\overline{P}(A_i^{\lambda_i}, A_j^{\lambda_j} \mid A_i^{\pi_i}, A_j^{\pi_j}) = \overline{P}(A_i^{\lambda_i} \mid A_i^{\pi_i})\overline{P}(A_j^{\lambda_j} \mid A_j^{\pi_j}).$$

Proof. The identities can be obtained by a chain of rewritings. The detailed rewriting steps can be found in the appendix. □

Theorem 1. *Under Assumption 2 the following inequalities hold any given formula ϕ with label ϕ^{λ_ϕ} and truth value ϕ^{π_ϕ}:*

$$\underline{P}(\phi^{\lambda_\phi} \mid \phi^{\pi_\phi}) \le P(\phi^{\lambda_\phi} \mid \phi^{\pi_\phi}) \le \overline{P}(\phi^{\lambda_\phi} \mid \phi^{\pi_\phi}).$$

Proof. Application of Lemma 4 on Eq. (1) yields the requested inequalities, see the appendix for further details. □

The derived inequalities now permit rigorous analysis of misperception rates of formulae comprising a non-trivial Boolean combination of occupancy atoms, as in guard conditions of safety-critical manoeuvres.

3.2 Estimating Classification Rates for Complex Boolean Formulae

The following central theorem summarises reducibility of classification rates for compound formulae to the respective rates of their atomic constituents.

Theorem 2. *Under Assumptions 1 and 2, the TP, FN, TN and FP rates of any Boolean formula Φ can be bounded by the minimum and maximum of polynomials over certain bounds of the respective rates of the atoms occurring in Φ.*

In particular the following inequalities hold for any formula ϕ, where $\mathcal{M}$ is a domain model, $m = (A_1^{\pi_1}, \ldots, A_n^{\pi_n})$ runs over all admissible truth assignments, and $l = (A_1^{\lambda_1}, \ldots, A_n^{\lambda_n})$ over all label assignments:

$$\min_{\substack{\mathcal{M},m \\ \mathbb{T} \\ \phi^{\pi_\phi}}} \sum_{l \models \phi^{\lambda_\phi}} \prod_{i=1}^{n} \underline{P}(A_i^{\lambda_i} \mid A_i^{\pi_i}) \le P(\phi^{\lambda_\phi} \mid \phi^{\pi_\phi}) \le \max_{\substack{\mathcal{M},m \\ \mathbb{T} \\ \phi^{\pi_\phi}}} \sum_{l \models \phi^{\lambda_\phi}} \prod_{i=1}^{n} \overline{P}(A_i^{\lambda_i} \mid A_i^{\pi_i})$$

or, slightly more explicit,

$$\min_{\mathcal{M},m\models\phi^\top} \sum_{l\models\phi^+} \prod_{i=1}^{n} \underline{P}(A_i^{\lambda_i} \mid A_i^{\pi_i}) \leq \mathrm{TPR}_\phi \leq \max_{\mathcal{M},m\models\phi^\top} \sum_{l\models\phi^+} \prod_{i=1}^{n} \overline{P}(A_i^{\lambda_i} \mid A_i^{\pi_i}),$$

$$\min_{\mathcal{M},m\models\phi^\top} \sum_{l\models\phi^-} \prod_{i=1}^{n} \underline{P}(A_i^{\lambda_i} \mid A_i^{\pi_i}) \leq \mathrm{FNR}_\phi \leq \max_{\mathcal{M},m\models\phi^\top} \sum_{l\models\phi^-} \prod_{i=1}^{n} \overline{P}(A_i^{\lambda_i} \mid A_i^{\pi_i}),$$

$$\min_{\mathcal{M},m\models\phi^\perp} \sum_{l\models\phi^-} \prod_{i=1}^{n} \underline{P}(A_i^{\lambda_i} \mid A_i^{\pi_i}) \leq \mathrm{TNR}_\phi \leq \max_{\mathcal{M},m\models\phi^\perp} \sum_{l\models\phi^-} \prod_{i=1}^{n} \overline{P}(A_i^{\lambda_i} \mid A_i^{\pi_i}),$$

$$\min_{\mathcal{M},m\models\phi^\perp} \sum_{l\models\phi^+} \prod_{i=1}^{n} \underline{P}(A_i^{\lambda_i} \mid A_i^{\pi_i}) \leq \mathrm{FPR}_\phi \leq \max_{\mathcal{M},m\models\phi^\perp} \sum_{l\models\phi^+} \prod_{i=1}^{n} \overline{P}(A_i^{\lambda_i} \mid A_i^{\pi_i}).$$

Proof. The reader is referred to the appendix.   □

To ease practical application we give the reader the following concretisations of the central theorem that allow a decomposition of a formula ϕ along its Boolean operators. While a decomposition along a negation is possible without restriction, for conjunction and disjunction we have to assume that the resulting subformulae have no common atoms. This requirement is given, e.g., after a Shannon expansion of the formula, or for binary decision trees (BDD) and their ordered and reduced variants (ROBDD).

Theorem 3. *For any formula $\neg\phi$ the following identities for the performance rates of $\neg\phi$ hold:*

$$\mathrm{TPR}_{\neg\phi} = \mathrm{TNR}_\phi, \qquad \underline{\mathrm{TPR}}_{\neg\phi} = \underline{\mathrm{TNR}}_\phi, \qquad \overline{\mathrm{TPR}}_{\neg\phi} = \overline{\mathrm{TNR}}_\phi,$$

$$\mathrm{FNR}_{\neg\phi} = \mathrm{FPR}_\phi, \qquad \underline{\mathrm{FNR}}_{\neg\phi} = \underline{\mathrm{FPR}}_\phi, \qquad \overline{\mathrm{FNR}}_{\neg\phi} = \overline{\mathrm{FPR}}_\phi,$$

$$\mathrm{TNR}_{\neg\phi} = \mathrm{TPR}_\phi, \qquad \underline{\mathrm{TNR}}_{\neg\phi} = \underline{\mathrm{TPR}}_\phi, \qquad \overline{\mathrm{TNR}}_{\neg\phi} = \overline{\mathrm{TPR}}_\phi,$$

$$\mathrm{FPR}_{\neg\phi} = \mathrm{FNR}_\phi, \qquad \underline{\mathrm{FPR}}_{\neg\phi} = \underline{\mathrm{FNR}}_\phi, \qquad \overline{\mathrm{FPR}}_{\neg\phi} = \overline{\mathrm{FNR}}_\phi.$$

Proof. By simple rewriting.   □

Theorem 4. *Let ϕ and ψ be two formulae such that ϕ and ψ have no atom in common. Then the following identities for the limiting performance rates of $\phi \wedge \psi$ and $\phi \vee \psi$ hold:*

$$\underline{\mathrm{TPR}}_{\phi\wedge\psi} = \underline{\mathrm{TPR}}_\phi\underline{\mathrm{TPR}}_\psi, \qquad\qquad \overline{\mathrm{TPR}}_{\phi\wedge\psi} = \overline{\mathrm{TPR}}_\phi\overline{\mathrm{TPR}}_\psi,$$

$$\underline{\mathrm{TNR}}_{\phi\vee\psi} = \underline{\mathrm{TNR}}_\phi\underline{\mathrm{TNR}}_\psi, \qquad\qquad \overline{\mathrm{TNR}}_{\phi\vee\psi} = \overline{\mathrm{TNR}}_\phi\overline{\mathrm{TNR}}_\psi,$$

$$\underline{\mathrm{FNR}}_{\phi\wedge\psi} = \underline{\mathrm{FNR}}_\phi + \underline{\mathrm{FNR}}_\psi - \underline{\mathrm{FNR}}_\phi\underline{\mathrm{FNR}}_\psi,$$

$$\overline{\mathrm{FNR}}_{\phi\wedge\psi} = \overline{\mathrm{FNR}}_\phi + \overline{\mathrm{FNR}}_\psi - \overline{\mathrm{FNR}}_\phi\overline{\mathrm{FNR}}_\psi,$$

$$\underline{\mathrm{FPR}}_{\phi\vee\psi} = \underline{\mathrm{FPR}}_\phi + \underline{\mathrm{FPR}}_\psi - \underline{\mathrm{FPR}}_\phi\underline{\mathrm{FPR}}_\psi,$$

$$\overline{\mathrm{FPR}}_{\phi\vee\psi} = \overline{\mathrm{FPR}}_\phi + \overline{\mathrm{FPR}}_\psi - \overline{\mathrm{FPR}}_\phi\overline{\mathrm{FPR}}_\psi.$$

Proof. The reader is referred to the appendix.   □

Theorem 5. *Let ϕ and ψ be two formulae such that ϕ and ψ have no atom in common. Then the following inequalities for the limiting performance rates of $\phi \wedge \psi$ and $\phi \vee \psi$ hold:*

$$\min \left\{ \begin{array}{l} \underline{\text{TPR}}_\phi + \underline{\text{TPR}}_\psi - \underline{\text{TPR}}_\phi \underline{\text{TPR}}_\psi, \\ \underline{\text{TPR}}_\phi + \underline{\text{FPR}}_\psi - \underline{\text{TPR}}_\phi \underline{\text{FPR}}_\psi, \\ \underline{\text{FPR}}_\phi + \underline{\text{TPR}}_\psi - \underline{\text{FPR}}_\phi \underline{\text{TPR}}_\psi \end{array} \right\} \le \underline{\text{TPR}}_{\phi \vee \psi},$$

$$\overline{\text{TPR}}_{\phi \vee \psi} \le \max \left\{ \begin{array}{l} \overline{\text{TPR}}_\phi + \overline{\text{TPR}}_\psi - \overline{\text{TPR}}_\phi \overline{\text{TPR}}_\psi, \\ \overline{\text{TPR}}_\phi + \overline{\text{FPR}}_\psi - \overline{\text{TPR}}_\phi \overline{\text{FPR}}_\psi, \\ \overline{\text{FPR}}_\phi + \overline{\text{TPR}}_\psi - \overline{\text{FPR}}_\phi \overline{\text{TPR}}_\psi \end{array} \right\},$$

$$\min \left\{ \underline{\text{FNR}}_\phi \underline{\text{FNR}}_\psi, \underline{\text{FNR}}_\phi \underline{\text{TNR}}_\psi, \underline{\text{TNR}}_\phi \underline{\text{FNR}}_\psi \right\} \le \underline{\text{FNR}}_{\phi \vee \psi},$$

$$\overline{\text{FNR}}_{\phi \vee \psi} \le \max \left\{ \overline{\text{FNR}}_\phi \overline{\text{FNR}}_\psi, \overline{\text{FNR}}_\phi \overline{\text{TNR}}_\psi, \overline{\text{TNR}}_\phi \overline{\text{FNR}}_\psi \right\},$$

$$\min \left\{ \begin{array}{l} \underline{\text{TNR}}_\phi + \underline{\text{TNR}}_\psi - \underline{\text{TNR}}_\phi \underline{\text{TNR}}_\psi, \\ \underline{\text{TNR}}_\phi + \underline{\text{FNR}}_\psi - \underline{\text{TNR}}_\phi \underline{\text{FNR}}_\psi, \\ \underline{\text{FNR}}_\phi + \underline{\text{TNR}}_\psi - \underline{\text{FNR}}_\phi \underline{\text{TNR}}_\psi \end{array} \right\} \le \underline{\text{TNR}}_{\phi \wedge \psi},$$

$$\overline{\text{TNR}}_{\phi \wedge \psi} \le \max \left\{ \begin{array}{l} \overline{\text{TNR}}_\phi + \overline{\text{TNR}}_\psi - \overline{\text{TNR}}_\phi \overline{\text{TNR}}_\psi, \\ \overline{\text{TNR}}_\phi + \overline{\text{FNR}}_\psi - \overline{\text{TNR}}_\phi \overline{\text{FNR}}_\psi, \\ \overline{\text{FNR}}_\phi + \overline{\text{TNR}}_\psi - \overline{\text{FNR}}_\phi \overline{\text{TNR}}_\psi \end{array} \right\},$$

$$\min \left\{ \underline{\text{FPR}}_\phi \underline{\text{FPR}}_\psi, \underline{\text{FPR}}_\phi \underline{\text{TPR}}_\psi, \underline{\text{TPR}}_\phi \underline{\text{FPR}}_\psi \right\} \le \underline{\text{FPR}}_{\phi \wedge \psi},$$

$$\overline{\text{FPR}}_{\phi \wedge \psi} \le \max \left\{ \overline{\text{FPR}}_\phi \overline{\text{FPR}}_\psi, \overline{\text{FPR}}_\phi \overline{\text{TPR}}_\psi, \overline{\text{TPR}}_\phi \overline{\text{FPR}}_\psi \right\}.$$

Proof. The reader is referred to the appendix.   □

The preceding theorems show how to estimate misevaluation risk for a given complex formula evaluating safety-critical situations against the misevaluation risk of the atomic classifiers involved. In particular, the theorems allow the true-positive and false-positive rate of the overall formula to be constrained by minima and maxima over polynomials of appropriate atomic classifier rates. In addition to the consequential identification of critical or noncritical atomic classifiers, this approach can also be used for deriving parameter setting of atomic classifiers that optimise the overall sensitivity and specificity of the given formula.

Concerning the question of whether our systems can be "safer than perception", a look at the above inequalities and thereby especially the bounds provided by Theorem 2 provide an affirmative answer: if enough atoms are symmetric in that setting one to true (false, resp.) has the same effect on the truth value of Φ than setting the other to true (false, resp.) then both true-positive and false-negative rates of evaluating Φ compare favourably to those of perceiving the underlying atoms. We claim that this property is inherent to many if not most of the safeguarding transitions encountered in well-designed safety-critical systems, as evidenced by the example from Sect. 2.

3.3   An Exemplary Computation

To demonstrate the derived formula and, as it were, as a continuation of the example from Sect. 2, let us consider ten atoms $A_1, \ldots, A_{10}$ observing the occupancy state of neighbouring cells on a lane segment as in $\phi \equiv \bigvee_{i=1}^{10} A_i$. The setting thus is equivalent to formula *necessary* from Sect. 2. Further assume that in the particular domain at least five cells are occupied by any vehicle, i.e., in any admissible assignment of the domain model $\mathcal{M}$ either none or at least five cells are occupied. We observe that over $\mathcal{M}$, the above condition ϕ is equivalent to the condition $|\{i \mid A_i\}| \geq k$, for any $k \in \{1, \ldots, 5\}$, in the sense that for each model $m \models \mathcal{M}$ it holds that $m \models \phi$ iff $m \models |\{i \mid A_i\}| \geq k$. We exploit this fact to obtain an equivalent, yet more robust observation formula g that is satisfied if and only if at least four cells are occupied, i.e., we replace ϕ by the $\mathcal{M}$-equivalent formula $|\{i \mid A_i\}| \geq 4$. Condition g constitutes a so-called pseudo-Boolean constraint [7], yet can also be encoded using classical Boolean connectives if desired. We would like to determine the total performance of g assuming that all atoms have the same performance rates with $\mathrm{TPR}_{A_i} = 0.8$, $\mathrm{FNR}_{A_i} = 0.1$, $\mathrm{TNR}_{A_i} = 0.7$, and $\mathrm{FPR}_{A_i} = 0.1$ (where the portions missing from 1 are assigned to inconclusive verdicts). Under the given domain model $\mathcal{M}$, we computed the following bounds using Theorem 2

$$\underline{\mathrm{TPR}}_g = 0.82537, \quad \overline{\mathrm{TPR}}_g = 0.99914, \quad \underline{\mathrm{FNR}}_g = 0.00086, \quad \overline{\mathrm{FNR}}_g = 0.17463,$$

$$\underline{\mathrm{TNR}}_g = \overline{\mathrm{TNR}}_g = 0.98720, \quad \underline{\mathrm{FPR}}_g = \overline{\mathrm{FPR}}_g = 0.01280.$$

In comparison with the atomic performance rates, even in the worst case, the true-positive rate has increased and at the same time the false-positive rate decreased significantly by almost an order of magnitude. Note that change of the threshold k in observation formula $|\{i \mid A_i\}| \geq k$ can be used to trade false-positive against true-positive rate: selecting $k = 3$ instead of 4, as used in g, would result in even higher and thus better true-positive rate at the price of also increased and thereby somewhat worse—though still considerably better than FPR_{A_i}—false-positive rate.

In fact, the true-positive rate will always, i.e. irrespective of the particular choice of $k \in \{1, \ldots, 5\}$, be better than TPR_{A_i}, which follows from the fact that a ground-truth positive features, due to $\mathcal{M}$, at least five positives: misperceiving it as a negative would thus require to perceive at least $5 - k + 1$ true atoms A_i as false while not perceiving a masking number of false atoms A_j as true. More exactly the false-negative rate of evaluating $g_k \equiv |\{i \mid A_i\}| \geq k$ can be bounded from above by

$$\mathrm{FNR}_{g_k} \leq \max_{m \in \{5, \ldots, 10\}} \sum_{n=m-k+1}^{m} \sum_{n'=0}^{n-(m-k+1)} \frac{m!}{n!} (\mathrm{FNR}_{A_i})^n \cdot \frac{(10-m)!}{n'!} (\mathrm{FPR}_{A_i})^{n'}$$

$$\leq (\mathrm{FNR}_{A_i})^{5-k+1} \leq \mathrm{FNR}_{A_i} ,$$

as misperceiving a satisfying assignment with $m \in \{5, \ldots, 10\}$ true atoms as false would require to perceive $n \in \{m - k + 1, \ldots, m\}$ true atoms as false and simultaneously at most $n - (m - k + 1)$ false atoms as true. The first inequality in the second line becomes strict if, as usual, FNR_{A_i} neither is 0 nor 1. Then

$$\text{TPR}_{g_k} = 1 - \text{FNR}_{g_k} > 1 - \text{FNR}_{A_i} = \text{TPR}_{A_i}$$

follows, i.e. the true-positive rate of the compound percept always is better than that of the atomic percepts if we deal with disjunctive statements ϕ.

For the false-positive rate, the situation is more complex. At first glance, a reduction of false-positive rate for disjunctive statements below that of the atomic percepts might seem implausible, but the numeric example from the previous page demonstrates that such a reduction can be achieved and can even be substantial. The amount of decrease (or, in the unlucky case, even increase) however depends on the particular value of FPR_{A_i} and the choice of the threshold k, where higher values for k obviously reduce the false-positive rate of the compound percept g'.

4   Related Work

Highly automated vehicles are typically learning-enabled cyber physical systems operating in an uncertain dynamic environment, where detection of properties about the dynamic environment is enabled through *inaccurate sensors* and subsequent *machine-learnt classifiers*. This renders an exact inference of the state of the environment infeasible, necessitating suitable representations of the *uncertainty* in such an inference about the dynamic environment. Appropriate representations of uncertainty in the inference have been investigated within the paradigm of probabilistic robotics [20], among others, particularly as applied to vehicle localization in urban environments [10,11,14], with localization being a special and historically more well-understood instance of the general problem of safe-guarding critical manoeuvre decisions. In these and related works such as [1,12], the environment uncertainty is represented as probabilistic beliefs. Applications of learning components in high assurance systems has been addressed in [18]. More recently, the challenge of assuring the autonomy of learning-enabled cyber physical systems has been considered in the works [2,8,13]. In particular, [2] considers the problem of falsifying signal temporal logic specifications for learning-enabled cyberphysical systems, with the technique demonstrated on a simplified model of an automatic emergency braking system with a perception component based on deep neural networks (DNNs). Contract-based compositional reasoning of learning-enabled autonomous systems is considered in [13], where DNNs constitute the learning components dealing with behavioural strategies. Markov Decision Processes form the operational basis of the models in [8] generated from reinforcement learning, where behavioural (not perceptive) strategies conforming to probabilistic temporal logic specifications are synthesised with the aim of enabling the safe navigation of autonomous systems among humans.

All the aforementioned approaches are based on assumptions concerning the quantitative reliability of perception component, and thus need to be complemented by approaches measuring or analytically determining the latter. Various approaches to combining multiple classifiers can be found in the literature, e.g., see [5,17] for an overview. The goal of such a combination is often to compensate for individual shortcomings in the performance by a better performance of the multitude of classifiers [17]. While in the pre-classification level the combination happens at the sensor or raw data level, the focus of this note is on fusion of classifiers at the post-classification level, as on-the-fly combinations of the decision of multiple atomic classifiers are considered. A major challenge for fusion on the decision level arises from the fact that the least genuine information about the object of observation is available at this level [9].

An important aid for the performance analysis on the decision level of adjustable classifiers is its empirical ROC curve (receiver operating characteristics) [4,15]. The ROC curve is obtained by plotting the true positive rate against the false positive rate for the different parameter settings into a graph. The coordinates of each point of the ROC curve reflect the true positive rate in the y-axis and the false positive rate in the y-axis for the respective threshold setting. The space spanned by these axes is referred to as the ROC space. The corresponding rates are measured against a test data set, which is independent from

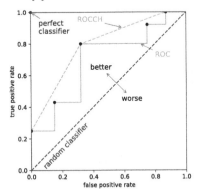

Fig. 3. Empirical ROC curve with convex hull (ROCCH).

the training data set used for establishing the classifiers. Empirically determined ROC curves are step-like functions that approximate the true curve as the sample size increases; see Fig. 3. The ROC space allows us to compare individual threshold settings. One point in the ROC space denotes a better threshold setting than another if its true positive rate is larger and its false positive rate is smaller. Thus, an optimal threshold setting is found in the upper left of the ROC space at those curve points which have the largest perpendicular distance to the diagonal spanned by (0,0) – (1,1) in their vicinity [15].

To contextualise the study of fusion of multiple classifiers at the decision level as found in [3,4,9,15,16,19], consider the optimal points of an empirical ROC curve identified above as individual classifiers. An important result is that each point of the convex hull curve (ROCCH) (see Fig. 3) of these points corresponds to a realizable classifier that can be obtained by a probabilistic linear interpolation of the decision of the convex hull generating classifiers [19]. Several papers [3,9,16] exploit that—under the assumption of conditional independence—Boolean combinations of the response of multiple classifier yield points in the ROC space that show a better performance than the ROCCH.

Despite the apparent relatedness of the presented approaches for classifier combinations, those works are mainly concerned with the consideration of the fusion of multiple classifiers with the goal of improving the overall performance of the classification of a single object of observation. Especially with respect to

Boolean combinations of such classifiers, the conditional independence assumption turns out to be problematic since all observations refer to a common object. In our approach, however, we consider complex Boolean combiners of diverse atomic classifiers, including different polarities, where each classifier refers to spatially separated cells, making the conditional independence assumption, here stated as Independent Labelling Assumption 1, less problematic. Altogether, work on improving the performance of generation and classification of atomic percepts, e.g. by sensor fusion, and our work showing a "safer than perception" property of combined safety-critical percepts are complementary in that advances in each of the two fields will combine to improve overall safety of autonomous systems.

5 Conclusion

While rigorously guaranteed safety of autonomous systems is a prerequisite for their sustained societal acceptance, providing such guarantees at the appropriate quantitative safety levels is intrinsically hard, given the currently as well as for the foreseeable future relatively high misperception rates of technical perception chains. When mapping an autonomous vehicle's vicinity, their error rates are generally much higher than the pertinent safety targets for autonomous operation. Consequently, to overcome the weakest link principle prevalent in current safety considerations, we need stringent arguments for why our designed systems actually are "safer than perception". More precisely, this requires a rigorous assessment of the likelihood that a safety-critical manoeuvre is erroneously adopted, and this assessment has to provide much tighter bounds for such manoeuvre adoption than for misperception. This note provides a mathematical framework supporting such an argument and indeed showing that for well-posed guard conditions, i.e. guard conditions that are not overspecific w.r.t. to their satisfying models but rather admit numerous satisfying and numerous violating models, as well as exhibit symmetry in that different atomic percepts share similar effect on the resultant logical value of the guard condition, "safer than perception" naturally applies. As the likelihood of misperception of a relevant, in the sense of safe-guarding a critical manoeuvre, property can thus be bounded to a considerably lower frequency than the risk of individual misclassifications of atomic percepts, the overall risk induced by an autonomous system can consequently be adjusted to a value less than a given level of societally accepted risk without imposing extraneous reliability demands on individual atomic percepts.

The analysis does only rely on the logical structure of the guard condition and could potentially be refined by also reflecting topology or geometry of models over the grid geometry of the occupancy grid: currently, all grid elements are considered as atomic carriers of occupancy information devoid of any geometry-induced relation. It would, however, be reasonable to refine analysis w.r.t. geometry, knowing that a slight misplacement of a detected object both is more likely to happen and more unlikely to change a guard's perceived truth value than a large displacement. This analysis, then obviously to be pursued in spatial logic, is subject of further research. The same applies for the obvious option of exploiting the derived analytical formulae concerning guard misevaluation probability within an optimization framework: here, the optimization would be used to automatically adjust the detection thresholds of individual sensor components on demand, i.e., derives from the analytic formula for a given guard condition g and a socially desired maximal false-negative rate an optimal assignment of the sensor thresholds along their receiver operating characteristic (ROC) curves such that maximal true-positive rate is obtained.

Acknowledgements. The research reported herein has been supported by the State of Lower Saxony within the Zukunftslabor Mobilität as well as by Deutsche Forschungsgemeinschaft under grant no. DFG FR 2715/5-1 "Konfliktresolution und kausale Inferenz mittels integrierter sozio-technischer Modellbildung". It furthermore benefit from technical discussions with Jan Peleska, and we dedicate it to him on the occasion of his 65th anniversary.

A   Proofs

Proof of Lemma 1. We use induction over n to show that the inequality

$$\min_{i=1,\ldots,n} \left\{ \frac{a_i}{b_i} \right\} \leq \frac{\sum_{i=1}^{n} a_i}{\sum_{i=1}^{n} b_i} \leq \max_{i=1,\ldots,n} \left\{ \frac{a_i}{b_i} \right\}$$

holds for any positive integer n and fractions $\frac{a_1}{b_1}, \ldots, \frac{a_n}{b_n}$ with real nominators $a_1, \ldots, a_n$ and positive real denominators $b_1, \ldots, b_n$. The base case $n = 1$ is trivial and the case $n = 2$ follows immediately from the mediant inequality $\frac{a}{b} \leq \frac{c}{d} \implies \frac{a}{b} \leq \frac{a+c}{b+d} \leq \frac{c}{d}$ for real numbers a, b and positive real numbers b, d. Assume that the induction hypothesis holds for $n - 1$. For any fraction $\frac{a_n}{b_n}$ with real $a_n, b_n > 0$ at least one of the inequalities (i) $\frac{\sum_{i=1}^{n-1} a_i}{\sum_{i=1}^{n-1} b_i} \leq \frac{a_n}{b_n}$ or (ii) $\frac{a_n}{b_n} \leq \frac{\sum_{i=1}^{n-1} a_i}{\sum_{i=1}^{n-1} b_i}$ holds. From case (i) it follows

$$\min_{i=1,\ldots,n} \left\{ \frac{a_i}{b_i} \right\} = \min_{i=1,\ldots,n-1} \left\{ \frac{a_i}{b_i} \right\} \leq \frac{\sum_{i=1}^{n-1} a_i}{\sum_{i=1}^{n-1} b_i} \overset{(*)}{\leq} \frac{\sum_{i=1}^{n} a_i}{\sum_{i=1}^{n} b_i} \overset{(*)}{\leq} \frac{a_n}{b_n} = \max_{i=1,\ldots,n} \left\{ \frac{a_i}{b_i} \right\}$$

and from case (ii) it follows

$$\min_{i=1,\ldots,n} \left\{ \frac{a_i}{b_i} \right\} = \frac{a_n}{b_n} \overset{(*)}{\leq} \frac{\sum_{i=1}^{n} a_i}{\sum_{i=1}^{n-1} b_i} \overset{(*)}{\leq} \frac{\sum_{i=1}^{n-1} a_i}{\sum_{i=1}^{n-1} b_i} \leq \max_{i=1,\ldots,n-1} \left\{ \frac{a_i}{b_i} \right\} = \max_{i=1,\ldots,n} \left\{ \frac{a_i}{b_i} \right\}$$

where $(*)$ denotes the application of the mediant inequality.   □

Proof of Lemma 2. We have to show that the inequalities

$$\min_{i=1,\ldots,n} \{ P(A \mid B_i) \} \leq P(A \mid \bigcup_{i=1}^{n} B_i) \leq \max_{i=1,\ldots,n} \{ P(A \mid B_i) \}$$

hold for all disjoint events $B_1, \ldots, B_n$. Using the identity $P(A \mid \bigcup_{i=1}^{n} B_i) = \frac{\sum_{i=1}^{n} P(A, B_i)}{\sum_{i=1}^{n} P(B_i)}$, an application of Lemma 1 yields

$$\min_{i=1,\ldots,n} \left\{ \frac{P(A, B_i)}{P(B_i)} \right\} \leq \frac{\sum_{i=1}^{n} P(A, B_i)}{\sum_{i=1}^{n} P(B_i)} \leq \max_{i=1,\ldots,n} \left\{ \frac{P(A, B_i)}{P(B_i)} \right\},$$

which finally rewrites to the asserted inequalities. □

Proof of Lemma 3. We have to show that the identity

$$P(A_i^{\lambda_i} \mid A_1^{\pi_1}, \ldots, A_n^{\pi_n}, A_j^{\lambda_j}) = P(A_i^{\lambda_i} \mid A_1^{\pi_1}, \ldots, A_n^{\pi_n}) \tag{3}$$

is equivalent to the identity

$$P(A_i^{\lambda_i}, A_j^{\lambda_i} \mid A_1^{\pi_1}, \ldots, A_n^{\pi_n}) = P(A_i^{\lambda_i} \mid A_1^{\pi_1}, \ldots, A_n^{\pi_n}) P(A_j^{\lambda_j} \mid A_1^{\pi_1}, \ldots, A_n^{\pi_n}) \tag{4}$$

for all positive integers n, atoms $A_1, \ldots A_n$, and $i \neq j$, $i \leq n$, $j \leq n$. Note that we implicitly assume the well-definedness of Eq. (3) and Eq. (4). I.e., both identities stipulate $P(A_1^{\pi_1}, \ldots, A_n^{\pi_n}) > 0$ and Eq. (3) additionally stipulates $P(A_j^{\lambda_j} \mid A_1^{\pi_1}, \ldots, A_n^{\pi_n}) > 0$. The equivalent transformation from Eq. (3) to Eq. (4) is obtained by multiplying both sides of Eq. (3) with $P(A_j^{\lambda_j} \mid A_1^{\pi_1}, \ldots, A_n^{\pi_n})$. The equivalent transformation from Eq. (4) to Eq. (3) by division is valid as long as the stronger stipulation $P(A_j^{\lambda_j} \mid A_1^{\pi_1}, \ldots, A_n^{\pi_n}) > 0$ imposed by Eq. (3) holds. Finally, note that for $P(A_j^{\lambda_j} \mid A_1^{\pi_1}, \ldots, A_n^{\pi_n}) = 0$ the identity Eq. (4) does not contain any deeper findings, as it degenerates to the trivial identity $0 = 0$ in this case. □

Proof of Lemma 4. We have to show that the identities

$$\underline{P}(A_i^{\lambda_i}, A_j^{\lambda_j} \mid A_i^{\pi_i}, A_j^{\pi_j}) = \underline{P}(A_i^{\lambda_i} \mid A_i^{\pi_i}) \underline{P}(A_j^{\lambda_j} \mid A_j^{\pi_j}),$$
$$\overline{P}(A_i^{\lambda_i}, A_j^{\lambda_j} \mid A_i^{\pi_i}, A_j^{\pi_j}) = \overline{P}(A_i^{\lambda_i} \mid A_i^{\pi_i}) \overline{P}(A_j^{\lambda_j} \mid A_j^{\pi_j})$$

hold for the limit probabilities $\underline{P}$ and $\overline{P}$ for all $i \neq j$. To see this consider the following chain of rewritings.

$$\underline{P}(A_i^{\lambda_i} \mid A_i^{\pi_i}) \underline{P}(A_j^{\lambda_j} \mid A_j^{\pi_j}) = \underline{P}(A_i^{\lambda_i} \mid A_i^{\pi_i}, A_j^{\pi_j}) \underline{P}(A_j^{\lambda_j} \mid A_i^{\pi_i}, A_j^{\pi_j})$$
$$= \underline{P}(A_i^{\lambda_i}, A_j^{\lambda_j} \mid A_i^{\pi_i}, A_j^{\pi_j}).$$

The corresponding identity for $\overline{P}$ follows analogously. □

Proof of Thm. 1. We have to show that

$$\underline{P}(\phi^{\lambda_\phi} \mid \phi^{\pi_\phi}) \leq P(\phi^{\lambda_\phi} \mid \phi^{\pi_\phi}) \leq \overline{P}(\phi^{\lambda_\phi} \mid \phi^{\pi_\phi})$$

holds for any formula ϕ with label ϕ^{λ_ϕ} and truth value ϕ^{π_ϕ}. In Eq. (1) we already showed

$$\min_{m \models \phi^{\pi_\phi}} \sum_{l \models \phi^{\lambda_\phi}} P(l \mid m) \leq P(\phi^{\lambda_\phi} \mid \phi^{\pi_\phi}) \leq \max_{m \models \phi^{\pi_\phi}} \sum_{l \models \phi^{\lambda_\phi}} P(l \mid m).$$

As all involved probabilities are nonnegative, monotonicity of $\leq$ yields

$$\min_{m \models \phi^{\pi_\phi}} \sum_{l \models \phi^{\lambda_\phi}} \underline{P}(l \mid m) \leq \min_{m \models \phi^{\pi_\phi}} \sum_{l \models \phi^{\lambda_\phi}} P(l \mid m)$$

$$\max_{m \models \phi^{\pi_\phi}} \sum_{l \models \phi^{\lambda_\phi}} P(l \mid m) \leq \max_{m \models \phi^{\pi_\phi}} \sum_{l \models \phi^{\lambda_\phi}} \overline{P}(l \mid m)$$

Combining the inequalities yields the asserted estimation.   □

Proof of Thm. 2. Let ϕ be an arbitrary formula with given label ϕ^λ_ϕ and truth value ϕ^{π_ϕ}. Further let $m = (A_1^{\pi_1}, \ldots, A_n^{\pi_n})$ be a truth assignment and $l = (A_1^{\lambda_1}, \ldots, A_n^{\lambda_n})$ a label assignment for all atoms A_i. In order to establish the theorem we show

$$\min_{m \models \phi^{\pi_\phi}} \sum_{l \models \phi^{\lambda_\phi}} \prod_{i=1}^n \underline{P}(A_i^{\lambda_i} \mid A_i^{\pi_i}) \leq P(\phi^{\lambda_\phi} \mid \phi^{\pi_\phi}) \leq \max_{m \models \phi^{\pi_\phi}} \sum_{l \models \phi^{\lambda_\phi}} \prod_{i=1}^n \overline{P}(A_i^{\lambda_i} \mid A_i^{\pi_i}).$$

The bounds

$$\min_{m \models \phi^{\pi_\phi}} \sum_{l \models \phi^{\lambda_\phi}} P(l \mid m) \leq P(\phi^{\lambda_\phi} \mid \phi^{\pi_\phi}) \leq \max_{m \models \phi^{\pi_\phi}} \sum_{l \models \phi^{\lambda_\phi}} P(l \mid m)$$

can be obtained without any further assumption and have already been established in Eq. (1). In Eq. (2) we already argued that the bounds

$$\min_{m \models \phi^{\pi_\phi}} \sum_{l \models \phi^{\lambda_\phi}} \prod_{i=1}^n P(A_i^{\lambda_i} \mid m) \leq P(\phi^{\lambda_\phi} \mid \phi^{\pi_\phi}) \leq \max_{m \models \phi^{\pi_\phi}} \sum_{l \models \phi^{\lambda_\phi}} \prod_{i=1}^n P(A_i^{\lambda_i} \mid m)$$

can be derived under the Independent Labelling Assumption 1. Finally, Assumption 2 allows us to bound each term of the form $P(A_i^{\lambda_i} \mid m) = P(A_i^{\lambda_i} \mid A_1^{\pi_1}, \ldots, A_n^{\pi_n})$ by its respective lower and upper bound $\underline{P}(A_i^{\lambda_i} \mid A_i^{\pi_i})$ and $\overline{P}(A_i^{\lambda_i} \mid A_i^{\pi_i})$. As all involved terms are nonnegative, we obtain

$$\min_{m \models \phi^{\pi_\phi}} \sum_{l \models \phi^{\lambda_\phi}} \prod_{i=1}^n \underline{P}(A_i^{\lambda_i} \mid A_i^{\pi_i}) \leq P(\phi^{\lambda_\phi} \mid \phi^{\pi_\phi}) \leq \max_{m \models \phi^{\pi_\phi}} \sum_{l \models \phi^{\lambda_\phi}} \prod_{i=1}^n \overline{P}(A_i^{\lambda_i} \mid A_i^{\pi_i}).$$

□

Proof of Thm. 4. We show the identities for the lower limiting rates $\underline{\text{TPR}}_{\phi \wedge \psi} = \underline{\text{TPR}}_\phi \underline{\text{TPR}}_\psi$ and $\underline{\text{FNR}}_{\phi \wedge \psi} = \underline{\text{FNR}}_\phi + \underline{\text{FNR}}_\psi - \underline{\text{FNR}}_\phi \underline{\text{FNR}}_\psi$. The identities for the upper limiting rates follow analogously. The remaining estimations for $\underline{\text{TNR}}_{\phi \vee \psi}$, $\underline{\text{FPR}}_{\phi \vee \psi}$, $\overline{\text{TNR}}_{\phi \vee \psi}$, and $\overline{\text{FPR}}_{\phi \vee \psi}$ can be obtained from the identity $\phi \vee \psi \equiv \neg(\neg \phi \wedge \neg \psi)$ and Thm. 3.

We decompose the conditional probabilities into proper assignments using Lemma 3 and Thm. 1.

$$\underline{\mathrm{TPR}}_{\phi\wedge\psi} = \underline{P}((\phi\wedge\psi)^+ \mid (\phi\wedge\psi)^\top) = \underline{P}(\phi^+,\psi^+ \mid \phi^\top,\psi^\top)$$
$$= \underline{P}(\phi^+ \mid \phi^\top)\underline{P}(\psi^+ \mid \psi^\top) = \underline{\mathrm{TPR}}_\phi\underline{\mathrm{TPR}}_\psi,$$

$$\underline{\mathrm{FNR}}_{\phi\wedge\psi} = \underline{P}((\phi\wedge\psi)^- \mid (\phi\wedge\psi)^\top)$$
$$= \underline{P}(\phi^- \mid \phi^\top,\psi^\top) + \underline{P}(\psi^- \mid \phi^\top,\psi^\top) - \underline{P}(\phi^- \mid \phi^\top,\psi^\top)\underline{P}(\psi^- \mid \phi^\top,\psi^\top)$$
$$= \underline{P}(\phi^- \mid \phi^\top) + \underline{P}(\psi^- \mid \psi^\top) - \underline{P}(\phi^- \mid \phi^\top)\underline{P}(\psi^- \mid \psi^\top)$$
$$= \underline{\mathrm{FNR}}_\phi + \underline{\mathrm{FNR}}_\psi - \underline{\mathrm{FNR}}_\phi\underline{\mathrm{FNR}}_\psi.$$

□

Proof of Theorem 5. We show the inequalities for the lower limiting rates only. The corresponding inequalities for the upper limiting rates follow analogously. Note that for the conditional probabilities $\underline{\mathrm{TPR}}_{\phi\vee\psi} = \underline{P}((\phi\vee\psi)^+ \mid (\phi\vee\psi)^\top)$ and $\underline{\mathrm{FNR}}_{\phi\vee\psi} = \underline{P}((\phi\vee\psi)^- \mid (\phi\vee\psi)^\top))$ the conditioning event $(\phi\vee\psi)^\top$ can be decomposed into disjoint models yielding

$$\underline{\mathrm{TPR}}_{\phi\vee\psi} = \underline{P}((\phi\vee\psi)^+ \mid \{\phi^\top,\psi^\top\} \cup \{\phi^\top,\psi^\perp\} \cup \{\phi^\perp,\psi^\top\}),$$
$$\underline{\mathrm{FNR}}_{\phi\vee\psi} = \underline{P}((\phi\vee\psi)^- \mid \{\phi^\top,\psi^\top\} \cup \{\phi^\top,\psi^\perp\} \cup \{\phi^\perp,\psi^\top\}).$$

Lemma 2 allows us to infer a lower estimate of the rates:

$$\min \left\{ \begin{array}{l} \underline{P}((\phi\vee\psi)^+ \mid \phi^\top,\psi^\top), \\ \underline{P}((\phi\vee\psi)^+ \mid \phi^\top,\psi^\perp), \\ \underline{P}((\phi\vee\psi)^+ \mid \phi^\perp,\psi^\top) \end{array} \right\} \leq \underline{\mathrm{TPR}}_{\phi\vee\psi},$$

$$\min \left\{ \begin{array}{l} \underline{P}((\phi\vee\psi)^- \mid \phi^\top,\psi^\top), \\ \underline{P}((\phi\vee\psi)^- \mid \phi^\top,\psi^\perp), \\ \underline{P}((\phi\vee\psi)^- \mid \phi^\perp,\psi^\top) \end{array} \right\} \leq \underline{\mathrm{FNR}}_{\phi\vee\psi}.$$

We decompose the labelling of $(\phi\vee\psi)^+$ and $(\phi\vee\psi)^-$ of each term in the minimum and maximum expression individually, where conjunctive events can further be decomposed into products using Lemma 3 E.g., the first term of the estimate for $\underline{\mathrm{TPR}}_{\phi\vee\psi}$ is rewritten as follows:

$$\underline{P}((\phi\vee\psi)^+ \mid \phi^\top,\psi^\top)$$
$$= \underline{P}(\phi^+ \mid \phi^\top,\psi^\top) + \underline{P}(\psi^+ \mid \phi^\top,\psi^\top) - \underline{P}(\phi^+,\psi^+ \mid \phi^\top,\psi^\top)$$
$$= \underline{P}(\phi^+ \mid \phi^\top) + \underline{P}(\psi^+ \mid \psi^\top) - \underline{P}(\phi^+ \mid \phi^\top)P(\psi^+ \mid \psi^\top)$$
$$= \underline{\mathrm{TPR}}_\phi + \underline{\mathrm{TPR}}_\psi - \underline{\mathrm{TPR}}_\phi\underline{\mathrm{TPR}}_\psi,$$

and the second term as follows:

$$\underline{P}((\phi\vee\psi)^+ \mid \phi^\top,\psi^\perp)$$
$$= \underline{P}(\phi^+ \mid \phi^\top,\psi^\perp) + \underline{P}(\psi^+ \mid \phi^\top,\psi^\perp) - \underline{P}(\phi^+,\psi^+ \mid \phi^\top,\psi^\perp)$$
$$= \underline{P}(\phi^+ \mid \phi^\top) + \underline{P}(\psi^+ \mid \psi^\perp) - \underline{P}(\phi^+ \mid \phi^\top)P(\psi^+ \mid \psi^\perp)$$
$$= \underline{\mathrm{TPR}}_\phi + \underline{\mathrm{FPR}}_\psi - \underline{\mathrm{TPR}}_\phi\underline{\mathrm{FPR}}_\psi.$$

After rewriting all terms accordingly, the lower bounds for $\underline{TPR}_{\phi \vee \psi}$ and $\underline{FNR}_{\phi \vee \psi}$ are established. The upper bounds for $\overline{TPR}_{\phi \vee \psi}$ and $\overline{FNR}_{\phi \vee \psi}$ follow analogously, and the remaining bounds for for $\underline{TNR}_{\phi \wedge \psi}$, $\overline{TNR}_{\phi \wedge \psi}$, $\underline{FPR}_{\phi \wedge \psi}$, and $\underline{FPR}_{\phi \wedge \psi}$ are obtained using De Morgan's law. $\square$

References

1. Baig, Q., Perrollaz, M., Laugier, C.: A robust motion detection technique for dynamic environment monitoring: a framework for grid-based monitoring of the dynamic environment. IEEE Robot. Automat. Mag. **21**(1), 40–48 (2014)
2. Dreossi, T., Donzé, A., Seshia, S.A.: Compositional falsification of cyber-physical systems with machine learning components. In: Barrett, C., Davies, M., Kahsai, T. (eds.) NFM 2017. LNCS, vol. 10227, pp. 357–372. Springer, Cham (2017). https://doi.org/10.1007/978-3-319-57288-8_26
3. Fawcett, T.: ROC graphs: notes and practical considerations for researchers. Mach. Learn. **31**(1), 1–38 (2004)
4. Fawcett, T.: An introduction to ROC analysis. Pattern Recogn. Lett. **27**(8), 861–874 (2006)
5. Galar, M., Fernandez, A., Barrenechea, E., Bustince, H., Herrera, F.: A review on ensembles for the class imbalance problem: bagging-, boosting-, and hybrid-based approaches. IEEE Trans. Syst. Man Cybernet. Part C (Appl. Rev.) **42**(4), 463–484 (2011)
6. Geirhos, R., Janssen, D.H.J., Schütt, H.H., Rauber, J., Bethge, M., Wichmann, F.A.: Comparing deep neural networks against humans: object recognition when the signal gets weaker. CoRR abs/1706.06969 (2017). http://arxiv.org/abs/1706.06969
7. Hammer, P.L., Rudeanu, S.: Pseudo-Boolean programming. Oper. Res. **17**(2), 233–261 (1969). https://doi.org/10.1287/opre.17.2.233
8. Junges, S., Jansen, N., Katoen, J.-P., Topcu, U., Zhang, R., Hayhoe, M.: Model checking for safe navigation among humans. In: McIver, A., Horvath, A. (eds.) QEST 2018. LNCS, vol. 11024, pp. 207–222. Springer, Cham (2018). https://doi.org/10.1007/978-3-319-99154-2_13
9. Khreich, W., Granger, E., Miri, A., Sabourin, R.: Iterative Boolean combination of classifiers in the ROC space: an application to anomaly detection with HMMs. Pattern Recogn. **43**(8), 2732–2752 (2010). https://doi.org/10.1016/j.patcog.2010.03.006
10. Levinson, J., Montemerlo, M., Thrun, S.: Map-based precision vehicle localization in urban environments. In: Proceedings of Robotics: Science and Systems. Atlanta, GA, USA, June 2007. https://doi.org/10.15607/RSS.2007.III.016
11. Levinson, J., Thrun, S.: Robust vehicle localization in urban environments using probabilistic maps. In: IEEE International Conference on Robotics and Automation, pp. 4372–4378 (2010)
12. Moras, J., Cherfaoui, V., Bonnifait, P.: Moving objects detection by conflict analysis in evidential grids. In: IEEE Intelligent Vehicles Symposium (IV 2011), pp. 1120–1125 (2011)
13. Păsăreanu, C.S., Gopinath, D., Yu, H.: Compositional verification for autonomous systems with deep learning components. In: Yu, H., Li, X., Murray, R.M., Ramesh, S., Tomlin, C.J. (eds.) Safe, Autonomous and Intelligent Vehicles. UST, pp. 187–197. Springer, Cham (2019). https://doi.org/10.1007/978-3-319-97301-2_10

14. Petrovskaya, A., Thrun, S.: Model based vehicle detection and tracking for autonomous urban driving. Auton. Robots **26**(2–3), 123–139 (2009)
15. Powers, D.: Evaluation: From precision, recall and f-measure to ROC, informedness, markedness & correlation. J. Mach. Learn. Technol. **2**(1), 37–63 (2011)
16. Radtke, P.V., Granger, E., Sabourin, R., Gorodnichy, D.O.: Skew-sensitive Boolean combination for adaptive ensembles – an application to face recognition in video surveillance. Inf. Fus. **20**, 31–48 (2014). https://doi.org/10.1016/j.inffus.2013.11.001
17. Sagi, O., Rokach, L.: Ensemble learning: a survey. WIREs Data Min. Knowl. Discovery **8**(4), e1249 (2018). https://doi.org/10.1002/widm.1249
18. Schumann, J., Liu, Y. (eds.): Applications of Neural Networks in High Assurance Systems, Studies in Computational Intelligence, vol. 268. Springer, Cham (2010). https://doi.org/10.1007/978-3-642-10690-3
19. Scott, M.J.J., Niranjan, M., Prager, R.W.: Realisable classifiers: improving operating performance on variable cost problems. In: Proceedings of the British Machine Vision Conference, pp. 31.1–31.10. BMVA Press (1998)
20. Thrun, S., Burgard, W., Fox, D.: Probabilistic Robotics (Intelligent Robotics and Autonomous Agents). The MIT Press, Cambridge (2005)
21. U.S. Department of Transportation, N.H.T.S.A.: Automated driving systems 2.0. a vision for safety (2017). www.nhtsa.gov/sites/nhtsa.dot.gov/files/documents/13069a-ads2.0_090617_v9a_tag.pdf

Supervision of Intelligent Systems: An Overview

Mario Gleirscher[1,2(✉)] (iD)

[1] Mathematics and Computer Science, University of Bremen, Bibliothekstr. 5, 28359 Bremen, Germany
`mario.gleirscher@uni-bremen.de`
[2] Assuring Autonomy International Programme, University of York, Deramore Lane, York YO10-5GH, UK

Abstract. Intelligent, online-learning, and other adaptive systems, such as the ones using reinforcement learning, have the potential to behave in an undesired way and are, thus, subjected to corrective external influence when they are used in critical contexts. We speak of *supervision* when referring to such influence, and of *supervisors* when talking of the components performing supervision. This work introduces core concepts in supervision and provides an overview of supervision techniques, highlighting recent applications in the supervision of intelligent systems. Furthermore, we will discuss the *synthesis and assurance of supervisors*, focusing on aspects of their modelling, verification, validation, and certification as well as their correct construction and the accompanying qualification of appropriate development tools. Our main conclusion is that reliable supervision offers a *separation of the concerns of correctness and autonomy*, enabling new options in the assurance and operation of intelligent and learning components in safety-critical applications.

Keywords: Intelligent systems · Cyber-physical systems · Safe autonomy · Reinforcement learning · Supervisory control · Controller synthesis · Sound development · Formal methods

1 Introduction

Systems have been controlled by software under human supervision for many decades and in many application domains. Our societies are, however, facing the quest for governance of machine intelligence used increasingly as a control technology in safety-critical public, industrial, and domestic areas. A wide variety of research hence deals with governance through *automated supervision by controllers responsible for fulfilling critical properties*. We call these controllers *supervisors*. Automated supervision is a software-intensive technology and, as such, subjected to corresponding software engineering and certification practices, including standard-compliant assurance, for example, according to IEC 61508 [30]. In this work, we examine the following three questions:

– What do adequate supervisors for intelligent systems look like?

A. E. Haxthausen et al. (Eds.): Peleska Festschrift 2023, LNCS 14165, pp. 202–221, 2023.
https://doi.org/10.1007/978-3-031-40132-9_13

- How can supervisors be constructed correctly?
- What are the criteria for supervisors to receive certification credit?

Accordingly, Sect. 2 introduces three running examples with the aim of aiding the discussion. Section 3 clarifies important terms as well as the specific viewpoint taken in this work. Section 4 gives an overview of several approaches to supervision, both in general and specific to intelligent systems. Section 5 summarises two universal approaches to the correct automated construction of supervisors, and Sect. 6 adds notes on the appropriate modelling for this purpose. Section 7 contains a brief account of industry-focused assurance workflows specific to supervisory control. Section 8 concludes with some key observations.

2   Examples of Supervised Intelligent Systems

The following three examples highlight categories of safety-critical systems with an increasing use of machine intelligence. These systems are, thus, subjected to supervision and should make the examination below more tangible.

In *robotic surgery* [9,28], robots assist in surgical tasks, usually under manual supervision or teleoperation by the surgeon. The *safety requirements* can, for example, include the avoidance of harm of any critical tissue to be left unaffected by the task. Moreover, a usual *performance goal* would be for the surgery to be minimally invasive. An intelligent robot in a surgical setting could learn to optimise parts of this performance goal while obeying hard safety constraints through automatic supervisory control. The supervisor could, for instance, be a separate embedded system deployed in the robot or a control infrastructure component with remote access to the robot's sensors and actuators.

In manufacturing automation, where *human-robot collaboration* has been around more or less since the early 1970s [54], modern intelligent control enables a wide range of interaction settings. Humans can collaborate on complex tasks in necessarily close vicinity to stationary robot arms, robotic utility vehicles, and other machines. Safety requirements usually pertain to the freedom of collision and clamping, while performance requirements can be about the avoidance of nuisance, quick progress, low energy consumption, and cost reduction in general [22]. Intelligent robots can then use safe learning techniques (explained later) to optimise multiple performance goals while guaranteeing task completion and safety constraints. Supervision is then, for example, taking care of the scenario-specific implementation of the completion goals and constraints [22].

Supervisory control also plays a critical role in *driving automation* [10,34]. The controllers of the lateral and longitudinal dynamics of autonomous vehicles receive inputs from a human driver or even a traffic information system in terms of set point changes to follow. Safety requirements in this domain include collision avoidance, keeping the lane, and dealing with dangerous internal hazards, such as running out of fuel or a failure of a control software component, dynamo, or battery. Performance requirements may include fuel efficiency and the minimisation of the estimated time to arrival. An intelligent vehicle can optimise its performance goals (e.g., specific to a geographical region) via learning. Meanwhile, a supervisor handles combinations of the mentioned hazards automatically or by falling back to an attentive human driver [11,26].

3   Background

Our discussion in this and the following sections will adopt some terminology from control theory and control engineering [53]. Readers from the software engineering domain unfamiliar with these terms are invited to have a look into the gentle software engineering related introduction in [38]. Here, we will not delve into the mathematics needed to properly apply control techniques.

Control theory aims at providing sound tools for control engineering. There, the central concept is that of the *process* to be controlled, often called "controlled process" or "plant". Section 2 presents three prominent types of safety-critical cyber-physical systems, where a process (e.g., surgery, industrial manufacturing, driving on a public road) is to be controlled by some control regime.

An important characteristic of a process is its *natural response*, its behaviour without external stimulus. We will see that it is useful to think of a discrete-event system, such as a software system, as such a process. In traditional control practice, the typical case considered is that of a *stable* system where the response to pulse (e.g., driving over a barrier) or step (e.g., holding the gas pedal down) signals stabilises at the original (e.g., chassis is straight) or a defined new (e.g., high speed) state, respectively, after an appropriate transition period without further interaction. To focus on controller design, a stable natural response can sometimes even be zeroed in (i.e., removed from) the used model. However, in more complex supervisory control settings, we need to consider *unstable* systems, that is, systems whose natural response is chaotic, occasionally more than some imposed safety constraints permit. These constraints allude to Leveson's fruitful notion of safety as an emergent property [36]. In our context, this chaotic natural response can be understood as an instance of *autonomy*. Hence, we will call the processes under supervision the *autonomous processes*.

An autonomous process can perform complex tasks, such as "driving from A to B", "resource efficient operation of a production line", or "fuel efficient heating of a building". Systems involved in performing this task might exhibit some, not necessarily human, *intelligence*. By "intelligent" or "smart", we refer to a comparatively rich ability of environmental perception of a system, the focus of human-machine interaction on non-trivial decision making or the exchange of final task results, and, thus, a corresponding autonomy of the process over a wide range of decisions. Moreover, this kind of intelligence is not necessarily present initially but might be the result of *learning*, a process of *adaptation* of the initially defined behaviour towards a behaviour that optimises some *cost (or fitness) functional*. This adaptation is normally driven by a series of interactions of components within an autonomous process and by these components receiving rewarding or penalising stimuli. A class of techniques widely-used in artificial intelligence (AI) applications and following these ideas is known as *reinforcement learning (RL)* [51, Chap. 21]. Because it is non-trivial to determine which was first, intelligence or the ability to learn, we could as well equate intelligence with the ability to adapt to new situations. For a discussion of the notion of machine intelligence, we refer the reader to Russell and Norvig's textbook [51, Sect. 1.1].

The state space reachable in an autonomous process will often include undesired or dangerous regions, for example, an autonomous vehicle could leave the road unsafely. This unsafe leaving of the road can be an undesired outcome of a driving action. Of particular interest is the situation where that action was one of several options to be chosen from by the vehicle's controller. But what were the circumstances for the undesired outcome? Was it

– some unexpected disturbance,
– the result of a (learned) decision, or
– a some other internal fault?

In each of these three cases, we encounter the notion of *risk* in the situation of interest. Qualitatively, risk can stem from an action with one or more (potentially uncertain) outcomes, of which at least one is undesired. Quantitatively, risk can be described as a function of

– the *probability of exposure* to a certain situation,
– the *probability of an undesired outcome* of an action enabled in that situation, and
– the *severity* of that outcome [27].

In more complicated settings not discussed here, one might not only consider risk of an action but also the chance of that action. Chance as the dual of risk is referring to the possibility (or probability) of desired outcomes. Note that we allow deterministic actions with exactly one undesired outcome. Moreover, the autonomous process usually has a choice between several actions enabled in a situation. This choice is one of the main entry points of influence for a supervisor.

Consequently, we view *supervision* as the separation of the concerns of *correctness* and *autonomy*. Here, correctness can comprise two independent aspects:

– *Safety* or, quantitatively, the degree of freedom from unacceptable risk, and
– *Progress* or, quantitatively, the degree of task performance or productivity.

As already hinted at, autonomy results from the process' natural response, its behaviour without (corrective) stimuli from the supervisor's perspective.

Hence, we use the term *supervisory control* to refer to the occasional—discrete or temporarily continuous—influence on an otherwise autonomous process with the goal to achieve or maintain correctness [46] while allowing the process to optimise some performance criteria given, for example, as a cost functional. Clearly, that process needs to be *observable* and *controllable* to the degree needed to successfully perform supervision (Fig. 1). Supervisory control can be performed manually and is traditionally done by human operators in, for example, chemical process plants, power stations, critical infrastructure, manufacturing (Sect. 2), and other domains of industrial automation, known as "supervisory control and data acquisition" (SCADA [14]).

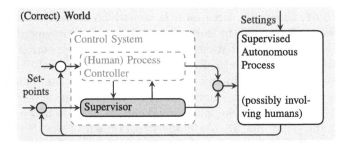

Fig. 1. A supervisor component embedded into a closed-loop system (the world) with an autonomous process and an optional process-external and task-specific, perhaps human or human-assisted, process controller

4 Supervision

This section introduces a light-weight taxonomy of supervision (Sect. 4.1), several universal techniques (Sect. 4.2), specialisations of these approaches suitable for the supervision of intelligent systems (Sect. 4.3), and closes with a discussion of the relationships to safety verification, controller synthesis (Sect. 4.4), and digital twins (Sect. 4.5).

4.1   A Taxonomy of Supervision

Our focus is on *automatic supervision and supervisory control*. First of all, supervision is characterised by being done *online*, that is, at run-time or during the operation of an autonomous process. Supervision can be performed passively or actively, with a soft global or hard local impact, and triggered based on events and/or applied permanently (Fig. 2).

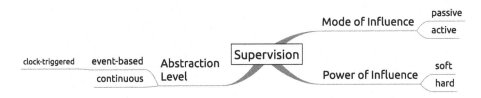

Fig. 2. A light-weight taxonomy of supervision

Regarding its *mode of influence* or response, *passive* supervision does not alter the process but raises awareness of anomalies, such as hazardous deviations from parameter reference intervals. Human operators (as indicated in Fig. 1) or a specific component of the autonomous process itself then have the possibility or even the responsibility to react to these anomalies (e.g., by single corrections or falling back to a mode of teleoperation or shared control [9]). *Active* supervision extends the passive mode by the capability to influence the process, normally through direct control (sometimes called "override") of certain process parameters otherwise controlled by the process itself. For example, the surgeon takes over the remote control of the robot arm, or the human driver takes over in a traffic situation with too much uncertainty for automatic control.

Considering the *power of influence*, a supervisor can perform *soft, indirect, or global* actions on the process. The supervisor acts as a moderator with a global impact on the process, that is, supervision and natural response are superimposed. The soft or indirect approach to supervision is typically exercised via the optimisation of a cost function in optimal and adaptive control and its applications to intelligent systems (e.g., in automated driving, a cost function could exponentially penalise fuel consumption). In contrast to that, we have the frequently practised *hard, direct, or local* supervision, where constraint mechanisms lead to a local influence aside from the natural response in critical regions of the process. Prominent examples for hard supervision are lane-keeping assistants, ADAS L1[1] functions used in modern cars for promptly correcting the trajectory and alerting the driver. Global and local influence have different properties regarding their ability to provide correctness guarantees. For example, it can be much harder to define a globally influencing supervisor to maintain an invariant than to define a locally acting supervisor to achieve safety [37].

One can distinguish two *abstraction levels* where supervision takes place. First, *event-based* (or high-level) supervision can be seen as a form of discrete-event control: the supervisor observes the process and influences it whenever some (e.g., dangerous or otherwise significant) events occur (e.g., an undesired lane change). Another example would be a safety system responsible for startup and shutdown routines triggered upon dangerous incidents, such as the handling of broken valves in a chemical process plant. A special case of this event-triggered control scheme is supervision at the occurrence of regular clock events (e.g., an equidistantly sampled comprehensive inspection of the patient's health status during the surgery). Second, *low-level* (or continuous) supervision is characterised by the (usually sampled) observation and temporarily continuous influence of the process (e.g., the low-level manoeuvre control for collision avoidance in a particular mode of the supervisor [20]). Low-level supervision can be implemented by standard approaches to control engineering. An example for this would be a corrective PID[2] controller used to locally stabilise an aeronautic system against wind, enabling a pilot to focus on more strategic decisions.

4.2 Fundamental Approaches to Supervision

The perhaps most widely-used class of approaches to supervision is called *safety monitoring* (e.g., SMOF [40]). There, usually simple but highly reliable monitoring mechanisms (also called "watchdogs", "policing functions", etc.) are triggered by hazardous events occurring in a process. These mechanisms then send

---

[1] Automated driving assistance system at autonomy level 1 [43].

[2] Proportional-Integral-Derivative; see, for example, [53].

warnings, for example, to a human supervisor or another higher-level (supervisory) control system. Passive supervision beyond the monitoring of formal safety properties [15] is also known as *run-time verification* [35].

A broad line of work gathers under the term of *run-time enforcement*. While run-time enforcement usually includes safety monitoring, its main purpose is to actively transform (e.g., ignore, correct, or otherwise modify) observed deficient discrete sequences or continuous signals such that they maintain a correctness specification [19,47,52] before being forwarded to some actuators in the process. One of the perhaps oldest and simplest mechanisms for intercepting and altering control inputs to the process is called *safety limiter*. In many cases, safety monitors and limiters are still manually engineered components.

Run-time verification and enforcement techniques are based on automata theory as well as qualitative and quantitative variants of temporal logic.[3] These techniques enable a variety of monitoring and enforcement schemes. Some of these schemes are amenable to prior deductive verification (e.g., the ModelPlex tool for the monitoring of hybrid systems [42]) and automated supervisor construction (e.g., the YAP tool for synthesising supervisors implementing risk-informed response properties [22]). Another example is *shielding* [7], motivated by the treatment of error-prone behaviour of complex electronic hardware. Shielding enables run-time enforcement by providing an approach to synthesising discrete supervisors (called *shields*) for fast output validation and correction in reactive control hardware. Shielding has already been investigated for use in intelligent and learning systems with uncertainties, as discussed in the next section.

4.3 Supervision of Intelligent Systems

As suggested in the above discussion, supervision is of particular interest in the context of autonomous, intelligent, and learning processes. There, the subject of supervision is not only the behaviour of a particular "snapshot" of a process but also the way how this process adapts itself to new situations, with the result of changing its behaviour in a rather subtle but potentially hazardous manner. Indeed, several techniques are available that can be understood as supervision techniques according to our characterisation in Sect. 4.1. Some of these techniques are natural extensions of the approaches introduced in Sect. 4.2.

In *risk-sensitive optimal control*, a technique also applicable in intelligent control systems, supervision occurs in a subtly indirect form as a weighting parameter of an exponential cost functional to be minimised [56]. That parameter's role is to heavily penalise disruptive or destabilising controls (e.g., produced by some state-feedback controller) with the expectation to increase robustness of the controlled process against chaotic disturbances or overly disruptive set point changes, while keeping track of performance goals. Risk-sensitive control can, thus, help in avoiding unnecessary overreactions, for example, when circumventing an obstacle on the road, or when touching critical tissue.

---

[3] For example, signal temporal logic, a variant of metric (time) temporal logic, particularly well-suited for reliable and efficient signal checking.

Supervision plays a central role in *safe reinforcement learning*. The wide success of reinforcement learning [51] is perhaps due to the advantage (over plain dynamic programming) of being able to learn merely from rather local reward stimuli, penalties, and observations and without complete prior knowledge of the process' internal dynamics or a global cost functional. There are several approaches implementing indirect and direct forms of supervision in RL applications. A soft form of RL supervision is based on *reward shaping* and *impact regularisation* [37]. These techniques aim at the creation of reward functions that penalise large—hence, potentially unsafe—state changes or any entrance of dangerous regions of the state space. As a result, the learning process is expected to avoid unsafe actions and highly likely or fully circumvent unsafe regions.

In contrast to soft RL supervision, *safety-constrained RL* [32] works in two stages. In the first stage, a safe sub-process of the Markov process describing the autonomous process is determined. That constrained sub-process then acts as a direct global supervisor for the RL agent's remaining learning episodes. In the second stage, the actual learning, the agent can then safely optimise some performance specification relative to the previously imposed constraint.

Shielding mechanisms (Sect. 4.2) have been extended to be used in RL applications. For example, to block locally unsafe actions available to the choice of an RL agent, a shield is computed online (using model checking) from the knowledge of states reachable by hypothetically performed actions in a locally modelled Markov process [33]. The result is an online-executable safety-constrained form of RL, with the learning forced to remain in the set of the safety invariant. Similar ideas have been developed for other control applications [1,5].

The overarching goal of the discussed approaches is the protection against hazardous events and their consequences with the potential of sacrificing performance under nominal conditions. The usual hypothesis is that incidents with harmful consequences—stemming from hazardous events in the autonomous process—would not have occurred or would have been far less likely when under supervision. In this sense, supervision can be intuitively defined to be effective by means of a, potentially probabilistic, counterfactual argument.

4.4   Relationship to Safety Verification and Controller Synthesis

While supervision is primarily understood as an online control technique, there are techniques, usually employed offline, with quite similar effects when applied to an autonomous process: safety verification and controller synthesis.

Safety verification aims at providing guarantees for the safety of the behaviour of an autonomous process, already *at design time*. There, a range of techniques (e.g., formal methods such as B, Z, VDM; automated reasoning such as temporal logic model checking or automated deduction; see, e.g., [48]) allow one to derive a firm conclusion about the correctness (here, safety) of *all possible executions* of that process. Accordingly, the safety verification problem is in many cases formulated as an *invariant property* that needs to hold along these executions, or, equivalently, as an *invariant set of states* that an execution must never leave, given it starts from an initial state in that set.

This characterisation can, of course, be seen as an indirect form of supervision. Now, would such a design-time approach make the use of separate supervisors redundant? Well, on the one hand, safety verification can bear the sometimes unrealistic assumption that the model used to formally reason about these executions faithfully captures all the relevant parts of the real autonomous process, down to a sufficient level of detail. On the other hand, if the model is reliably conservative and allows the transfer of the safety guarantees to the process implementation, it might still be practical or even be required to separate supervisory control from task control.

Controller synthesis is another offline technique aiming at the computation of controllers, more specifically, control policies applicable to the whole state space and lifetime of a process. For example, the winning region[4] of a safety game (as, e.g., used in shielding [7]) has to be computed fully *in advance* in order to know how the process needs to be safely initialised and influenced on-the-fly.

Although, at the same level of abstraction, off- and online techniques can be quite different, techniques such as controller synthesis, mainly used offline, can serve the construction of a supervisor (even online as, e.g., shown in [2]) that then performs online to reduce or avoid hazards in an autonomous process.

4.5   Relationship to Digital Twins

Recent developments in simulation and virtual prototyping and commissioning culminated in the rise of *digital twins* employed in a variety domains [55]. Digital twins enable a more or less strongly *coupled execution* of a primary system in operation (i.e., the process or physical twin) and a, not necessarily fully equivalent, secondary system (i.e., the digital twin). While not much is genuinely new about digital twins, the latter can be seen as a modern instance of a multipurpose environment with a high-bandwidth connection to the primary system. Digital twins can thus be useful in a range of tasks in data-intensive (model-based) systems engineering and operation. Among these tasks are, for example:

- Flexible *integration testing* by model-, software-, or hardware-in-the-loop testing, whilst offering various modes of co-simulation (e.g., [17, 22, 39]).
- *Conformance testing* of critical components (e.g., supervisors) by using appropriate abstractions and coupled test execution (e.g., [23]).
- Simulation-informed *teleoperation* or *shared control*, perhaps as a form of SCADA with a multi-modal human-machine interface (Sect. 3).
- *Supervision* by using the digital twin as a reference model and comparing complex observations between primary and secondary systems (e.g., [57]).
- *Active supervision* going beyond safety monitoring and teleoperation.

Consequently, it can be beneficial to build digitally twinned supervisors in order to test these critical parts in parallel to their operation in the real process [22]. As opposed to that, the whole digital twin itself could be understood and used as a

---

[4] The set of states from where it is always and indefinitely possible for the controller to win (here, to maintain an invariant) by exercising its previously computed policy.

supervisor, given the appropriate instrumentation built into it. However, it needs to be examined on a case-by-case basis, whether the complexity of a practical digital twinning architecture (e.g., taking advantage of a heavy-weight computing infrastructure) gets in the way of using it reliably in a critical supervision task.

5   Synthesis of Supervisors

As already hinted at in Sect. 4.1, it is reasonable to think of complex supervisors as discrete-event or hybrid controllers. Controller design automation then immediately raises the question of the automated synthesis of supervisors. Controller or program synthesis is a traditional multi-disciplinary and, thus, well-researched area. In the Sects. 5.1 and 5.2, we will briefly examine two main approaches, dynamic programming and the solving of dynamic games, with a focus on their respective discrete variants. These approaches became available from over seven decades of research. However, a historical perspective is out of scope here.

5.1   Dynamic Programming of Supervisors

Dynamic programming refers to a wide class of dynamic optimisation techniques that can find a controller from a potentially infinite set of possible controllers. This set is sometimes called the *design space*. The solution of the corresponding search problem is guided by evaluating a cost functional for all possible executions of a process model. These executions result from applying a range of admissible control signals to the model of the process dynamics.

More specifically, the cost-optimal controller can, for example, be easily constructed by a comparatively simple numerical algorithm called value iteration [51, Sect. 17.2]. This algorithm computes optimal control inputs backwards for the whole (admissible) state space and the considered lifetime of the process. The result is a control policy defined for all (initial) states of the admissible state space and for the chosen time interval. Dynamic programming can be applied in continuous and discrete settings. Hence, it is suitable for synthesising supervisors for both event-based or high-level supervision [22] and for low-level supervision.

Two advantages of dynamic programming over other dynamic optimisation techniques are of interest here: Particularly, when using value iteration for supervisor synthesis, discrete dynamic programming can approximate autonomous processes with non-linear natural response reasonably well. Moreover, value iteration allows for a simple yet useful mechanism to locally constrain control policies such that they avoid moving the process into an unsafe area. Clearly, discrete dynamic programming has important limits, especially when executed online, if the precision and lifetime requirements lead to very large state and input spaces. For a broader introductory treatment of this quite well-researched area, readers may consider [51, Sect. 17].

5.2 Game-Based Supervisor Synthesis

Game-based supervisor synthesis refers to a class of approaches, building on and generalising dynamic programming and other control techniques. One of the main differences of dynamic game theory over plain dynamic programming is that the controller construction directly takes into account adversarial behaviour—in control theory, usually referred to as "disturbance"—of the autonomous process. For example, a patient moves their body during the surgery, or a vehicle's lane positioning sensors are bounded inaccurate.

From solving such games, we can obtain controllers that work as desired under worst-case assumptions about the process. The cost functionals used for these games then become quite critical because they carry the hypothesis that, in less adversarial situations, the controllers should perform even better, that is, even safer. The circumstance creating this hypothesis is due to the completeness of the search problem (in the discrete game) or the convexity of the optimisation problem (in the weighted game). In other words, it is assumed that this completeness or convexity reflects reality. In fact, in many practical applications this assumption was proven to be justified. Our focus in the remainder of this section lies on discrete games (e.g., [47]).

Worth mentioning are automata-based games with qualitative winning conditions, for example, the specific class of discrete games suitable for constructing controllers that provably maintain a finite state invariant. Such games are called *safety games* and their winning conditions are of the kind "never leave the invariant". The result of such a game can be a permissive policy (i.e., a still non-deterministic controller) that exerts *corrective influence* only if it is needed, for example, whenever the autonomous process is about to approach the boundary of an invariant set. Safety games are, for example, used for determining the corrective influence applied in shields [7], as already described in Sect. 4.2.

There are other classes of games allowing more expressive [47] and quantitative [6] winning conditions. Imagine an autonomous process with hazards or incidents that cannot be fully avoided but are occasionally occurring. Further envisage that the process' capabilities are insufficient or insufficiently incentivised to mitigate such events and leave the corresponding region of the state space. Moreover, consider that the supervisor, perhaps because of a lack of resources, only observes the process at sparse points in time but can, on demand, devote more effort in supervision. The required type of corrective influence in this scenario usually goes beyond the capacity of a safety game. However, a combination of a *reachability game* with a safety game might be able to address this situation. The winning condition of this combined game leads the synthesis algorithm looking for supervisors that can always return (i.e., progress) to the safe region from some unsafe state. An instance of these ideas is investigated in [22,47].

6 Modelling for Supervisor Construction

It does not matter which approach to supervision is chosen or whether one manually constructs a supervisor or wants to use synthesis for that. A frequent cross-cutting concern is the *modelling* for the purposes of *supervisor specification, synthesis, and verification*. The main question is: What needs to be included in a desirable model, for example,

- to feed a synthesis procedure for correct-by-construction supervisors,
- to aid an embedded software developer or control system engineer in implementing a validated supervisor design, or
- to help a verification engineer in examining a supervisor implementation?

The following model ingredients appear to be generally useful in this context:

1. A model of the autonomous process (i.e., the *world* or control loop model), in particular, with descriptions of the relevant actors performing in that domain (e.g., the surgeon, a transport robot, an oncoming vehicle; cf. Sect 2). These actors may describe human behaviour and mental models thereof to capture human-machine interaction being subject of supervision.
2. A parametric description of the *design space* for the supervisor or some kind of *specification* of the *monitoring and control capabilities* (e.g., the event and action alphabet) of any supervisor to be constructed.
3. A model of the *uncertainties* arising from both the world model and the supervisor specification. For example, the actors of the world model to be influenced may react with uncertainty, they can be fallible. Moreover, the supervisor could have faulty sensors or actuators. These phenomena justify the use of stochastic modelling as, for example, exemplified in [22].
4. A model of the *supervision requirements*, perhaps derived from standards for safety-critical systems [31] or from a domain-specific hazard analysis and risk assessment (HARA) of the autonomous process.

The world model (1), the design space (2), and the uncertainty model (3) can then be integrated into a model of the closed-loop system, as depicted in Fig. 1 and discussed in more detail in [22,23]. In a next step, the integrated model can be validated by checking it against the supervision requirements (4). These four ingredients have the potential to be core assets in industry-strength supervisor development workflows and life cycles [34], useful to all participating stakeholders (e.g., robotics and AI engineers, analysts, and assessors) and amenable to certification. The latter immediately leads us to the next section.

7   Certifiable Assurance of Supervisors

One of the crucial questions with systems used for critical purposes is that of whether these systems are dependably correct, that is, whether they are performing the right tasks in a highly reliable, available, and secure manner? Clearly, supervisors are systems subjected to all these requirements.

So far, we have dealt with supervision both as a control technique and as a run-time assurance mechanism, without looking into the details of how supervisors are implemented correctly and how they are certified. In this section, we view supervisors from a *verification and certification perspective* [48], that is, as *critical components under development*. Observing that supervisors perform critical tasks, their operation is subject to certification before entry into service.

Section 7.1 examines world model validation, correct supervisor synthesis, and supervisor verification with a focus on complete testing [45]. Section 7.2 explores the domain of supervisor certification and the accompanying qualification [50] of the tools used in supervisor engineering.

7.1 Correct-by-Construction Supervisors

Model Validation. The normally desired use of models obviously raises the question of model validation. Supervisor models themselves need to be checked for potential incompleteness, their parameters identified using appropriate techniques and empirical data, all with the aim to close the so-called "reality gap".[5] An advantage of supervisors is that they are sometimes, and preferably, orders of magnitude simpler than the autonomous process to be supervised, such that it might be comparatively easy to detect and close the reality gap.

Depending on the language or formalism, the world model (Sect. 6, Fig. 1) is provided in, model validation can be tackled

- by (tool-supported) reviews or formal inspection, if the world model is, for example, provided as a (textual) SysML or UML model and the supervision requirements remain informal statements;
- by (temporal logic or stochastic) model checking, if the world model is given as a lower-level (probabilistic) transition system with supervision requirements encoded as (probabilistic) temporal logic formulas [22]; or
- by deductive verification, if the world model is represented as a more abstract program or state machine and the supervision requirements are given, for example, as a Hoare triple or dynamic logic formula.

The *correctness and well-formedness properties* required for model validation can usually be derived from process and component HARAs as well as from the modelling formalisms used. An important aspect when using formalisms to specify these properties and the models is the *avoidance of vacuous checks* [12], that is, checks that do not contribute positive evidence to an assurance effort.

Correct Automated Construction. Tightly interwoven with the question of developing correct supervisors from valid world models is that of the correct automatic construction of supervisors (Sect. 5), in particular, the correct construction of supervisor implementations (i.e., program code, micro-controller code, or a circuit description for electronic hardware synthesis)[6] and intermediate representations (e.g., the input formalism of some model checker or proof assistant). For example, supervisors resulting from discrete game-based controller synthesis

---

[5] An undesired conceptual or representational gap between a real object and a usually fully independent representation of it, a typical side-effect of any modelling with a potentially huge impact on the overall validity of a model.

[6] For example, a C++, PLC, or VHDL program.

and discrete dynamic programming require as inputs a world model given as some kind of non-deterministic transition system. The synthesised supervisors can, thus, be represented straightforwardly as deterministic transition systems, amenable to temporal logic model checking. It is worth noting that the latter technique is frequently used in industrial practice. Hence, it is likely that certification authorities will have gained useful experiences with such formal techniques in a regulatory context (see [24] for a more detailed discussion).

Supervisor Verification. Depending on the complexity of the development steps to be made to get from a non-deterministic world model including a supervisor specification or design space to a particular supervisor implementation, the latter will at some point need to be verified against the initial world model and supervision requirements. We speak of supervisor verification. This verification might even be necessary if part of the supervisor development is based on correct-by-construction synthesis [23].

According to several widely-used industrial standards (e.g., DO-178 [30,49], IEC 61508, ISO 26262), the primary way of achieving certification credit for a supervisor implementation is *testing*, as examined in [34, p. 93] and illustrated in [44] for sensor systems in train supervisors. Among the variety of (normally incomplete) testing techniques used in practice, the testing of critical systems, such as supervisors, is typically accompanied with the requirement of being *complete*. Completeness, inherent to formal verification, means showing the absence of faults under all circumstances. Accordingly, complete in the context of testing then means that a supervisor test suite is able to detect *every possible fault* in a certain (usually quite large) formalism-induced[7] fault domain.

Complete testing can be used to formally verify refinement [45] and observation equivalence [41]. The latter can be accomplished, for example, by the W- [13] or H-methods [16]. These methods work by deriving a test suite (a set of input sequences) from a specification (e.g., a minimal deterministic Mealy machine or I/O automaton) that is able to detect every faulty state machine implementation, given the latter has a limited number of additional states. This form of testing suffers particularly from a problem similar to that of state space explosion in model checking. Because supervisors can often be designed as relatively simple state machines, this issue might not be a limiting factor. Moreover, many supervisors can be abstracted into non-deterministic symbolic transition systems where complete equivalence class testing techniques are available [29]. Non-determinism as an abstraction technique can strongly reduce the complexity in complete testing of supervisors for autonomous processes as encountered in intelligent cyber-physical and socio-technical systems. However, complete testing often requires an automata-based specification, which can be hard to craft manually. Hence, it is crucial to be able to synthesise abstract supervisors from even more abstract (e.g., property-based) supervisor specifications.

---

[7] If automata are used to represent the test reference, every faulty automaton possible in the fault domain can be detected by at least one test case of the suite.

7.2   Industrial Certification of Supervisors

Certification of supervisors according to IEC 61508 [30] or related standards involves a number of tasks.

First of all, supervisor specifications will usually be the result of a regulatory *process HARA* for an autonomous process. The outcome of such a HARA can be a range of (supervision) requirements, some of which specify the safety measures or corrective influence to be implemented in the (synthesised) supervisor.

Moreover, supervisors as critical components are subjected to a *component HARA* and, consequently, to safety integrity level (SIL) classification. A SIL represents a set of assurance requirements with the goal to reduce the failure likelihood of a supervisor. As already mentioned, the failures of interest here can be caused by faulty sensors, planning or decision algorithms, and actuators. Thus, the SIL determines the assurance measures (e.g., testing, formal verification, delivery of an assurance case) to be taken—according to the applicable standard—to receive certification credit for the supervisor implementation.

Importantly, in the context of artificially intelligent systems, such credit is to be achieved with respect to AI safety requirements and AI regulations. The safety requirements can capture known failure modes of AI components used in the autonomous process, as summarised in, for example, [3,8]. The regulations can include, for instance, recent EU directives [18], the novel ANSI/UL 4600 standard [4], or general safety-critical system standards, such as IEC 61508 [30].

The regulations mandate the creation of evidence (e.g., test verdicts, mathematical proofs) and a documented argument demonstrating that the designed and implemented supervisors are correct and compliant. Such an argument needs the correctness properties of the autonomous process and the supervisor to be derived from the aforementioned AI failure modes and the HARAs. Part of these properties need to be translated into supervisor models [44], appropriate proof obligations (e.g., temporal logic formulas used in model checkers, theorems initialising proof efforts in proof assistants), and exhaustive test campaigns to be run against supervisor implementations [23]. The aim of all stakeholders should then be to turn the resulting argument into an explicit, well-structured, and rigorously [21] challenged and evidenced *assurance case*.

Tool Qualification. In most situations, engineers are interested in using tools for design automation and the aforementioned development and assurance stages. In a certification context (e.g., where DO-178C is applicable), this desire quickly leads to the task of tool qualification as required by the corresponding standards (e.g., DO-330 [50]), that is, the assurance of the software tools used for supervisor development and assurance. Especially, we need to rule out, for example, that a synthesis tool introduces faults in the generated supervisor implementations, faults subsequently encountered during operation.

As already mentioned, supervisors are critical components and their failure can have catastrophic consequences. The same holds of tools directly involved in the automated construction of supervisors. Erroneous verification tools do not directly introduce but perhaps only mask potential supervisor faults. Hence, they are subjected to a less[8] stringent qualification regime [24]. However, erroneous synthesis tools can directly introduce faults into supervisors. Consequently, these tools need to undergo a stringent qualification, applying the assurance measures described in the Sects. 4.4 and 7.1, in particular, formal proofs of property or semantics preservation across the involved transformations and translations.

8   Conclusions

This work outlines and highlights important issues and questions to be dealt with when engineering supervisors for intelligent systems, accompanied by an approach to the *certifiable synthesis and verification of supervisors.*

In coherence with Leveson's notion of safety as an emergent property [36], we made the assumption that autonomy can be treated as a chaotic natural response in a sufficiently observable and controllable process. An important observation based on this assumption is that, after *separating the concerns of correctness and autonomy* resulting from reliable supervision, the circumstance of whether or not an autonomous process exhibits intelligence or learning abilities, can take on a less critical and more manageable role in system assurance. Moreover, the criticality of supervision in intelligent cyber-physical systems will likely demand lean, fast, and easy to verify supervisor implementations with a highly direct connection to the process. Consequently, the domain of automatic supervision and supervisory control is in need of sound workflows for supervisor development [34], specifically to cope with new challenges in supervising intelligent systems.

A valuable goal of this endeavour addressing the Manifesto of Applicable Formal Methods [25] could be to provide engineers developing intelligent control systems and AI safety practitioners in industry with a formally-integrated [21] workflow for supervisor engineering, including development, synthesis, and assurance. Finally, it will also be worthwhile to further examine how recent platforms, for example, digital twins, could be used as a versatile supervision instrument, accompanied with high-fidelity simulation and data processing capabilities.

Acknowledgements. It is my pleasure to thank Jan Peleska for his proactive professional mentoring, his warm and friendly attitude, a very welcoming work atmosphere in his formal methods group, and a solid portion of jazz music during my time as a postdoctoral researcher at the University of Bremen. Furthermore, I would like to thank the anonymous reviewers for their helpful suggestions.

References

1. Alshiekh, M., Bloem, R., Ehlers, R., Könighofer, B., Niekum, S., Topcu, U.: Safe reinforcement learning via shielding. In: AAAI Conference on Artificial Intelligence, vol. 32 (2018). https://ojs.aaai.org/index.php/AAAI/article/view/11797

---

[8] Nevertheless, when using verification tools, tool qualification ideally amounts to the verification of the verification results.

2. Althoff, M., Dolan, J.M.: Online verification of automated road vehicles using reachability analysis. IEEE Trans. Robot. **30**(4), 903–918 (2014). https://doi.org/10.1109/TRO.2014.2312453

3. Amodei, D., Olah, C., Steinhardt, J., Christiano, P., Schulman, J., Mané, D.: Concrete problems in AI safety. CoRR (2016)

4. ANSI/UL 4600: Standard for safety for the evaluation of autonomous products. Standard, Underwriters Laboratories (2019). http://UL4600.com

5. Bastani, O., Li, S., Xu, A.: Safe reinforcement learning via statistical model predictive shielding. In: Robotics: Science and Systems (RSS). RSS Foundation (2021). https://doi.org/10.15607/rss.2021.xvii.026

6. Bersani, M.M., Soldo, M., Menghi, C., Pelliccione, P., Rossi, M.: PuRSUE – from specification of robotic environments to synthesis of controllers. Form. Asp. Comput. **32**(2-3), 187–227 (2020). https://doi.org/10.1007/s00165-020-00509-0

7. Bloem, R., Könighofer, B., Könighofer, R., Wang, C.: Shield synthesis. In: Baier, C., Tinelli, C. (eds.) TACAS 2015. LNCS, vol. 9035, pp. 533–548. Springer, Heidelberg (2015). https://doi.org/10.1007/978-3-662-46681-0_51

8. Bommasani, R., Liang, P., et al.: On the opportunities and risks of foundation models. CoRR (2021). https://doi.org/10.48550/arXiv.2108.07258

9. Boyraz, P., Dobrev, I., Fischer, G., Popovic, M.B.: Robotic surgery. In: Biomechatronics, pp. 431–450. Elsevier (2019). https://doi.org/10.1016/b978-0-12-812939-5.00015-x

10. Broy, M.: Challenges in automotive software engineering. In: 28th International Conference on Software Engineering (ICSE). ACM Press (2006). https://doi.org/10.1145/1134285.1134292

11. Calinescu, R., Alasmari, N., Gleirscher, M.: Maintaining driver attentiveness in shared-control autonomous driving. In: 16th International Symposium on Software Engineering for Adaptive and Self-Managing Systems (SEAMS). IEEE (2021). https://doi.org/10.1109/seams51251.2021.00021

12. Chockler, H., Kupferman, O., Vardi, M.: Coverage metrics for formal verification. Int. J. Softw. Tools Technol. Trans. **8**(4), 373–86 (2006). https://doi.org/10.1007/s10009-004-0175-4

13. Chow, T.S.: Testing software design modeled by finite-state machines. IEEE Trans. Softw. Eng. **4**(3), 178–187 (1978). https://doi.org/10.1109/TSE.1978.231496

14. Dey, C., Sen, S.K.: Industrial Automation Technologies. CRC Press (2020). https://doi.org/10.1201/9780429299346

15. Diekert, V., Leucker, M.: Topology, monitorable properties and runtime verification. Theor. Comput. Sci. **537**, 29–41 (2014). https://doi.org/10.1016/j.tcs.2014.02.052

16. Dorofeeva, R., El-Fakih, K., Yevtushenko, N.: An improved conformance testing method. In: Wang, F. (ed.) FORTE 2005. LNCS, vol. 3731, pp. 204–218. Springer, Heidelberg (2005). https://doi.org/10.1007/11562436_16

17. Douthwaite, J., et al.: A modular digital twinning framework for safety assurance of collaborative robotics. Front. Robot. AI **8**, 402 (2021). https://doi.org/10.3389/frobt.2021.758099

18. European Commission: Report on the safety and liability implications of artificial intelligence, the internet of things and robotics. Technical report, COM/2020/64, EU (2020). https://eur-lex.europa.eu/legal-content/en/TXT/?uri=CELEX:52020DC0064

19. Falcone, Y., Mounier, L., Fernandez, J.C., Richier, J.L.: Runtime enforcement monitors: composition, synthesis, and enforcement abilities. Form. Method. Syst. Des. **38**(3), 223–262 (2011). https://doi.org/10.1007/s10703-011-0114-4

20. Foster, S., Gleirscher, M., Calinescu, R.: Towards deductive verification of control algorithms for autonomous marine vehicles. In: 25th International Conference on Engineering of Complex Computer Systems, ICECCS 2020 Singapore, pp. 113–118 (2020). https://doi.org/10.1109/ICECCS51672.2020.00020

21. Foster, S., Nemouchi, Y., Gleirscher, M., Wei, R., Kelly, T.: Integration of formal proof into unified assurance cases with Isabelle/SACM. Formal Aspects Comput. **33**(6), 855–884 (2021). https://doi.org/10.1007/s00165-021-00537-4

22. Gleirscher, M., et al.: Verified synthesis of optimal safety controllers for human-robot collaboration. Sci. Comput. Program. **218**, 102809 (2022). https://doi.org/10.1016/j.scico.2022.102809

23. Gleirscher, M., Plecher, L., Peleska, J.: Sound development of supervisors. Working paper, U Bremen (2022). https://arxiv.org/abs/2203.08917

24. Gleirscher, M., Sachtleben, R., Peleska, J.: Qualification of proof assistants, checkers, and generators: where are we and what next? Sci. Comput. Program. **226**(3), 102930 (2023). https://doi.org/10.1016/j.scico.2023.102930

25. Gleirscher, M., van de Pol, J., Woodcock, J.: A manifesto for applicable formal methods. Softw. Syst. Model., 1–17 (2023, in press). https://arxiv.org/abs/2112.12758

26. Gold, C., Damböck, D., Bengler, K., Lorenz, L.: Partially automated driving as a fall-back level of high automation. In: Fahrerassistenzsysteme, 6. Tagung, vol. 28 (2013). https://mediatum.ub.tum.de/doc/1187198/

27. Hansson, S.O.: Risk. In: Zalta, E.N. (ed.) The Stanford Encyclopedia of Philosophy. Metaphysics Research Lab, Stanford University (2018). https://plato.stanford.edu/entries/risk/

28. Howe, R.D., Matsuoka, Y.: Robotics for surgery. Annu. Rev. Biomed. Eng. **1**(1), 211–240 (1999). https://doi.org/10.1146/annurev.bioeng.1.1.211

29. Huang, W., Peleska, J.: Complete model-based equivalence class testing for nondeterministic systems. Formal Aspect. Comput. **29**(2), 335–364 (2016). https://doi.org/10.1007/s00165-016-0402-2

30. IEC 61508: Functional safety of electrical/electronic/programmable electronic safety-related systems. Standard, The 61508 Association (2011). http://www.61508.org/

31. ISO/PAS 21448: Road vehicles - safety of the intended functionality (SOTIF). Standard, ISO (2019). https://www.iso.org/standard/70939.html

32. Junges, S., Jansen, N., Dehnert, C., Topcu, U., Katoen, J.-P.: Safety-constrained reinforcement learning for MDPs. In: Chechik, M., Raskin, J.-F. (eds.) TACAS 2016. LNCS, vol. 9636, pp. 130–146. Springer, Heidelberg (2016). https://doi.org/10.1007/978-3-662-49674-9_8

33. Könighofer, B., Rudolf, J., Palmisano, A., Tappler, M., Bloem, R.: Online shielding for stochastic systems. In: Dutle, A., Moscato, M.M., Titolo, L., Muñoz, C.A., Perez, I. (eds.) NFM 2021. LNCS, vol. 12673, pp. 231–248. Springer, Cham (2021). https://doi.org/10.1007/978-3-030-76384-8_15

34. Koopman, P., Wagner, M.: Autonomous vehicle safety: an interdisciplinary challenge. IEEE Intell. Transp. Syst. Mag. **9**(1), 90–96 (2017). https://doi.org/10.1109/MITS.2016.2583491

35. Leucker, M., Schallhart, C.: A brief account of runtime verification. J. Logic Algebr. Progr. **78**(5), 293–303 (2009). https://doi.org/10.1016/j.jlap.2008.08.004

36. Leveson, N.G.: A systems-theoretic approach to safety in software-intensive systems. IEEE Trans. Dependable Secure Comput. **1**(1), 66–86 (2004). https://doi.org/10.1109/tdsc.2004.1

37. Lindner, D., Matoba, K., Meulemans, A.: Challenges for using impact regularizers to avoid negative side effects. In: Espinoza, H., et al. (eds.) 3rd SafeAI Workshop. AAAI (2021). http://ceur-ws.org/Vol-2808/

38. Litoiu, M., et al.: What can control theory teach us about assurances in self-adaptive software systems? In: de Lemos, R., Garlan, D., Ghezzi, C., Giese, H. (eds.) Software Engineering for Self-Adaptive Systems III. Assurances. LNCS, vol. 9640, pp. 90–134. Springer, Cham (2017). https://doi.org/10.1007/978-3-319-74183-3_4

39. Löcklin, A., Müller, M., Jung, T., Jazdi, N., White, D., Weyrich, M.: Digital twin for verification and validation of industrial automation systems - a survey. In: 25th International Conference on Emerging Technologies and Factory Automation (ETFA). IEEE (2020). https://doi.org/10.1109/etfa46521.2020.9212051

40. Machin, M., Guiochet, J., Waeselynck, H., Blanquart, J.P., Roy, M., Masson, L.: SMOF: a safety monitoring framework for autonomous systems. IEEE Trans. Syst., Man, Cybern., Syst. **48**(5), 702–715 (2018). https://doi.org/10.1109/tsmc.2016.2633291

41. Milner, R.: Communication and Concurrency. International Series in Computer Science. Prentice-Hall (1989)

42. Mitsch, S., Platzer, A.: ModelPlex: verified runtime validation of verified cyber-physical system models. Form. Method. Syst. Des. **49**(1-2), 33–74 (2016). https://doi.org/10.1007/s10703-016-0241-z

43. On-Road Automated Driving (ORAD) Committee: Taxonomy and definitions for terms related to driving automation systems for on-road motor vehicles. Standard J3016_201806, SAE International (2018). https://www.sae.org/standards/content/j3016_201806/preview/

44. Peleska, J., Haxthausen, A.E., Lecomte, T.: Standardisation considerations for autonomous train control. In: Margaria, T., Steffen, B. (eds.) Leveraging Applications of Formal Methods, Verification and Validation. Practice, ISoLA 2022. LNCS, vol. 13704. Springer, Cham (2022). https://doi.org/10.1007/978-3-031-19762-8_22

45. Peleska, J., Huang, W., Cavalcanti, A.: Finite complete suites for CSP refinement testing. Sci. Comput. Program. **179**, 1–23 (2019). https://doi.org/10.1016/j.scico.2019.04.004

46. Ramadge, P.J., Wonham, W.M.: Supervisory control of a class of discrete event processes. SIAM J. Control. Optim. **25**(1), 206–230 (1987). https://doi.org/10.1137/0325013

47. Renard, M., Rollet, A., Falcone, Y.: Runtime enforcement of timed properties using games. Form. Asp. Comput. **32**(2–3), 315–360 (2020). https://doi.org/10.1007/s00165-020-00515-2

48. Roggenbach, M., Cerone, A., Schlingloff, B.H., Schneider, G., Shaikh, S.: Formal Methods for Software Engineering. EATCS. Springer, Switzerland (2020). https://doi.org/10.1007/978-3-030-38800-3

49. RTCA/DO-178C: Software considerations in airborne systems and equipment certification. Standard, RTCA SC-205 (2011). http://www.rtca.org/

50. RTCA/DO-330: Software tool qualification considerations. Standard, Radio Technical Commission for Aeronautics (RTCA) (2011). https://standards.globalspec.com/std/1461615/RTCADO-330

51. Russell, S., Norvig, P.: Artificial Intelligence: A Modern Approach, 3 edn. Pearson International (2014)

52. Schneider, F.B.: Enforceable security policies. ACM Trans. Inf. Syst. Secur. **3**(1), 30–50 (2000). https://doi.org/10.1145/353323.353382

53. Schwarzenbach, J.: Essentials of Control. Longman (1999)
54. Sugimoto, N.: Safety engineering on industrial robots and their draft standards for safety requirements. In: 7th International Symposium on Industrial Robots, pp. 461–470 (1977)
55. Tao, F., Cheng, J., Qi, Q., Zhang, M., Zhang, H., Sui, F.: Digital twin-driven product design, manufacturing and service with big data. Int. J. Adv. Manuf. Technol. **94**(9), 3563–3576 (2018). https://doi.org/10.1007/s00170-017-0233-1
56. Whittle, P.: Risk-sensitive linear/quadratic/gaussian control. Adv. Appl. Probab. **13**(04), 764–777 (1981). https://doi.org/10.2307/1426972
57. Woodcock, J., Gomes, C., Macedo, H.D., Larsen, P.G.: Uncertainty quantification and runtime monitoring using environment-aware digital twins. In: Margaria, T., Steffen, B. (eds.) ISoLA 2020. LNCS, vol. 12479, pp. 72–87. Springer, Cham (2021). https://doi.org/10.1007/978-3-030-83723-5_6

Fault Injection in Co-simulation and Digital Twins for Cyber-Physical Robotic Systems

Peter Gorm Larsen[1]([⊠])[iD], Lukas Esterle[1][iD], John Fitzgerald[2][iD], and Mirgita Frasheri[1][iD]

[1] DIGIT, Department of Electrical and Computer Engineering, Aarhus University, Aarhus, Denmark
{pgl,lukas.esterle,mirgita.frasheri}@ece.au.dk
[2] School of Computing, Newcastle University, Newcastle upon Tyne, UK
john.fitzgerald@ncl.ac.uk

Abstract. The model-based engineering of dependable robotic systems brings challenges that include the need to work effectively with a range of models, owners and operators, and addressing the extent to which the systems evolve over time. This paper explores the linking of co-simulation, which allows for the exploration of models composed of multiple diverse simulation units, with the concept of a digital twin, which provides a framework for coupling virtual models with the real, evolving systems that they are intended to represent. We describe a systematic and generic approach to fault injection in multi-formalism models that use the Functional Mockup Interface standard, alongside the embedding of such multi-models in digital twins. We illustrate the potential and challenges of such an approach using a small "desktop" version of a commercial semi-autonomous agricultural robot. Inspired by the work of Jan Peleska on test automation, we identify directions for future research and innovation in this setting.

1 Introduction

In domains such as agriculture, increasing reliance is being placed on 'smart' cyber-physical robot systems that have a degree of autonomy. Techniques and tools for designing and maintaining such systems should assist engineers in delivering the level of dependability demanded by the application. Model-Based Design (MBD) is an attractive option for offering the evidence and rationale required to deliver dependability, but it faces some challenges in this setting. We focus on two of these. First, such systems are often composed of separate subsystems that are documented to varying levels of detail and that may have highly diverse models. Second, such systems may operate over a long period in a wide range of physical environments, and may be adapted, repaired and maintained so that, over time, the systems 'as built' diverge from their original design models.

We aim to contribute to meeting these challenges by proposing: (i) the use of co-simulation technology to allow smart Cyber-Physical Systems (CPSs) to be described by clusters of diverse models, coupled with (ii) the use of a Digital Twin (DT) concept which provides a framework for linking virtual models with the real, evolving systems that they purport to represent [8]. In this setting, we describe a systematic and

A. E. Haxthausen et al. (Eds.): Peleska Festschrift 2023, LNCS 14165, pp. 222–236, 2023.
https://doi.org/10.1007/978-3-031-40132-9_14

generic approach to fault injection in multi-formalism models alongside the embedding of such multi-models in DTs. Our goal here is to provide techniques that allow a DT to provide a level of supervisory control that enhances dependability in the presence of autonomy [7].

In order to ensure the dependability of robots and other autonomous systems, a significant body of research has focussed on synthesising supervisory controllers and devoting test regimes to ensure that they are correct [15]. Much of the work in this area tends to abstract away from some types of fault in the physical devices, as well as communications delays over networks. This is done in order to be able to express completeness and soundness, but from a practical perspective additional analysis is needed. For example, in [37], the authors propose a two-stage ROS-based verification mechanism that consists in static verification for multi-goal multi-agent decision-making using probabilistic model-checking, and runtime verification which uses invariant checking and focuses on the processing of real-time data. Finding the right granularity for the decision-making, i.e., having a proper mapping between high-level decisions and low-level abilities (of the agent/robot), remains a challenge.

In this paper we present work in progress towards the development of dependable robots utilising DTs. Specifically, we describe work on model-based fault injection allowing us to explore the limitations of a CPS by introducing various types of faults into its simulation. With a dedicated wrapper, which can be used on generic models implementing the Functional Mockup Interface (FMI) standard[1], we can inject virtual faults at runtime and interact with physical robots executing in real-time.

Section 2 briefly introduces the background technologies of co-simulation and DTs. We then present an overview of the techniques we propose to allow analysis of the dependability-related properties of CPSs (Sect. 3). Later in the paper, we describe the provision of support for analysing faults and failures using these approaches. These are exemplified in Sect. 4 on a small case study simulating Robotti – a real commercial agricultural robot[2]. Finally, Sect. 5 reviews these first steps and considers research directions towards enhanced CPS dependability through DTs coupled in test automation.

2 Background: Co-simulation and Digital Twins

The goal of our work is to facilitate the MBD of dependable cyber-physical robotic systems. In this context, dependability encompasses properties including reliability, safety, integrity and availability [1]. Engineering for dependability covers both the provision of evidence and arguments to justify the reliance placed on a system and the ability to avoid unacceptably serious or frequent failure. Research on engineering dependable CPSs therefore includes techniques, tools, processes and standards that provide for modelling, analysis and tolerance of faults, errors and failures, as well as the verification of designs and implementations.

For the reasons outlined in Sect. 1, our work builds on techniques for simulation of multiple diverse models describing different aspects of CPSs (described in Sect. 2.1) and the potential of DTs for maintaining models in line with the evolving CPS (described in Sect. 2.2).

---

[1] https://fmi-standard.org/.

[2] https://agrointelli.com/.

2.1 Co-simulation

Our work is focussed on enabling simulation of abstract CPS models as an element of design. A CPS is composed of computational and physical processes. We therefore expect that a CPS is described with multiple diverse models often generated by many different tools, some using discrete event formalisms, and some over continuous time domains. In practice, some of these constituent models will come from providers who may not wish to release full descriptions, and so we require to be able to coordinate the execution of diverse simulation units without necessarily requiring the full release of intellectual property. In order to ensure that the models are sufficiently faithful it may be necessary to perform different kins of calibration.

Our approach uses collaborative/coupled simulation (co-simulation) [20]. This technique brings individual simulation units of the CPS constituents together into a simulation of the CPS as a whole. This is achieved through coordinated time progression and exchange of values between the constituent simulations. Thus, a co-simulation typically consists of a repetitive procedure of setting inputs on the simulation units, making them progress in time, and retrieving their outputs. An introduction to and survey of work on co-simulation has been provided by Gomes et al. [16].

Although it is possible to define simulation composition for each potential pair of formalisms, a more open and general simulation approach requires that the units conform to a standard supporting interoperability. Our work is based on the FMI version 2 (FMI2) de-facto standard [2,3]. The individual simulation units in an FMI-based co-simulation are referred to as Functional Mockup Units (FMUs). Each FMU is expected to implement a set of C-interfaces conforming to the standard, provide a static description file describing the given simulation unit, and be packaged in a defined fashion.

The realisation of a co-simulation, and thereby a composition of FMUs, is carried out by a Co-simulation Orchestration Engine (COE) employing an orchestration algorithm. In the work reported here we used the Maestro2 COE [34,35] which for example contains its own language for controlling the orchestration.

2.2 Digital Twins

Advances in data gathering technology, networks and computational power have made it possible to think of real-world systems having their own *Digital Twins (DTs)* – including virtual models of reality that are continually updated about the actual state of their physical counterparts and which can enable decision-making that in turn leads to changes in the real world. The DT concept has garnered significant attention, driven by the potential to bring benefits such as visualisation, what-if analysis, preventive maintenance, performance optimisation and design space exploration [6]. Crucially for the work described here, fault diagnosis, safety monitoring [10], reconfiguration [23] and autonomy [18,30] are also seen as potential benefits of deploying DTs.

A feature of the DT concept is that the twin is added to the system being twinned, enhancing it, offering improvements over the original system's operation. These improvements emerge from the interaction between the original system and the DT. Consequently, we regard the engineering of the DT to deliver these improvements as a *systems engineering* task.

A DT is a system built around virtual representations (different models) of a 'real-world' system of interest. In this paper, we call the real-world system the *Physical Twin* *(PT)* to contrast it with the DT, although it can in fact be a combination of computational and physical processes and thus be a CPS. The representations at the heart of a DT could make a number of different abstractions to support different analyses, for example of performance or of safety. It is for this reason that we are interested in DTs built around multiple models. The DT also receives data about the PT, and these data can be used to update the models or to conduct analyses using those models. A DT delivers its added value by supporting analysis and reasoning services over the models and data, ultimately delivering capabilities such as anomaly detection, what-if analysis, visualisation or adaptation.

Kritzinger et al. [19] categorise reports of DTs according to the level of integration of the DT into the system of interest. A *digital model* is a representation of a PT that does not benefit from any automatic data exchange with the PT. A *digital shadow* is a model that receives an automated data flow from the PT so that the model is able to reflect changes in the observed state of the PT. A full-fledged DT is then a digital shadow that has the ability to send data to the PT, providing the DT with a level of control. An important aspect here is that the time delay in the data streamed from the PT to the DT is under control at an acceptable rate in order to still act as a DT [13].

Initial considerations for the engineering of DTs using a combination of models inside the DT that could be coupled together using co-simulation were presented in [9]. We make use of the INTO-CPS[3] multi-model toolchain [21]. Subsequently the streaming of data from a PT (possibly filtered for noise) using the FMI standard was established using RabbitMQ wrapped into an FMU [12]. This was taken further in [5] with an increased level of autonomy, where safety becomes even more important. This is the underlying technology we use for our fault injections as described below.

3   Fault Injection in Co-simulations

As we indicated in Sect. 2, the ability to analyse faults, errors and failures is an important aspect of ensuring dependability. In order to do this, it is important to be able model faults so that we can observe potential causal chains and examine alternatives for tolerating, limiting or mitigating their consequences. However, in the multi-formalism, multi-owner environment of a CPS project, the introduction of faults into closed-IP models is a particular challenge since the inherit behaviour of such models are unknown. In this section, we describe an approach to Fault Injection (FI) in our INTO-CPS multi-model toolchain.

FI techniques are used across software and hardware domains to analyse the robustness and dependability of system designs. In recent years, there has been a focus shift towards software FI [29], which can be applied at different levels, from changes that emulate bugs injected into code, to data injection for manipulating memory states and registers, and interface injections that target the inputs and outputs of the injected components. In any case, it is necessary to construct adequate fault models, that define the

---

[3] https://into-cps.org/.

what, when, and where of the faults being injected, with trade-offs on representation, usability, and efficiency [29]. These techniques have also been applied to MBD, i.e., Model-Implemented FI, where the response to faults is evaluated in simulation (e.g., Simulink [31], LabVIEW [17] and dSPACE [27] models). Nevertheless, there are some known drawbacks, such as:

1. FI artefacts are integrated in the system model [25, 28, 32], thus leading to high intrusion of the methods in the actual system model.
2. The FI has to be adapted each time the original model changes, as a consequence of the previous point.
3. External tools are required for performing the FI, which means that these tools are not seamlessly integrated in the modelling process.

We propose an FI approach that is FMI-compliant and extends our co-simulation framework based on Maestro through a configurable plugin. This allows faults to be injected at the interface points of FMUs, alleviating the drawbacks of current model-implemented FI. Additionally, the framework enables hardware-in-the-loop testing with FI, as described in Sect. 4.

Using co-simulation to implement a DT utilises MBD, allowing to perform fault-injection at the interface points between individual models and components (FMUs). An initial exploration of this has been reported by Frasheri et al. [14]. In our proposed approach, Maestro (the COE) is extended through a plugin to support fault injection of FMUs during run-time[4]. The plugin creates a wrapper around the FMU(s) of interest (Fig. 1), which can be configured through an xml file. In this xml file, one can specify different events that can be applied at different periods of time during the co-simulation, affecting one or several inputs/outputs, of one or more FMUs. The wrapper injects the specified values if the time conditions are satisfied, otherwise it simply serves as a proxy by setting inputs, and getting outputs [13]. Examples of such a file are given below:

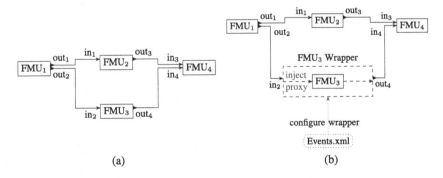

(a)   (b)

Fig. 1. (a) High-level schematic of the connections between FMUs; (b) High-level schematic of the fault injection mechanism. Adapted from [14].

---

[4] The repository for the plug-in is to be found at https://github.com/INTO-CPS-Association/fault-injection-maestro.

```
1   <events>
2     <event id="1" when="(t>=0.2)&(t<0.4)">
3       <variable valRef="3" type="real" newVal="57.0+t"
4       vars=""/>
5     </event>
6   </events>
```

An event entry is characterised by the *id* field (line 2), used to specify which FMU is affected by this event, and the *when* field (line 2), used to specify the timing condition, i.e., interval under which the fault is to be injected. Within this event, one or more inputs/outputs can be injected with specifiable values (line 3), where *valRef* is the value reference of the desired input/output, *type* refers to the type (among int, bool, string, and double), and *newVal*, specifying the new value to be injected. An arbitrary value can be given, as well as a function dependent on time as in this example. Events targeting different FMUs can be given as well, within the same file, as shown below:

```
1   <events>
2     <event id="id-A_1" when="(t>=0.2)&(t<0.5)" >
3       <variable valRef="3" type="real" newVal="t+2*var_3" vars="var_3," />
4     </event>
5
6     <event id="id-A_2" when="t=8.0" >
7       <variable valRef="1" type="bool" newVal="~var_1" vars="var_1," />
8     </event>
9
10    <event id="id-B_1" when="t>=10.0" >
11      <variable valRef="5" type="int" newVal="var_5+35" vars="var_5," />
12    </event>
13
14    <event id="id-B_2" when="t=12.0" >
15      <variable valRef="7" type="string" newVal="halloj" vars=""/>
16    </event>
17  </events>
```

The first two events (Lines 2–8) will be applied to the FMU identified by *id-A_**, whereas the other two (lines 10–16) will affect the FMU identified by *id-B_**. Additionally, the injected values can be calculated based on the state of other variables in the system, e.g., as in line 3, where the injected value for variable with value reference 3 is calculated based on the previous value of the same variable. In this case, this variable should be declared in the *vars* field so that the plugin is able to interpret it correctly. The time variable does not need to be declared. Similar operations can be done for the other types, except for the string type, where it is only possible to provide the plugin with an arbitrary string. It is also possible to write more complex timing conditions that depend on the values of the involved variables as shown below (line 1):

```
1   <event id="1" when="(t>=0.2)&(t<0.4)" other="var_2>0" vars="var_2,">
2     <variable valRef="2" type="real" newVal="t+36" vars="var_2," />
3   </event>
```

The interaction between Maestro and the FI plugin is depicted in Fig. 2. Typically, three phases characterise co-simulation: initialisation, execution and termination. We omit the termination phase here for simplicity. Maestro loads and instantiates the involved FMUs during initialisation. Thereafter, a wrapper is created for each FMU the user wants to fault inject. A list of FMU instances and the xml file are provided to the plugin. Maestro concludes the initialisation phase, by initialising each FMU and wrapper such that the starting point of each is coordinated.

The execution phase corresponds to a loop, where each iteration is in fact a simulation step, moving the co-simulation from time t to $t + h$, where h is the step-size.

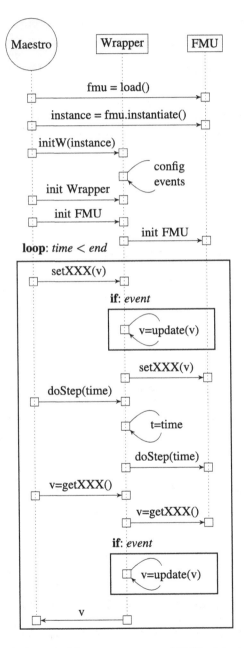

Fig. 2. Interaction between Maestro, wrapper, and FMU. Adapted from [14].

The execution phase will continue until a termination condition is met, or in other words the pre-specified end time is reached. At the beginning of each iteration, Maestro sets the inputs of the FMUs through setXXX calls. Thereafter, Maestro requests a doStep from each FMU. This effectively progresses the simulation in time with the given step-size. Before the iteration concludes, Maestro gets the outputs of all involved FMUs through getXXX calls. The fault injected FMUs are operated through their wrappers, i.e., Maestro requests the different calls, setXXX, doStep, getXXX through the wrapper interface. The wrapper itself can operate in inject and proxy mode. In inject mode, the wrapper will tamper with the values given by Maestro through setXXX calls, and the outputs provided by the FMU before passing them to Maestro through getXXX calls, if so specified in the configuration file. If no injection is specified at some t, the wrapper simply proxies the values.

4   A Case Study: The Desktop Robotti

In this section we first briefly explain the Desktop Robotti (DR) platform in Sect. 4.1. After that Sect. 4.2 describes how the PT is operating in parallel with the DT which is monitoring the operation of the PT. Finally Sect. 4.3 and Sect. 4.4 both illustrates how the FI techniques presented in this paper can be used to inject faults during the PT operation and how the monitoring capability can pretend additional obstacles being present in front of the DR.

4.1   Platform Description

The DR, shown in Fig. 3, is a 4-wheel robot that serves as a prototype of the Robotti field robot developed by AgroIntelli [11]. The DR is under continuous development, in terms of both hardware and software upgrades, as such in the following we provide the description that is relevant for the experiments and results reported in this paper, also discussed in [24]. It is possible to operate the DR through a teleoperation interface executing in a ROS2 network [26] within a virtual machine, acting as the system controller. Movement commands, consisting of a desired speed and heading angle, can

Fig. 3. The Desktop Robotti.

be sent to the robot via this interface. These values are calculated initially for a virtual bicycle model [36], thereafter translated into values for each wheel and sent to a dedicated ROS2 node running on the Raspberry Pi 4 Model B+, that serves as the brain of the DR. The real wheels have dedicated control loops in order to regulate the speed which run on an Arduino UNO, and continuously receive control parameters from the ROS2 node running on the Pi. Localisation is supported by processing the planar scans coming from a 2D lidar, that allow tracking of how the robot moves as compared to the initial pose. In later versions of the robot, the Marvelmind indoor positioning system has also used for localisation.

4.2   Parallel Operation and Monitoring

A characteristic of a DT is the ability to follow the operation of its PT during run-time by determining the state of the said twin in real-time. To achieve this, the DT utilises sensory data from the PT and applies filtering and time-series prediction approaches. In our setting, the state refers to the position of the robot expressed in (x, y) coordinates. It is therefore crucial to evaluate the accuracy of these predictions, and potentially determine bounds within which the error is expected to be. To this end, we have conducted initial tests, where the DT is run alongside its PT for a time window of $30s$. The DT in these experiments (Fig. 4) consists of an actuation and kinematic model used for prediction, and a monitor that visualises the predicted and real data. The communication with the PT is realised through the ROS network, by utilising an FMU setup with

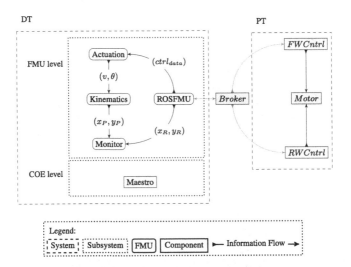

Fig. 4. The DT is composed of the actuation and kinematic models used to predict the position of the robot given the control commands sent from the user. The monitor displays the predicted and real data that come from the robot. The data is propagated through the ROS network, where a dedicated ROS-compatible FMU serves as the external interface point of the DT. The broker component gets the user commands and propagates it to both the DT and PT, as well as has access to the real position of the robot which is sent to the DT.

UniFMU [22] that encapsulates a ROS node. The Broker node forwards the user commands to both the DT and PT, while also forwarding the position of the robot to the DT. During the defined time window, both are fed with the same teleoperation commands that were intended to drive the robot through a three point turn.

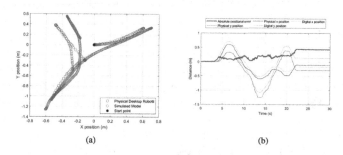

(a)   (b)

Fig. 5. Trajectories are illustrated as executed by the robot (in blue), and as predicted by the DT (in red) in Fig. a. Figure b shows the absolute positional error as well as the error of the physical robot and the digital model along the x- and y-axis. (Color figure online)

The outcome of this experiment is shown in Fig. 5a. Note that the error increases quickly as the robot starts moving, although there is a clear overall resemblance between the two trajectories. These discrepancies can be attributed to (i) the difference of start and break times between the twins as seen in the first, second and fourth stops, and (ii) a faster change of the heading angle performed by the PT as can been seen in during the middle left turn. The discrepancy regarding the break time could partly be caused by not including the mechanical delay caused by the DC motors in the actuation model. It still is unclear why the model stops before the actual PT. This can also be seen in direct comparison of the position along the x- and y-axis and the absolute positional error as illustrated in Fig. 5b. This experiment sheds more light into the challenge of achieving high fidelity on the DT side during parallel operation, and is an area that clearly requires future work.

4.3 Hardware-in-the-Loop Fault Injection

A DT setup can be used to perform hardware-in-the-loop testing, and support the injection of faults in order to evaluate the robustness of the fault-tolerance mechanisms in place. Below we describe a simple example of such an experiment, in order to provide an idea of what can be realised with our toolset. Assume as in the case of the parallel operation that the DT is coupled to the DR, with a two-way communication in place, and that the robot receives the target speed from a user. In such a case, it would be of interest to evaluate how the robot behaves should it receive distorted control signals, that make it jump back and forth, while it is following some trajectory. It is possible to simulate this scenario at the DT level (Fig. 6), by placing within the DT a controller to which fault injection is applied using the same tools as described in Sect. 3. The target speed provided by the user is also sent to the DT, which is then forwarded to the controller. The latter will output distorted values that are afterwards sent to the robot, received by the MockCntrl node which controls the robot, for a specific period of time. This scenario is depicted in Fig. 7. On the left side, under normal conditions, the controller will simply relay the speed set by the user, whereas on the right side, the output of the controller is fault injected from time step 5 s to 11.1 s, where values jump from -20 to 40 cm/s.

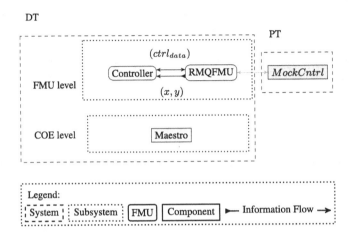

Fig. 6. The DT is composed of the controller, which can be fault injected. The communication with the PT is done through RMQFMU. On the PT a mock controller is placed which will simply rely the commands sent by the controller in the DT.

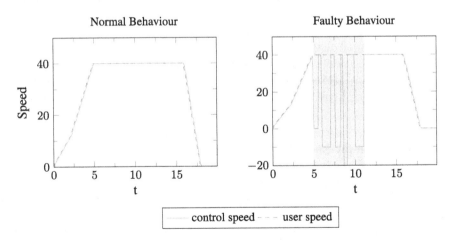

Fig. 7. Normal operation (left), where the controller in the DT relays the user speed, and fault injected conditions (right), where the controller outputs bad values that are thereafter sent to the robot, red shaded area.

While still a simple setup, this experiment gives a sense of what can be achieved with DTs that support FI capabilities, where it is possible to perform experiments with hardware, as soon as it becomes available.

4.4 Emergency Stop at the DT Level

A DT can be used in a variety of ways after being deployed alongside its PT, e.g., for prediction (as seen in Sect. 4.2), reconfiguration of the system as a whole, and for adding a supervisory monitoring layer, able to kick in should the PT behave in way that is not desired. Below we describe a simple setup for an emergency stop scenario, where the DT sends such a command to the robot if the native monitor on the PT malfunctions (is not able to correctly detect an obstacle ahead)[5]. In order to simulate this scenario, without the need of developing a faulty monitor for the PT, we follow a similar method to Sect. 4.3. Specifically, we place the native monitor (PTM) in the DT and use FI to simulate faulty behaviour of the component (Fig. 8). Additionally, in the DT there is the supervisory level component (DTM), as well as the RMQFMU which enables the communication with the PT. A mock of the native monitor is placed in the PT itself, that simply relays the data to the controller. While the robot is running, in this case moving ahead towards a virtual obstacle, its position data, and the perceived position of the obstacle are continuously being sent to the DT. They are used both at the PTM and DTM to evaluate whether an emergency stop should be issued. The latter will take place if the distance to the known obstacle is smaller than a predefined threshold. Without the FI, both monitors will send a stop command, whichever is processed first will cause the robot to stop. However, when the PTM is injected, by tampering its output (changing the stop command to a go ahead), as expected only the command from the DTM consists in a stop. In a simple manner, we are able to test, with the hardware in the loop, the expected behaviour of the DTM. It is clear that, at the time the DT would be deployed, it would be possible to let the PTM reside within the PT itself.

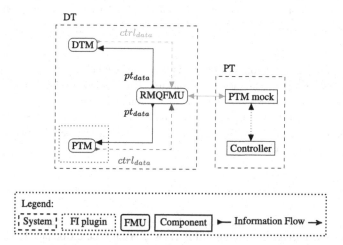

Fig. 8. PT-DT system configured with a faulty PTM. pt_{data} refers to the positions of the robot and obstacle, whereas $ctrl_{data}$ refers to the eventual emergency stop command sent from DTM/PTM.

---

[5] Note that the work regarding this experiment is at the time of writing under review.

5 Looking Forward

The interest in robotic systems with increasing levels of autonomy naturally gives rise to a concern for dependability, and particularly safety. DTs coupled with the co-simulation of multi-formalism models have potential to help ensure the levels of dependability required of such smart systems with their physical and computational elements. In our future work, we plan to integrate the FI primitives described in this paper with the test automation process. This allows us to explore tolerances of the system under test against different kinds of faults, following the approaches pioneered by Jan Peleska. Specifically, we will utilise Design Space Exploration (DSE) approaches [4] to perform controlled exploration of potential faults with multiple FIs. Integrated feedback loops will enable us to identify and explore corner cases in more detail where necessary.

In a DT context, incorporation of results from the run-time verification community makes a lot of sense [33]. In this way the desired properties are not only examined at the time of developing a PT but also examined after its deployment on the DT side. We expect that the FI work presented here can be used at development time and in a deployment setting in order to not just detect that a fault has occurred but to be able to diagnose it by seeing that the pattern is similar to what was experienced during FI.

Acknowledgements. We are grateful to the Poul Due Jensen Foundation for supporting the establishment of a Centre for Digital Twin Technology at Aarhus University, advancing the principles, tools and applications of Digital twin Engineering. We thank Jakob Levisen, Gill Lumer-Klabbers, Jacob Odgaard Hausted and Malthe Faurschou Tøttrup for their contributions for the Desktop Robotti case-study. We gratefully acknowledge Innovation Foundation Denmark for funding the AgroRobottiFleet project and ITEA for funding the UPSIM project. Finally we would like to thank the anonymous reviewers for valuable feedback on the original version of this paper.

Dedication. It is a pleasure to offer this paper in honour of Jan Peleska, whose leadership in the formal methods and the test automation communities has enabled collaborations research like ours. His work on formal approaches and their application in the rail sector will have a profound and long-lasting impact. Reflecting in particular on our collaboration on formal approaches in systems-of-systems, we thank Jan for the many lessons we have learned from him and for the friendship that he has shown us.

References

1. Avizienis, A., Laprie, J.C., Randell, B., Landwehr, C.: Basic concepts and taxonomy of dependable and secure computing. IEEE Trans. Depen. Secure Comput. **1**, 11–33 (2004). https://doi.org/10.1109/TDSC.2004.2
2. Blochwitz, T., et al.: The functional mockup Interface 2.0: the standard for tool independent exchange of simulation models. In: Proceedings of the 9th International Modelica Conference, Munich, Germany, September 2012
3. Blochwitz, T.: Functional mock-up interface for model exchange and co-simulation, July 2014. https://www.fmi-standard.org/downloads

4. Bogomolov, S., et al.: Tuning Robotti: the machine-assisted exploration of parameter spaces in multi-models of a cyber-physical system. In: Fitzgerald, J.S., Oda, T. (eds.) Proceedings of the 18th International Overture Workshop, pp. 50–64. Overture, December 2020

5. Esterle, L., Gomes, C., Frasheri, M., Ejersbo, H., Tomforde, S., Larsen, P.G.: Digital twins for collaboration and self-integration. In: 2021 IEEE International Conference on Autonomic Computing and Self-Organizing Systems Companion (ACSOS-C). IEEE (2021)

6. Feng, H., Gomes, C., Thule, C., Lausdahl, K., Iosifidis, A., Larsen, P.G.: Introduction to digital twin engineering. In: The Annual Modeling and Simulation Conference, Virginia, USA, pp. 1–12 (2021)

7. Feng, H., et al.: Integration of the MAPE-K loop in digital twins. IEEE, 18–20 July 2022. https://doi.org/10.23919/ANNSIM55834.2022.9859489

8. Feng, H., Gomes, C., Thule, C., Lausdahl, K., Iosifidis, A., Larsen, P.G.: Introduction to digital twin engineering. In: Proceedings of the 2021 Annual Modeling and Simulation Conference, Virtual Conference. IEEE, July 2021

9. Fitzgerald, J., Larsen, P.G., Pierce, K.: Multi-modelling and co-simulation in the engineering of cyber-physical systems: towards the digital twin. In: ter Beek, M.H., Fantechi, A., Semini, L. (eds.) From Software Engineering to Formal Methods and Tools, and Back. LNCS, vol. 11865, pp. 40–55. Springer, Cham (2019). https://doi.org/10.1007/978-3-030-30985-5_4

10. Flammini, F.: Digital twins as run-time predictive models for the resilience of cyber-physical systems: a conceptual framework. Phil. Trans. R. Soc. A **379**(2207), 1–11 (2021)

11. Foldager, F., Balling, O., Gamble, C., Larsen, P.G., Boel, M., Green, O.: Design Space Exploration in the Development of Agricultural Robots. In: AgEng Conference, Wageningen, The Netherlands, July 2018

12. Frasheri, M., Ejersbo, H., Thule, C., Esterle, L.: RMQFMU: bridging the real world with co-simulation for practitioners. In: Macedo, H.D., Thule, C., Pierce, K. (eds.) Proceedings of the 19th International Overture Workshop. Overture, October 2021

13. Frasheri, M., et al.: Addressing time discrepancy between digital and physical twins. Robot. Auton. Syst. **161**, 104347 (2023). https://doi.org/10.1016/j.robot.2022.104347

14. Frasheri, M., Thule, C., Macedo, H.D., Lausdahl, K., Larsen, P.G., Esterle, L.: Fault injecting co-simulations for safety. In: The 5th International Conference on System Reliability and Safety, ICSRS 2021 (2021)

15. Gleirscher, M., Peleska, J.: Complete test of synthesised safety supervisors for robots and autonomous systems. In: Farrell, M., Luckcuck, M. (eds.) Proceedings 3rd Workshop on Formal Methods for Autonomous Systems, pp. 101–109. FMAS, October 2021. https://arxiv.org/abs/2110.12589

16. Gomes, C., Thule, C., Broman, D., Larsen, P.G., Vangheluwe, H.: Co-simulation: a survey. ACM Comput. Surv. **51**(3), 49:1–49:33 (2018)

17. He, D., Hu, N., Wang, M.: Study on real-time fault injection and simulation of mechanic-electronic-hydraulic control system based on AMESim and LabVIEW. In: 2014 Prognostics and System Health Management Conference, PHM-2014 Hunan, pp. 446–450. IEEE (2014)

18. Hribernik, K., Cabri, G., Mandreoli, F., Mentzas, G.: Autonomous, context-aware, adaptive digital twins: state of the art and roadmap. Comput. Industr. **133**, 103508 (2021). https://doi.org/10.1016/j.compind.2021.103508. https://www.sciencedirect.com/science/article/pii/S0166361521001159

19. Kritzinger, W., Karner, M., Traar, G., Henjes, J., Sihn, W.: Digital twin in manufacturing: a categorical literature review and classification. IFAC-PapersOnLine **51**, 1016–1022 (2018)

20. Kübler, R., Schiehlen, W.: Two methods of simulator coupling. Math. Comput. Model. Dyn. Syst. **6**(2), 93–113 (2000)

21. Larsen, P.G., et al.: The INtegrated TOolchain for Cyber-Physical Systems (INTO-CPS): a Guide. Technical report, INTO-CPS Association, October 2018. www.into-cps.org

22. Legaard, C.M., Tola, D., Schranz, T., Macedo, H.D., Larsen, P.G.: A universal mechanism for implementing functional mock-up units. In: Wagner, G., Werner, F., Ören, T.I., Rango, F.D. (eds.) Proceedings of the 11th International Conference on Simulation and Modeling Methodologies, Technologies and Applications, SIMULTECH 2021, Online Streaming, 7–9 July 2021, pp. 121–129. SCITEPRESS (2021). https://doi.org/10.5220/0010577601210129

23. Leng, J., et al.: Digital twin-driven rapid reconfiguration of the automated manufacturing system via an open architecture model. Robot. Comput. Integr. Manuf. **63**, 101895 (2020). https://doi.org/10.1016/j.rcim.2019.101895

24. Lumer-Klabbers, G., Hausted, J.O., Kvistgaard, J.L., Macedo, H.D., Frasheri, M., Larsen, P.G.: Towards a digital twin framework for autonomous robots. In: The 5th IEEE International Workshop on Software Engineering for Smart Systems (SESS), COMPSAC 2021. IEEE, July 2021

25. Macedo, H.D., Rasmussen, M.B., Thule, C., Larsen, P.G.: Migrating the INTO-CPS application to the cloud. In: Sekerinski, E., et al. (eds.) FM 2019. LNCS, vol. 12233, pp. 254–271. Springer, Cham (2020). https://doi.org/10.1007/978-3-030-54997-8_17

26. Macenski, S., Foote, T., Gerkey, B., Lalancette, C., Woodall, W.: Robot Operating System 2: design, architecture, and uses in the wild. Sci. Robot. **7**(66) (2022). https://doi.org/10.1126/scirobotics.abm6074

27. Markwirth, T., Jancke, R., Sohrmann, C.: Dynamic fault injection into digital twins of safety-critical systems. In: 2021 Design, Automation & Test in Europe Conference & Exhibition (DATE), pp. 446–450 (2021). https://doi.org/10.23919/DATE51398.2021.9474066

28. Moradi, M., Gomes, C., Oakes, B.J., Denil, J.: Optimizing fault injection in FMI co-simulation through sensitivity partitioning. In: SummerSim, pp. 32–1 (2019)

29. Natella, R., Cotroneo, D., Madeira, H.S.: Assessing dependability with software fault injection: a survey. ACM Comput. Surv. (CSUR) **48**(3), 1–55 (2016)

30. Rosen, R., Wichert, G., Lo, G., Bettenhousen, K.: About the importance of autonomy and digital twins for the future of manufacturing. IFAC Papersonline **48**(3), 567–572 (2015)

31. Silveira, A.M., Araújo, R.E., de Castro, R.: FIEEV: a co-simulation framework for fault injection in electrical vehicles. In: 2012 IEEE International Conference on Vehicular Electronics and Safety, ICVES 2012, pp. 357–362. IEEE (2012)

32. Svenningsson, R., Eriksson, H., Vinter, J., Törngren, M.: Generic fault modelling for fault injection. In: Aichernig, B.K., de Boer, F.S., Bonsangue, M.M. (eds.) FMCO 2010. LNCS, vol. 6957, pp. 287–296. Springer, Heidelberg (2011). https://doi.org/10.1007/978-3-642-25271-6_15

33. Temperekidis, A., Kekatos, N., Katsaros, P.: Runtime verification for FMI-based co-simulation. In: Dang, T., Stolz, V. (eds.) Runtime Verification, pp. 304–313. Springer, Cham (2022). https://doi.org/10.1007/978-3-031-17196-3_19

34. Thule, C., et al.: Building custom, extensible, fast and verifiable, co-simulations with Maestro2 (2022, submitted)

35. Thule, C., Lausdahl, K., Gomes, C., Meisl, G., Larsen, P.G.: Maestro: the INTO-CPS co-simulation framework. Simul. Model. Pract. Theor. **92**, 45–61 (2019). https://doi.org/10.1016/j.simpat.2018.12.005. http://www.sciencedirect.com/science/article/pii/S1569190X1830193X

36. Woodcock, J., Gomes, C., Macedo, H.D., Larsen, P.G.: Uncertainty quantification and run-time monitoring using environment-aware digital twins. In: Margaria, T., Steffen, B. (eds.) ISoLA 2020. LNCS, vol. 12479, pp. 72–87. Springer, Cham (2021). https://doi.org/10.1007/978-3-030-83723-5_6

37. Yang, Y., Holvoet, T.: Generating safe autonomous decision-making in ROS. Electron. Proc. Theoret. Comput. Sci. **371**, 184–192 (2022). https://doi.org/10.4204/eptcs.371.13

Towards a Unifying Framework for Uncertainty in Cyber-Physical Systems

Jim Woodcock[✉]

University of York, York, England
jim.woodcock@york.ac.uk

Abstract. This paper is dedicated with affection to Jan Peleska on the occasion of his 65th birthday. We discuss a unifying theory of uncertainty in robotics based on Hoare & He's unifying theories of programming and Hehner's probabilistic predicative programming. We start a long-term research agenda with a semantics for Prism and end with many questions.

Dedication

I have known Jan for many years. We first met in 1991 when he was with DST in Hamburg. He invited me to give a course for his development team on using formal methods. DST were developing the Airbus Interphone System. I went with my colleague Joy Reed to Hamburg with my lectures and practicals well-prepared in advance. Jan had different ideas and made me work hard! He asked me to adapt the examples and practicals. Every night I revised my course and worked on the problem. We found a significant error in the specification of the Interphone. Cabin crew members could get locked out of a conference call during an emergency. We found this error by writing the formal specification in Z [35,39] and then reasoning about important scenarios. Jan and I became firm friends, meeting at conferences and visiting each other in Bremen, Oxford, and York. We worked together on European projects, such as INTO-CPS, influential in cyber-physical systems. I am constantly impressed by Jan's ability to develop and apply formal methods in real-world applications. Jan is one of those enviable people who always make progress on challenging problems.

In 2015, Jan developed a runtime verification technique for CSP by translating CSP to Kripke structures [25]. He checks that a system under test satisfies properties over CSP failures. This depends on the soundness of the translation and on traceability of the analysis back to the CSP model. With Ana Cavalcanti and Wen-ling Huang, we formalised the soundness argument. We unified the languages involved: normalised graphs in CSP model checking, action systems, and Kripke structures [4]. When Wen-ling asked me to contribute to Jan's Festschrift, I decided to revisit this work. I wanted to unify formalisms for treating uncertainty in robotics and to formalise Prism's semantics in particular.

A. E. Haxthausen et al. (Eds.): Peleska Festschrift 2023, LNCS 14165, pp. 237–253, 2023.
https://doi.org/10.1007/978-3-031-40132-9_15

1   Introduction

1.1   Uncertainty in Robotics

To motivate robotic uncertainty, here are two scenarios [28]. (i) An autonomous vehicle tries to drive quickly through an intersection with no signals. Instead of accelerating, it slows down. It gathers information on the intentions of pedestrians and other traffic. This helps the vehicle coordinate actions with others. It achieves its goal faster. (ii) A robotic arm pushes an irregular object to a designated pose. The robot must minimise the number of actions. It decides not to push the object directly towards the final pose. It uses the first few pushes to gather information on the object's centre of mass. Later actions are more effective. Both robots are uncertain. They learn more about their environment so they can achieve their goals. How do we model and reason about uncertainty?

1.2   A Unifying Framework for Uncertainty?

Our problem is how to model and solve robot decision and control tasks under uncertainty. This includes noisy sensing, imperfect control, environment changes, and inaccurate models. Applications include localisation and navigation, search and tracking, autonomous driving, multi-robot systems, object manipulation, and human-robot interaction. Robots must reason about outcomes of actions with limited sensor information. Actions have short-term rewards and inform long-term success. Notations for modelling uncertainty include pGCL [19], MDPs [13], POMDPs [28], dynamic epistemic logic [22], and the epistemic mu-calculus [34]. What would a unifying theory look like?

Research Hypothesis. We can unify different theories of uncertainty using: probabilistic relations [20,41]; Bayesian semantics [21]; and information theory [33].

1.3   Candidate Theory for Unification: POMDPs

POMDPs are partially observable Markov decision processes [28], generalising standard MDPs. POMDPs model an agent decision process with MDP dynamics, but the agent cannot observe the underlying state. It must maintain a sensor model and the underlying MDP. The sensor model is a probability distribution of observations, given the current state. An MDP policy function maps states to actions. A POMDP policy maps the observation history (the belief states) to actions. POMDPs have discrete states, actions, observations, and time. Robots operate in the physical world and need continuous control models. A unifying semantics could address the generalisation from discrete to continuous.

1.4   Unifying Semantics for Prism

Our first step towards a unifying theory of uncertainty is to outline semantics for Prism. We propose specification-oriented semantics for probabilistic proof and refinement. We use Hoare & He's Unifying Theories of Programming (UTP) [5, 24, 36, 37] and Hehner's Probabilistic Predicative Programming (PPP) [20]. These provide a probabilistic relational calculus, a Bayesian interpretation, and a link to information theory. We start with discrete-time Markov chains and extend this in later work to MDPs, POMDPs, continuous-time Markov chains, probabilistic automata, probabilistic timed automata, and partially ordered probabilistic timed automata. The semantics can unify Prism and a wide variety of other modelling languages. The denotational semantics that we define is the gold standard. Galois connections [18, 24] link our denotational semantics for individual languages. We derive operational semantics from denotational semantics, guaranteeing soundness. The derivation and soundness proofs for the operational semantics provide laws for algebraic semantics. We will establish a probabilistic Hoare logic [7] and a refinement theory and calculus [29]. We will complement the verification theory with a testing theory for practical systems (cf. Gaudel [17]). Finally, we will mechanise everything in the Isabelle/UTP theorem prover [15].

1.5   This Paper

We give a small motivating example of a Prism DTMC in Sect. 2. We discuss why we need a formal semantics for Prism in Sect. 3. In Sect. 4, we present a non-probabilistic Kripke-style semantics for the Unity programming language, which has a similar structure to the non-probabilistic part of Prism's language. We describe the existing system module semantics for Prism in Sect. 5. We present Hehner's Predicative Programming technique in Sect. 6 as a notation for defining Kripke semantics. We present Hehner's Probabilistic Predicative Programming technique in Sect. 7 as a notation for defining probabilistic semantics. We describe a simple example of reasoning about probabilistic specifications in Sect. 8. We give a description of related work in Sect. 9. We discuss where we go from here in Sect. 10.

2   A Prism Example

We start with an example of a simple Prism program solving a DTMC.

Example 1 (Prism DTMC Example). Throw a pair of six-sided dice until they are equal. How long will this take? A Prism program to answer this is in Fig. 1.

```
1  dtmc
2  module TwoDice
3    u: [1..6];
4    v: [1..6];
5    s: [0..3] init 0;
6    [] s=0 -> 1/6: (u'=1) & (s'=1) + 1/6: (u'=2) & (s'=1)
7              + 1/6: (u'=3) & (s'=1) + 1/6: (u'=4) & (s'=1)
8              + 1/6: (u'=5) & (s'=1) + 1/6: (u'=6) & (s'=1) ;
9    [] s=1 -> 1/6: (v'=1) & (s'=2) + 1/6: (v'=2) & (s'=2)
10             + 1/6: (v'=3) & (s'=2) + 1/6: (v'=4) & (s'=2)
11             + 1/6: (v'=5) & (s'=2) + 1/6: (v'=6) & (s'=2) ;
12   [] s=2 & u=v  -> (s'=3);
13   [] s=2 & u!=v -> (s'=0);
14   [] s=3 -> true;
15 endmodule
16 rewards "total_time"
17   s=0 : 1;
18 endrewards
```

Fig. 1. Prism program simulating throwing two six-sided dice until equal.

So we have a Prism model, but what properties does it have? How many throws, on average, do we need to terminate? The reward structure gives us the time steps: what is the expected time taken to reach, from the initial state, s=3? Prism says: you need 5.99997028280834 throws (with apologies for the spurious accuracy). But what if we have 10 dice? How many throws do we now need? We can generalise the program in Fig. 1, but that does not help us much: the resulting DTMC is too large and Prism cannot provide the answer. We need to reason outside the model checker.

3   Why Do We Need Another Formal Semantics for Prism?

An anonymous paper describes the semantics of the Prism language [32]. The semantics is not compositional because variables are shared between modules. Process algebraic operators combine modules. The semantics shows first how to flatten this structure into a single system module. This module is then given a semantics as a probabilistic Kripke structure. So why do we need yet another formal semantics for Prism?

Kwiatkowska et al. describe the combination of Prism's modules using "the standard CSP parallel composition": modules synchronise over all their common actions [27]. They describe Prism's support for several other CSP parallel operators, including alphabetised parallel and interleaving. But Prism's existing semantics is not straightforward. Its process algebraic operators may well be CSP-based, but some aspects are only syntactic, not semantic. For instance, action labels are not CSP events. Deadlock is not CSP deadlock. The hiding operator is not CSP's hiding operator.

Formal semantics can help us find more powerful probabilistic verification and validation techniques. Refinement theory can enable correctness by construction. Assertional reasoning can enable design by contract and runtime checking. Formal semantics can integrate tools, such as combining model checking and theorem proving. Testing theory can enable scalable validation and verification of practical systems. To extend Marie-Claude Gaudel's insight [17], probabilistic testing can be formal, too. We explain this below.

3.1   Prism Action Labels Are Not CSP Events

In Prism, an unlabelled guarded command is a kind of silent action similar to τ in CCS. Consider the example in Fig. 2a. Perhaps this behaves like the process $\tau \rightarrow P \, \square \, b \rightarrow Q$. Since τ is not part of CSP, how else might this behaviour arise? The answer lies in the hiding operator. The τ event could result from hiding the event a: $(a \rightarrow P \, \square \, b \rightarrow Q) \setminus \{a\}$. But the algebraic semantics of CSP has a law that says what happens when we hide an event in an external choice:

$$(a \rightarrow P \, \square \, b \rightarrow Q) \setminus \{a\} \; = \; P \setminus \{a\} \sqcap ((P \setminus \{a\}) \, \square \, (b \rightarrow (Q \setminus \{a\})))$$

```
1  mdp
2  module
3     s: [...];
4     []   s=0 -> (s'=sp);
5     [b]  s=0 -> (s'=sq);
6     ...
7  endmodule
```

```
1  mdp
2  module hide
3     s: [0..1] init 0;
4     []   s=0 -> (s'=1);
5     [a]  s=0 -> (s'=1);
6     []   s=1 -> true;
7  endmodule
```

(a) Prism example with labelled and unlabelled guarded commands.

(b) Prism module choosing between labelled and unlabelled commands.

Fig. 2. Labelled and unlabelled guarded commands.

The silent, internalised a event might occur so fast that the environment cannot choose the b event. This is the behaviour $P \setminus \{a\}$. The other behaviour $(P \setminus \{a\}) \, \square \, (b \rightarrow (Q \setminus \{a\}))$ gives the environment the possibility of the b event. The choice between these two behaviours is nondeterministic. This is not what is happening in the Prism code. The issue of action labels (events) is a red herring, since action labels are eliminated in the semantics once the translation reaches the system module [32].

3.2   Prism Deadlock Is Not CSP Deadlock

Deadlock (in the CSP sense) is structurally forbidden in Prism. Why? Because Prism's formalism has (probabilistic) Kripke semantics. This is important for the semantics of Prism's logics. Prism's property specification language has aspects of PCTL (probabilistic computation tree logic), CSL (continuous stochastic logic), PLTL (probabilistic linear temporal logic) and PCTL* (unified CTL and LTL). PCTL specifies discrete-time DTMCs and PTAs and real-time PTAs. CSL extends PCTL for CTMCs. LTL and PCTL* specify discrete-time and untimed CTMCs. Prism supports most of CTL. Semantics for these logics requires infinite sequences. CSP deadlock represents a bounded behaviour. For this reason, a Prism program cannot deadlock. Every state must have at least one outgoing transition. This also guarantees proper distributions in the transition probability matrix. If we need deadlock in a probabilistic program, we must model it in some way. We represent deadlock with a state with a single self-transition. Reaching these states is the same as deadlocking. Prism automatically searches models for deadlocks and fixes them by adding these self-loops.

3.3   Prism Hiding Is Not CSP Hiding

Hiding an event in CSP makes that event internal and urgent. Is this also true for Prism? Consider the module in Fig. 2b choosing between labelled and unlabelled commands. This does not prioritise the first command over the second.

1. For each command [] g -> p1: u1+ ... + pn: un of M'
   add [] g -> p1: u1+ ... + pn: un to the commands of M
2. For each a ∉ A and command [a] g -> p1: u1+ ... + pn: un of M'
   add [a] g -> p1: u1+ ... + pn: un to the commands of M
3. For each a ∈ A and command [a] g -> p1: u1+ ... + pn: un of M'
   add [] g -> p1: u1+ ... + pn: un to the commands of M

This is not the semantics of CSP hiding.

3.4   Refinement Theory

Correctness by construction (CbyC) is sound stepwise development. Examples include the refinement calculi of Back [2], of Morgan [30], and of Morris [31]. We want to extend the refinement calculus to probabilistic programs. Probabilistic CbyC (pCbyC) applies rules preserving correctness. It relies on probabilistic program refinement. This is important because probabilistic correctness is notoriously unintuitive [29].

3.5   Programming Logic

Morgan & McIver define a weakest pre-expectation calculus for pGCL [19]. This generalises Dijkstra's weakest precondition calculus [9]. Den Hartog's thesis proposes a probabilistic logic: pH [7]. This is a sound and complete calculus extending Hoare logic [23]. Both are variations of Dijkstra's Guarded Command Language GCL [8]. They include probabilistic choice $Q \oplus_p R$, selecting Q with probability p and R with probability $1 - p$.

3.6   Testing Theory

The seminal paper on principled system testing is by Gaudel: Testing Can Be Formal, Too (1995) [17]. Given specification *SP* and system under test *SUT*, testing uses a satisfaction (conformance) relation: *SUT* **sat** *SP*. The *SUT* is executable, raising issues of observability and controllability. Can probabilistic testing be formal, too? How?

3.7   Example: Decision Support

Suppose you are in a maze with three doors in front of you. Which door should you choose fairly to make further progress in the maze? You have a one-euro coin in your pocket to help you. What is your strategy? You have an idea: transform the coin's distribution with rejection sampling [3]: transform uniform$(0 .. 1)$ to uniform$(0 .. 2)$. This is the acceptance-rejection method. (Compare with Knuth-Yao's algorithm [26]):

1. Flip the coin twice. Interpret the outcome as a binary number.
2. Accept if the result is in $0 .. 2$ (a door number). Finish.
3. Reject if the outcome is out of range. Repeat.

Is this fair? What is the average time to choose a door? Consider yourself as the system under test. Assume you behave like the Prism code in Fig 3. Note the implicit assumption in the program code that your coin is not biased.

```
1   dtmc
2   module CoinDoors
3       s:  [0..3] init 0;
4       d:  [0..2] init 0;
5       b0: bool   init false;
6       b1: bool   init false;
7       [] s=0 -> 0.5:(s'=1) & (b0'=true) + 0.5:(s'=1) & (b0'=false);
8       [] s=1 -> 0.5:(s'=2) & (b1'=true) + 0.5:(s'=2) & (b1'=false);
9       [] s=2 & !b0 & !b1 -> (s'=3) & (d'=0);
10      [] s=2 & !b0 &  b1 -> (s'=3) & (d'=1);
11      [] s=2 &  b0 & !b1 -> (s'=3) & (d'=2);
12      [] s=2 &  b0 &  b1 -> (s'=0);
13      [] s=3 -> true;
14  endmodule
```

Fig. 3. Prism program using a coin to choose between doors.

3.8   How Do We Assess Your Strategy?

We want to test the SUT's behaviour. Two questions must be answered by any theory of probabilistic testing: (i) Correctness: Is the strategy fair? (ii) Performance: What is the average time needed for a choice?

Morgan & McIver ask the question, what is the issue about testing probabilistic systems [29]? Dijkstra said that program testing can be used effectively to show the presence of bugs [10]. Morgan & McIver said that for probabilistic programs, we cannot even establish that presence. Odd behaviours may occur in correctly operating probabilistic systems. Correctness is about the distribution of outputs. Are bugs sufficiently rare? Evidence of quantitative errors requires many traces and statistical analysis. Debugging probabilistic programs is a challenge, even with that evidence.

4   Unity

Chandy & Misra describe an experimental programming language: Unity [6]. Unity describes what is computed, not where, when, or how. Program commands execute nondeterministically with no control-flow. Programs can run indefinitely. Execution ceases if the program converges on a fixed point. Commands are (simultaneous) condi-

```
1   module SortThree
2       x: int init 3;
3       y: int init 2;
4       z: int init 1;
5       [] x>y       -> (y'=x) & (x'=y);
6       [] y>z       -> (z'=y) & (y'=z);
7       [] x<=y<=z -> true;
8   endmodule
```

Fig. 4. Unity code to sort three numbers.

tional assignments. There are no other commands, but there is a module structure. This model is asynchronous computation: an unstructured set of guarded assignments with nondeterministic selection. See also Alur & Henzinger's Reactive Modules [1] and Dill's MURϕ [11]. The Unity program in Fig. 4 sorts three numbers into ascending order. The program has a Kripke structure semantics that provides two infinite traces.

4.1   Kripke Structures

A Kripke structure describes models with propositionally labelled states. Temporal logic semantics uses Kripke structures. The essence is a transition relation. Nodes represent reachable states and edges state transitions. A labelling function maps nodes to sets of properties holding in that state. Kripke structures represent closed finite-state models with observability related to real executions. A trace is a sequence of observable parts of states.

Ordinary Kripke models are not reactive [16]. A reactive process executes internally before pausing for interaction with its environment. A Kripke model does not react, respond, or change while we evaluate it.

AP is a set of atomic propositions over variables, constants, and predicate symbols. A Kripke structure over AP is a quadruple $M = (S, I, R, L)$, as follows. (i) A finite set of states S and a set of initial states $I \subseteq S$. (ii) A left-total transition relation $R \subseteq S \times S, \forall s : S \bullet \exists s' : S \bullet (s, s') \in R$. (iii) A labelling function $L : S \to \mathbb{P} AP$. Left-totality ensures an infinite path exists through the structure. Deadlocked states are modelled by single outgoing self-loops. For state $s \in S$, the set $L(s)$ defines atomic propositions valid in s. Every path is an infinite state-sequence: $\rho = \langle s_1, s_2, s_3, \ldots \rangle$, such that for each $i > 0$, $R(s_i, s_{i+1})$ holds. A path ρ corresponds to word w, a sequence of sets of atomic propositions: $w = \langle L(s_1), L(s_2), L(s_3), \ldots \rangle$, an infinite sequence over alphabet $\mathbb{P}\,AP$.

4.2 Unity Module Semantics

Let C be the multiset of commands in a module and let $V = \{v_1, \ldots, v_m\}$ be the set of its local and global variables. States are tuples $(x_1, \ldots, x_m)$, where x_i is a value for v_i. The set of all states S consists of valuations of variables in V. The set of initial states is given either by explicit values for each variable or by implicit values defined by a predicate over variables (the init ... endinit construct). An unspecified initial value for a variable is simply the minimum value in the range.

4.3 Unity Single Command Semantics

Consider a guarded command $c \in C$ []g->u. The guard g is a predicate over variables in V. This command is enabled in a sub-state space $S_c = \{\, s \in S \mid s \models g \,\}$. In UTP, this is simply g. The command u is a (simultaneous) assignment to the variables in V: $u : S_c \to S$. Unmentioned variables stay the same.

5 Prism System Module Semantics

We start by considering the semantics for single commands. The assumptions are the same as for Unity. Command c of C is schematically: $[a]\ g \to p_1 : u_1 + \cdots + p_n : u_n$. The action label a is needed only for flattening process-algebraic operators. It has no semantics purpose once that has been done. Guard g is a predicate over the variables in V. Each state of the system is a variable valuation. g defines a subset of the global state $S_c = \{\, s \in S \mid s \models g \,\}$. In UTP, this is simply g. Update u_j of c is a transition assigning values to variables $u_j : S_c \to S$. Let $u_j = \bigwedge i : 1 .. m \bullet (v_i' = e_i)$. Each $s \in S_c$, is an m-tuple: $i \in 1 .. m \Rightarrow (ti = e_i(s))$. Update u_j in c occurs with probability p_j. c defines, for $s \in S_c$, a function $\mu_{c,s} : S \to \mathbb{R}_{\geq 0}$, for $t \in S$: $\mu_{c,s}(t) \mathrel{\hat{=}} \sum j : 1 .. n \bullet [\, u_j(s) = t\,] * p_j$. DTMC and MDP syntax guarantees $\mu\,c, s$ is a probability distribution over S.

    A discrete-time Markov chain is defined by a transition probability matrix. Define the matrix, for any $s, t \in S$: $\overline{P}(s, t) \mathrel{\hat{=}} \sum c : C \bullet \mu_{c,s}(t)$. The rows of $\overline{P}$ may sum to more than 1. Why? Local nondeterminism in a module arises from overlapping guards. Prism warns when local nondeterminism is detected in a DTMC. Nondeterministic choice is randomised. A probability distribution is obtained by normalising $\overline{P}$: $P(s, t) \mathrel{\hat{=}} \overline{P}(s, t) / \sum u : S \bullet \overline{P}(s, u)$. This replaces nondeterminism by uniform probabilistic choice between transitions.

6   Predicative Programming

Predicative Programming (PP) is Hehner's CbyC technique [20], related to Hoare & He's UTP [24]. Variables model observations. State variables are either before- (x) or after-variables (x'). Specifications are predicative relations over observations and state variables. PP uses pointwise relational calculus: $\forall$, $\exists$, $=$, $\Rightarrow$, $\wedge$, $\vee$, $\neg$, $;$, $\cdots$. The implementation relation is refinement: $P \sqsubseteq Q = [Q \Rightarrow P]$. (Here the brackets universally close the alphabet of P, which is the alphabet of Q.) Refinement requires every behaviour of Q is a behaviour of P. Refinement is transitive. P is implementable if $\forall \sigma \bullet \exists \sigma' \bullet P$. Here $\sigma = x, y, \cdots$ is the alphabet of before-variables and $\sigma' = x', y', \cdots$ is the alphabet of after-variables. P is deterministic just in case each before-state has a unique after-state.

6.1   Notation

Identity. $\mathbb{I} = (\sigma' = \sigma)$, for state vector σ.

Assignment. $x := e = (x' = e) \wedge (y' = y) \wedge \cdots$.

Conditional Composition. if b then P else $Q = b \wedge P \vee \neg b \wedge Q$.

Sequential Composition. $P \;;\; Q = \exists \sigma'' \bullet P[\sigma''/\sigma'] \wedge Q[\sigma''/\sigma]$. Where $\sigma = x, y, \cdots$ are initial values, $\sigma'' = x'', y'', \cdots$ are intermediate, and $\sigma' = x', y', \cdots$ are final.

Execution Time. Variable t records execution starting time. Variable t' records execution termination time. Nontermination has $t' = \infty$. In partial correctness, a program must produce a correct result whenever it terminates. In total correctness a program must terminate, and when it does it must produce a correct result. PP introduces super-total correctness: a program must terminate within a specified time, and when it does it must produce a correct result.

A guarded command in PP is just conjunction: $g \to P = g \wedge P$. The Unity program in Fig. 4 has the semantics defined by the recursive PP program in Fig. 5. The transition matrix is defined by the body of the program without the recursive calls. Refinement of Unity programs is simply PP refinement.

$$
\begin{array}{l}
x, y, z := 3, 2, 1 \;; \\
ST = \begin{array}{lll} x > y & \to y, x := x, y \;; & ST \\ y > z & \to z, y := y, z \;; & ST \\ x \le y \le z \to & true \;; & ST \end{array}
\end{array}
$$

Fig. 5. Semantics of program in Fig. 4.

7   Probabilistic Predicative Programming

Definition 1 (Discrete distribution). *Let e be an expression with free variables v. It is a discrete distribution if it satisfies two criteria: (i) Its value (for all assignments to v) is a probability: $[0 \le e \le 1]$. (ii) Its sum (for all assignments to v) is 1: $\sum v \bullet e = 1$.*

Example 2. Suppose n and m are strictly positive integers. Then $(\frac{1}{2})^{n+m}$ is a discrete distribution because it satisfies the two criteria:

1. values: $\forall\, n, m : 1\,..\,\infty \bullet 0 \leq (\frac{1}{2})^{n+m} \leq 1$;
2. sum: $(\sum n, m : 1\,..\,\infty \bullet (\frac{1}{2})^{n+m}) = 1$.

Example 3. Suppose n and m are nonnegative integers (in contrast to the last example). $(\frac{1}{2})^{n+m}$ is not a distribution, because it fails the second criterion: $(\sum n, m : 0\,..\,\infty \bullet (\frac{1}{2})^{n+m}) \neq 1$.

A distribution is the frequency of occurrence of values of variables. Example 2^{-n}: says n has value 3 for $\frac{1}{8}$ of the time. Example $(\frac{1}{2})^{n+m}$: says state $(n = 3) \wedge (m = 1)$ occurs $\frac{1}{16}$ of the time. If $n, m : \mathbb{N}_1$ are distributed as $(\frac{1}{2})^{n+m}$, then $\sum m : \mathbb{N}_1 \bullet (\frac{1}{2})^{n+m} = (\frac{1}{2})^n$ gives the frequency of occurrence of values of n. Independent variables are the product of distributions partitioning variables. Example: $(\frac{1}{2})^{n+m} = (\frac{1}{2})^n * (\frac{1}{2})^m$, so n and m are independent. Average value of e as v varies according to distribution p is $\sum v \bullet e * p$. Example: average value of n^2 as n varies over $\mathbb{N}_1$ with $(\frac{1}{2})^n$ is $\sum n : \mathbb{N}_1 \bullet n^2 * (\frac{1}{2})^n = 6$. Average value of $n - m$ as n and m vary over $\mathbb{N}_1$ with distribution $(\frac{1}{2})^{n+m}$ is $\sum n, m : \mathbb{N}_1 \bullet (n - m) * (\frac{1}{2})^{n+m} = 0$.

Definition 2 (Iverson bracket). $[P] = (1 \lhd P \rhd 0) = $ **if** P **then** 1 **else** 0.

This maps a predicate into a function of its free variables to the set $[0, 1]$. In UTP, $[P]$ has free variables up to αP. A mapping exists in the opposite direction: from probabilities to predicates. We define the inverse Iverson mapping implicitly in a Galois connection (but see Law 1 for an explicit definition).

Definition 3 (Inverse Iverson bracket). $\langle N \rangle_\mathcal{I} \sqsupseteq P = [N \leq [P]_\mathcal{I}]$.

Law 1 (Iverson)

$$\langle N \rangle = N > 0 \qquad\qquad [\neg \langle N \rangle] = [N = 0]$$
$$\langle 1 \rangle = \textbf{true} \qquad\qquad \langle 0 \rangle = \textbf{false}$$
$$[N \leq [\langle N \rangle]] \qquad\qquad \langle [P] \rangle \sqsupseteq P$$
$$P \sqsupseteq Q \Rightarrow [P] \leq [Q] \qquad (M \leq N) \Rightarrow (\langle M \rangle \sqsupseteq \langle N \rangle)$$
$$[P \wedge Q] = [P] * [Q] \qquad [P \vee Q] = [P] + [Q] - [P] * [Q]$$
$$[\neg P] = 1 - [P]$$

$$[k \in A] + [k \in B] = [k \in A \cup B] + [k \in A \cap B]$$
$$[x \in A \cap B] = [x \in A] * [x \in B]$$
$$[\forall m \bullet P(k, m)] = \prod m \bullet [P(k, m)]$$
$$[\exists m \bullet P(k, m)] = \min\{1, \sum m \bullet [P(k, m)]\}$$

Suppose the variables are x and y in the following commands.

Null Statement. skip changes no variable and immediately terminates. Its semantics is the one-point distribution of final states: $(x' = x) * (y' = y)$. On termination, the after-state is equal to the before-state with probability 1. All other assignments to the after-state have probability 0. $skip \mathrel{\widehat{=}} [x' = x] * [y' = y]$.

Assignment $x := e$ is the one-point distribution of the final state (Dirac). $x := e \mathrel{\widehat{=}} [\, x' = e \,] * [\, y' = y \,]$.

Conditional statement **if** c **then** A **else** B composes weighted distributions of A and B. Example **if** $1/3$ **then** $x := 0$ **else** $x := 1$. With probability $1/3$, assign value 0 to x. With probability $2/3$, assign 1 to x. **if** c **then** A **else** $B \mathrel{\widehat{=}} c * A + (1 - c) * B$.

Sequential composition $A \; ; \; B$ composes A with B. It is the conditional probability of B, given A. $A \; ; \; B \mathrel{\widehat{=}} \sum x_0, y_0 \bullet A[x_0, y_0/x', y'] * B[x_0, y_0/x, y]$.

Parallel composition $A \parallel B$ normalises the product A with B. It is the joint probability of A and B. In its most general form, neither A nor B need to be proper distributions, but the result will be. $A \parallel B \mathrel{\widehat{=}} \mathbf{N}\,(A * B)$.

Let E be an expression: (i) Whose value (for all assignments of values) is nonnegative. (ii) Whose sum (over all assignments of values) is strictly between 0 and ∞. Then, the normalisation $\mathbf{N}\,(E)$ is a distribution. Its values are in the same proportion as the values of E.

Definition 4 (Normalisation). $\mathbf{N}\,(E) \;\mathrel{\widehat{=}}\; E \,/\, (\sum n \bullet E)$ *(for free variable* n*).*

Definition 5 (Distribution of Final States). *Suppose S is a deterministic, probabilistic specification. Let p be a distribution describing the initial state σ. Then the distribution describing the final state σ' is $\sum \sigma \bullet S * p$*

Example 4. Let x and y be integer variables. Suppose that x starts with value 7 for $1/3$ of the time and 8 for $2/3$ of the time. The initial distribution is $X = 1/3 * (x = 7) + 2/3 * (x = 8)$. Suppose y also starts with 7 for $1/3$ of the time and 8 for $2/3$ of the time. Initial distribution is $Y = 1/3 * (y = 7) + 2/3 * (y = 8)$. Distribution of initial states is the product $X * Y$. Let $S = (\,$**if** $x = y$ **then** $x, y := 0, 0$ **else** $x, y := abs(x - y), 1\,)$. This is a deterministic specification (and trivially probabilistic). It has the following distribution of final states:

$$\sum x, y \bullet S * X * Y \;=\; 5/9 * ((x', y') = (0, 0)) + 4/9 * ((x', y') = (1, 1))$$

The right-hand side is exactly the semantics of the Prism command

```
5/9: (x'=0) & (y'=0) + 4/9: (x'=1) & (y'=1);
```

8 Example: Killer Robots

Two robots, *cyberman* and *dalek*, attack the *Tardis* daily. *cyberman* has probability $1/2$ of a successful attack. *dalek* has probability $3/10$ of a successful attack. *cyberman* attacks more often than *dalek*. *cyberman* attacks with probability of

```
1   dtmc
2   const int cyber=1;
3   const int dalek=2;
4   const int succ=1;
5   const int fail=2;
6   module Tardis
7     robot   : [1..2] init 1;
8     attack  : [1..2] init 1;
9     s       : [0..3] init 0;
10    [] s=0 -> 3/5: (robot'=cyber)&(s'=1)
11             + 2/5: (robot'=dalek)&(s'=2);
12    [] s=1 -> 1/2: (attack'=succ)&(s'=3)
13             + 1/2: (attack'=fail)&(s'=3);
14    [] s=2 -> 3/10:(attack'=succ)&(s'=3)
15             + 7/10:(attack'=fail)&(s'=3);
16    [] s=3 -> true;
17  endmodule
```

$Tardis =$
  if ⅗ **then**
    ($robot$:= cyber ;
    if ½ **then**
      $attack$:= succ
    else
      $attack$:= fail)
  else
    ($robot$:= dalek ;
    if ³⁄₁₀ **then**
      $attack$:= succ
    else
      $attack$:= fail)

(a) Prism program for the attack on the Tardis.

(b) PPP program for the attack on the Tardis.

Fig. 6. Prism program and semantics for the attack on the Tardis.

⅗ on a particular day. *dalek* attacks with probability ⅖ on that day. What is the probability that there is a successful attack today? This is a problem in conditional probability: $P(A \wedge B) = P(A) * P(B \mid A)$.

$$P(cyber) = ⅗, P(succ \mid cyber) = ½, P(dalek) = ⅖, P(succ \mid dalek) = ³⁄₁₀$$

$$P(succ) = P(cyber \wedge succ) + P(dalek \wedge succ)$$
$$= P(cyber) * P(succ \mid cyber) + P(dalek) * P(succ \mid dalek)$$
$$= ⅗ * ½ + ⅖ * ³⁄₁₀$$
$$= ²¹⁄₅₀$$

The problem is described by the Prism program in Fig. 6a and the PPP program in Fig. 6b.

This program has the following semantics:

$Tardis = $ **if** ⅗ **then** ($robot$:= cyber ; **if** ½ **then** $attack$:= succ **else** $attack$:= fail)
    else ($robot$:= dalek ; **if** ³⁄₁₀ **then** $attack$:= succ **else** $attack$:= fail)
   $= $ ³⁄₁₀ * ($robot, attack$:= cyber, succ) + ³⁄₁₀ * ($robot, attack$:= cyber, fail)
    + ⁶⁄₅₀ * ($robot, attack$:= dalek, succ) + ¹⁴⁄₅₀ * ($robot, attack$:= dalek, fail)

The final line is equivalent to the Prism program in Fig. 7 (modulo the state variables s and t). We can see that the probability of a successful attack is ³⁄₁₀ + ⁶⁄₅₀ = ²¹⁄₅₀, the same answer as before.

```
1  module Tardis
2    robot  : [1..2] init 1;
3    attack : [1..2] init 1;
4    t      : [0..1] init 0;
5    [] t=0 -> 3/10:  (robot'=cyber) & (attack'=succ) & (t'=1)
6               3/10:  (robot'=cyber) & (attack'=fail) & (t'=1)
7               6/50:  (robot'=dalek) & (attack'=succ) & (t'=1)
8               14/50: (robot'=dalek) & (attack'=fail) & (t'=1)
9    [] t=3 -> true;
10 endmodule
```

Fig. 7. Prism program for the abstract attack on the Tardis.

9 Related Work

The only formal semantics for Prism is that contained in the anonymous document describing the translation and the system module [32]. Conserva Filho et al. analyse RoboChart with probabilities [14]. Woodcock et al. [38] give a different account of the probabilistic semantics of RoboChart. Ye et al. [41] describe probabilistic modelling and verification using RoboChart and Prism. Ye et al. [42] describe a UTP semantics for reasoning about probabilistic sequential programs with theorem proving. Woodcock et al. [40] discuss uncertainty quantification and runtime monitoring using environment-aware digital twins. Esterle et al. [12] discuss verification and uncertainties in self-integrating systems.

10 Conclusions and Further Work

What would a unifying theory for uncertainty look like? What connects the semantics and tools that support different approaches? Can we establish more connections? Can we support probabilistic and statistical model checking with theorem proving? Can we support theorem proving with probabilistic and statistical model checking? Can we establish uncertainty properties using CbyC? What about probabilistic refinement model checking? Can we qualify an analysis tool for high assurance? What's the formal testing theory for a system with unknown MDP semantics? What are the testability hypotheses? How do we exploit testing, proof, and model checking together? What about uncertainty and runtime verification? How do we develop, apply, and evaluate uncertain systems? We described preliminary work towards answering these questions.

Acknowledgements. This work has benefited from extensive discussions with Radu Calinescu, Ana Cavalcanti, Simon Foster, Rob Hierons, Peter Gorm Larsen, Zhiming Liu, Mohammad Mousavi, and Kangfeng Ye. The work is supported by (i) EPSRC EP/R025479/1 RoboTest: Systematic model-based testing and simulation of mobile autonomous robots; and (ii) EPSRC EP/V026801/2 UKRI Trustworthy Autonomous Systems Node in Verifiability.

References

1. Alur, R., Henzinger, T.A.: Reactive modules. Formal Methods Syst. Des. **15**(1) (1999)
2. Back, R.-J., von Wright, J.: Refinement Calculus – A Systematic Introduction. Graduate Texts in Computer Science. Springer (1998). https://doi.org/10.1007/978-1-4612-1674-2
3. Casella, G., Robert, C.P., Wells, M.T.: Generalized Accept-Reject Sampling Schemes. University of Michigan, Institute of Mathematical Statistics Lecture Notes Series (2004)
4. Cavalcanti, A., Huang, W., Peleska, J., Woodcock, J.: CSP and kripke structures. In: Leucker, M., Rueda, C., Valencia, F.D. (eds.) ICTAC 2015. LNCS, vol. 9399, pp. 505–523. Springer, Cham (2015). https://doi.org/10.1007/978-3-319-25150-9_29
5. Cavalcanti, A., Woodcock, J.: A tutorial introduction to CSP in *unifying theories of programming*. In: Cavalcanti, A., Sampaio, A., Woodcock, J. (eds.) PSSE 2004. LNCS, vol. 3167, pp. 220–268. Springer, Heidelberg (2006). https://doi.org/10.1007/11889229_6
6. Chandy, K.M., Misra, J.: Parallel Program Design: A Foundation. Addison Wesley (1988)
7. den Hartog, J., de Vink, E.P.: Verifying probabilistic programs using a Hoare like logic. Int. J. Found. Comput. Sci. **13**(3), 315–340 (2002)
8. Dijkstra, E.W.: Guarded commands, nondeterminacy and formal derivation of programs. Commun. ACM **18**(8), 453–457 (1975)
9. Edsger, W.: Dijkstra, A Discipline of Programming. Prentice-Hall (1976)
10. Dijkstra, E.W.: On the reliability of programs. In: Apt, K.R., Hoare, T.D. (eds.) Edsger Wybe Dijkstra: His Life, Work, and Legacy, pp. 359–370. ACM / Morgan & Claypool (2022)
11. Dill, D.L.: The Murphi verification system. In: Alur, R., Henzinger, T.A. (eds.) CAV 1996. LNCS, vol. 1102, pp. 390–393. Springer, Heidelberg (1996). https://doi.org/10.1007/3-540-61474-5_86
12. Esterle, L., Porter, B., Woodcock, J.: Verification and uncertainties in self-integrating system. In El-Araby, E., Kalogeraki, V. (eds.) IEEE International Conference on Autonomic Computing and Self-Organizing Systems, ACSOS 2021, pp. 220–225. IEEE (2021)
13. Feinberg, E.A., Shwartz, A. (eds.) Handbook of Markov Decision Processes. Kluwer (2002)
14. Conserva Filho, M.S., Marinho, R., Mota, A., Woodcock, J.: Analysing robochart with probabilities. In: Massoni, T., Mousavi, M.R. (eds.) SBMF 2018. LNCS, vol. 11254, pp. 198–214. Springer, Cham (2018). https://doi.org/10.1007/978-3-030-03044-5_13
15. Foster, S., Baxter, J., Cavalcanti, A., Woodcock, J., Zeyda, F.: Unifying semantic foundations for automated verification tools in Isabelle/UTP. Sci. Comput. Program. **197**, 102510 (2020)
16. Gabbay, D.M.: Introducing reactive Kripke semantics and arc accessibility. Ann. Math. Artif. Intell. **66**(1–4), 7–53 (2012)
17. Floyd, C.: Theory and practice of software development. In: Mosses, P.D., Nielsen, M., Schwartzbach, M.I. (eds.) CAAP 1995. LNCS, vol. 915, pp. 25–41. Springer, Heidelberg (1995). https://doi.org/10.1007/3-540-59293-8_185 pg

18. Harwood, W., Cavalcanti, A., Woodcock, J.: A theory of pointers for the UTP. In: Fitzgerald, J.S., Haxthausen, A.E., Yenigun, H. (eds.) ICTAC 2008. LNCS, vol. 5160, pp. 141–155. Springer, Heidelberg (2008). https://doi.org/10.1007/978-3-540-85762-4_10

19. He, J., Seidel, K., McIver, A.: Probabilistic models for the guarded command language. Sci. Comput. Program. **28**(2–3), 171–192 (1997)

20. Hehner, E.C.R.: Probabilistic predicative programming. In: Kozen, D. (ed.) MPC 2004. LNCS, vol. 3125, pp. 169–185. Springer, Heidelberg (2004). https://doi.org/10.1007/978-3-540-27764-4_10

21. Hehner, E.C.R.: A probability perspective. Formal Aspects Comput. **23**(4), 391–419 (2011)

22. Hintikka, J.: Knowledge and Belief. Cornell University Press (1962)

23. Hoare, C.A.R.: An axiomatic basis for computer programming (reprint). Commun. ACM **26**(1), 53–56 (1983)

24. Hoare, C.A.R., Jifeng, H.: Unifying Theories of Programming. Prentice Hall (1998)

25. Huang, W., Peleska, J.: Complete model-based equivalence class testing. Int. J. Softw. Tools Technol. Transf. **18**(3), 265–283 (2016)

26. Knuth, D., Yao, A.: Algorithms and Complexity: New Directions and Recent Results, chapter The complexity of nonuniform random number generation. Academic Press (1976)

27. Kwiatkowska, M.Z., Norman, G., Parker, D.: Quantitative analysis with the probabilistic model checker PRISM. In: Cerone, A., Wiklicky, H. (eds.) Proceedings of the Third Workshop on Quantitative Aspects of Programming Languages, QAPL 2005, Edinburgh, UK, 2–3 April 2005, vol. 153. ENTCS, pp. 5–31. Elsevier (2005)

28. Lauri, M., Hsu, D., Pajarinen, J.: Partially observable Markov decision processes in robotics: A survey. CoRR, abs/ arXiv: 2209.10342 (2022)

29. McIver, A., Morgan, C.: Correctness by construction for probabilistic programs. In: Margaria, T., Steffen, B. (eds.) ISoLA 2020. LNCS, vol. 12476, pp. 216–239. Springer, Cham (2020). https://doi.org/10.1007/978-3-030-61362-4_12

30. Morgan, C.: Programming from Specifications, 2nd edn., International series in computer science. Prentice Hall (1994)

31. Morris, J.M.: A theoretical basis for stepwise refinement and the programming calculus. Sci. Comput. Program. **9**(3), 287–306 (1987)

32. Prism. The PRISM language — semantics. www.prismmodelchecker.org/doc/semantics.pdf

33. Shannon, C.L., Weaver, W.: Mathematical Theory of Communication. University of Illinois (1963)

34. Shilov, N.V., Garanina, N.O.: Combining knowledge and fixpoints. Technical Report Preprint 98, A.P. Ershov Institute of Informatics Systems, Novosibirsk (2002).www.iis.nsk.su/files/preprints/098.pdf

35. Woodcock, J.C.P.: Properties of Z specifications. ACM SIGSOFT Softw. Eng. Notes **14**(5), 43–54 (1989)

36. Woodcock, J.: Hoare and He's unifying theories of programming. In: Jones, C.B., Misra, J., (eds.) Theories of Programming: The Life and Works of Tony Hoare, pp. 285–316. ACM / Morgan & Claypool (2021)

37. Woodcock, J., Cavalcanti, A.: A tutorial introduction to designs in unifying theories of programming. In: Boiten, E.A., Derrick, J., Smith, G. (eds.) IFM 2004. LNCS, vol. 2999, pp. 40–66. Springer, Heidelberg (2004). https://doi.org/10.1007/978-3-540-24756-2_4

38. Woodcock, J., Cavalcanti, A., Foster, S., Mota, A., Ye, K.: Probabilistic semantics for robochart. In: Ribeiro, P., Sampaio, A. (eds.) UTP 2019. LNCS, vol. 11885, pp. 80–105. Springer, Cham (2019). https://doi.org/10.1007/978-3-030-31038-7_5

39. Woodcock, J., Davies, J.: Using Z – Specification, Refinement, and Proof. Prentice Hall international series in computer science. Prentice Hall (1996)

40. Woodcock, J., Gomes, C., Macedo, H.D., Larsen, P.G.: Uncertainty quantification and runtime monitoring using environment-aware digital twins. In: Margaria, T., Steffen, B. (eds.) ISoLA 2020. LNCS, vol. 12479, pp. 72–87. Springer, Cham (2021). https://doi.org/10.1007/978-3-030-83723-5_6

41. Ye, K., Cavalcanti, A., Foster, S., Miyazawa, A., Woodcock, J.: Probabilistic modelling and verification using RoboChart and PRISM. Softw. Syst. Model. **21**(2), 667–716 (2022)

42. Ye, K., Foster, S., Woodcock, J.: Automated reasoning for probabilistic sequential programs with theorem proving. In: Fahrenberg, U., Gehrke, M., Santocanale, L., Winter, M. (eds.) RAMiCS 2021. LNCS, vol. 13027, pp. 465–482. Springer, Cham (2021). https://doi.org/10.1007/978-3-030-88701-8_28

Tools and Techniques for Specification, Verification and Code Generation

Source-Code-to-Object-Code Traceability Analysis for Airborne Software: A Case for Tool Support

Jörg Brauer[(✉)]

Verified Systems International GmbH, Bremen, Germany
brauer@verified.de
https://www.verified.de

Abstract. Industrial practise frequently warrants small, not so common verification activities, where dedicated tool support can significantly ease the workload associated with these activities, even though the verification activities cannot be automated fully. Source-code-to-object-code (STO) traceability analysis, which is one form of structural coverage analysis required by RTCA DO-178C for avionic software of development assurance level A (DAL-A), is one of these not so common verification activities. The purpose of STO analysis is to ensure that the entire object code has been exercised by requirements-based tests. However, performing the STO analysis manually is very time-consuming and requires a lot of expertise in the domain. In this paper, we argue that dedicated special-purpose tools, which implement only a few specific analyses, can to a great extent be used to automate the STO analysis activity and contribute to the certification of airborne software.

1 Introduction

One question that frequently arises during the development of safety-critical software is: Has the software been tested sufficiently? This is not an easy question, and indeed, development standards such as RTCA DO-178C [17] for airborne software contain detailed guidance on the completeness of verification activities [17, Tab. A-7]. While many of the objectives and techniques described in [17, Tab. A-7] can be considered common knowledge nowadays—for example, verification of exhaustive requirements coverage by testing via the examination of traceability matrices—there is one daunting objective for Design Assurance Level A (DAL-A):

> *"Verification of additional code, that cannot be traced to Source Code, is achieved."*

Additional code may be introduced during the compilation process, which means that 100% structural coverage on source code level does not necessarily mean 100% structural coverage on object code level. Even though the requirements-based tests indicate 100% structural coverage on source code level, the binary may still contain code that has not been verified. Satisfaction of the above DAL-A objective thus relies on two activities:

- Identification of additional object code which was introduced during compilation and cannot be traced to source code.
- Verification of additional object code.

Establishing a tracing between source code and object code is thus a prerequisite for the identification of additional code. Unfortunately, compilers used in aviation typically do not provide such tracing information, for which reason it must be derived. Once the additional code has been identified, it shall be verified. Observe that DO-178C does not enforce verification of additional code by testing. As an alternative to testing, the additional code can thus be verified by some kind manual or automatic analysis.

A connected topic that is frequently raised by certification authorities is confidence in the correctness of the compiler, as many verification activities are performed on source code level, and the validity of these verification results depends on the consistency of source code and object code. In some application domains, this issue is addressed by utilising validated compilers. This approach, however, is not accepted in aviation, and pure testing can be considered insufficient to substantiate confidence in correctness of the compiler. For instance, a requirements-based test typically contains assertions on some outputs of the software in order to show that the outputs are consistent with the software requirements. However, a test does not verify that *all outputs* are consistent with *all software requirements*, but only exercises a subset of the output state. The compiler could have introduced an undesired store operation, which would not be detected by requirements-based unit testing, which could ultimately lead to a critical failure of the software.

1.1   Objectives and Contributions

In this paper, we describe an automated approach to STO traceability analysis. We discuss how variants of adding, removing, or transforming code can be detected by a combination of several static analyses, namely: (a) control flow analysis, (b) memory allocation analysis, (c) hidden call detection, and (d) store analysis. Pass (a) detects all variants of branches added or removed during compilation, (b) identifies data structures allocated with insufficient memory, (c) detects untraceable function calls, and (d) finds untraceable accesses to memory and registers. The analyses have been implemented in the industrial tool RTT-STO and applied for the STO traceability analysis of DAL-A code for a commercial avionics control system. We also identify the tool qualification needs for RTT-STO and present a strategy for tool qualification as a verification tool according to the guidelines of DO-330 [18].

The overall flow of analyses implemented in RTT-STO is depicted in Fig. 1. The control flow analysis is the prequisit for all other analyses, which rely on matched representations of object code and source code. All analysis passes produce verification sheets, which consist of two sections:

- One section contains all the verification details that could be automated by RTT-STO. For example, this could be a traceability matrix, which maps all traceable branches in source code to the corresponding object code statements.
- The other section contains those branches in source code and object code that could not be traced. This section needs to be edited by a verification engineer.

After the manual edits have been completed, the verification evidence is complete and can serve as evidence for the certification authorities. Since RTT-STO is qualified, the tool support for the generation of the verification sheets provides a guarantee that all relevant branches have been covered.

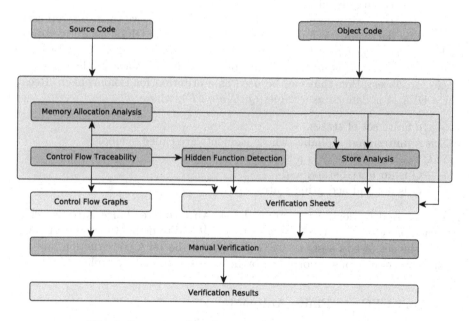

Fig. 1. Sequence of analyses implemented in RTT-STO.

1.2   Outline

In what follows, Sect. 2 discusses the branching analysis, which is used to match control flow representations on source code and object code level. The key steps of the approach are discussed by means of a worked example. Next, Sect. 3 discusses the remaining three static analyses for memory allocation analysis, hidden call detection and store analysis, before the topic of tool qualification is covered in Sect. 5. Details on the verification sheets produced by RTT-STO for the certification process are provided in Sect. 4. The paper concludes with a presentation of related in work in Sect. 6 and a discussion in Sect. 7.

2   Control Flow Traceability

As discussed before, STO analysis using RTT-STO is structured into four successive analysis passes. The base of these analysis passes is the branching analysis, the purpose of which is to associate branches on source code and object code level. If successful, control flow in both program representations is indistinguishable, and the control flow graphs (CFGs) can be considered *isomorphic*.[1] The key idea of branching analysis in the context of STO analysis is thus to provide a technique that derives an *isomorphism* between the CFGs, a technique that is familiar when comparing different versions of the same executable program [9,10,12]. This section thus addresses the question of how isomorphisms between source and object code CFGs can be established.

In order to detect whether two CFGs are isomorphic, we turn to a representation using deterministic finite automata (DFAs). The DFAs are derived from a CFG so as to represent the control flow of the underlying CFG. Then, two or more CFGs can be considered isomorphic if their DFAs accept the same languages, an observation that can be used as a criterion for isomorphism. Recall that a DFA $\mathcal{A}$ is defined as a tuple $(Q, \Sigma, \delta, q_0, F)$, where

- Q is a finite set of states,
- Σ is a finite input alphabet whose elements are called symbols,
- $\delta : Q \times (\Sigma \cup \{\varepsilon\}) \to Q$ is a transition function,
- $q_0 \in Q$ is an initial state, and
- $F \subseteq Q$ is a set of accepting states.

Here, ε is used to denote the empty label. An intuitive choice is to associate with each basic block in the CFG a state $q \in Q$ and to define the input alphabet of $\mathcal{A}$ as the set of edges of the CFG. We sketch the DFA construction and the decision procedure for isomorphism by means of a worked example.

2.1   From CFGs to Finite Automata

Figure 3 depicts the C code for a function f() that serves as the running example. This function is part of a simple state machine, where the current state is evaluated using a switch statement, and the respective handlers are called in sub-functions. The CFG generated from the above source code is shown in Fig. 2.

---

[1] CFG reconstruction from source code and object code is not the scope of the paper, and we thus assume that CFGs for both representations are readily available; see Sect. 6 for further details on this issue.

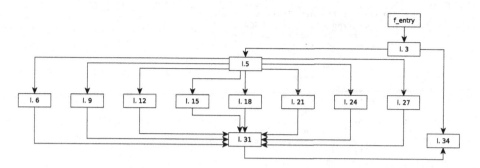

Fig. 2. Control flow graph extracted from the code of a function that uses a `switch` statement with seven `case` branches and one `default` branch, see Fig. 3.

It consists of an entry node and 12 basic blocks[2], each of which is represented by a single node. The exit node 1.34 corresponds to the `return` statement in line 34. Note that the if-statement represented by 1.3 induces an explicit `then`-branch to the `switch`-statement in 1.5 as well as an implicit `else`-branch that targets the `return`-statement represented by 1.34.

As sketched before, a DFA $\mathcal{A}$ can be extracted by adding a state for each basic block and then labelling the edges with unique descriptions of their role. In the running example, we choose labels IfThen and IfElse for the edges induced by the if statement in line 3 and Case_i with $i \in \{0, \dots 7\}$ for the edges from the `switch` statement to the `case` and `default` branches. All other edges receive the empty label ε. As accepting state, we additionally introduce a distinguished exit-node _end, whose incoming edge is labelled with E. We likewise add an initial state _start. This way, we obtain the DFA $\mathcal{A}$ given in Fig. 4, where the fresh nodes are highlighted using dashed lines. Likewise, we obtain a CFG and a DFA from the object code of the function in Fig. 3. The DFA is depicted in Fig. 5. Whilst this DFA looks quite similar to the one generated from source code, it is yet to decide whether both DFAs implement isomorphic control flow.

2.2 Deciding CFG Isomorphism

The final step is thus a decision procedure for isomorphism of two or more CFGs represented by their DFAs. The comparison of two DFAs $\mathcal{A}_1$ and $\mathcal{A}_2$ is implemented using a variant of Hopcroft's algorithm [13], which ensures that two DFAs which accept the same language are equal up to isomorphism. Minimised DFAs can thus be compared using graph traversal. In the worked example, the verdict is that the control flow of the CFGs differs because the resulting DFAs are not isomorphic due to the transition from b0 to L236 in Fig. 5 labelled by Case_8.

---

[2] In the example, nodes are labelled with their line numbers from the listing. However, the choice of a labelling is inconsequential as long as the node labels are unique.

```
1  ReturnType f(const State_t state) {
2    ReturnType status = SUCCESS;
3    if (state != currentState) {
4      previousState = currentState;
5      switch(state) {
6      case STATE_INIT:
7        status = toInit();
8        break;
9      case STATE_PREACTIVE:
10       status = toPreactive();
11       break;
12     case STATE_PROCESSING:
13       status = toProcessing();
14       break;
15     case STATE_UPLOADING:
16       status = toUploading();
17       break;
18     case STATE_ERROR:
19       status = toError();
20       break;
21     case STATE_FAILED:
22       status = toFailed();
23       break;
24     case STATE_DEBUG:
25       status = toDebug();
26       break;
27     default:
28       status = ERR_PARAM;
29       break;
30     }
31     stateTime = getTimeStamp();
32     performEntryAction = TRUE;
33   }
34   return status;
35 }
```

Fig. 3. C code for the worked example.

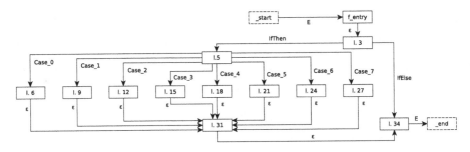

Fig. 4. DFA derived from the CFG in Fig. 2.

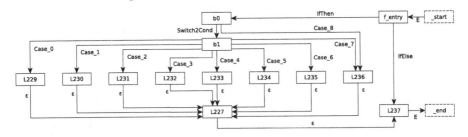

Fig. 5. DFA derived from the object code generated from the source code in Fig. 3.

Now that the branching analyzer has shown that the source code and the object code implementation of function f() implement a differing branching structure, additional effort has to be put into understanding the reason for this deviation. It turns out that the least value handled in the switch-statement, STATE_INIT is defined as holding the integer value 1. The compiler—even though it has been configured to perform no optimisations at all—thus produces code that preventively checks whether the value of parameter state is at least 1; if not so, control is passed directly to the default-branch without exercising all the possible branches in the switch-statement itself (in the DFA in Fig. 5, this branch is represented by the transition b0 $\xrightarrow{\text{Case\_8}}$ L236, for which no counterpart is found on source code level). This form of control flow is invisible from source code level. However, the branch is reachable and legitimate, and thus two distinguished test cases are required: one that passes value 0 for parameter state and thus triggers the additional branch, and another one that passes another unhandled value so as to trigger the actual default-branch.

2.3 Limitations of Branching Analysis Using DFAs

The alert reader will have observed that the chosen representations of the control flow using CFGs and DFAs are not equivalent. Indeed, the described transformation from CFGs to DFAs inevitably leads to a loss in precision. As an example, let us return to Fig. 5. Suppose the compiler has by mistake generated code that gives a transition b0 $\xrightarrow{\text{Case\_8}}$ L235 instead of b0 $\xrightarrow{\text{Case\_8}}$ L236. The branching analysis based on comparison of automata does not uncover this flaw, which may appear to be a serious problem of the approach; it is not. Branching analysis in the context of DO-178C is not a stand-alone analysis, but *complements* requirements-based testing activities. Such erroneous edges would thus have been uncovered using requirements-based tests beforehand.

3 Additional Analyses

As argued before, one of the key aspects of STO analysis is to provide evidence that the branching structure of the compiled object code of a program correctly models the branching structure induced by the source code. However, tracing branches in both representations is only the first step required to receive certification credit. This section focuses on further subtleties that need to be analysed.

3.1 Hidden Call Detection

Even if the branching structure of the object code matches the source code, this does not imply that the compiler has not introduced additional function calls. Naively, one could argue that the compiler is not allowed to do so. This is not true. For example, suppose a program on a 32-bit PowerPC (PPC) platform uses a 64-bit integer division, which is not natively supported by the processor.

The compiler then *should* replace this operation by a call to a built-in function, which in turn leads to a different calling structure and stack layout compared to what is expected from source code. The identification of such *hidden calls* is straightforward, given the information about the program structure that has been derived during branching analysis.

Recall that for branching analysis, we have determined a mapping between basic blocks in both source code and object code. Hence, it suffices to check whether all basic blocks invoke the same sub-functions in exactly the same order in both program representations. If this is not the case, a traceability issue has been detected, thereby requiring additional verification.

As an example, consider the following assembly fragment generated by a PPC compiler, which contains calls to two functions getMsgTime() and __udiv64(). The function getMsgTime() returns an unsigned 64-bit integer value.

```
 1: bl    getMsgTime
 2: mr    r12, r4
 3: mr    r11, r3
 4: mr    r4, r12
 5: mr    r3, r11
 6: lis   r6, 15
 7: addi  r6, r6, 16960
 8: li    r5, 0
 9: bl    __udiv64
10: mr    r12, r4
11: mr    r11, r3
12: stw   r12, 16(r31)
```

This basic block could directly be traced to the following C block, which contains just one call:

```
msg->timestamp = (uint32) (getMsgTime() / MILLI_TO_NANO);
```

The function __udiv64() called in the assembly has been inserted by the compiler to implement the unsigned 64-bit division. The code is thus not traceable, yet correct, and additional verification measures have to be taken. With the traceability data for basic blocks, it is straightforward to point verification engineers to program locations that need to be examined.

3.2   Memory Allocation Analysis

The memory allocation analysis checks whether the object code contains data allocations (on the heap, on the stack, or in form of registers) where the size of the allocated memory region does not conform to the size expected from the type declarations in the source code. The concept behind this analysis is thus simple: Sound expectations have to be derived from the source code, and an object code analysis has to determine whether the object code meets these expectations. The size-allocation strategies for data structures are usually laid out in the application binary interface (ABI) of the target processor, cf. [19], and can thus be mimicked by the STO traceability analyzer to infer the expected values. Moreover, compilers typically provide information as to how they set up stack frames. For the example from Fig. 3, for instance, we obtain the following information:

```
#function:                    f
#stack frame size:            16
#link area offset:            0
#local storage area offset:   12
#gpr save area offset:        12
#status                       r31    local
#state                        r11    param
```

These outputs indicate that the overall size of the stack frame of f() is 16, that parameter state is passed via register r11, and that status is stored locally in register r31. Along with the declarations of global data in the .data respectively .rodata sections the object code, this information needs to be analyzed. Of course, one also has to check whether the object code correctly allocates the data regions, in particular the setup of the stack frame. However, such an analysis comes for free when performing a dedicated store analysis, which is discussed in the following section.

3.3   Store Analysis

A quite subtle observation is that an erroneous compiler may have inserted undesired store operations targeting some memory addresses. Since requirements-based tests typically only examine the effects of desired store operations in the expected results—but not all possible alterations of the memory state—such malicious behaviour is likely to be missed during testing.

On RISC processors, all accesses to memory are implemented using explicit load and store operations such as stw r12, 4(r31), which stores the contents of register r12 in the memory cell addressed in r31 with an offset of 4. It is therefore important that the store analysis traces the values of those registers that are used as sources respectively targets in the load and store operations. The abstract interpretation is thus implemented as an intraprocedural fixed-point iteration on assembly code [1,6] with an abstract domain specifically designed to trace variable addresses. We thus build on the side-effect analysis for PPC assembly of Flexeder et al. [11], which infers side-effects of procedure calls onto the runtime stack, and straightforwardly extend it to heap-based data.

A noteworthy characteristic of PPC assembly is that loading addresses of variables into registers is distributed over multiple instructions. Suppose that label .L42 in the assembly refers to a global variable x. Then, the code fragment

```
lis r4, %hiadj(.L42)
addi r4, r4, %lo(.L42)
```

loads the address of x into register r4, that is, it corresponds to the C-expression &x: first, the upper half word of the address is loaded into r4, and then its lower half word is added. This address handling pattern has to be tracked during abstract interpretation.

4   Verification Sheets and Application

Prior to the development of RTT-STO, we identified three key requirements for the successful application of RTT-STO, all of which are *soft, non-functional requirements*:

Req #1 RTT-STO shall produce a low number of false positive warnings, thus promising a significant reduction of the verification efforts.

Req #2 RTT-STO shall support verification engineers during the challenging manual verification activities.

Req #3 RTT-STO shall generate evidence that can convincingly be presented to the certification authorities.

While **Req #1** is addressed by the analyses described in Sect. 2 and Sect. 3, the latter two have not been addressed thus far. Addressing **Req #3**, from our industrial experience, spreadsheets provide a well-established way to convincingly present verification results. Important activities such as searching, filtering checking for completeness, etc. are natively supported and understood by all participants of the verification process, which is why we prefer spreadsheets over customized documents. It is much simpler to ensure completeness of evidences in a spreadsheet than in a customized document. Therefore RTT-STO should generate spreadsheets—here called verification sheets. For DAL-A verification projects, the structure of the verification sheets and how verification engineers should generate and edit the verification sheets have to be defined in the process definitions of the project. We defined so-called *verification procedures*, which are guidelines/instructions that define the different tasks of the verification engineers for STO analysis and how these tasks have to be executed.

We addressed **Req #2** by ensuring that the presentation of outputs is helpful for verification staff. For example, for hidden function call analysis, the verification sheet would contain columns as follows:

- The name of the assembly file that contains a hidden function call [auto-generated].
- The line number in the assembly file thatn contains a hidden function call [auto-generated].
- The name of the hidden library function that is called [auto-generated].
- The name of the source code file that contains the hidden function call [auto-generated].
- The line number in the source code file that is traced to the hidden function call [auto-generated].

- The name of the function in the source code that contains the hidden function call [auto-generated].
- The name of the responsible verification engineer [manually assigned].
- The verdict chosen by the verification engineer [manually edited].
- A reference to the manual analysis that serves as justification for the verdict [manually edited].
- The name of the reviewer of the justification and verdict [manually assigned].
- The verdict chosen by the reviewer [manually edited].

This way, it is virtually impossible that manual activities are missed. The aforementioned verification procedures contain precise instructions on how the manually edited cells have to be processed. By using such kinds of verification sheets with detailed instructions, our verification team was able to produce complete verification results with (relatively) little effort, as the verification duties were already prepared by RTT-STO and served as input to the manual verification activities.

We have applied RTT-STO for the STO analysis of an avionic control system, which has been certified for DAL-A. This section discusses our experiences from this project. The software itself is written in C and targets a 32-bit PPC platform. The overall codebase consists of about 300 functions. The overall warning rate was low. For example, RTT-STO detected 28 untraceable control flows, which were caused more or less by two constructs:

- The compiler uses two different strategies for generating object code from `switch` statements: it either implements a binary decision tree to compare the switch variable with the specified cases (including the `default` case), or produces a jump table. In both cases, the compiler may produce untraceable object code. If the different cases refer to integer values $c_1, \ldots, c_n$ and there exists a value $c_0 < c_1$, the object code may contain an additional branch for handling this situation in addition to the implementation of the `default` branch. We have seen this situation in Sect. 2.1.
- As a 32-bit platform, the PPC target naturally has to emulate 64-bit arithmetic using a sequence of operations that may contain additional branching. For example, if a 64-bit unsigned integer x is compared to a 32-bit unsigned integer variable y, the compiler emits code to first compare the most significant 32 bits of x to 0 and subsequently compare the least significant 32 bits of x to y. The compiler thus generates branches that are not directly traceable to source code, and that have not been exercised during requirements-based testing.

The additional code inserted by the compiler could easily be verified correct be experienced verification engineers, with guidance provided through the verification sheets that exactly highlighted the differing control flows. Our experiences with respect to the other analysis passes are similar.

5 Tool Qualification

The DO-330 [18] clarifies tool qualification considerations for tools applied in the software development life cycle according to DO-178C. Intuitively, the DO-178C requires evidence that a tool applied during the development satisfies its needs and is reliable, given the safety-critical context. All in all, the DO-330 specifies tool life cycle processes for the development and application of software tools in airborne software development [18, Fig. 1-1]. The exact needs for tool qualification depend on the impact of the software tool on the software life cycle process, for which several criteria are defined [18, App. B]. Depending on the impact and the design assurance level of the software, a tool qualification level is determined. The criteria are (cp. [18, App. B]):

Criteria 1 The output of RTT-STO is not part of the resulting software and thus could not insert an error.

Criteria 2 The output of RTT-STO is not used to justify the elimination or reduction of other development activities than STO-analysis.

Criteria 3 RTT-STO is a tool that, within the scope of its intended use, could fail to detect an error.

Only criteria 3 is fulfilled, hence the applicable tool qualification level is TQL-5 [18, App. D, Chap. 1.5.3.3.4], the least rigorous level. As described in [18, App. D, Chap. 1.5.3.3.4], TQL-5 is a replacement for the category of *verification tools* used in DO-178B developments. The tool qualification evidence required for TQL-5 tools mainly consists of the tool operational requirements, data to show that the tool satifies its tool operational requirements in the installed environment, configuration management and a verification/validation report. Further details are provided in [18, App. D, Chap. 1.6].

RTT-STO could successfully be qualified for DAL-A using the above evidences. The most critical part was the development of an automated tool qualification test suite, which consists of a collection of (both automatic and manual) verification cases and covers the entire set of tool operational requirements of RTT-STO. The tool qualification suite is executed using RT-TESTER [20] in the operating environment of RTT-STO.

6 Related Work

According to the DO-178C [17, Tab. A-7], STO traceability analysis is part of structural coverage analysis. It is important to note that structural coverage analysis is performed to identify any functionality that was not exercised during the requirements-based testing activities [16, Chap. 9.7.4]. Structural coverage analysis must thus not be confused with structural testing (which is considered inadequate for projects in the domain of DO-178C), the purpose of which is to systematically exercise a software based on the structure of its code. Important sources of information regarding STO analysis in avition are the Certification Authorities Software Team (CAST) position papers on STO analysis [7,8].

To the best of our knowledge, little effort has so far been put into the automation of the STO traceability analysis process, which may be explained by the fact that STO analysis is indeed a niche topic, which is only relevant for a small subset of systems—that is, DAL-A software systems—in aviation. The tool COUVERTURE [4] uses QEMU [3]—which performs dynamic binary translation—to provide a virtualized execution environment for the target software on a host rather than the actual target. The software is then executed and coverage is measured. The approach can be seen as diametrically opposed to ours. Whereas our work is based on static analysis—and possibly additional tests on the target for verification of additional code—COUVERTURE relies on dynamic measurements. However, to us it is unclear how the approach followed by COUVERTURE could actually be integrated into the software development lifecycle to obtain certification credit for DAL-A. Other tools, such as OSMOSE [2] use dynamic symbolic execution to generate test cases directly on the level of object code. An interesting aspect of OSMOSE is that it identifies potentially infeasible branches directly in the binary, and the authors argue that tools such as OSMOSE are useful to complement to source-level testing activities.

The commercial tool RAPICOVER ZERO [15] measures branch traces produced by the system-under-test without access to source code. For STO analysis, the debug information produced by the compiler is used to trace between source code and object code. Another commercial tool for STO analysis and object code verification is TBOBJECTBOX [14], which generates tracing data between object code and source code so as to identify uncovered object code fragments. Further, this paper is based on our own previous work [5], which describes the underlying algorithms.

7   Conclusion

We argue that the automation of very specialized verification activities such as STO analysis can significantly ease the certification of DAL-A avionics software. The RTT-STO tool described in this paper builds upon a set of well-understood and well-established techniques from the areas of program analysis, abstract interpretation and automata theory to address one very specific challenge, and thereby deviates from the established processes. Rierson [16, Chap. 9.7.4.4] describes the way STO analysis is usually performed in practise as follows:

> "The analysis is usually applied using a sample of the actual code, rather than 100% of the code. The sample used should include all constructs that are allowed in the source code and comprise at least 10% of the actual code base. [...] The analysis requires an engineer with knowledge of the specific language, assembly, machine code, and compilers."

This brief summary directly exposes the contributions of our work compared to the state-of-the-art and our proposal for the integration of formal methods into industrial processes. RTT-STO performs the analysis on the *entire code* base rather than a sample, and, consequently *covers all constructs* used in the source code, and requires *less engineering man-power* with expertise in assembly language, due to a high degree of automation. The savings by tool-based automation in terms of workload—and thus cost—are significant.

There are certain situations in which RTT-STO fails to detect traceability even though the code is traceable. In practise, discussions with certification authorities often circle around the question how completeness of the verification activities can be proven. A simple but very valuable side-effect of tool-supported STO analysis, even if the tools produce some false positive warnings, is that it guides verification engineers to locations that warrant manual verification, and guarantees that there are no gaps in the verification activities and evidence.

References

1. Balakrishnan, G., Reps, T.W.: WYSINWYX: what you see is not what you execute. ACM Trans. Program. Lang. Syst. **32**(6), 1–87 (2010)
2. Bardin, S., Herrmann, P., Védrine, F.: Refinement-based CFG reconstruction from unstructured programs. In: Jhala, R., Schmidt, D. (eds.) VMCAI 2011. LNCS, vol. 6538, pp. 54–69. Springer, Heidelberg (2011). https://doi.org/10.1007/978-3-642-18275-4_6
3. Bartholomew, D.: Qemu: a multihost, multitarget emulator. Linux J. **2006**(145) (2006)
4. Bordin, M., Comar, C., Gingold, T., Guitton, J., Hainque, O., Quinot, T.: Object and source coverage for critical applications with the couverture open analysis framework. In: ERTS (2010)
5. Brauer, J., Dahlweid, M., Pankrath, T., Peleska, J.: Source-code-to-object-code traceability analysis for avionics software: don't trust your compiler. In: Koornneef, F., van Gulijk, C. (eds.) SAFECOMP 2015. LNCS, vol. 9337, pp. 427–440. Springer, Cham (2015). https://doi.org/10.1007/978-3-319-24255-2_31
6. Brauer, J., Noll, T., Schlich, B.: Interval analysis of microcontroller code using abstract interpretation of hardware and software. In: SCOPES. ACM (2010)
7. Certification Authorities Software Team (CAST): Guidelines for Approving Source Code to Object Code Traceability - Position Paper CAST-12. CAST (2002)
8. Certification Authorities Software Team (CAST): Structural Coverage of Object Code - Position Paper CAST-17. CAST (2003)
9. Dullien, T., Rolles, R.: Graph-based comparison of executable objects. SSTIC **5**, 1–13 (2005)
10. Flake, H.: Structural comparison of executable objects (2004)
11. Flexeder, A., Petter, M., Seidl, H.: Side-effect analysis of assembly code. In: Yahav, E. (ed.) SAS 2011. LNCS, vol. 6887, pp. 77–94. Springer, Heidelberg (2011). https://doi.org/10.1007/978-3-642-23702-7_10
12. Gao, D., Reiter, M.K., Song, D.: BinHunt: automatically finding semantic differences in binary programs. In: Chen, L., Ryan, M.D., Wang, G. (eds.) ICICS 2008. LNCS, vol. 5308, pp. 238–255. Springer, Heidelberg (2008). https://doi.org/10.1007/978-3-540-88625-9_16
13. Hopcroft, J.: An n log n algorithm for minimizing states in a finite automaton. Technical report, DTIC Document (1971)
14. LDRA Inc.: TBobjectbox. https://ldra.com/products/tbobjectbox

15. Rapita Systems Ltd.: RapiCover Zero. https://www.rapitasystems.com/products/rapicoverzero
16. Rierson, A.: Developing Safety-Critical Software. CRC Press, Boca Raton (2013)
17. RTCA SC-205/EUROCAE WG-71: Software Considerations in Airborne Systems and Equipment Certification. No. RTCA DO-178C, RTCA Inc, 1140 Connecticut Avenue, N.W., Suite 1020, Washington, D.C. 20036 (2011)
18. RTCA SC-205/EUROCAE WG-71: Software Tool Qualification Considerations. No. RTCA DO-330, RTCA, Inc. (2011)
19. Sobek, S., Burke, K.: Power PC Embedded Application Binary Interface (EABI): 32-Bit Implementation. Freescale Semiconductor Inc. (2004)
20. Verified Systems International GmbH: RT-Tester. https://www.verified.de/products/rt-tester

Space Telemetry Analysis with PyContract

Bevin Duckett, Klaus Havelund[(✉)], and Luke Stewart

Jet Propulsion Laboratory, California Institute of Technology, Pasadena, USA
klaus.havelund@jpl.nasa.gov

Abstract. PYCONTRACT is a Python library for trace analysis, also characterized as an internal DSL (Domain-Specific Language). It combines flavors of state machines and rule-based programming, supporting states that can carry data, thus allowing for monitoring of events that carry data. The fact that it is a Python library offers full expressiveness, and access to a vast amount of libraries, which becomes useful for realistic situations. This is in this paper illustrated by its real life application to data analysis of telemetry logs obtained during testing of NASA's Europa Clipper flight computer. The mission will place a spacecraft in orbit around Jupiter in order to perform a detailed investigation of its moon Europa. The analysis includes not only verifying functional correctness but also, and especially, performance analysis such as execution times and rates of change. This includes generation of data in table format and visualization as graphs. The important message is that runtime verification and data analysis are closely related topics, which can only be addressed with highly expressive specification languages.

1 Introduction

Runtime Verification (RV) is normally seen as a discipline of verifying whether a system/program execution is correct wrt. a given set of properties, yielding a Boolean true/false flavored verdict[1]. It can with this view be seen as a lightweight formal method, where the specification is formal, but where only single executions are checked, in contrast to all executions, or even necessarily many executions. Runtime verification is complementary to test case generation but can be used for formulating test oracles, or it can be applied after deployment of the system in the real world to verify that the system performs as desired during operation. Properties are usually expressed in formal Domain-Specific Languages (DSLs) of temporal nature, such as e.g. various forms of temporal logic, regular expressions, state machines, grammars, rule-based systems, and stream processing formalisms. Runtime verification can be applied *online*, monitoring a system

The research performed was carried out at Jet Propulsion Laboratory, California Institute of Technology, under a contract with the National Aeronautics and Space Administration.

[1] Some RV theories operate with extensions of the Boolean domain with a small finite set of additional values, e.g. [6].

© The Author(s), under exclusive license to Springer Nature Switzerland AG 2023
A. E. Haxthausen et al. (Eds.): Peleska Festschrift 2023, LNCS 14165, pp. 272–288, 2023.
https://doi.org/10.1007/978-3-031-40132-9_17

as it executes, or it can be applied *offline*, analysing a log produced by a previous run of a system. In this paper we shall study offline RV, combining classical Boolean verdict RV with data analysis, where the focus is on producing data from logs.

A classical distinction amongst DSLs is that of external versus internal DSLs [17]. An *external* DSL is a "small language" with its own grammar and parser. An *internal* DSL (sometimes referred to as an *embedded* DSL) is a library in a general purpose programming language. Numerous external RV DSLs have been developed over time, including [1,2,4,5,9,12,15,22,23,25]. Internal DSLs are usually again grouped into deep and shallow [18]. In a *deep* internal DSL, data structures in the host language are used to represent DSL constructs in an explicit manner, e.g., as an AST (Abstract Syntax Tree), which can then be processed by writing either an interpreter or a compiler for execution. Some examples are [19,30]. A *shallow* internal DSL includes the constructs of the host language as part of the DSL, using the host language's native runtime system to execute them. Examples of shallow internal DSLs in Scala include [3,20,21,24].

PYCONTRACT [10] is a very expressive internal shallow DSL for runtime verification. In this work we present its application to data analysis of telemetry from NASA's Europa Clipper mission [16] flight computer during real life testing of its performance. We present sketches of five such monitors. The purpose is not only to check functional correctness of temporal properties, but also to analyze and visualize non-functional properties, such as performance wrt. time and data volumes. The possible advantages of using PYCONTRACT for such data analysis has been previously suggested in [11]. The mentioned advantages include the fact that Python is already highly popular in the field of data analysis, and e.g. used extensively within NASA's Jet Propulsion Laboratory (JPL) for telemetry analysis on ground, examining data coming from spacecraft and rovers. An internal DSL is "just" another library in a familiar language. It allows to use favorite development tools (such as IDEs) and other libraries for the host language. It is expressive, and implementation and maintenance of the DSL is easier. A disadvantage of shallow internal DSLs (when compared to external DSLs and deep internal DSLs) is lack of *analyzability*. However, Python supports powerful metaprogramming features allowing a program to inspect its own AST. We use this for visualizing specifications.

Although only briefly touched upon in the paper, our work includes a web-based interface to the use of PYCONTRACT, programmed using the Dash visualization library [13]. It provides a unified convenient framework for requesting analyses to be performed as well as for visualizing and tabulating results.

The paper is organized as follows. Section 2 introduces the PYCONTRACT library. Section 3 describes how it is applied to the five different data analysis problems, each resulting in a PYCONTRACT monitor. Section 4 concludes the paper.

2   The PyContract Core Library

PyCONTRACT allows to specify first-order temporal properties over a trace of events. A temporal property relates events occurring at different points in the trace. The first-order capability allows to also relate the data occurring in events across different points in the trace, turning the logic very expressive. The fact that PyCONTRACT is a Python library furthermore augments the expressiveness, allowing to combine temporal properties and general purpose programming, making it Turing complete. PyCONTRACT is inspired by rule-based programming [4,21] in that the memory of a monitor is a set of facts, where a fact in its basic form is a named data record. However, facts, like states in state machines, can have transitions which, upon triggering, can generate other facts, while removing the fact who's transition is taken. In the following we shall demonstrate how this looks like. PyCONTRACT is inspired by the Scala DSL Daut [14,20] and is developed for Python 3.10 that supports pattern matching [29]. PyCONTRACT is available under the Apache 2.0 open-source license at [28].

The general approach is to define a monitor as a sub-class of the Monitor class, create an instance of it, and then feed it with events, as shown in Fig. 1. Events can be fed, one by one, using the evaluate(event: object) method. In the case of a finite sequence of observations, for example when examining a log file, a call of the end() method tells the monitor that the sequence has ended. Note that end() may not be called when monitoring is online, but if it is called, any outstanding obligations that have not been satisfied (expected events that did not occur) will be reported as errors. Events can be provided by the user in different ways. If examining a log file for example, they can be read from any file format such as e.g. CSV, JSON, XSML, etc. This would in the example in Fig. 1 take place in line 7, where we instead of providing the trace explicitly, as done here, would read it from a file.

```
1  import pycontract as pc
2
3  class M(pc.Monitor):
4      ... body of monitor ...
5
6  monitor = M()
7  trace = [event₁, event₂, ..., eventₙ]
8  for event in trace:
9    monitor.evaluate(event)
10 monitor.end()
```

Fig. 1. General approach for defining and using a PyContract monitor.

As an example we will define a monitor for verifying command execution on board the spacecraft. The example yields a Boolean verdict, in the tradition of classical RV. Commands are submitted to the spacecraft, and on board dispatched, followed hopefully by a completion. Commands have a name and each command dispatch has in addition a number. Events can in PyContract be any data object. We shall in this paper focus on events represented as dictionaries: mapping from fields to values. E.g. the dispatch of a command may be represented by the event:

{ "name" : "dispatch", "cmd" : "TURN", "nr" : 3, "time" : 382649}

We shall verify the following property:

Commands: *The dispatch of a command, with a number, must be followed by a completion within 3 seconds, and no failure of that command dispatch must be observed in between. In addition, a dispatch number can only be completed once (no double execution).*

Note that the "*within 3 s*" constraint can have two interpretations: either that a failure is reported exactly after 3 s without having seen a completion, or that a failure is reported when observing an event occurring after 3 s without having seen a completion within 3 s. The former interpretation requires an internal clock in the monitor, whereas the latter interpretation can rely on the time stamps carried by events. We adopt the latter interpretation, which is suitable for log analysis. For online runtime verification, however, the former interpretation would be more appropriate.

The property is implemented as the monitor in Fig. 2. First we import the PyContract module (line 1). The monitor is defined as a class extending the Monitor class (line 3). The body of the monitor defines a transition function (lines 4–7), and two states: DoComplete (lines 10–20) and Executed (lines 23–29). The outer transition function (lines 4–7) processes all events submitted to the monitor. It takes an event as argument and matches it against possible patterns, using the pattern matching features provided in Python from version 3.10 [29]. In this case just one pattern matches if the name of the command is "dispatch". If so it binds the command id, number, and time to the variables c, n, and t respectively, and returns a new state: DoComplete with these bindings as arguments. This state is now added to the memory of the monitor. The actual type of the transition function is:

```
def transition(self, event: Event) ->
    Optional[State | List[State]]
```

where Event is the type of events (dictionaries in this case). It returns either None (corresponding to no match), a state, or a list of states. We leave out the types in the remaining transition function definitions.

The DoComplete state extends HotState, meaning that it must eventually be removed, otherwise an error is reported when the end() method is called at the end of the trace. It will e.g. be removed when the command it monitors completes. The state is parameterized with a command id, a dispatch number, and the time of dispatch. The body defines a transition function applicable when the state is active, which offers three options for processing an incoming event (if none match the state remains in the monitor memory). The first case matches if the command (with the same id and number) fails[2]. In this case an error is reported. The second case matches if any event is observed with a time stamp more than 3 s from the dispatch time. This also results in an error being reported. The third case matches if the command completes, in which case an Executed state, parameterized with the dispatch number, is returned, and recorded in the monitor memory (while the DoComplete state is removed). The Executed state itself is just a State, meaning that it is ok to terminate in this state. It monitors that the dispatch number does not complete again.

We mentioned above that the outermost transition function (lines 4–7) is applied to all events submitted to the monitor. Behind the scenes it is translated to an initial so-called AlwaysState, as shown in Fig. 3 (lines 2–7). An AlwaysState state is always active. The former style is, however, more convenient to write.

PyContract offers other features, such as allowing to return a list of states from a transition, next-states (failing if no transition cases match an event), querying the fact memory (used for expressing past time properties), grouping of monitors, and user-defined indexing (slicing) to optimize monitoring, similar to what is supported in RV systems such as MOP [25] and QEA [30]. In addition one can of course add any Python code to be executed in transition actions, and use general Python expressions as transition conditions. PyContract was evaluated against other systems in [10], performing reasonably by processing 4 million events in under 100 s.

PyContract visualizes a monitor using PlantUML [27] by first analyzing the AST of the monitor (using Python's meta-programming capabilities) and then generating PlantUML text. Figure 4 is such a visualization of the monitor in Fig. 2. Green states (the initial state) are always active, and safe to terminate in. Bright yellow states, the DoComplete state, indicate danger: they must be left eventually. Faded yellow states, the Executed state, are safe to terminate in as well. Finally red states are error states. Transitions out of a state are numbered to indicate the order of evaluation caused by the semantics of Python's **match**-statements.

3 Data Analysis Scripts

In this section we present five different monitors using the PyContract library for performing various forms of combined property checking and data analysis. We show only essential code fragments that provide the general idea. The scripts offer user options for different behaviours, which we largely ignore in this presentation. A spacecraft reports telemetry to ground as individual messages. There are three general types of spacecraft data sent to ground [7]:

---

[2] In Python's pattern matching, dotted names, such as self.cmd, must match the incoming value, whereas non-dotted names, such as c, are binding the incoming value.

```
 1  import pycontract as pc
 2
 3  class Commands(pc.Monitor):
 4    def transition(self, event):
 5      match event:
 6        case {'name':'dispatch','cmd':c,'nr':n,'time': t}:
 7          return Commands.DoComplete(c, n, t)
 8
 9    @pc.data
10    class DoComplete(pc.HotState):
11      cmd: str; nr: int; time: int
12
13      def transition(self, event):
14        match event:
15          case {'name':'fail','cmd':self.cmd,'nr':self.nr}:
16            return pc.error('failed')
17          case {'time':t} if t - self.time > 3000:
18            return pc.error('time')
19          case {'name':'complete','cmd':self.cmd,'nr':self.nr}:
20            return Commands.Executed(self.nr)
21
22    @pc.data
23    class Executed(pc.State):
24      nr: int
25
26      def transition(self, event):
27        match event:
28          case {'name':'complete','nr':self.nr}:
29            return pc.error('double_completion')
```

Fig. 2. A monitor for property **Commands**.

- *Time series data* (EHAs[3]) representing onboard measurements of spacecraft state over time. JPL missions generally refer to this type of data as "channelized telemetry" or "channels", with each channel representing a time series of measurements from spacecraft hardware sensors, as well as data reported by software components (e.g. onboard memory states).
- *Event Records* (EVRs) representing single events that occur onboard the spacecraft. Rather than the single data value of a channel record, each EVR record contains a message string, which contains further spacecraft state information embedded in that message.
- *Data Products* (DPs), each containing a range of types of information, depending on the need. There are a wide variety of data products used by projects, including snapshots of state such as memory and data management states.

---

[3] EHA stands for 'Engineering Housekeeping & Accountability'.

```
 1  class Commands(pc.Monitor):
 2      @pc.initial
 3      class Start(pc.AlwaysState):
 4          def transition(self, event):
 5              match event:
 6                  case {'name':'dispatch','cmd':c,'nr':n,'time':t}:
 7                      return Commands.DoComplete(c, n, t)
 8
 9      @pc.data
10      class DoComplete(pc.HotState):
11          ...
12
13      @pc.data
14      class Executed(pc.State):
15          ...
```

Fig. 3. Translation of the outermost transition function of the **Commands** monitor in Fig. 2 to an AlwaysState containing the transition function.

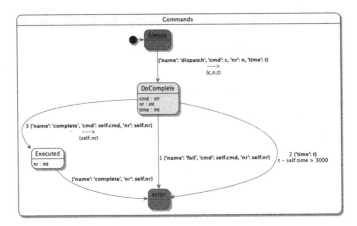

Fig. 4. Visualization of the monitor in Fig. 2, generated by PyContract.

In this work we are only concerned here about the first two kinds (EHAs and EVRs). The five monitors will analyze logs containing sequences of such spacecraft data. These include (1) counting of EHAs per 5 s, illustrating a very basic monitor not using state machines; (2) reporting of EVRs that occur within a certain time frame after having been reported missing, illustrating a temporal property formulated as state machine with multiple states active, as well as the handling of time in such a state machine; (3) file uplink to the spacecraft, consisting of several events that must occur in order, and where at the end several statistics are computed, illustrating data storage, many states, and hot states; (4) verification that issued commands are followed by expected responses (success, failure), and the durations of these (minimal, maximal, average, median), illustrating trace slicing for optimization and modeling of past time properties; and finally (5) measuring rates with which sampled values change, illustrating a more complicated past time property. The examples are non-trivial, and demonstrate the combination of Boolean first-order temporal properties combined with data analysis going beyond Boolean verdicts.

3.1   The Sample Counting Monitor

Our first monitor shows the number of channel values (EHAs) that are received per 5 s. Figure 5 shows the first lines of an example CSV file[4]. Each row reports the reading of a channel in a particular software module on board the spacecraft. Specifically, column D contains channel IDs of the form `<module>-<chan>`, consisting of a module name and a channel number. Column J contains time stamps of the form `<year>-<day>T<hour>:<min>:<sec>.<ms>`. To process this we can import and use various Python libraries, in this case `csv` (for reading CSV files), `re` (regular expressions), `datetime` (handling of time stamps), `statistics` (for statistics), and the substantial data analysis and visualization libraries `pandas` [26] and `dash` [13], illustrating why an internal programming oriented monitoring library is useful.

	A	B	C	D	E	F	G	H	I	J	K
1	...	...	...	M1-1	...	...	...	...	...	2022-277T01:59:28.526153	...
2	...	...	...	M2-2	...	...	...	...	...	2022-277T01:59:28.526153	...
3	...	...	...	M3-3	...	...	...	...	...	2022-277T01:59:29.027038	...
4	...	...	...	M3-4	...	...	...	...	...	2022-277T01:59:29.027038	...
5	...	...	...	M3-5	...	...	...	...	...	2022-277T01:59:29.027038	...
6	...	...	...	M3-6	...	...	...	...	...	2022-277T01:59:29.027038	...
7	...	...	...	M4-7	...	...	...	...	...	2022-277T01:59:30.151107	...
8	...	...	...	M4-8	...	...	...	...	...	2022-277T01:59:30.151107	...
9	...	...	...	M4-9	...	...	...	...	...	2022-277T01:59:30.151107	...
10	...	...	...	M4-10	...	...	...	...	...	2022-277T01:59:30.151107	...
11	...	...	...	M4-11	...	...	...	...	...	2022-277T01:59:30.151107	...
12	...	...	...	M4-12	...	...	...	...	...	2022-277T01:59:30.151107	...
13	...	...	...	M4-13	...	...	...	...	...	2022-277T01:59:30.151107	...

Fig. 5. An example of a log represented as a CSV file.

Figure 6 shows the type of events (used for all scripts), namely that of dictionaries from CSV column names to values. The function `convert` (line 8–12) takes as argument an event and augments it with additional fields, in this case the module in which the channel is sampled, and the time. This approach of extending events with additional "columns" is used as a general approach to deal with data fields, who's composition needs processing before being referred to in monitors.

Figure 7 illustrates a statistics module that our monitor will instantiate and update. The essence here is that of going beyond Boolean verdict monitoring. The statistics module maintains a list of channel reading counts per 5 s, and a mapping from module names to the number of channel readings in that module. Finally the results can be shown textually and in graphs, implemented using Python's `dash` library.

---

[4] Data have been left out or renamed to keep sensitive data hidden.

```
1   Event = Dict[str, object]
2
3   def stamp_to_datetime(cls, timestamp: str) -> DateTime:
4     return datetime.strptime(timestamp, '%Y-%jT%H:%M:%S.%f')
5
6   chan_pat = re.compile(r'(\w+)-(\d+)')
7
8   def convert(self, event: Event) -> Event:
9     module = chan_pat.match(event['D'])[1]
10    date_time = Time.stamp_to_datetime(event['J'])
11    event.update({'Module': module, 'Time': date_time})
12    return event
```

Fig. 6. The event type and functions for extending events.

```
1 class Statistics:
2   def __init__(self):
3     self.counts: List[int] = []
4     self.modules: Dict[str, int] = {}
5
6   def to_text(self): ...
7   def to_graph(self): ...
```

Fig. 7. The statistics class.

Finally, our monitor can be programmed as shown in Fig. 8. Note that this monitor represents a basic case where no states are needed, only the top level transition function. It corresponds to basically just writing a program. We have shown it here to illustrate how also such a monitor can be made to fit into the library's vocabulary, extending the Monitor class and defining the transition function. The result of running the monitor is statistics about how many channels were read per 5 s, an example is visualized in Fig. 9, as well as various tables, including e.g. one showing how many readings that were observed per module, see Fig. 10.

3.2   The Missed Event Monitor

The second monitor in Fig. 11 highlights (as its output) any row that reports a missing EVR (line 4), which then occurs anyway (line 19) with a matching name later within 5 s, and without any intervening rows reporting a timeout (line 13), another failure report for the same EVR (line 15), or a success report for that EVR (line 17). This monitor is temporal in nature in that upon detection of a reported missing event (line 4), it creates a new Watch-state, parameterized with the EVR name and the time. The Watch-state subsequently watches rows relevant for that EVR. Note that if several EVRs are missing a Watch-state will

```
1  class EHACount(pc.Monitor):
2    def __init__(self):
3      super().__init__()
4      self.previous_time: DateTime = None
5      self.current_time: DateTime = None
6      self.eha_count: int = 0
7      self.statistics = Statistics()
8
9    def transition(self, event):
10     module = event['Module']
11     self.statistics.update_modules(module)
12     time = event['Time']
13     if self.previous_time is None:
14       self.previous_time = time
15     self.current_time = time
16     seconds = diff(self.previous_time, self.current_time)
17     if seconds < 5:
18       self.eha_count += 1
19     else:
20       self.statistics.update_counts(self.eha_count, seconds)
21       self.eha_count = 1
22     self.previous_time = self.current_time
23
24    def end(self):
25      self.statistics.to_text()
26      self.statistics.to_graph()
```

Fig. 8. The channel sample counting monitor.

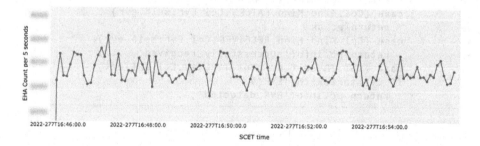

Fig. 9. Graphing of channel counts per 5 s.

be created for each. The monitor demonstrates a temporal property combined with reporting, via calls of the info method, of events that modify its state.

3.3 The File Uplink Monitor

The objective of the next monitor is to report on file uplinks from Earth to spacecraft. A file uplink is recorded in the telemetry as a sequence of EVRs,

Module	Count
M23	234
M6	235
M11	821
M13	826
M1	1,054
M20	1,989

Fig. 10. Tabulation of channel counts per module.

```
1  class MissingEVR(pc.Monitor):
2    def transition(self, event):
3      match event:
4        case {Col.Kind:Kind.FAILED,Col.Evr:evr,Col.ERT:ert}:
5          return MissingEVR.Watch(evr, ert)
6
7    @data
8    class Watch(State):
9      evr: str; ert: str
10
11     def transition(self, event):
12       match event:
13         case {Col.ERT:ert} if diff(self.ert, ert) > 5:
14           return pc.info('timed_out', ...)
15         case {Col.Kind:Kind.FAILED,Col.Evr:self.evr}:
16           return pc.ok
17         case {Col.Kind:Kind.RECEIVED,Col.Evr:self.evr}:
18           return pc.info('successfully_received', ...)
19         case {Col.ID:self.evr,Col.TYPE:ty,Col.ERT:ert}
20         if ty.startswith('EVR'):
21           return pc.info('EVR_detected', ...)
```

Fig. 11. The missing EVR monitor.

each providing additional information about the uplink. This information must be gathered and shown, including durations between EVRs, the total duration, the file size, and file size divided by duration, etc. In addition various statistics across file uplinks must be tabulated.

Figure 12 sketches the monitor for this analysis. Upon detecting the start of a file uplink (line 8) a ReceiveMeta state is created, that now looks for the next relevant event in the file uplink process. The monitor illustrates a number of points that one normally does not see in temporal specifications. First, we define storage to keep track of statistics across file uplinks (line 4). This resembles the variable state of an extended finite state machine [8]. Second, instead of passing numerous parameters to each state, a single object containing all data for a particular uplink sequence is created and passed as argument (line 9). This is then parameter to each state (e.g. line 13), and can be updated (line 21) before being passed on. Three more states are needed (lines 24–31), all following the same pattern that one is replaced by the next upon a certain event, and where in the final Finish state, upon detecting the end of the uplink, statistics is printed out. Note that the pc.ok return state (line 18) indicates that monitoring of this particular file uplink is terminated, a FIT_INFO event aborts the monitoring of this particular uplink.

3.4   The Command Execution Monitor

The next monitor examines the execution of commands and tabulates their execution time (minimal, maximal, average, median). The monitor also verifies that expected responses (success, failure) follow the dispatch of commands. That is, a dispatched command must be followed by a success or failure, with command id and number (and other parameters) matching (all extracted by regular expressions from data columns). Furthermore, a success or failure of a command that has not been dispatched should cause an error.

The monitor in Fig. 13 performs this analysis. The monitor creates a Succeed state upon detection of a command dispatch (line 19), which then watches for success or failure of the command. The monitor illustrates a few points. First of all, as previously, we notice the statistics updating (lines 4 and 32). The monitor also shows the definition of the key function (lines 6–9), which overrides its definition in the Monitor class (where it returns None) to return the hash value of an event. This is used for storing Succeed states in hash buckets for faster lookup. As mentioned before, this corresponds to slicing as found in systems such as MOP [25] and QEA [30]. A final comment concerns the definition of the monitored function (lines 11–14), which is called as a transition condition (line 21), returning true if a Succeed state exists in the monitor memory, with appropriate command code and number. It is here used to flag if a command succeeds or fails without a previous dispatch.

3.5   The Sample Rate Monitor

The last analysis reports, amongst other things, the rates with which channels change per second, measured for each channel in periods of 15 s, called *rate events*. The data can be collected in two modes chosen by the user with an option: (1) across the entire log, or (2) in so-called autopsy windows only. Autopsy windows are 60 s periods where the spacecraft records autopsy information in a buffer, which is then later dumped to a data product and sent to ground, indicated by a *recording off* EVR at the end of the window. During analysis, however, we do not know when a 60 s window begins until we see the *recording off* EVR, complicating the analysis from a temporal point of view. Events overlapping an autopsy window are considered relevant if they terminate

```
1  class Uplink(pc.Monitor):
2    def __init__(self):
3      super().__init__()
4      self.statistics = Statistics()
5
6    def transition(self, event):
7      match event:
8        case {Col.TYPE:Val.FIT_INFO,Col.Cmd:c,Col.File:f}:
9          return Uplink.ReceiveMeta(UplinkInfo(c, f))
10
11  @pc.data
12  class ReceiveMeta(pc.HotState):
13    info: UplinkInfo
14
15    def transition(self, event):
16      match event:
17        case {Col.TYPE:Val.FIT_INFO,Col.Cmd:self.info.cmd}:
18          return pc.ok
19        case {Col.SOURCE:source,Col.ID:Val.RECEIVE_META, ...}
20          if source in [Val.FSW_RT, Val.FSW_REC]:
21            self.info.source = source
22            return Uplink.ReceiveEOF(self.info)
23
24  @pc.data
25  class ReceiveEOF(pc.HotState): ...
26
27  @pc.data
28  class Succeed(pc.HotState): ...
29
30  @pc.data
31  class Finish(pc.HotState): ...
```

Fig. 12. The file uplink monitor.

within 60 s after the *recording off* EVR. The monitor reports in table format statistics such as time periods of autopsy windows, rates of change for each channel, and file compression rates.

Figure 14 shows fragments of this monitor. The main transition function (lines 2–10) creates different kinds of states, depending on what the incoming event is. Specifically an EventBegun (line 6, expiring on a 15 s timeout in line 19) when a channel is read, and a DumpBegun (line 10) when a autopsy window end has been detected (expiring on a 60 s timeout in line 28). Note that rate event monitoring is not initiated in the 60 s *after* the autopsy *recording off* event, ensured by a call of the dumping function (defined in a similar manner as the monitoring function in Fig. 13 line 11) in the transition condition (line 5). Note how we record each 60 s autopsy window (line 9) upon detecting the end of the window with a *recording off* event. Due to the fact that we only know the windows at their end, we need to re-access all information produced

```
1  class CommandDur(pc.CSVMonitor):
2    def __init__(self):
3      super().__init__()
4      self.statistics = Statistics()
5
6    def key(self, event) -> Optional[object]:
7      match event:
8        case {Col.CmdCode:c,Col.CmdNr:n}:
9          return int(n)
10
11   def monitored(self, code: str, nr: str):
12     return self.exists(
13       lambda state: isinstance(state,CommandDur.Succeed) and
14         state.code == code and state.nr == nr)
15
16   def transition(self, event):
17     match event:
18       case {Col.ID:Val.DISPATCH,Col.SCLK:t,Col.Code:c,Col.Nr:n}:
19         return CommandDur.Succeed(t, c, n)
20       case {Col.ID:Val.FAILURE|Val.SUCCESS,Col.Code:c,Col.Nr:n}
21         if not monitored(c, n):
22           return pc.error()
23
24 @pc.data
25 class Succeed(pc.HotState):
26   sclk: str; code: str; nr: str
27
28   def transition(self, event):
29     match event:
30       case {Col.ID:Val.CMD_SUCCESS|Val.CMD_FAILURE,
31         Col.SCLK:t,Col.CmdCode:self.code,Col.CmdNr:self.nr}:
32         self.statistics.record_duration(self.code,self.sclk,t)
33         return pc.info(...)
```

Fig. 13. The command execution monitor.

during monitoring once we know the windows. PYCONTRACT stores all messages produced with the methods error and info internally, which can be extracted with a call of the method get_all_messages(). These are then processed again, this time taking the now known windows into account. The fact that we have to process the messages again illustrates a weakness in the PYCONTRACT library wrt. expressing past time properties. Note, however, that even if PYCONTRACT could express past time properties conveniently, there is still the data analysis aspect which complicates matters.

```
 1  class EHARates(pc.CSVMonitor):
 2    def transition(self, event):
 3      match event:
 4        case {Col.TYPE:Val.EHA,Col.ID:c,Col.SCLK:t,Col.DATA:d}
 5        if not self.dumping():
 6          return EHARates.EventBegun(c, float(d), float(t))
 7        case {Col.ID:Val.HEALTH_AUT_RECORDING_OFF, ...}
 8        if Options.AUTOPSY:
 9          windows.add_window(float(sclk))
10          return EHARates.DumpBegun(float(sclk))
11
12  @pc.data
13  class EventBegun(pc.State):
14    channel: str; value1: float; sclk1: float
15
16    def transition(self, event):
17      match event:
18        case {Col.ID:self.channel,Col.SCLK:t,Col.DATA:d}
19        if float(t) - self.sclk1 >= 15:
20          ...; return pc.info(...)
21
22  @pc.data
23  class DumpBegun(pc.State):
24    sclk: float
25
26    def transition(self, event):
27      match event:
28        case {Col.SCLK:t} if float(t) - self.sclk > 60:
29          ...; return pc.ok
```

Fig. 14. The sample rate monitor.

4   Conclusion

We presented an application of the RV library PyContract in Python to the
analysis of log files from NASA's Europa Clipper flight computer. The analysis
had as purpose to evaluate functional as well as non-functional (performance)
properties. The effort demonstrates how such a temporal formalism can be used
for data analysis, where the objective is not only to produce Boolean yes/no
verdicts as in classical runtime verification, but also to produce richer forms of
data. PyContract supports writing temporal properties. Adding data analysis
to these becomes easy due to the fact that PyContract is a Python library,
allowing to mix temporal specifications with code. Current work includes further
development of the web-based interface using Dash, allowing easier construction
and application of monitors as plugins. The interface allows to select monitors
and logs to which they are applied. The logs are extracted from a database. The
interface allows convenient browsing (filtering and coloring) of logs as well as

visualization and tabulation of results. Wrt. longer term future work, there are rich opportunities for log analysis visualization.

References

1. Ancona, D., Franceschini, L., Ferrando, A., Mascardi, V.: RML: theory and practice of a domain specific language for runtime verification. Sci. Comput. Prog. **205**, 102610 (2021)
2. Barringer, H., Goldberg, A., Havelund, K., Sen, K.: Rule-based runtime verification. In: Steffen, B., Levi, G. (eds.) VMCAI 2004. LNCS, vol. 2937, pp. 44–57. Springer, Heidelberg (2004). https://doi.org/10.1007/978-3-540-24622-0_5
3. Barringer, H., Havelund, K.: TraceContract: a Scala DSL for trace analysis. In: Butler, M., Schulte, W. (eds.) FM 2011. LNCS, vol. 6664, pp. 57–72. Springer, Heidelberg (2011). https://doi.org/10.1007/978-3-642-21437-0_7
4. Barringer, H., Rydeheard, D., Havelund, K.: Rule systems for run-time monitoring: from Eagle to RuleR. In: Sokolsky, O., Taşıran, S. (eds.) RV 2007. LNCS, vol. 4839, pp. 111–125. Springer, Heidelberg (2007). https://doi.org/10.1007/978-3-540-77395-5_10
5. Basin, D., Klaedtke, F., Marinovic, S., Zălinescu, E.: Monitoring of temporal first-order properties with aggregations. Formal Method. Syst. Des. **46**(3), 262–285 (2015). https://doi.org/10.1007/s10703-015-0222-7
6. Bauer, A., Leucker, M., Schallhart, C.: The good, the bad, and the ugly, but how ugly is ugly? In: Sokolsky, O., Taşıran, S. (eds.) RV 2007. LNCS, vol. 4839, pp. 126–138. Springer, Heidelberg (2007). https://doi.org/10.1007/978-3-540-77395-5_11
7. Castano, R., et al.: Operations for autonomous spacecraft. In: 2022 IEEE Aerospace Conference (AERO). IEEE (2022)
8. Cheng, K.-T., Krishnakumar, A.: Automatic functional test generation using the extended finite state machine model. In: 30th ACM/IEEE Design Automation Conference, pp. 86–91 (1993)
9. Colombo, C., Pace, G.J., Schneider, G.: LARVA – safer monitoring of real-time Java programs (tool paper). In: Proceedings of the 2009 Seventh IEEE International Conference on Software Engineering and Formal Methods (SEFM 2009), Washington, DC, pp. 33–37. IEEE Computer Society (2009)
10. Dams, D., Havelund, K., Kauffman, S.: A Python library for trace analysis. In: Dang, T., Stolz, V. (eds.) Proceedings of the 22nd International Conference on Runtime Verification (RV). LNCS, vol. 13498, pp. 264–273. Springer, Cham (2022). https://doi.org/10.1007/978-3-031-17196-3_15
11. Dams, D., Havelund, K., Kauffman, S.: Runtime verification as documentation. In: Margaria, T., Steffen, B. (eds.) Leveraging Applications of Formal Methods, Verification and Validation. Software Engineering (ISoLA). LNCS, vol. 13702, pp. 157–173. Springer, Cham (2022). https://doi.org/10.1007/978-3-031-19756-7_9
12. D'Angelo, B., et al.: LOLA: runtime monitoring of synchronous systems. In: Proceedings of TIME 2005: The 12th International Symposium on Temporal Representation and Reasoning, pp. 166–174. IEEE (2005)
13. Dash. https://plotly.com/dash
14. Daut. https://github.com/havelund/daut
15. Decker, N., Leucker, M., Thoma, D.: Monitoring modulo theories. Softw. Tools Technol. Transf. **18**(2), 205–225 (2016)

16. Europa Clipper Mission. https://europa.nasa.gov
17. Fowler, M., Parsons, R.: Domain-Specific Languages. Addison-Wesley (2010)
18. Gibbons, J., Wu, N.: Folding domain-specific languages: deep and shallow embeddings (functional pearl). In: Proceedings of the 19th ACM SIGPLAN International Conference on Functional Programming (ICFP 2014), New York, pp. 339–347. Association for Computing Machinery (2014)
19. Hallé, S., Villemaire, R.: Runtime enforcement of web service message contracts with data. IEEE Trans. Serv. Comput. **5**(2), 192–206 (2012)
20. Havelund, K.: Data automata in Scala. In: 2014 Theoretical Aspects of Software Engineering Conference, TASE 2014, Changsha, 1–3 Sept 2014, pp. 1–9. IEEE Computer Society (2014)
21. Havelund, K.: Rule-based runtime verification revisited. Softw. Tools Technol. Transf. **17**(2), 143–170 (2015)
22. Kauffman, S., Havelund, K., Joshi, R.: nfer – a notation and system for inferring event stream abstractions. In: Falcone, Y., Sánchez, C. (eds.) RV 2016. LNCS, vol. 10012, pp. 235–250. Springer, Cham (2016). https://doi.org/10.1007/978-3-319-46982-9_15
23. Kim, M., Kannan, S., Lee, I., Sokolsky, O.: Java-MaC: a run-time assurance tool for Java. In: Proceedings of the 1st International Workshop on Runtime Verification (RV 2001). Electronic Notes in Theoretical Computer Science, vol. 55, no. 2. Elsevier (2001)
24. Kurklu, E., Havelund, K.: A flight rule checker for the LADEE lunar spacecraft. In: Pun, V.K.I., Stolz, V., Simao, A. (eds.) ICTAC 2020. LNCS, vol. 12545, pp. 3–20. Springer, Cham (2020). https://doi.org/10.1007/978-3-030-64276-1_1
25. Meredith, P.O., Jin, D., Griffith, D., Chen, F., Roşu, G.: An overview of the MOP runtime verification framework. Int. J. Softw. Techniq. Technol. Transf. 249–289 (2011)
26. Pandas. https://pandas.pydata.org
27. PlantUML. http://plantuml.com
28. PyContract. https://github.com/pyrv/pycontract
29. Python Pattern Matching. https://peps.python.org/pep-0636
30. Reger, G., Cruz, H.C., Rydeheard, D.: MARQ: monitoring at runtime with QEA. In: Baier, C., Tinelli, C. (eds.) TACAS 2015. LNCS, vol. 9035, pp. 596–610. Springer, Heidelberg (2015). https://doi.org/10.1007/978-3-662-46681-0_55

An Intermediate Language-Based Approach to Implementing and Verifying Communicating UML State Machines

Alexander Knapp$^{(\boxtimes)}$ (iD)

Universität Augsburg, Augsburg, Germany
`alexander.knapp@uni-a.de`

Abstract. UML state machines provide a rich language for specifying and realising reactive and timed parts of software systems. When targeting diverse back-ends for system integration, the interplay of the various language features make code generation for different implementation and verification tasks challenging. We describe the "State Machine Intermediate Language" SMILE that combines constructs for capturing the main control flow of executing a UML state machine with abstract primitives for communication with the environment and handling underlying data. SMILE is at the basis of the UML translation tool HUGO/RT which can generate Java and C++ code for implementations as well as PROMELA and timed automata specifications for model checking in SPIN and UPPAAL. We illustrate HUGO/RT and SMILE for different UML state machine features in several case studies.

1 Introduction

In model-based software development, models as the central artefacts not only serve as documentary specifications but are the source for code generation, system analysis, and verification [5, 11]. Typically, different model transformations have to be applied for obtaining model views from different viewpoints, like executable code, quantitative analysis, or model checking. The more these transformations share in their semantic basis beyond the model syntax only, the more the results of the different views are aligned and compatible. As in compiler design [1], intermediate representations and virtual runtime environments may bridge the gap between the various targets and back-ends of the model transformations [13].

We describe the "State Machine Intermediate Language" SMILE for implementing and verifying the state machine dialect of the "Unified Modeling Language" (UML [15]) that is also part of the "Systems Modeling Language" (SysML [17]). This behavioural model has evolved from ROOM charts that introduced the notion of a "run-to-completion" (RTC) step [21, 22]. Differing from Harel's state charts [7], when reacting to an event, a UML state machine only focuses on executing a transition from one state configuration to another and does not consider any other events during the reaction. On the other hand, UML state machines comprise a rich vocabulary for behaviour specification, like hierarchical states, orthogonal regions, compound transitions, dynamic choices, or history states. The intermediate language SMILE offers constructs for capturing the main control flow of executing a UML state machine together

A. E. Haxthausen et al. (Eds.): Peleska Festschrift 2023, LNCS 14165, pp. 289–307, 2023.
https://doi.org/10.1007/978-3-031-40132-9_18

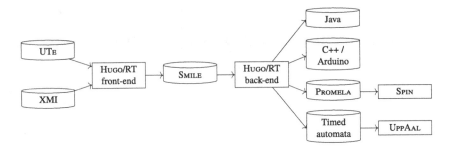

Fig. 1. Overview of Hugo/RT

with abstract primitives for communication with a virtual UML environment that also handles underlying data. Smile is at the basis of the open-source UML translation tool Hugo/RT[1], see Fig. 1: Hugo/RT reads a UML model from a standard "XML-based Metamodel Interchange" (XMI) or a proprietary "UML Text" (UTe) file, transforms the state machines of the UML model into Smile, and then generates Java and C++ code for implementations as well as Promela and timed automata specifications for model checking in Spin[2] and UppAal[3].

UML/SysML state machines have been widely employed in the model-based development of reactive and embedded systems [11]. For their implementation, libraries and internal domain-specific languages, like MSM[4] or QP[5]; code generation, like Umple[6]; or direct model-based execution, like xUML [19], have been considered. The "dynamic metamodelling" approach [6] advocates to extend the abstract syntax of the UML metamodel by semantic concepts that can be used in an operational semantics, which has been taken up by the GEMOC initiative[7] and OMG's "Precise Semantics of UML State Machines" [16]. For verification, mainly by model checking, a host of proposals supporting different sublanguages and offering rather various tool support exists—the survey by É. André et al. [3] lists 24 translational approaches and 12 approaches based on a separate operational semantics. For the case of simple, non-hierarchical state machines executable state machine code has also been combined with monitoring and a model checker for verification [4]. In contrast to these approaches, the Smile-based scheme aims at providing a common, uniform semantic tier for supporting different translation targets for implementation and verification.

---

[1] https://bitbucket.org/knappale/hugo-rt/.

[2] https://spinroot.com.

[3] https://uppaal.org.

[4] https://boost.org/doc/libs/release/libs/msm.

[5] https://sourceforge.net/projects/qpc/.

[6] https://umple.org.

[7] https://gemoc.org.

Synopsis. In Sect. 2, we briefly summarise the concrete and abstract syntax of communicating UML state machines as well as their semantics mainly by means of an example. Section 3 introduces SMILE and demonstrates its use in capturing one of the example's state machines. HUGO/RT's overall translation process is described in Sect. 4 illustrating also the SMILE representation of some special UML features. Section 5 explains how HUGO/RT translates SMILE further into programming languages (Java, C++/Arduino) and for model checkers (SPIN, UPPAAL). Finally, Sect. 6 concludes and gives an outlook to future work.

2   Communicating UML State Machines

We briefly recapitulate the main syntactic and semantic concepts of UML state machines by means of modelling the commonly used case study of the "Generalised Railroad Crossing" problem (GRC [8]; see, e.g., [9, 14, 18]): A gate shall be operated at a railroad crossing for several tracks. Whenever a train passes the gate, the gate must be closed. Moreover, within some tolerance, the gate must be open when not occupied; as soon the gate initiates opening, it must become fully open and must stay open for a certain period.

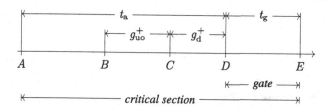

Fig. 2. "Generalised Railroad Crossing" timing annotations

The modelling problem, see Fig. 2, assumes that around the gate there are sensors for each track indicating whether a train is entering (position A) or exiting (position E). All trains pass this critical section around the gate from left to right. Inside the critical section there is at most one train on any track, but trains on different tracks may travel at different speeds. The time a train takes to pass from the entry sensor at A to the gate at D is at least t_a and at most T_a; the minimal resp. maximal time a train takes to pass the gate from D to E is t_g resp. T_g. The gate bars take the time g_u resp. g_d to go from fully closed resp. open to fully open resp. closed. The period the gate has to stay open is denoted by g_o.

Accounting for possible communication delays $\Delta \geq 0$, the gate has to start closing at $g_d^+ = g_d + \Delta$ before the fastest train may reach the gate after passing A, i.e., at location C. In order to avoid the gate opening only partly, the gate may only initiate opening when at least the time $g_{uo}^+ = g_u + g_o + \Delta$ remains before the next closing is scheduled, that is, when there is no train beyond location B (requiring that $t_a - g_d^+ - g_{uo}^+ > \Delta$).

2.1   Modelling the GRC in UML

We model the GRC problem in UML by three *classes* Track, Gate, and Controller, that also show dynamic behaviour specified by *state machines*, see Fig. 3.

Statically, every (instance of) Controller refers to a single Gate and, vice versa, every Gate is controlled by a single Controller. Moreover, every Controller is connected to k instances of Track, each Track knowing its Controller via ctrl and holding its number in num. A Controller records the number of trains currently in the critical region in the attribute trains. A Gate reacts to the *signals* open and close for opening and closing of the gate. A Controller reacts to the signals enter(i) and exit(i) for an integer i reporting a train entering or exiting the critical section on track i, as well as to the signals doOpen and doClose for internal requests to open or close the gate.

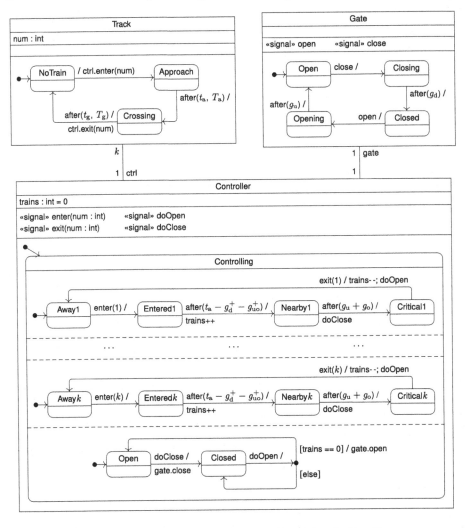

Fig. 3. UML model of the "Generalised Railroad Crossing" problem

The dynamics of each instance of Gate, Track, and Controller is governed by a separate instantiation of its respective state machine. The state machine for Gate shows an *initial pseudostate* and four *simple states* Open, Closing, Closed, and Opening. The *transition* from *source state* Open to *target state* Closing can only be *fired* when a *signal event* for close is present as its *trigger*. The transition from Closing to Closed will be fired when a *time event* occurs, which is raised after g_d time units have elapsed since Closing has been *activated*. The transitions from Closed to Open via Opening work analogously such that, in particular, closing and opening a gate takes the required amount of time.

Analogously, the state machine for Track sojourns, once having activated Approach, in this state at least for the time t_a before firing the transition to Crossing and at most the time T_a. The transition from NoTrain to Approach is triggered by a *completion event* which occurs when all activities of a state, of which there are none in this case, have finished. This transition also shows an *effect*, viz., that signal enter(num) is raised for the instance of Controller referred to as ctrl. Hence, the state machines for the tracks simulate the entering and exiting of trains in the critical section; the minimal time a train may take for this distance is $t_a + t_g$, the maximal time is $T_a + T_g$.

Finally, the state machine for Controller shows an *orthogonal composite state* consisting of several *orthogonal regions*. The upper k orthogonal regions, the ith region handling the entering and exiting of a train on the ith track, all provide the same behaviour: When a train on track i has entered the critical region, an internal signal doClose requesting the closing of the gate is raised after $t_a - g_d^+ - \Delta$, and when a train on track i leaves the critical region an internal signal doOpen requesting the opening of the gate is raised. The last orthogonal region actually handles closing and opening of the gate: When in Open and receiving a signal event for doClose, a signal event for close to the instance in gate is sent. However, when in Closed only a signal event for doOpen is reacted to—should a signal event for doClose arrive in this state it is discarded by the whole state machine as there is no other transition taking such an event as its trigger. The transition fired by a signal event for doOpen has two possible target states, linked by a *junction pseudostate*: If the guard trains == 0 is true on firing the transition indeed a signal event for open on gate is raised and Open is activated; otherwise the other branch is taken: Closed is first *deactivated* but becomes activated immediately again.

2.2   UML Metamodel and Semantics

The abstract syntax of the UML is captured by its *metamodel* (see [15]), which also forms the basis for describing the meaning of a UML model. Figure 4 shows the main concepts and relationships for UML state machines as supported by HUGO/RT and SMILE.

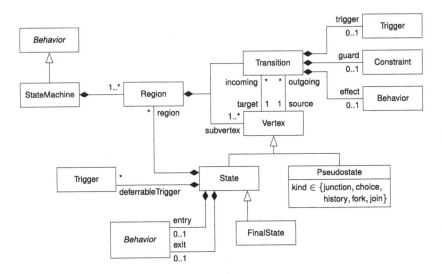

Fig. 4. Excerpt of the UML metamodel for state machines

A StateMachine consists of at least one top-level Region. Regions contain Vertexes linked by Transitions; a Vertex may be a State or a Pseudostate. A State without inner Regions is called *simple* otherwise it is *composite*; if it contains a single Region it is *simple composite*, if several then *orthogonal composite*. Each Pseudostate has a kind, which may be junction, choice, (shallow) history, fork, or join. Transitions can be chained by connecting Pseudostates into *compound transitions*. This may start with a join for synchronously exiting states in different orthogonal regions. Then some junctions and choices may follow, where guards at junctions are evaluated before any effect along the compound transition is executed and decisions at choices are taken dynamically based on previously executed effects. A compound transition can have a fork as one of its Pseudostates from which then different orthogonal regions are targeted. It can stop at States or at a history for activating the most recently recorded State. A simple or composite state is deactivated inside-out w.r.t. its regions, executing all exit Behaviors in this order; conversely, a state is activated outside-in executing entry Behaviors. A compound transition has a single Event as its trigger, which may be a signal, a call, a time, or a completion; signal events are handled asynchronously, whereas call events have to be acknowledged.

Semantically, the actual state of a state machine is given by its *active state configuration* and by the contents of its *event pool*. The active state configuration is the tree of active states; in particular, for every active composite state one state in each of its regions has to be active. The event pool holds the events that have not yet been handled by the machine. In a state configuration, an *event dispatcher* chooses some event from the pool, mainly in a queue-like fashion, but always prioritising completion and time events; the event is then processed in a *run-to-completion* (RTC) step: First, a maximal conflict-free, prioritised set of enabled compound transitions is chosen. A compound transition is *enabled* if all of its source states are contained in the active state configuration, its trigger is matched by the current event, and its guard evaluates to true; two enabled compound transitions are in *conflict* if they share a source state; and a compound transition takes *priority* over another if it starts at a deeper hierarchical level than the other. From all the compound transitions in the set, the *least common ancestor* (LCA) is determined that is the lowest composite state that contains all the compound transition's source and target states. The overall *main source state*, that is the direct substate of the LCA containing the source states, is then deactivated, the transition's actions are executed, and its target states are activated. If there is no enabled compound transition, the event may be marked as *deferred* in the active state configuration such that it is put back into the event pool; otherwise the event is discarded.

3 SMILE

SMILE (State Machine Intermediate Language) is an abstract guarded-command language for capturing the semantics of UML state machines. The language provides a simple set of control structures, like conditionals and loops, and several primitives for interacting with a state machine's environment of data and event pools. The language has been modelled on SPIN's input language PROMELA (PROtocol MEta LAnguage). However, rather than yielding a general-purpose language with rich data structures, SMILE programs always are to be interpreted in a UML environment. This environment on the one hand determines the particular implementation of the event pools and the communication between state machines. On the other hand, SMILE delegates the evaluation of UML expressions and the execution of UML actions to the surrounding implementation of data attributes. Thus, SMILE programs yield an alternative representation of UML state machines with the same dependencies on an abstract execution environment as state machines, but reducing the semantic control structures to simpler terms.

Table 1. SMILE grammar

$$
\begin{aligned}
Stm ::= \; &; \mid Var = Expr; \mid Stm\ Stm \mid \texttt{break}; \\
&\mid \texttt{if } (:: Expr \texttt{ -> } Stm)^* \; [:: \texttt{else -> } Stm] \; \texttt{fi}; \\
&\mid \texttt{do } (:: Expr \texttt{ -> } Stm)^* \; [:: \texttt{else -> } Stm] \; \texttt{od}; \\
&\mid \texttt{execute}(Action^{\text{UML}}); \mid \texttt{initialisation}(); \mid \texttt{success}(); \mid \texttt{fail}(); \\
&\mid \texttt{fetch}(); \mid \texttt{acknowledge}(); \mid \texttt{defer}(); \mid \texttt{chosen}(); \\
&\mid \texttt{complete}(State^{\text{UML}}); \mid \texttt{uncomplete}(State^{\text{UML}}); \\
&\mid \texttt{starttimer}(Event^{\text{UML}}); \mid \texttt{stoptimer}(Event^{\text{UML}}); \\
Expr ::= \; &\texttt{true} \mid \texttt{false} \mid State^{\text{UML}} \mid Transition^{\text{UML}} \mid Var \\
&\mid Expr \texttt{ == } Expr \mid Expr \texttt{ != } Expr \mid \texttt{!}\,Expr \mid Expr \texttt{ \&\& } Expr \mid Expr \texttt{ || } Expr \\
&\mid \texttt{eval}(Expression^{\text{UML}}) \mid \texttt{match}(Event^{\text{UML}}) \\
&\mid \texttt{isCompleted}(State^{\text{UML}}) \mid \texttt{isTimedOut}(Event^{\text{UML}})
\end{aligned}
$$

Table 1 summarises the grammar of SMILE. All non-terminals marked with ᵁᴹᴸ denote entities external to SMILE. This comprises state, transition, and event constants, as well as UML expressions and actions. The internal data state of a SMILE program is given by `state`, `transition`, and `flag` variables.

We do not detail the formal semantics of SMILE programs, but rather illustrate the language idioms by means of the simple UML state machine for Track depicted in Fig. 3 (in fact, the code presented does not differ much from what is produced by HUGO/RT, see Sect. 4). All SMILE code is to be executed in a virtual UML environment that contains an event pool for each system object and representations of the object states as given by the attribute valuations. The full state of each Track object thus consists of an integer value for num, an object ctrl, an event pool for the completion event for NoTrain and the time events after(t_a, T_a) and after(t_g, T_g), and, in particular, a `state` variable `top_state` recording the currently active state.

An initialisation block calls the primitive `initialisation()` for setting up the attributes, sets the `top_state` state to the constant `<NoTrain>`, and signals by the primitive `complete()` that this state is immediately complete such that a completion event is added to the event pool by the environment:

```
initialisation();
top_state = <NoTrain>;
complete(<NoTrain>);
```

The main loop for executing the remaining state machine amounts to fetching an event from the object's event pool and reacting to the selected event in a run-to-completion step until termination; in fact, Track does not show a final state. An implementation of the `fetch()` command has to respect the rules of UML event pools that require completion events to be prioritised. The fetched event for Track must be one of the time events or the only completion event. A conditional `if ... fi` or an indefinite loop `do ... od` blocks if none of its branches can be chosen. On the other hand, also several branches may be enabled such that an exhaustive execution has to consider backtrack points.

```
do
:: else ->
   event = fetch();
   if
   :: match(event, <time Approach after [ta, Ta]>) -> ...
   :: match(event, <time Crossing after [tg, Tg]>) -> ...
   :: match(event, <completion NoTrain>) -> ...
   fi;
od;
```

The reaction to each of the events found by a `match()` first checks whether the machine is in a state where this event can be consumed by an outgoing transition; otherwise the event is discarded. Subsequently the state configuration is changed accordingly executing the transition effects on the way. For the completion event for NoTrain, an enter signal with the Track's num has to be sent to the Track's ctrl, a timer for the approaching train has to be started and the configuration has to be updated to Approach:

```
if
:: top_state == <NoTrain> ->
   execute(ctrl.enter(num));
   starttimer(<time Approach after [ta, Ta]>);
   top_state = <Approach>;
:: else -> ;
fi;
```

The primitive execute() delegates the handling of the attribute evaluation and the sending proper to the environment. It is also the obligation of the environment to raise a time event for after(t_a, T_a) in between t_a and T_a time units. The reaction to this time event starts a new timer for the train crossing; the configuration is updated to Crossing:

```
if
:: top_state == <Approach> ->
   starttimer(<time Crossing after [tg, Tg]>);
   top_state = <Crossing>;
:: else -> ;
fi;
```

Finally, the reaction to the time event after(t_g, T_g) sends the signal exit with the Track's num to the Track's ctrl and moves to NoTrain, which is also immediately again completed:

```
if
:: top_state == <Crossing> ->
   execute(ctrl.exit(num));
   top_state = <NoTrain>;
   complete(<NoTrain>);
:: else -> ;
fi;
```

All the remaining SMILE primitives also communicate with the surrounding UML environment. The commands success() and fail() signal (un-)successful overall execution; acknowledge() means an acknowledgement of the reception of an operation call as the current event on a state machine; defer() puts the current event back to the event pool; chosen() signals that some event has been consumed and not deferred such that now deferred events may be re-considered; uncomplete() ensures that some state is not marked as completed any more, stoptimer() that some timer cannot elapse any more. For the expressions, eval() evaluates a UML expression; isCompleted() checks whether a state is currently marked as complete; and isTimedOut() checks whether some timer has elapsed.

4   Representing UML State Machines in SMILE

The translation of UML state machines into SMILE as used by HUGO/RT directly generates code for executing a run-to-completion step as briefly summarised in Sect. 2.2.

The template for this procedure acting on an active state configuration *conf* stored in SMILEstate variables is shown in Algorithm 1. We first discuss the transition selection (*steps*) and the transition firing part (*handleTransition*) of *RTC*. Some more details on handling the deferring and acknowledging of events as well as the treatment of choice and history pseudostates are given in Sects. 4.1 to 4.3.

After fetching an event (1. 2 of Algorithm 1) a maximal conflict-free, prioritised set of compound transitions, called a *step*, is chosen (1. 3); if there are no reacting compound transitions, then *step* is the empty set. In HUGO/RT, the choice of a step is achieved by a SMILEif...fi conditional. All possibilities are computed by the algorithm for *steps* given an active state configuration *conf* and the chosen *event*, shown in Algorithm 2. The algorithm works like the computation of all configurations in a *prime event structure* (cf. [23]): if some next compound transition (1. 7) is in conflict with the previously selected transitions and also has a higher priority, then the transition selection is only valid if the guard of the next transition is false. For orthogonal regions all possible combinations of simultaneously enabled compound transitions are thus considered. However, their number may rise exponentially with the number of regions. For example, in the GRC Controller for k tracks, see Fig. 3, when disregarding the parameters for enter and exit, there are 2^k possibilities for each of the events.

In HUGO/RT's translation, any trying to add a prioritised compound transition later on is avoided by considering all the transitions "inside-out", starting with the inner-most transitions with the highest nesting level. Conflicts are detected by updating flags r_chosen for all regions r and ensuring that no two transitions leaving the same region are selected. Additionally, it is statically checked whether parameter conditions are contradictory, such that for enter and exit only the following clauses remain:

Algorithm 1. Run-to-completion step

---

1   $RTC(conf) \equiv$
2   ⌈$event \leftarrow$ fetch()
3    $step \in steps(conf, event)$
4   if $step = \emptyset \wedge event \in deferred(conf)$
5   then defer($event$) fi
6   for $transition \in step$ do
7     $conf \leftarrow handleTransition(conf, transition)$ od
8   if $isCall(event) \wedge event \notin deferred(conf)$
9   then acknowledge($event$) fi
10 $conf$⌋

Algorithm 2. Maximal conflict-free, prioritised set of (compound) transitions

```
1   steps(conf, event) ≡
2   ⌈{step | (guard, step) ∈ steps(conf, enabled(conf, event)) ∧ ⊨ guard}⌋

3   steps(conf, transitions) ≡
4   ⌈steps ← {(ff, ∅)}
5   for transition ∈ transitions do
6       for (guard, step) ∈ steps(conf, transitions \ {transition}) do
7           if inConflict(conf, transition, step)
8               then if higherPriority(conf, transition, step)
9                   then guard ← guard ∧ ¬guard(transition) fi
10              else step ← step ∪ {transition}
11                  guard ← guard ∧ guard(transition) fi
12          steps ← steps ∪ {(guard, step)} od od
13  steps⌋
```

Algorithm 3. Compound transition handling

```
1   handleTransition(conf, transition) ≡
2   ⌈for state ∈ insideOut(exited(transition))
3       uncomplete(state)
4       for timer ∈ timers(state) do stopTimer(timer) od
5       execute(exit(state))
6       conf ← conf \ {state} od
7   execute(effect(transition))
8   for state ∈ outsideIn(entered(transition)) do
9       execute(entry(state))
10      for timer ∈ timers(state) do startTimer(timer) od
11      conf ← conf ∪ {state}
12      complete(state) od
13  conf⌋
```

```
if
:: match(event, <send entering>) ->
   if
   :: Ctrl1_state == <Controller.Ctrl1.Away1> && eval(num == 0) -> ...
   :: Ctrl2_state == <Controller.Ctrl2.Away2> && eval(num == 1) -> ...
   :: else -> ;
   fi;
:: match(event, <send exit>) ->
   if
   :: Ctrl1_state == <Controller.Ctrl1.Critical1> && eval(num == 0) -> ...
   :: Ctrl2_state == <Controller.Ctrl2.Critical2> && eval(num == 1) -> ...
   :: else -> ;
   fi;
:: ...
fi;
```

For firing all selected transitions Algorithm 3 is used. The generated code takes care of deactivating all exited states and activating the entered states. The stopping of timers and the marking of states as not being completed is needed if a state is not left by the dedicated time or completion event and discards pending events in the event pool.

The separation of transition selection and transition handling reflects the general UML procedure of the run-to-completion step but may lead to rather inefficient code. HUGO/RT mitigates this by employing partial evaluation and data-flow analysis to infer possible values of its state, transition, and flag variables and to reduce the code accordingly. For example, the generated code for the Controller is reduced from 366 to 99 lines of SMILE code. However, reduction is sometimes more limited if more complicated UML patterns are used, see Sect. 4.2.

4.1 Deferring and Acknowledging

Calls of operations, as opposed to the raising of signals, have to be handled synchronously such that the callee acknowledges the processing of a call to the caller. While waiting for this acknowledgement the caller is suspended; in particular, any self-call leads to a deadlock of the caller. An acknowledgement is also sent if the call event is simply discarded since it cannot be handled in the active state configuration. If, however, the call event is marked as deferred, the acknowledgement is delayed (1. 4 and 1. 8 of Algorithm 1).

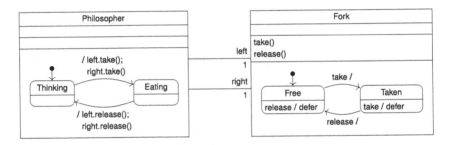

Fig. 5. UML model for the "Dining philosophers" problem

Consider, for example, the model of the well-known "Dining Philosophers" problem (see [12,20]) in Fig. 5. Only if a Fork fetches a call event for take in Free, it will send an acknowledgement such that the calling Philosopher makes progress. The SMILE code generated for the completion of the state Thinking of a Philosopher is

```
if
:: top_state == <Thinking> ->
   execute(left.take(this)); execute(right.take(this));
   top_state = <Eating>; complete(<Eating>);
:: else -> ;
fi;
```

Waiting for an acknowledgement has to be handled by the surrounding UML environment when a call is executed. The SMILE code generated for handling a call to take in a Fork combines deferring and acknowledging:

```
if
:: top_state == <Free> ->
   chosen(); top_state = <Taken>; acknowledge(event);
:: else -> defer(event);
fi;
```

Here, the primitive chosen() tells the UML environment that some event has been consumed and that hence deferred events may be reconsidered. Without this hint, an event may be repeatedly deferred and then immediately reconsidered by the event dispatcher.

4.2 Choice Pseudostates

A compound transition may target one or several choice pseudostates. When reaching a choice some outgoing (compound) transition has to be chosen based on the guards; if none is enabled, the current execution fails. The enabledness of an outgoing transition, however, may depend on the previous execution sequence of transition effects in the same RTC step. As transitions outgoing from a choice may leave the containing state, conflicts may arise with the previously chosen transitions. Whether a conflict will arise is statically undecidable, in general, since transitions between choice pseudostates make for a Turing complete language. For dynamic conflict detection, the regions r left by transitions are recorded in flag variables r_chosen. Before executing a transition outgoing from a choice, the flags for regions in conflict with the main source state of the transition are checked; if a conflict is detected the execution fails.

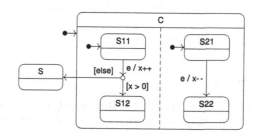

Fig. 6. Sample UML state machine with choice pseudostate

Consider the (rather artificial) example in Fig. 6. If event e occurs in the configuration containing S11 and S21, the only maximal conflict-free set of compound transitions leads to S22 and the choice pseudostate, leaving S11 and S21. If x is greater than zero, no conflict will occur, as the transition from the choice to S12 does not leave any new state. If x is less than zero, a conflict is bound to occur, as now the transition from the choice to S has to be fired, which also leaves C, in conflict with S21. The most intricate case occurs when x is zero on leaving S11 and S21: A conflict will only happen, if the transition from S21 to S22 is fired before the choice is left. This transition selection for event e and the subsequent transition firing are represented in SMILE as follows:

```
if
:: top_state == <C> ->
   if
   :: R1_state == <C.R1.S11> -> R1_transition = <C.R1.S11_2_C.R1.Choice>;
      if
      :: R2_state == <C.R2.S21> -> R2_transition = <C.R2.S21_2_C.R2.S22>;
      :: else -> ;
      fi;
   :: R1_state != <C.R1.S11> && R2_state == <C.R2.S21> ->
      R2_transition = <C.R2.S21_2_C.R2.S22>;
   :: else -> ;
   fi;
   do
   :: R1_transition == <C.R1.S11_2_C.R1.Choice> ->
      R1_transition = <empty>; execute(x++;);
      R1_state = <C.R1.Choice>; R1_chosen = false;
      if
      :: eval(x > 0) ->
         if :: !top_chosen || R2_chosen -> ; fi;
         R1_chosen = true; top_chosen = true; R1_state = <C.R1.S12>;
      :: eval(x <= 0) ->
         R1_state = <empty>; R2_state = <empty>; if :: !top_chosen -> ; fi;
         top_chosen = true; top_state = <S>;
      :: !eval(x <= 0) && !eval(x > 0) -> fail();
      fi;
   :: R2_transition == <C.R2.S21_2_C.R2.S22> ->
      R2_transition = <empty>; execute(x--;);
      if :: R2_chosen && !top_chosen || !R2_chosen && R1_chosen -> ; fi;
      R2_chosen = true; top_chosen = true; R2_state = <C.R2.S22>;
   :: R1_transition == <empty> && R2_transition == <empty> -> break;
   od;
   top_chosen = false; R1_chosen = false; R2_chosen = false;
:: else -> ;
fi;
```

4.3   History Pseudostates

A history pseudostate in a region records the state of this region which has been last active when the region is left; if this last active state is a final state, the history pseudostate is reinitialised to being empty. When reaching such a pseudostate on a transition the last active state is restored and activated. If, however, there is no state recorded then either there are outgoing transitions from the history and one of these is fired or the default entry of the history's region is used, i.e., some transition outgoing from the region's initial pseudostate is fired.

Consider the "CD Player" example in Fig. 7 (see [2, 24]). The reaction to play has to consider the history in the state Busy and is represented in SMILE as follows:

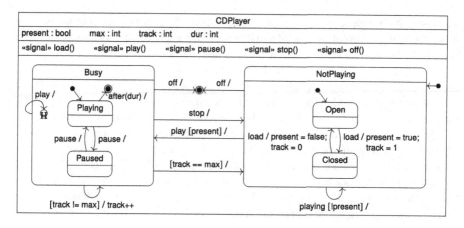

Fig. 7. UML model of the "CD Player"

```
if
:: top_state == <Busy> ->
   if
   :: Busy_history == <empty> ->
      Busy_state = <Busy.Playing>; Busy_history = <Busy.Playing>;
      complete(<Busy.Playing>);
   :: Busy_history == <Busy.Paused> -> Busy_state = <Busy.Paused>;
   :: Busy_history == <Busy.Playing> ->
      Busy_state = <Busy.Playing>; complete(<Busy.Playing>);
   fi;
:: top_state == <Final> -> ;
:: eval(present) && top_state == <NotPlaying> ->
   NotPlaying_state = <empty>; top_state = <Busy>; Busy_state = <Busy.Playing>;
   Busy_history = <Busy.Playing>; complete(<Busy.Playing>);
:: eval(!present) && top_state == <NotPlaying> ->
   NotPlaying_state = <NotPlaying.Closed>;
fi;
```

5   Code Generation and Verification

For a SMILE-based generation of executable code from UML state machines in a particular programming language it suffices to represent the control structures provided by
SMILE in the target language, to support `eval` and `execute` for some UML expression
and action language, and to implement the remaining SMILE primitives by an event pool
library.

HUGO/RT directly supports Java and C++ in this manner. Each object of a class with a
state machine is executed in a separate thread and all these threads communicate through
the event pools attached to the objects. The task code of each thread implements the
main loop of `fetch`ing and `match`ing, the reaction to each event is delegated to different
methods for readability. Such a split can be conveniently obtained by employing partial
evaluation for all possible events on the overall SMILE code. The event pool library in
both cases supports timers and realises a queue in which completion and time events are

prioritised. Although each active object is represented by a thread, the mutual exchange of synchronous call events may lead to a deadlock; for a self-call a deadlock is inevitable (see Sect. 4.1) and HUGO/RT issues a warning about this fact.

HUGO/RT also offers a more specialised translation for producing code that can be directly executed on an Arduino[8]. The model of execution on an Arduino, however, is single-threaded. Unlike the general C++-translation, several communicating state machines are thus run in a round-robin fashion. Moreover, synchronous operation calls now have to be handled differently, as the caller would always keep polling for an acknowledgement from the callee and thus would block all machines. HUGO/RT hence generates additional events for acknowledging operation calls and splits the SMILE code into resumption blocks where a caller would block. For the Philosopher's transition from Thinking to Eating (see Fig. 5) three methods for first handling the completion event and then resuming after acknowledgements are generated:

```
void Philosopher::completion_Thinking() {
  if (top_state == THINKING) {
    ep->waitforacknowledgement(ackLEFT_TAKE_THIS__);
    this->left->take(ep, this);
  }
}
void Philosopher::resume_left_take_this__() {
  ep->waitforacknowledgement(ackRIGHT_TAKE_THIS__);
  this->right->take(ep, this);
}
void Philosopher::resume_right_take_this__() {
  top_state = EATING;
  ep->insertcompletion(COMPLETION_EATING);
}
```

For verifying communicating UML state machines, HUGO/RT implements a SMILE-based generation of input for the model checker SPIN (for untimed Linear Time Logic, LTL) and the model checker UPPAAL (for timed Computation Tree Logic, TCTL). Generating PROMELA code, the input language of SPIN, is rather straightforward as SMILE has been designed along the lines of PROMELA. Only the event pool functionality has to be provided, where PROMELA's channel functionality can be reused directly. The translation of SMILE into timed automata as used by UPPAAL is somewhat more expensive as all control structures have to be turned into automata terms which often leads to a thicket of locations and transitions. The translation of the Controller of the GRC problem (see Fig. 3), for instance, results in 28 locations and 68 transitions. HUGO/RT splits the event pool of a state machine into an internal buffer for the prioritised completion and time events and an external separate timed automaton for buffering signal and call events. Each event in the external buffer can be delayed by an adjustable amount of time, only events with the same sender are delivered in their order of arrival. Also the sizes of both buffers can be adjusted, where the size of the external buffer grows quadratically with its number of places.

---

[8] https://arduino.cc.

For the properties to be verified, HUGO/RT offers special variants of LTL and TCTL using UML terms directly as well as UML interactions [10] for describing timed traces of events. For example, the safety property of the GRC can be expressed as

```
AG (track1.inState(Crossing) or track2.inState(Crossing)) implies
   gate.inState(Closed);
```

It is verified with UPPAAL 64 4.1.26-2 for two tracks with all internal and external buffer sizes set to 2 on an i7-system with 2.80 GHz and 16 GB in 0.13 s. That the gate stays open at least g_o time units can be expressed by a UML interaction that asks for an execution with less time elapsed between a gate.open() and a gate.close(); here UPPAAL reports that this impossible in 0.37 s.

6   Conclusions

We have described the "State Machine Intermediate Language" SMILE and its use in the UML translation tool HUGO/RT. On the one hand, SMILE is an abstract guarded-command language for capturing the main control flow of the run-to-completion step of UML state machines. On the other hand, SMILE comprises primitives for delegating object data handling and the communication between state machines via event pools to an underlying UML environment. HUGO/RT uses SMILE as a common abstraction for aligned and compatible translations of UML state machines to Java, C++, SPIN, and UPPAAL from a single source.

SMILE should be extended to cover the remaining UML state machine features, most notably activity Behavior that runs while a state machine is in a state, and entry and exit point Pseudostates for structuring compound transitions. The flexibility of the translation scheme offered by SMILE, like in which order state entry and exit Behavior is executed on a compound transition, should be made available to the user, for example by using templates. More generally, the intermediate representation could be made a stand-alone language such that external translation could start with (a) SMILE.

Dedication. This article is dedicated to Jan Peleska on the occasion of his 65th birthday. It is a pleasure to collaborate now with him on SysML 2, in particular, and modelling, in general. Jan is a rôle model both for making deep theoretical research insights applicable in usable tools and as an academic teacher explaining all topics profoundly and vividly.

References

1. Aho, A.V., Lam, M.S., Sethi, R., Ullman, J.D.: Compilers: Principles, Techniques, and Tools, 2nd edn. Addison-Wesley, Boston (2006)
2. André, É., Benmoussa, M.M., Choppy, C.: Translating UML state machines to coloured Petri nets using acceleo: a report. In: Pang, J., Liu, Y. (eds.) Proceedings of 3rd International Workshop Engineering Safety and Security Systems (ESSS). Electrics, Processing and Theoretical Computer Science, vol. 150, pp. 1–7 (2014). https://doi.org/10.4204/EPTCS.150.1
3. André, É., Liu, S., Liu, Y., Choppy, C., Sun, J., Dong, J.S.: Formalizing UML state machines for automated verification – a survey (2014). draft, https://lipn.fr/~andre/UML-SMD-survey.pdf

306   A. Knapp

4. Besnard, V., Teodorov, C., Jouault, F., Brun, M., Dhaussy, P.: Unified verification and monitoring of executable UML specifications. Softw. Syst. Model. **20**(6), 1825–1855 (2021). https://doi.org/10.1007/s10270-021-00923-9
5. Brambilla, M., Cabot, J., Wimmer, M.: Model-Driven Software Engineering in Practice. Synthesis Lectures on Software Engineering, Morgan & Claypool Publ. (2012). https://doi.org/10.2200/S00441ED1V01Y201208SWE001
6. Engels, G., Hausmann, J.H., Heckel, R., Sauer, S.: Dynamic meta modeling: a graphical approach to the operational semantics of behavioral diagrams in UML. In: Evans, A., Kent, S., Selic, B. (eds.) UML 2000. LNCS, vol. 1939, pp. 323–337. Springer, Heidelberg (2000). https://doi.org/10.1007/3-540-40011-7_23
7. Harel, D.: Statecharts: a visual formalism for complex systems. Sci. Comput. Program. **8**(3), 231–274 (1987). https://doi.org/10.1016/0167-6423(87)90035-9
8. Heitmeyer, C.L., Lynch, N.A.: The generalized railroad crossing: a case study in formal verification of real-time systems. In: Proceedings of 15th IEEE Real-Time Systems Symposium (RTSS), pp. 120–131. IEEE (1994). https://doi.org/10.1109/REAL.1994.342724
9. Knapp, A., Merz, S., Rauh, C.: Model checking timed UML state machines and collaborations. In: Damm, W., Olderog, E.-R. (eds.) FTRTFT 2002. LNCS, vol. 2469, pp. 395–414. Springer, Heidelberg (2002). https://doi.org/10.1007/3-540-45739-9_23
10. Knapp, A., Wuttke, J.: Model checking of UML 2.0 interactions. In: Kühne, T. (ed.) MODELS 2006. LNCS, vol. 4364, pp. 42–51. Springer, Heidelberg (2007). https://doi.org/10.1007/978-3-540-69489-2_6
11. Kordon, F., Hugues, J., Canals, A., Dohet, A. (eds.): Embedded Systems: Analysis and Modeling with SysML, UML and AADL, Wiley-ISTE (2013)
12. Liu, S., et al.: A formal semantics for complete UML state machines with communications. In: Johnsen, E.B., Petre, L. (eds.) IFM 2013. LNCS, vol. 7940, pp. 331–346. Springer, Heidelberg (2013). https://doi.org/10.1007/978-3-642-38613-8_23
13. Mellor, S.J., Scott, K., Uhl, A.: MDA Distilled: Principles of Model-driven Architecture. Addison-Wesley Professional, Boston (2004)
14. Niewiadomski, A., Penczek, W., Szreter, M.: A new approach to model checking of UML state machines. Fund. Inform. **93**(1–3), 289–303 (2009). https://doi.org/10.3233/FI-2009-0103
15. Object Management Group: Unified Modeling Language. Standard formal/2017-12-05, OMG (2017). https://www.omg.org/spec/UML/2.5.1
16. Object Management Group: Precise semantics of UML state machines. Standard formal/2019-05-01, OMG (2019). https://www.omg.org/spec/PSSM/1.0
17. Object Management Group: Systems Modeling Language. Specification ptc/22-08-02, OMG (2022) https://www.omg.org/spec/SysML/1.7
18. Okalas Ossami, D.D., Mota, J.M., Thiry, L., Perronne, J.M., Boulanger, J.L., Mariano, G.: A method to model guidelines for developing railway safety-critical systems with UML. In: Filipe, J., Shishkov, B., Helfert, M. (eds.) Proceedings of 2nd International Conference on Software and Data Technologies (ICSOFT), vol. SE, pp. 236–243. INSTICC Press (2007)
19. Raistrick, C., Francis, P., Wright, J., Carter, C., Wilkie, I.: Model Driven Architecture with Executable UML. Cambridge University Press, Cambridge (2004)
20. Rodríguez, R.J., Åke Fredlund, L., Herranz, Á.: From UML state-machine diagrams to Erlang. In: Proceedings of 13th Spanish Conference on Programming and Computer Languages (PROLE), pp. 288–299 (2013)
21. Selic, B.: An efficient object-oriented variation of the statecharts formalism for distributed real-time systems. In: Agnew, D., Claesen, L.J.M., Camposano, R. (eds.) Proc. 11th IFIP WG10.2 International Conference on Computer Hardware Description Languages and their Applications (CHDL), IFIP Transactions, vol. A-32, pp. 335–344. North-Holland (1993)

22. Selic, B., Gullekson, G., Ward, P.T.: Real-Time Object-Oriented Modeling. Wiley Professional Computing, Wiley, Hoboken (1994)
23. Winskel, G., Nielsen, M.: Models for concurrency. In: Abramsky, S., Gabbay, D.M., Maibaum, T.S.E. (eds.) Semantic Modelling, Handbook of Logic in Computer Science, vol. 4, pp. 1–148. Clarendon Press (1995)
24. Zhang, S.J., Liu, Y.: An automatic approach to model checking UML state machines. In: Proceedings of 4th International Conference on Secure Software Integration and Reliability Improvement, Companion, vol. pp. 1–7 (2010). https://doi.org/10.1109/SSIRI-C.2010.11

Polynomial Formal Verification of Complex Circuits Using a Hybrid Proof Engine

Alireza Mahzoon[1]([✉]) [iD] and Rolf Drechsler[1,2] [iD]

[1] Institute of Computer Science, University of Bremen, Bremen, Germany
{mahzoon,drechsler}@uni-bremen.de
[2] Cyber-Physical Systems, DFKI GmbH, Bremen, Germany

Abstract. The size and complexity of digital circuits are increasing; thus, they are becoming more and more error-prone. In order to prevent the bugs from escaping to silicon, formal verification is a mandatory and important phase after the design. In particular, *Polynomial Formal Verification* (PFV) has gotten a lot of attention in recent years, since it makes the verification process scalable and predictable in terms of memory usage and run-time. However, applying PFV is not always easy, especially when it comes to complex circuits.

In this paper, the concept of PFV is reviewed. Then, we introduce a hybrid proof engine to attack the problem of verifying complex modern systems in polynomial space and time. The engine takes advantage of several verification techniques, such as combinational equivalence checking based on bit-level approaches, like SAT and *Binary Decision Diagrams* (BDDs), as well as word-level verification based on e.g. *Symbolic Computer Algebra* (SCA) and *Word-Level Decision Diagrams* (WLDDs). The correctness of each block or system task can be ensured in polynomial time using a specific verification technique from the environment. Thus, we overcome the shortcomings of using only one verification method and pave the way toward polynomial verification of highly complex architectures.

Keywords: Polynomial Formal Verification · Complexity · Proof Engine · Binary Decision Diagram · Symbolic Computer Algebra

1 Introduction

Recently, the verification community has achieved many successes in proving the correctness of a wide variety of digital circuits. Several formal methods based on equivalence checking, model checking, and theorem proving have been proposed to verify both combinational and sequential circuits. Particularly, the formal verification of arithmetic circuits has gotten a lot of attention due to the high complexity and big size of these circuits: (a) *Binary Decision Diagram* (BDD) [21] and SAT-based [22] verification methods report very good results for different types of adder architectures, (b) *Multiplicative Binary Moment Diagrams* (*BMDs) [4,13] are used to verify multipliers, and (c) *Symbolic Computer Algebra* (SCA) [15,20,25] is employed to verify multipliers and dividers.

A. E. Haxthausen et al. (Eds.): Peleska Festschrift 2023, LNCS 14165, pp. 308–319, 2023.
https://doi.org/10.1007/978-3-031-40132-9_19

However, the main shortcoming of these techniques is unpredictability in performance, leading to several verification problems:

- It cannot be predicted before actually invoking the verification tool whether it will successfully terminate or run for an indefinite amount of time.
- The scalability of these techniques remains unknown, i.e., it is not predictable how much the run-time and the required memory increase when the size of the circuit grows.
- It is not possible to compare the performance of verification methods for a specific design and choose the best one.

In order to resolve the unpredictability of a verification method, its time and space complexities have to be calculated. Knowing the complexity bounds for a verification technique alleviates the three aforementioned verification problems. We are particularly interested in space and time complexities with the smallest possible polynomial order, i.e. $O(n^c)$, where n is a circuit parameter (e.g. the number of input bits) and c is a positive number. The concept of *Polynomial Formal Verification* (PFV) was first introduced in [6], where the author proved that PFV can be applied to three adder architectures using BDDs. Shortly, the complexity bounds for the verification of various circuits were calculated and new PFV techniques were proposed. A formal verification method with polynomial complexity bounds (time and space), where the exponent in the polynomial is not too high, is scalable and can be carried out successfully for different circuit sizes.

Modern digital circuits consist of several sub-components. For example, an *Arithmetic Logic Unit* (ALU) is made of several sub-components to carry out logic and arithmetic operations. It is usually the case that a monolithic proof engine cannot ensure the correctness of the entire circuit in polynomial space and time. For example, a word-level proof engine cannot be used for the PFV of the entire ALU. In this paper, we propose a hybrid proof engine to make the PFV of complex modern systems possible. The engine takes advantage of both bit- and word-level formal approaches. Thus, the correctness of each block or system task can be ensured in polynomial space and time using a specific verification approach from the environment. We take advantage of two case studies, i.e., an ALU and a structurally complex multiplier, in order to demonstrate the success of our hybrid proof engine in PFV of complex circuits. It is an important step toward PFV of highly complex designs, e.g., *Central Processing Units* (CPUs), *Digital Signal Processing* (DSP) blocks, and AI-synthesized architectures.

1.1   Related Works

In the last few years, researchers have come up with various PFV methods to resolve the verification unpredictability. They involve 1) proving the polynomial bounds for existing verification methods and 2) improving and extending existing formal methods to obtain polynomial upper-bound complexities [10].

PolyAdd [6] for the first time proved that the formal verification of three adder architectures (i.e., ripple carry adder, conditional sum adder, and carry

look-ahead adder) is possible in polynomial time using BDDs. The proof is based
on the fact that underlying BDDs remain polynomial during the whole construction process. However, PolyAdd did not provide the upper-bound complexities.
The authors of [18] and [19] extended PolyAdd by obtaining the upper-bound
time complexities of conditional sum adder and parallel prefix adders (i.e., serial
prefix adder, Ladner-Fischer adder, and Kogge-Stine adder). They calculated the
time complexities by adding up the computational complexity of *If-Then-Else*
(ITE) operation in each step of the symbolic simulation. Formal verification
of AI-generated prefix adders in polynomial time was investigated in [9]. The
authors of [12] proved that PFV of a simple ALU, consisting of arithmetic and
logic operations, is possible. Authors of [23] focused on the PFV of approximate adders. They proved that the upper-bound time complexities of verifying
approximate ripple carry adder, conditional sum adder, and carry look-ahead
adder, as well as handcrafted approximate adders, are polynomial using BDDs.

The authors of [5,17] proposed a BDD-based verification technique to ensure
the correctness of multipliers. They also proved that the output BDD sizes are
polynomial. However, they did not calculate the verification complexity. The
work of [16] considered the PFV of a multiplier for the first time. The authors
demonstrated that the verification of a Wallace-tree like multiplier can be carried out in polynomial space and time using *BMDs. The proof was extended
by [1] to arithmetic circuits consisting of multiplication and addition operations.
Moreover, the authors showed that PFV can be also performed using SCA. The
authors of [11] proved that SCA-based methods have exponential upper-bound
complexities when it comes to verifying structurally complex multipliers. Then,
they came up with a hybrid formal method based on SCA and BDDs to achieve
polynomial bounds.

In addition to arithmetic circuits, there have been some efforts to make PFV
possible for other types of circuits. The authors of [8] and [7] proved that ensuring the correctness of symmetric functions and tree-like circuits is possible in
polynomial space and time using BDDs. The work of [24] proposed two methods
to generate polynomially verifiable circuits for an approximate function.

In this paper, we highlight the limitations of a monolithic proof engine in
PFV of complex digital circuits. Then, we propose a hybrid proof engine that
takes advantage of bit- and word-level verification approaches to overcome these
limitations.

2   Background

In this section, we first review the bit-level verification methods with a focus on
BDDs. Then, we give an overview of word-level methods, particularly SCA.

2.1   Verification Using Bit-Level Techniques

In a bit-level verification method, a circuit is described in the Boolean domain,
i.e., the functions receive the intermediate and input signals as individual

Boolean variables and return the outputs in the Boolean domain as well. The verification method based on BDDs is one of the examples of bit-level verification. In this section, we focus on BDD-based verification.

We first briefly summarize some basics of BDD:

- **Binary Decision Diagram (BDD):** a directed, acyclic graph whose nodes have two edges associated with the values of the variables 0 and 1. A BDD contains two terminal nodes (leaves) that are associated with the values of the function 0 or 1.
- **Ordered BDD (OBDD):** a BDD, where the variables occur in the same order along each path from the root to a leaf.
- **Reduced OBDD (ROBDD):** an OBDD that contains a minimum number of nodes for a given variable order.

We refer to ROBDD as BDD in the rest of the paper, since it is the canonical representation that is used in the verification of arithmetic circuits.

The ITE operator (If-Then-Else) [2] is used to calculate the results of the logic operations in BDDs:

$$ITE(f, g, h) = (f \wedge g) \vee (\overline{f} \wedge h), \tag{1}$$

The basic binary operations can be presented using the ITE operator:

$$\begin{aligned} f \wedge g &= ITE(f, g, 0), \\ f \vee g &= ITE(f, 1, g), \\ f \oplus g &= ITE(f, \overline{g}, g), \\ \overline{f} &= ITE(f, 0, 1). \end{aligned} \tag{2}$$

In order to formally verify a circuit, we need to have the BDD representation of the outputs. Symbolic simulation helps us to obtain the BDD for each primary output. In a simulation, an input pattern is applied to a circuit, and the resulting output values are observed to see whether they match the expected values. On the other hand, symbolic simulation verifies a set of scalar tests (which usually covers the whole input space) with a single symbolic test. Symbolic simulation using BDDs is done by generating corresponding BDDs for the input signals. Then, starting from primary inputs, the BDD for the output of a gate (or a building block) is obtained using the ITE operation. This process continues until we reach the primary outputs. Finally, the output BDDs are evaluated to see whether they match the BDDs of the circuit.

2.2   Verification Using Word-Level Techniques

In a word-level verification method, a circuit is described in the integer domain, i.e., the functions receive the intermediate and input signals as individual Boolean variables and return the outputs in the integer domain. The verification method based on SCA is one of the examples of word-level verification.

We now summarize some basics of SCA:

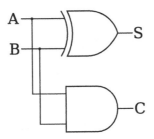

Fig. 1. Half-adder

- **Monomial:** power product of the variables, i.e. $M = x_1^{a_1} x_2^{a_2} \ldots x_n^{a_n}$, where $a_i \geq 0$.
- **Polynomial:** finite sum of monomials, i.e. $P = c_1 M_1 + \cdots + c_j M_j$ with coefficients in field k.
- **Division:** Assuming p is a polynomial and F is a set of polynomials, the division of p by F is denoted by $p \xrightarrow{F} r$, where r is called a remainder.

The goal of SCA-based verification is to formally prove that all signal assignments consistent with the gate-level or *AND Inverter Graph* (AIG) representation evaluate the *Specification Polynomial* (*SP*) to 0. The *SP* determines the word-level function of an arithmetic circuit based on its inputs and outputs, e.g. for the half-adder of Fig. 1 $SP = 2C + S - (A + B)$, where $2C + S$ represents the word-level representation of the 2-bit output, and $A + B$ represents the addition of the 1-bit inputs.

Before verification, the gates of the circuit should be modeled as polynomials describing the relation between inputs and outputs. If the circuit is built from basic logic gates (e.g., NOT, AND, OR, and XOR), four different operations might happen in the circuit. Assuming z is the output, and a and b are the inputs of a gate, the polynomials for the basic logic gates are as follows:

$$
\begin{aligned}
z &= \neg a \Rightarrow p_g := z - 1 + a, \\
z &= a \wedge b \Rightarrow p_g := z - a \cdot b, \\
z &= a \vee b \Rightarrow p_g := z - a - b + a \cdot b, \\
z &= a \oplus b \Rightarrow p_g := z - a - b + 2a \cdot b.
\end{aligned}
\tag{3}
$$

The extracted gate polynomials are in the form $P_g = x - tail(P_g)$, where x is the gate's output, and $tail(P_g)$ is a function based on the gate's inputs. Similarly, the polynomials for the nodes can be extracted in an AIG representation (see [20, 26]).

Based on the Gröbner basis theory, all signal assignments consistent with the AIG evaluate the specification polynomial SP to 0, iff the remainder of dividing SP by the gate polynomials is equal to 0 (see [15] for more details).

The step-wise division of SP by gate polynomials for the half-adder of Fig. 1 is as follows:

$$SP := 2C + S - (A + B),$$

$$SP \xrightarrow{P_{AND}} SP_1 = 2AB + S - (A + B),$$

$$SP_1 \xrightarrow{P_{XOR}} r = 0. \tag{4}$$

Since the remainder is zero, the circuit is bug-free. In arithmetic circuits, dividing SP_i by a gate polynomial $P_{g_i} = x_i - tail(P_{g_i})$ is equivalent to substituting x_i with $tail(P_{g_i})$ in SP_i. For example, dividing SP_1 by P_{XOR} in Eq. (4) is equivalent to substituting S with $tail(P_{XOR}) = A + B - 2A \cdot B$ in SP_1. In the results, we always replace powers $x_i^{a_i}$ with $a_i > 1$ by x_i, since x_i can only take values from $\{0, 1\}$. In the theory, this corresponds to adding $x_i^2 - x_i$ to the gate polynomials. The process of step-wise division (substitution) is called *backward rewriting*.

3   PFV Using a Hybrid Proof Engine

In this section, we first introduce our hybrid proof engine that uses both bit- and word-level approaches for PFV. Then, we present two case studies to illustrate the applications of our hybrid proof engine.

3.1   Overview

Despite the progress in PFV of various circuits, most of the works are still limited to the polynomial verification of individual components, e.g., adders, and are based on a monolithic proof engine. Thus, the PFV of complex systems, consisting of many different sub-components, is an almost unexplored area. The challenge originates from the fact that a verification method (e.g., equivalence checking using BDDs) might verify a sub-component (e.g., an adder) in polynomial time but have an exponential verification complexity for another sub-component (e.g., a multiplier).

We propose a hybrid proof engine that integrates both bit- and word-level approaches in an environment. As a result, the verification is not limited to a single formal method. Each sub-component or system task can be verified using a suitable formal approach that ensures PFV. Consequently, PFV can be applied to complex circuits which could not be verified using a single formal method in polynomial space and time. We take advantage of BDDs and SCA as our bit-level and word-level verification methods in our hybrid proof engine, since their polynomial upper-bounds have been proven for a wide variety of circuits (see e.g., [1,11,18,19]).

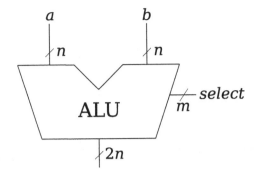

Fig. 2. Symbolic representation of the ALU

Table 1. List of supported operations

s_2	s_1	s_0	function
0	0	0	$0\ldots0$
0	0	1	$b - a$
0	1	0	$a - b$
0	1	1	$a + b$
1	0	0	$a \times b$
1	0	1	$a \oplus b$
1	1	0	$a \vee b$
1	1	1	$a \wedge b$

3.2   Case Study I: PFV of an ALU

An ALU is a combinational digital circuit that performs arithmetic and bitwise operations on integer binary numbers. The type and the number of supported operations in an ALU depend on the application. Figure 2 shows the symbolic representation of a general ALU. It receives two n-bit inputs a and b. The operation between the inputs is determined by an m-bit *select*. Finally, the result of the operation is returned as a $2n$-bit output.

In this paper, we consider an ALU with 8 operations, i.e. the *select* signal has 3 bits. The complete list of supported operations is depicted in Table 1. The ALU can perform three arithmetic operations (i.e., addition, subtractions, and multiplication) as well as three bitwise logic operations (i.e., XOR, OR, and AND).

The addition and subtraction are implemented based on the carry look-ahead algorithm. On the other hand, the architectures for the three stages of the multiplier (see Fig. 3) are as follows: simple partial product generator, array, and ripple carry adder. The multiplier is structurally simple, since the second and third stages are only made of half-adders and full-adders.

We now discuss the results of verifying the ALU using a monolithic proof engine based on BDDs and SCA:

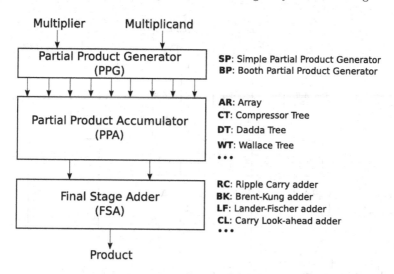

Fig. 3. Multiplier structure

- BDD-based verification reports very good results when it comes to ensuring the correctness of various adder architectures. It has been proven in [6] that carry look-ahead adder can be verified in polynomial space and time using BDDs. PFV can be also applied to the subtractor, since it is built by adding XOR gates to the inputs of the adder. However, BDD-based verification runs out of memory when it comes to the verification of multipliers. It has been proven in [3] that the size of output BDDs becomes exponential for a multiplier. As a result, a monolithic proof engine based on BDDs cannot be used for the PFV of the entire ALU.
- SCA-based verification has shown very good results for the verification of structurally simple multipliers. The experimental results demonstrated the efficiency of SCA-based verification in proving the correctness of million-gate multipliers [20]. In addition, it has been shown that the PFV of structurally simple multipliers is possible using SCA [11]. However, SCA-based methods run quickly out of memory when it comes to the verification of adders that are not only made of half-adders and full-adders. The authors of [11] have proven that the size of intermediate polynomials becomes exponential during the verification of a carry look-ahead adder. As a result, a monolithic proof engine based on SCA cannot be used for the PFV of the entire ALU.

We can overcome the limitations of monolithic proof engines in verifying the ALU by using our hybrid proof engine. The verification of logic operations (AND, OR, and XOR) as well as addition and subtraction is performed using BDDs in polynomial space and time. Moreover, the SCA-based method is used for the PFV of the multiplication operation. As a result, the entire ALU can be verified polynomially using our hybrid proof engine.

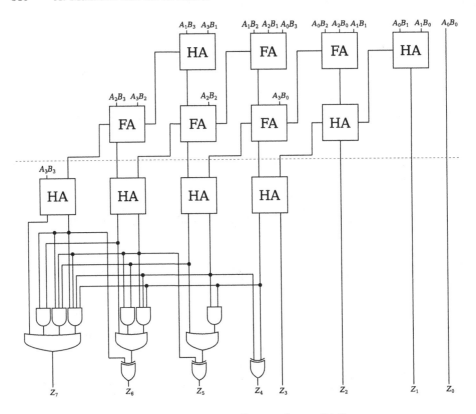

Fig. 4. 4×4 structurally complex multiplier

3.3   Case Study II: PFV of a Structurally Complex Multiplier

If the second and third stages of a multiplier (see Fig. 3) are not only made of half-adders and full-adders, it is called a structurally complex multiplier. Figure 4 depicts a 4×4 structurally complex multiplier, where the final stage adder has a carry look-ahead adder architecture. Ensuring the correctness of structurally complex multipliers is a big challenge for the verification community. Several formal verification methods based on SCA have been proposed to overcome the challenges [14,20]. However, it is not trivial to prove their polynomial complexity for all multiplier architectures due to some heuristics in their flow.

We now discuss the results of verifying the complex multiplier using a monolithic proof engine based on BDDs and SCA:

– Similar to the structurally simple multipliers, the size of output BDDs becomes exponential for structurally complex multipliers. Several techniques have been proposed to make the verification of multipliers possible using BDDs. The work of [5] considers the partial products as new input variables and constructs the output BDDs based on them. As a result, the size of output BDDs becomes polynomial with respect to the input width. However, it is

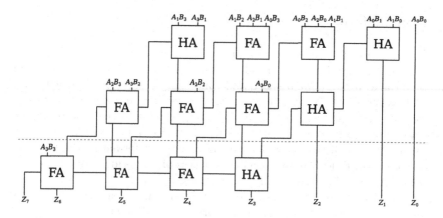

Fig. 5. 4×4 structurally simple multiplier

still not clear whether the size of intermediate BDDs is polynomially bounded during the symbolic simulation. Thus, BDD-based verification cannot ensure the PFV of structurally complex multipliers.

– Although SCA-based verification has shown very good results for the verification of structurally simple multipliers, it fails when it comes to ensuring the correctness of structurally complex multipliers. It has been shown experimentally that the size of intermediate polynomials grows drastically during backward rewriting. The authors of [11] proved that the size of intermediate polynomials increases exponentially for structurally complex multipliers. As a result, a monolithic proof engine based on SCA cannot be used for the PFV of a structurally complex multiplier.

If the design hierarchy, including the boundaries between the three stages of the multiplier (i.e. PPG, PPA, and FSA) and the components in each stage are available, we can take advantage of our hybrid proof engine to ensure the correctness of the structurally complex multiplier. Our method consists of three main steps:

1. the final stage of the multiplier, i.e. FSA, is replaced with a ripple carry adder,
2. the new multiplier architecture is verified using SCA,
3. the FSA is verified using BDDs.

If both verification methods ensure correctness, the multiplier is bug-free. Otherwise, it is buggy.

It is now possible to calculate the space and time complexity of SCA and BDD-based methods separately and prove their polynomial upper-bounds with respect to the multiplier size: After replacing the FSA with a ripple carry adder, the new multiplier is structurally simple, since the second and third stages are made of half-adders and full-adders (see Fig. 5). It has been proven in [11] that structurally simple multipliers can be verified in polynomial space and time using SCA. On the other hand, PFV can be applied to the original FSA using BDDs as proven in [6]. As a consequence, PFV of structurally complex multipliers becomes possible.

4   Conclusions

In this paper, we illustrated the importance of using a hybrid proof engine for PFV. Complex digital circuits usually consist of many sub-components, which can be verified in polynomial space and time using a suitable verification technique. However, the PFV cannot be guaranteed using a monolithic proof engine. This problem can be alleviated by introducing a hybrid proof engine that integrates bit- and word-level formal methods in an environment. Thus, each sub-component or system task is verified using one of the formal methods in polynomial space and time. We discussed the success of a hybrid proof engine in the PFV of an ALU and a structurally complex multiplier.

In the future, we plan to investigate the PFV of other complex digital circuits such as CPUs and DSP blocks using a hybrid verification engine.

Acknowledgements. This paper has been dedicated to the 65th birthday of Jan Peleska. Parts of this work have been supported by DFG within the Reinhart Koselleck Project *PolyVer: Polynomial Verification of Electronic Circuits* (DR 287/36-1).

References

1. Barhoush, M., Mahzoon, A., Drechsler, R.: Polynomial word-level verification of arithmetic circuits. In: ACM and IEEE International Conference on Formal Methods and Models for Codesign, pp. 1–9 (2021)
2. Brace, K.S., Rudell, R.L., Bryant, R.E.: Efficient implementation of a BDD package. In: Design Automation Conference, pp. 40–45 (1990)
3. Bryant, R.E.: On the complexity of VLSI implementations and graph representations of Boolean functions with application to integer multiplication. IEEE Trans. Comput. **40**(2), 205–213 (1991)
4. Bryant, R.E., Chen, Y.A.: Verification of arithmetic circuits with binary moment diagrams. In: Design Automation Conference, pp. 535–541 (1995)
5. Burch, J.: Using BDDs to verify multipliers. In: Design Automation Conference, pp. 408–412 (1991)
6. Drechsler, R.: PolyAdd: polynomial formal verification of adder circuits. In: IEEE Symposium on Design and Diagnostics of Electronic Circuits and Systems, pp. 99–104 (2021)
7. Drechsler, R.: Polynomial circuit verification using BDDs. In: International Conference on Electrical, Electronics, Communication, Computer Technologies and Optimization Techniques, pp. 466–483 (2021)
8. Drechsler, R., Dominik, C.: Edge verification: Ensuring correctness under resource constraints. In: Symposium on Integrated Circuits and System Design, pp. 1–6 (2021)
9. Drechsler, R., Mahzoon, A.: Towards polynomial formal verification of AI generated arithmetic circuits. In: International Symposium on Devices, Circuits and Systems (2023). https://ieeexplore.ieee.org/document/10153522
10. Drechsler, R., Mahzoon, A.: Polynomial formal verification: Ensuring correctness under resource constraints. In: International Conference on Computer-Aided Design, pp. 70:1–70:9 (2022)

11. Drechsler, R., Mahzoon, A., Goli, M.: Towards polynomial formal verification of complex arithmetic circuits. In: IEEE Symposium on Design and Diagnostics of Electronic Circuits and Systems, pp. 1–6 (2022)

12. Drechsler, R., Mahzoon, A., Weingarten, L.: Polynomial formal verification of arithmetic circuits. In: International Conference on Computational Intelligence and Data Engineering, pp. 457–470 (2021)

13. Hamaguchi, K., Morita, A., Yajima, S.: Efficient construction of binary moment diagrams for verifying arithmetic circuits. In: International Conference on Computer-Aided Design, pp. 78–82 (1995)

14. Kaufmann, D., Beame, P., Biere, A., Nordström, J.: Adding dual variables to algebraic reasoning for gate-level multiplier verification. In: Design, Automation and Test in Europe, pp. 1431–1436 (2022)

15. Kaufmann, D., Biere, A., Kauers, M.: Verifying large multipliers by combining SAT and computer algebra. In: Formal Methods in Computer-Aided Design, pp. 28–36 (2019)

16. Keim, M., Drechsler, R., Becker, B., Martin, M., Molitor, P.: Polynomial formal verification of multipliers. Formal Method. Syst. Des. Int. J. **22**(1), 39–58 (2003)

17. Kumar, J., Miyasaka, Y., Srivastava, A., Fujita, M.: Formal verification of integer multiplier circuits using binary decision diagrams. IEEE Trans. Comput. Aided Des. Circuit. Syst. (2022). https://ieeexplore.ieee.org/document/9832648

18. Mahzoon, A., Drechsler, R.: Late breaking results: polynomial formal verification of fast adders. In: Design Automation Conference, pp. 1376–1377 (2021)

19. Mahzoon, A., Drechsler, R.: Polynomial formal verification of prefix adders. In: Asian Test Symp, pp. 85–90 (2021)

20. Mahzoon, A., Große, D., Drechsler, R.: RevSCA-2.0: SCA-based formal verification of non-trivial multipliers using reverse engineering and local vanishing removal. IEEE Trans. Comput. Aided Des. Circuit. Syst. **41**(5), 1573–1586 (2022). https://ieeexplore.ieee.org/document/9440537

21. Malik, S., Wang, A.R., Brayton, R.K., Sangiovanni-Vincentelli, A.L.: Logic verification using binary decision diagrams in a logic synthesis environment. In: International Conference on Computer-Aided Design, pp. 6–9 (1988)

22. Mishchenko, A., Chatterjee, S., Brayton, R.K.: DAG-aware AIG rewriting a fresh look at combinational logic synthesis. In: Design Automation Conference, pp. 532–535 (2006)

23. Schnieber, M., Fröhlich, S., Drechsler, R.: Polynomial formal verification of approximate adders. In: EUROMICRO Symposium on Digital System Design, pp. 761–768 (2022)

24. Schnieber, M., Fröhlich, S., Drechsler, R.: Polynomial formal verification of approximate functions. In: IEEE Annual Symposium on VLSI, pp. 92–97 (2022)

25. Yu, C., Brown, W., Liu, D., Rossi, A., Ciesielski, M.: Formal verification of arithmetic circuits by function extraction. IEEE Trans. Comput. Aided Design Circuit. Syst. **35**(12), 2131–2142 (2016)

26. Yu, C., Ciesielski, M., Mishchenko, A.: Fast algebraic rewriting based on and-inverter graphs. IEEE Trans. Comput. Aided Design Circuit. Syst. **37**(9), 1907–1911 (2017)

Debugging Frame Conditions

Thomas Santen[(✉)]

Formal Assurance, Aachen, Germany
santen@formalassurance.com
http://www.formalassurance.com

Abstract. Frame conditions play an important role in formal specifications of system behavior or software operations. A frame condition specifies that a particular part of the data in a system state will not change during a state transition. In abstract system specifications, explicit equations of the form $x' = x$ describe frame conditions, whereas in contracts of imperative or object-oriented programs, frame conditions can also be described implicitly by specifying a set of heap locations that are allowed to change whereas the content of other heap locations must not change during an operation execution.

Too liberal or too strong framing is a notorious source of error during the development of a formal specification. Based on experience from customer projects, this article describes common framing errors in abstract system models, expressed in Alloy, and an approach using model finding to systematically debug such erroneous specifications.

Keywords: Framing · Debugging Formal Specifications · Formal Verification

1 Introduction

Consider a system that manipulates its data state by way of a number of operations. A formal specification of such a system can abstractly describe the data that the system holds, possibly with data invariants, and transition predicates that describe operations by their effect on the data. If a specific implementation in a programming language is to be considered, a contract-style specification of an imperative or object-oriented program describes the effect of the operation implementations by pre-/post-condition contracts.

For both kinds of specification, the concept of *framing* plays an important role. It refers to the fact that an operation specification not only describes the desired change of data in the system state, but it must also describe the part of the system state that *does not* change when the operation is executed.

Various concepts of object-ownership have been developed to ease the formal specification of the heap frame in contract-style formal specifications of imperative or object-oriented programs [5]. They particularly strive to address the complexity of program behavior caused by pointer aliasing or concurrency.

© The Author(s), under exclusive license to Springer Nature Switzerland AG 2023
A. E. Haxthausen et al. (Eds.): Peleska Festschrift 2023, LNCS 14165, pp. 320–332, 2023.
https://doi.org/10.1007/978-3-031-40132-9_20

Abstracting from specific programming features, a formal system model can describe the data held in a system state and system operations manipulating that data without referring to programming concepts like heap memory. Languages such as Alloy [7] in its latest Version 6 [1], VDM [8], or Z [13] support this style of specification. In such a model, system operations may be specified in terms of transition relations between the valuations of variables in the states before and after execution of the system operation. Here, *framing equations* of the form $x' = x$ serve to specify that the value of a state component x is not changed by the operation.

Framing is a common source of error when developing system models or program contracts. Framing equations are easily forgotten when specifying the effect of an operation. This results in too liberal a specification that allows certain parts of the state to change arbitrarily. Dually, a too narrow heap frame or framing equations that are too strong may contradict state changes required by the desired effect of the operation, thus precluding certain desired behavior or resulting in an inconsistent specification.

This paper focusses on erroneous framing equations in abstract system specifications, and approaches how to debug them. The discussion draws on experience from customer projects comprising several tens of thousands lines of formal specification code. To respect customers' non-disclosure requirements, and to keep the presentation self-contained, a simple mockup system is used for illustration purposes: a rover maneuvering around obstacles on a plain.

For a simple system like this, an experienced verification engineer will easily spot and correct framing errors. For a sizeable specification of a real system, however, it is challenging to keep track of the different parts of a specification that contribute to a particular frame and spot inconsistencies just by inspection. Consequently, debugging framing errors often is time consuming and tedious. Under change of the system functionality or its requirements, and consequently their formal representations, debugging framing errors may be even more challenging. Identifying a single erroneous framing equation in the process of integrating a new feature into a sizeable formal specification can easily require several person days of debugging effort.

The structure of the presentation in Sects. 2 to 4 mimics a formal specification effort leading to a defective specification. Section 5 discusses why standard approaches to debugging such a specification do not provide adequate support to identify the erroneous part of the specification. Section 6 introduces a more systematic approach to debugging inconsistent abstract system specifications, which has the potential to considerably reduce the time and effort needed to fix erroneous framing equations. Section 7 discusses related work, and Sect. 8 concludes with suggestions for future work.

2   A System Model in Alloy

For system modeling, this paper uses the formal language Alloy [7], which is a temporal first-order relational logic. The Alloy analyzer uses the Kodkod relational model finder and several SAT solvers to explore Alloy models and verify

Listing 1. Alloy signatures of the *Rover* system

```
1  sig Coord {
2    adjacent : some Coord
3  }
4
5  fact adjacentFacts {
6    irreflexive[adjacent]
7    symmetric[adjacent]
8  }
9
10 abstract sig Thing {
11   var position : Coord
12 }
13
14 one sig Rover extends Thing {}
15 sig Obstacle extends Thing {}
16
17 one sig theSystem {
18   r : Rover,
19   os : set Obstacle
20 }{
21   all t : r+os | t.position not in (r+os−t).position
22 }
```

assertions about them. The latest Version 6 of the Alloy language and analyzer [1] comes with new features allowing one to specify and assess behavioral models natively. It allows one to mark the mutable data of a system state, specify the transition relation between system states, and assert temporal properties of the resulting set of system traces. In addition to checking bounded traces with SAT solving, standard model checkers like NuSMV [2,3] can be used to verify temporal properties of unbounded traces.

The running example illustrating framing errors and their debugging is a *rover* maneuvering around obstacles on a plain. A set of abstract coordinates and an adjacency relation between them describes the topology of the plain. The positions of the rover and the obstacles are coordinates locating them on the plain. The positions of all objects on the plain must be distinct.

In Alloy, *signatures* define new types. Listing 1 shows the signatures formally representing the concepts of the rover example. The signature Coord has a field adjacent, which is a non-empty set of coordinates. In the Alloy semantics, a field of a signature is a globally visible relation mapping the signature type to the declared type of the field, i.e., the semantics of adjacent is a binary relation on Coord. Referring to that global semantics, the axiom adjacentFacts states that the adjacency relation between coordinates is irreflexive and symmetric, i.e., a coordinate it not adjacent to itself, and adjacency is not directed.

Listing 2. Transition predicates and system traces

```
1   pred moveTo [ p : Coord ]{
2     p in theSystem . r . position . adjacent
3     theSystem . r . position ' = p
4     all o : theSystem . os | o . position ' = o . position
5   }
6
7   pred move {
8     some p : theSystem . r . position . adjacent |{
9       moveTo [ p ]
10      }
11  }
12
13  pred init {
14    theSystem . os = Obstacle
15  }
16
17  pred step {
18    move
19  }
20
21  fact traces {
22    init
23    always step
24  }
```

The abstract signature Thing generalizes rovers and obstacles. The keyword **var** declares its field position to be mutable, i.e., its value may change in a state transition, whereas fields that are not marked with **var** remain constant during the entire lifetime of a system. The signatures Rover and Obstacle extend Thing. The former has exactly **one** instance whereas the number of obstacles is not constrained in the signature declaration.

The signature theSystem contains the state of the entire system, i.e., one rover and a set of obstacles. Its invariant requires that the rover and all obstacles have distinct positions.

The definitions in Listing 2 describe how the rover moves around the plain while avoiding obstacles. The predicate moveTo[p] moves the rover to a position p, provided p is adjacent to the current position of the rover. The primed version of a mutable field, such as theSystem.r. position ' denotes the value of the field in the post-state of a state transition. The universally quantified framing equations o. position ' = o.position specify that all obstacles keep their positions while the rover moves. The predicate move non-deterministically chooses a position adjacent to the rover and requires it to move to that position. The system invariant (Line 21 of Listing 1) ensures that the rover does not attempt to move to a position that is occupied by an obstacle.

Listing 3. Operation push

```
1  pred push {
2    some o : theSystem.os |{
3      o.position in theSystem.r.position.adjacent
4      moveTo[o.position]
5      o.position' in o.position.adjacent−theSystem.r.position
6      all oo : theSystem.os−o | oo.position' = oo.position
7    }
8  }
9
10 pred step {
11   move
12   ||
13   push
14 }
```

The axiom traces defines the set of traces of the rover system by way of a temporal formula, where the predicate init requires that in an initial system state all obstacles are placed somewhere on the plain, and the predicate step says that each state transition consists of a single move of the rover.

A number of desired properties of the rover system, omitted in Listing 2, serve as sanity checks for the formal specification. They include a check of the consistency of the specification as well as a model exploration showing that the desired moves of the rover indeed form the set of specified traces. Assertions requiring that the rover only moves to free adjacent positions, and that the positions of obstacles never change are other sanity checks validating the rover specification. Specific examples of sanity checks are further discussed in Sect. 4.

3 A New Feature

After a thorough analysis of the rover system presented in Sect. 2, a new feature is to be added to the system: the rover is enhanced to be able to push obstacles out of its way. Listing 3 shows the modifications to integrate this feature into the formal specification. In addition to the operation move, which moves the rover to a free adjacent position, the new operation push allows the rover to move to an adjacent position that is occupied by an obstacle, provided that the obstacle can itself be moved to a free adjacent position.

The specification of push requires that there exists an obstacle o that is adjacent to the rover. It uses the predicate moveTo to update the position of the rover, and it moves the obstacle o to an adjacent position (Line 5). The framing equations in Line 6 of Listing 3 ensure that all other obstacles remain at their original positions. Like for the specification of move, the system invariant ensures that the obstacle o is moved to a free position.

The modified definition of step in Listing 3 reflects the extended behavior of the rover system: each single state transition is a move or a push operation.

Listing 4. Validation of the modified rover system

```
1  run {} for 10
2  run {eventually push} for 10
3  run push for 10
```

4   Specification Validation

As for the original version of the specification, sanity checks must be performed to validate the formal specification. Listing 4 shows some of them.

The **run** command in Line 1 tells the Alloy Analyzer to find a model that satisfies the true predicate and in which all signatures have at most 10 instances. Thus the consistency of the specification as a whole is verified. This sanity check is successful.

Since the modified step predicate is a case distinction, sanity checks should demonstrate that each case is reachable, i.e., for each system operation, there is an initial system state such that the operation can eventually be applied. For step this means that both system operations should be executed in some traces of the system. In particular, there should exist a trace from an initial system configuration to a state in which push is performed. The predicate **eventually** push in Line 2 formalizes that sanity check as a temporal proposition. Model finding for this sanity check fails: there is no trace of the modified system that eventually executes push.

This motivates the final sanity check in Line 3, which also fails. The maximal cardinality of 10 specified for each type in the **run** command is sufficient to exhibit a model satisfying push, if there is one. Therefore, the failing sanity check shows that the predicate push is inconsistent, i.e., there is no state transition executing push, not even for a pre-state that may not be reachable from an initial state.

5   Approaches to Debugging

The failing sanity checks indicate that the definition of push in Listing 3 is faulty, but they do not easily provide a clue as to what part of the specification is wrong or how to correct it. The failure occurs in an attempt to find a model for push, i.e., the SAT solver invoked by the Alloy Analyzer does not find a model for this predicate.

The standard means to debug an inconsistent specification is to inspect a minimal unsatisfiable core [10] of the failing model finding attempt. This is a minimal contradictory set of clauses of the specification. The Alloy Analyzer provides a version of MiniSAT [6] with the ability to compute a minimal unsatisfiable core.

For the specification of the modified rover system, the unsatisfiable core of push consists of three formulas: the system invariant (Line 21 of Listing 1), the rover position update and the framing equations of moveTo (Line 3 and Line 4 of

Listing 2). This core can be instrumental in debugging the specification, because it is quite concise and it does include the erroneous framing predicate of moveTo that makes the specification of push inconsistent: The obstacle o in the definition of push is "pushed" to an adjacent position and therefore does change its position in contradiction with the framing predicate of moveTo.

However, the unsatisfiable core tends to provide useful information for debugging only for specifications of very limited size and predicates of limited complexity. Already the unsatisfiable core of **eventually** push (Line 2 of Listing 4) is too large, relative to the size of the specification, to be of much use: it includes the complete definitions of moveTo, move, and push, as well as the system invariant; it highlights only the system invariant and the rover position update. Therefore, it is of little help for debugging the specification.

For a specification of a real system of considerable size and complexity, like the one that motivated the present work, the unsatisfiable core often is of no use at all. In a situation where a specification comprising several thousand lines of code is modified to incorporate a new feature, the unsatisfiable core tends to comprise the newly specified functionality and the parts of the specification it depends on. Given the project context, namely that the modification builds on a thoroughly validated specification, the unsatisfiable core thus only provides the redundant information that the newly added code is not consistent with the parts of the existing specification to which it refers.

Systematic inspection is another way of debugging an inconsistent specification. For an experienced person, it will be easy to find the fault in the tiny specification of the rover system just by inspection. They will first convince themselves that the update predicates of the specification correctly capture the intended effect of the operation. Then, they will focus on framing equations as a known source of specification errors, and will easily spot the contradiction between Line 5 of Listing 3 and Line 4 of Listing 2.

However, if the specification is so large that it is hard to mentally keep track of all details necessary to identify an error, and if the offending framing equation resides several levels down in the reference hierarchy of predicate definitions in some remote part of the code base, the erroneous framing equation will not be so easy to spot. Under these circumstances, debugging is reduced to tedious manual slicing of the code base until a sufficiently small part of the specification can be inspected to find the offending framing predicate. This process is time consuming, and therefore expensive, because model finding takes considerably more time to terminate for an inconsistent specification than for a consistent one since the solver must in essence explore the complete model space to make sure that no model of the specification can be found.

6   Systematic Frame Equation Debugging

A more systematic approach to debugging an inconsistent specification exploits the fact that usually only a few lines of the specification contribute to the contradiction, in particular, if it is related to framing. Assuming such a situation,

Listing 5. Instrumented rover specification

```
1  one sig _moveTo_00, _push_00, _push_01
2    extends BlameLabel{}
3
4  pred moveTo [ p : Coord ]{
5    p in theSystem.r.position.adjacent
6    theSystem.r.position' = p
7    all o : theSystem.os |
8      _bl[o.position' = o.position , _moveTo_00]
9  }
10
11 pred push {
12   some o : theSystem.os |{
13     o.position in theSystem.r.position.adjacent
14     moveTo[o.position]
15     _bl[o.position'
16        in o.position.adjacent—theSystem.r.position ,
17        _push_01]
18     all oo : theSystem.os — o |
19       _bl[oo.position' = oo.position , _push_00]
20   }
21 }
```

successive weakening of the specification, one predicate at a time, is promising. With some instrumentation of the specification code, model finding can support a process of successive weakening steps, and thus become a valuable debugging aid. The general idea of this approach is to identify a class of predicates that likely contribute to the inconsistency, framing equations in our case, and form disjunctions of those predicates with a set of *blame predicates* to which model finding will assign truth values in a controlled way. If model finding assigns true to a blame predicate, then the original specification predicate in the respective disjunction is effectively removed from the specification. Conceptually, blame predicates are similar to *clause selectors* [10] used to compute minimal unsatisfiable cores, but they are used in a dual way.

6.1 Instrumentation

Listing 5 shows how the signature BlameLabel and the macro _bl [.,.] are used to instrument the definition of push and moveTo. Their definitions and the supporting Alloy code are shown in Listing 6. They are explained in the remainder of this section. The *blame labels* _moveTo_00, _push_00, and _push_01 provide markers for parts of the specification that are considered likely candidates contributing to the detected inconsistency. The first two blame labels mark framing equations, whereas the label _push_01 marks the position update of the obstacle o, which is not a framing equation. It is included for illustration purposes only.

Listing 6. Instrumentation Support for Debugging

```
1   abstract sig BlameLabel {}
2
3   abstract sig BlameCard {}
4   one sig blameZero, blameOne, blameTwo extends BlameCard {}
5
6   one sig theBlame {
7     card : one BlameCard,
8     toBlame : set BlameLabel,
9     required : set BlameLabel,
10    knownSingles : set BlameLabel,
11    knownPairs : set BlamePair
12  }{
13    no (toBlame & required)
14    no (toBlame & knownSingles)
15    all bp : knownPairs | toBlame & bp.p != bp.p
16    {
17      card = blameZero => no toBlame
18      card = blameOne  => one toBlame
19      card = blameTwo  => card2[toBlame]
20    }
21  }
22
23  pred blame [ lbl : BlameLabel ]{
24    lbl in theBlame.toBlame }
25
26  pred blameScenario [ c : BlameCard, r : set BlameLabel,
27    s : set BlameLabel, p : set BlamePair ]{
28    theBlame.card = c        && theBlame.required = r
29    theBlame.knownSingles = s && theBlame.knownPairs = p }
30
31  let _bl[prd,lbl] = {(blame[lbl] || (prd))}
```

The Alloy code in Listing 6 defines the semantics of the instrumentation. It introduces the abstract signature BlameLabel as the type of labels like _push_00 that are declared in the instrumentation of a specification.

The sub-signatures of BlameCard allow one to specify how many labeled predicates model finding should remove from the specification in order to make it consistent. For example, blameTwo specifies that two predicates should be removed from the specification.

The signature theBlame maintains information to control the search for a consistent sub-specification. The field card specifies the number of labeled predicates to remove from the specification. The field toBlame contains a set of labels referring to predicates that make the specification inconsistent. Thus, for card = blameOne the cardinality of toBlame is required to be one. This relationship is expressed in the signature invariant.

The other fields of theBlame further constrain the possible values of toBlame. The set of required blame labels denotes predicates that must not be removed from the specification. The sets knownSingles and knownPairs are used in the debugging process to accumulate single blame labels and pairs of blame labels, respectively, referring to predicates that cause inconsistencies. Together, the fields of theBlame but toBlame describe a *blame scenario*. The predicate blameScenario[c,r,s,p] describes a blame scenario, requiring the fields of theBlame to be equal to the respective parameter values.

Finally, the macro _bl[prd, lbl] forms a disjunction of the predicate prd and a blame[lbl] with the provided label lbl. Thus, if a model of the instrumented specification assigns true to blame[lbl], then the original specification predicate prd is (semantically) removed from the specification. The definition of blame[lbl] says that the parameter is a member of the set of labels "to blame", and thus establishes the logical connection to the blame scenario described in theBlame.

6.2 Process

The search for predicates that make the original specification inconsistent proceeds by adding blame scenarios (as axioms) in turn to the original specification. For the rover example, this process works as follows:

A first exploration focusses on framing equations. Therefore, the blame label _push_01 is required in all scenarios of this exploration. In a first step of the exploration, model finding for the sanity check Line 3 of Listing 4 with the axiom

fact blameScenario[blameOne, _push_01,**none**,**none**]

provides a model where theBlame.toBlame = _moveTo_00. Thus, already this first exploration step exhibits the actually erroneous framing predicate.

Considering _moveTo_00 a member of knownSingles, the second step uses the axiom

fact blameScenario[blameOne, _push_01, _moveTo_00,**none**]

to search for a different predicate that might cause an inconsistency while keeping the original framing equation labeled _moveTo_00. It turns out that model finding fails, i.e., just relaxing the other framing predicate labeled _push_00 does not yield a consistent specification.

This analysis provides sufficient information to correct the specification. With minimal effort, it correctly identifies the erroneous frame condition, from which an experienced verification engineer can easily derive a fix of the specification.

The following exploration of scenarios of cardinality two just serves as an illustration of a debugging process for a more complex specification error. Without requiring any predicate, model finding with the axiom

fact blameScenario[blameTwo,**none**,**none**,**none**]

searches for *two* predicates to be removed from the specification in order to make it consistent. The SAT solver finds a model where theBlame.toBlame contains the two labels _moveTo_00 and _push_00, which in turn are provided as a known pair by the axiom

fact blameScenario[blameTwo,**none**,**none**,bp[_moveTo_00,_push_00]]

to another round of model finding. This yields another pair of blame labels: _moveTo_00 and _push_01. The final model finding run with the axiom

fact blameScenario[blameTwo,**none**,**none**,
bp[_moveTo_00,_push_00]+bp[_moveTo_00,_push_01]]

does not succeed and thus confirms that no other pairs of labeled predicates can be weakened to yield a consistent specification.

6.3   Generalization and Automation

The use of the blame label _push_01 shows that the technique described in this section is not restricted to debugging frame conditions. Blame labels may be attached to any predicate. For example, when debugging large specifications with a deep call hierarchy within predicate definitions, it may be useful to first label calls to predicates within the top-level definitions of transition relations, and once predicates contributing to an inconsistency are identified, label specific types of predicates, e.g., framing equations, in the definitions of those predicates.

If the types of predicates to be labeled have a specific syntactic form, such as framing equations do, it is easy to automatically instrument a specification with blame labels. This can either be done by directly modifying the source code, or more elegantly by augmenting the parse tree of a specification.

Likewise, the exploration described in Sect. 6.2 can be automated by successively generating the model exploration commands and accumulating the results, which can be mapped back to the source code to highlight the predicates that cause an inconsistency without explicitly presenting blame labels at the user interface.

7   Related Work

Technically, the use of blame labels is similar to clause selectors [10] used in computing a minimal unsatisfiable core, or activation variables [4] proposed for debugging unrealizable assume/guarantee temporal specifications. However, in those approaches, these variables serve to mark an *inconsistent* subset of specification clauses, whereas the approach presented in Sect. 6 aims at finding a *consistent* sub-specification by removing just one or two predicates from an inconsistent specification.

There is comprehensive research on computing an unsatisfiable core for inconsistent or unrealizable temporal specifications, e.g., [11,12]. The general assumption underlying that work is that an algorithmically determined unsatisfiable set of clauses of a specification will provide verification engineers with sufficient information to find specification errors. Experience from our customer projects show, however, that this is often not the case in practice.

Könighofer et al. [9] consider not just one but all unsatisfiable cores to compute counterstrategies to debug unrealizable assume/guarantee specifications. This work targets application scenarios in the context of hardware design with error patterns that concern the (global) reactive behavior of a system. Their approach is conceptually and computationally more complex than the present work, and, if applicable, would require much more effort to support the scenario of debugging framing equations.

8 Discussion

Inconsistent abstract system specifications of non-trivial size are hard to debug. In particular, contradictions of framing equations and other predicates determining a transition relation form a common error pattern. In such a situation, model finding for the original specification does not succeed and computing a minimal unsatisfiable core often does not yield useful information. This is a quite common case in formal specification efforts for real systems.

Section 6 presents a proof of concept of a computationally light-weight but practically useful way of using model finding to debug inconsistent specifications. The underlying hypothesis is that, in a real-life project, large parts of a specification that evolves over time are adequate, and if an inconsistency occurs in an updated version of a specification, then only very few places in the specification contribute to that inconsistency. Thus, it is more productive to search for the erroneous part of the specification by removing small parts from it until it is consistent, rather than trying to derive debugging information from one or all (minimal) unsatisfiable cores.

Current tool support for abstract formal system specifications, like the Alloy Analyzer, provide little support for debugging inconsistencies. Implementing the present work as a feature of those tools – as sketched in Sect. 6.3 – would provide a valuable debugging aid to practitioners.

Acknowledgements. Since the early 1990 s,s, when I first met him, Jan Peleska has been a pioneer in applying Formal Methods to industrial software systems. His work has been and continues to be a source of inspiration throughout my professional life. Thank you! Thanks also to the anonymous reviewers and to Maritta Heisel for valuable comments on an earlier draft of this paper.

References

1. Alloy analyzer version 6 (2021). https://allytools.org/alloy6.html
2. Cimatti, A., et al.: NuSMV 2: an opensource tool for symbolic model checking. In: Brinksma, E., Larsen, K.G. (eds.) CAV 2002. LNCS, vol. 2404, pp. 359–364. Springer, Heidelberg (2002). https://doi.org/10.1007/3-540-45657-0_29

3. Cimatti, A., Clarke, E., Giunchiglia, F., Roveri, M.: NuSMV: A new symbolic model verifier. In: Halbwachs, N., Peled, D. (eds.) CAV 1999. LNCS, vol. 1633, pp. 495–499. Springer, Heidelberg (1999). https://doi.org/10.1007/3-540-48683-6_44

4. Cimatti, A., Roveri, M., Schuppan, V., Tchaltsev, A.: Diagnostic information for realizability. In: Logozzo, F., Peled, D.A., Zuck, L.D. (eds.) VMCAI 2008. LNCS, vol. 4905, pp. 52–67. Springer, Heidelberg (2008). https://doi.org/10.1007/978-3-540-78163-9_9

5. Dietl, W., Müller, P.: Object ownership in program verification. In: Clarke, D., Noble, J., Wrigstad, T. (eds.) Aliasing in Object-Oriented Programming. Types, Analysis and Verification. LNCS, vol. 7850, pp. 289–318. Springer, Heidelberg (2013). https://doi.org/10.1007/978-3-642-36946-9_11

6. Eén, N., Sörensson, N.: An extensible SAT-solver. In: Giunchiglia, E., Tacchella, A. (eds.) SAT 2003. LNCS, vol. 2919, pp. 502–518. Springer, Heidelberg (2004). https://doi.org/10.1007/978-3-540-24605-3_37

7. Jackson, D.: Software Abstractions: Logic, Language, and Analysis. Revised edition. MIT Press (2011)

8. Jones, C.B.: Systematic Software Development using VDM, 2nd edn. Prentice Hall (1990)

9. Könighofer, R., Hofferek, G., Bloem, R.: Debugging formal specifications: a practical approach using model-based diagnosis and counterstrategies. Int. J. Softw. Tools Technol. Transf. **15**(5-6), 563–583 (2013). https://doi.org/10.1007/s10009-011-0221-y

10. Lynce, I., Silva, J.P.M.: On computing minimum unsatisfiable cores. In: SAT 2004 - The Seventh International Conference on Theory and Applications of Satisfiability Testing, Online Proceedings (2004). http://www.satisfiability.org/SAT04/programme/110.pdf

11. Roveri, M., Ciccio, C.D., Francescomarino, C.D., Ghidini, C.: Computing unsatisfiable cores for LTLf specifications. In: Giacomo, G.D., Guzzo, A., Montali, M., Limonad, L., Fournier, F., Chakraborti, T. (eds.) Proceedings of the Workshop on Process Management in the AI Era (PMAI 2022). CEUR Workshop Proceedings, vol. 3310, pp. 81–84. CEUR-WS.org (2022). http://ceur-ws.org/Vol-3310/paper12.pdf

12. Schuppan, V.: Enhanced unsatisfiable cores for QBF: weakening universal to existential quantifiers. Int. J. Artif. Intell. Tools **29**(03n04), 2060012:1–2060012:27 (2020). https://doi.org/10.1142/S021821302060012X

13. Spivey, J.M.: The Z Notation - A Reference Manual, 2nd edn. Prentice Hall (1992)

Author Index

A. E. Haxthausen et al. (Eds.): Peleska Festschrift 2023, LNCS 14165, pp. 333–334, 2023.
https://doi.org/10.1007/978-3-031-40132-9

Printed in the United States
by Baker & Taylor Publisher Services

Printed in the United States
by Baker & Taylor Publisher Services